Cybercrime

Cybercrime

The Transformation of Crime in the Information Age

2nd edition

DAVID S. WALL

polity

First published in 2007 by Polity Press
This 2nd edition first published in 2024 by Polity Press.

Polity Press
65 Bridge Street
Cambridge CB2 1UR, UK

Polity Press
111 River Street
Hoboken, NJ 07030, USA

ISBN-13: 978-0-7456-5352-5
ISBN-13: 978-0-7456-5353-2 (pb)

A catalogue record for this book is available from the British Library.

Library of Congress Control Number: 2023945979

Typeset in 9.5 on 12pt Utopia
by Cheshire Typesetting Ltd, Cuddington, Cheshire
Printed and bound in Great Britain by TJ Books Ltd, Padstow, Cornwall

For further information on Polity, visit our website:
politybooks.com

Contents

Figures, Tables and Boxes

Figures

Tables

Boxes

Preface and Acknowledgements to the Second Edition

So much has happened in the world since the first edition of this book was published in 2007, and yet many of its initial observations are still valid. In this preface, I note the main changes that have occurred since the first edition was written and also point out what has remained the same.

The advent of social media, cloud technologies, the 'Internet of Things' and cryptocurrencies have augmented already emerging technological trends to lead to a marked step-change in the threat landscape, arising from malware (malicious software) and social engineering. Alongside the botnets were information-guzzling malware (to quote *The Register*) such as Zeus, Emotet and Trickbot. Then came the nation-state attacking Stuxnet, and more recently scareware, ransomware, data extortion and ransomhacks (automated malware which deceives individuals into paying a ransom directly to the criminals). Of worldwide concern in the middle of the third decade of the twenty-first century has been the increased use of data as the focus of cybercrime, and also the use of cybercrime in geopolitical conflicts which may direct its future trajectory. Data breaches are now commonplace in many cybercrimes and have become a major driver of crime as the importance of data is so much greater to its owners today. Infrastructure as well as the financial sector are now common targets, which indicates that the criminal actors often have political as well as financial motivations. Since the first edition of this book was published, these four technological developments have changed the cybercrime threat landscape to a point where some of the more fanciful predictions made about cybercrime in the late twentieth and early twenty-first centuries are now becoming very real and harmful. Many new attack vectors, for example, seek to victimize the organizational infrastructure in ways that were initially imagined in science fiction books. Many of the largely unfounded claims that were made in previous decades, which I was once critical of, are now starting to come true.

Whereas the first edition showed how networked and digital technologies enabled a single criminal to commit many different crimes simultaneously, this edition illustrates how we have witnessed a gradual division of labour in the organization of cybercrime in the second and third decades of the twenty-first century that has led to the emergence of a supply chain of skills for hire. This cybercrime ecosystem helps and enables cybercriminals to commit their acts. Perhaps one of the bigger changes in approach since the first edition is that, whereas I used to warn against reading cybersecurity reports (the grey literature) as they were little more than 'weather reports from umbrella manufacturers', 15 years later I would now advise everyone to read them, although always with a wary and critical eye.

There are times when one wonders what has actually changed in the field, because so many of the key issues that prevailed in the early 2000s are still very alive today, but bigger. New technological developments are continually being introduced and converging with others to create new creative, educational, commercial, leisure possibilities. But the main difference is that not only has the technological environment changed through cloud technologies and the Internet of Things, which speed up communications and create new information paths, but social media and cryptocurrencies have also created new ways of interaction and transaction which have shaped the social, financial and political environments in which we live. Of course, along with these opportunities (or affordances[1]) come new and often unintended opportunities for crime and malevolent behaviour. It is the same with the growth in popularity of social media which now dominates societal usage of the internet, followed by a revolution in internet sales and banking, which have jointly expanded the cyber-threat landscape. Moreover, its many platforms have also contributed to increases in the scale of offending and new and novel opportunities for cybercriminals. Yet, in response to these changes, most countries have now introduced national cybersecurity strategies and associated cybercrime policies, and the UN and other international bodies are exploring the development of international norms and treaties. There also exist a range of formal institutional responses for policing and prosecuting the various types of cybercrime across borders. Yet the march of progress always seems to keep offenders one step ahead of law enforcement, which still largely acts upon reports of victimization. So, it still feels as though those charged with protecting society from wrongdoing are always one step behind.

Alongside technological development has been a change in social and political cyberspace. Social media technology has become a serious force, especially in the wrong hands, where it has contributed to the fermentation of political unrest. In more tolerant regimes, flash mobbing has been used to signal disquiet both online, through distributed denial of service attacks, and also offline by enabling crowds to organize and assemble physically. Social network media (Facebook, Twitter/X, Threads, Telegram, Instagram, Snapchat, Whatsapp, TikTok and so on) were a twinkle in the technologist's eye 15 years ago, and now they are principal forms of communication for the digital generation – many of whom now work in cybersecurity and the criminal justice system, especially policing agencies. These digital natives are no longer perplexed by new technologies but embrace them as a part of their lives without thinking about it. Access to communications technology and social media is now a 'given' rather than a 'desirable' aspect of life today, which diminishes the power of democratic governments to restrict its usage. So, when you thought it was all bad, one factor remains reassuring, which is that, just as criminals have become networked, then so have the police and the various policing agencies, so there is hope, especially as the lag between criminal and police use of technologies has reduced and new forms of artificial intelligence-driven 'policing' methods to assist police are being experimented with – though not without concerns for privacy. There has also not been the anticipated radical transformation in police, government and most corporate structures, because echoes of many of the cultural and organizational issues identified in the first edition of this book still linger today over a decade and a half later. So, although technology has advanced and the cyber-threat landscape has changed considerably, and the cybercrimes described have changed in terms of size and volume, as has their complexity, many of the observations made in the earlier version still stand today.

This (admittedly long overdue) second edition updates the first edition and, although the explanation and analysis of events remain much the same, new information about events and comment have been added. Moreover, a new story emerges, mentioned above, which shows how cybercrime has become a sophisticated business that now has its own dedicated supply chain and supportive ecosystem. I have, however, retained some of the earlier examples to demonstrate the lingering importance of many of the original issues and events, and also that many of the new events that scare us today are variations on a familiar theme. Not least, the internet is no longer 'new' and is now over 35 years old and spanning 5 decades, and it has started to develop its own history. So, I have retained examples that are still relevant and added new ones. (N.B.: an important note to students, please do not start your essays with the phrase 'Cybercrimes are a new phenomenon caused by the internet . . .' – they are not new!)

I still owe the same debts to the folk mentioned in the preface to the first edition, but I must now add to that original list my colleagues in the criminology group at Durham University between 2010 and 2015; in computer science at Newcastle University, at CEPOL and the UNODC; and also on the various research projects that I have been involved with in the past 15 years. Then there are the many others whom I have omitted because of space, but who nevertheless matter. Also, I must thank my various research colleagues over the years who have worked with me on my cybercrime research projects, including Drs Lena Connolly, Roberto Musotto, Yanna Papadodimitraki, Maria Grazia Porcedda and Harrison Whitehouse-Wall, who are now part of a new generation of academic researchers that are taking this field forward.

My family still provide loving support, entertainment and also a welcomed disruption to my endeavours, although one wonderful new development is that I am now able to discuss some of the ideas in this book with my children, who (allegedly!) are now mature adults. Between 2010 and 2015, I moved up the A1M from Leeds to Durham University, but then moved back to Leeds in 2015 to a more research-oriented position. I made a wonderful new set of colleagues in Durham and still keep in touch with many, but it is great to be back with my old and new colleagues at Leeds. I still do not, however, dedicate this book to my colleagues or family as is the custom – rather, this dedication still goes to the train drivers between York and Leeds (and for 5 years between York and Durham) and the good folk of Rosedale Abbey who have kept me sane and provided me that much needed few hours of solitude each day to have a cup of coffee and ponder on research ideas and the text of this book. I would also like to thank Jonathan Skerrett, commissioning editor at Polity, and his colleagues Karina Jákupsdóttir, Neil de Cort and Leigh Mueller for their patience over the years, and especially when bringing this edition together; plus, of course, the anonymous reviewers whose comments and observations were extremely useful.

With my pessimistic hat on, it looks as though aspects of everybody's personal data will soon be leaked online at some point, and we will become prey to cybercriminals or even warring nations! But can I also say, with my happy hat on, that the advantages of the new technologies still far outweigh the disadvantages and there have been some incredible advances in responding to the cyber-threat field? While I would not call myself a digital native, I do love (most) streamed TV, I love using GPS devices to guide me when I am walking in the wilds, I love mobile banking and email and social media, I love being able to switch on my water heater remotely (not that I do very often), I love being able to buy a washing machine from my phone and, as a diabetic, I love being able to use my 'phone' to check my blood glucose levels. I, like most on this planet, would be lost in life without cyberspace, so we need to work hard to preserve the good parts of it, especially as we cannot switch it off!

David S. Wall, Leeds, 16 August 2023

Preface and Acknowledgements to the First Edition

When I was young, there was a programme on British TV called *Tomorrow's World* which presented new technologies and inventions. It symbolized the 'White Heat of Technology' of the 1960s and made the viewer privy to an exciting world of whirring and clicking computers administered by people in white coats. This was a world of hovercrafts, jet packs, cures for this, that and the other – James Bond stuff for real. The show was inherently optimistic in tone and promoted technologies either as benign or in terms of the ways they could advance the human cause. Unfortunately, the youthful optimism it bred in me was later shattered by my academic study which made me realize that the chilling reality of the real *Tomorrow's World* was quite different because the technologies are by no means benign. Yes, they may do good, interesting and useful things and I still retain some optimism to this effect, but they can also put people out of work, victimize individuals, and potentially threaten our liberties. Moreover, technologies are now becoming more pervasive, especially when they converge, and they are beginning to frame our lives in ways that are both good and bad. It is therefore from this perspective of critical optimism that I approach the subject of this book.

With the benefit of 20:20 hindsight, this was not an easy book to write because the subject matter changed so rapidly. Indeed, it was the very nature of this change that subsequently became an important part of the narrative. Because of this, the book possibly tries to achieve too much. Furthermore, it is also a snapshot of the state of play in 2006, so by the time of its publication in 2007, new events may have either confirmed the predictions or even superseded them. Such is the risk in writing about the internet. Then why bother? The answer is simple: the account within this book is a thematic history of cybercrime's present. Epistemologically, without an historical awareness of the behaviour we call cybercrime how can we understand what it is and in what direction it is developing?

This book is intended for upper-level undergraduates and graduates. It contains a monograph style narrative that can be read in its entirety, but also contains much specific information that can be accessed via the index to search out particular issues, or through the list of cases and references to follow up any reference streams.

It will be apparent from my institutional affiliation that I live and work in the UK. However, where possible, I have sought to provide cross-jurisdictional information and examples. Since one of the book's central arguments is that the internet is a global information and networked medium, it is no surprise that the broader findings show thematic similarities across jurisdictions.

In writing this book there are many people I need to thank. Some have been directly involved, others indirectly. So, the first group to thank are the funders. The School of Law at the University of Leeds gave me research leave during which I brought together many of the ideas that had been informed by prior research projects funded by the bodies I list in the introduction. An AHRC award then provided additional funding to extend my period of research (Award APN18143).

I must then thank my immediate colleagues at the University of Leeds, especially Yaman Akdeniz, Adam Crawford, Paul Taylor, Clive Walker, but also Anthea Hucklesby, Sam Lewis, Stuart Lister, Norma Martin Clement, Emma Wincup and the others in the School of Law and Centre for Criminal Justice Studies. In the broader academy I have to thank for their friendship, help, or just inspiration (in alphabetical order): Richard Ericson, Peter Grabosky, Kevin Haggerty, Yvonne Jukes, Tony Krone, Mike Levi, David Lyon, Peter Manning, Sam McQuade III, Soumyo Moitra, Hedi Nasheri, April Pattavina, Ken Pease, Ernesto Savonna, Jackie Schneider, Clifford Shearing (Clifford and Jennifer Wood gave particularly insightful comments on an earlier draft of chapter 8), Russell Smith, Mike Sutton, Matt Williams, Maggi Wykes, Majid Yar. And, of course, there are the providers of information about events that is so important to the narrative, such as the staff at *The Register* and *Wired*, and the various columnists at the *BBC News Online* site.

Moving on to others, I am indebted to Emma Longstaff, commissioning editor at Polity, for her forbearance and very useful editorial input; Ann Bone (desk editor) and Anne Dunbar-Nobes (copy editor); plus, of course, the anonymous reviewers whose comments were invaluable.

Finally, I thank Helen, Harrison, Sophie and James for their support and for being there for me. Sophie (aka Bubble-Pop Electric) and Harri enlightened me as to how central the internet is to the world of teenagers. Unfortunately, in so doing, they also showed me just how hard it is to remove malicious software in the form of trojans, viruses and worms from their computer – kids eh!

But, contrary to tradition, I do not dedicate this book to them, or to my colleagues, funders, friends, helpers or inspiration. Instead, I would like to dedicate this book to the 7.06 am and 6.55 pm trains between York and Leeds which gave me that much needed hour or so of solitude each day to have a cup of coffee and ponder on the text.

David S. Wall, Leeds 2007

Acronymns

AHRC	Arts and Humanities Research Council
AI	Artificial Intelligence
APACS	Association for Payment Clearing Services (now UK Payments)
APIG	All Party Internet Group
APP	authorized push payment
APWG	Anti-Phishing Working Group (UK)
ARP	Address Resolution Protocol
BBFC	British Board of Film Classification
BBS	bulletin board services
BEC	business email compromise
BGP	Border Gateway Protocol
BPI	British Phonographic Industry
BTC	Bitcoin
CaaS	crimeware as a service
CAUCE	Coalition Against Unsolicited Commercial Email
CEPOL	European Union Agency for Law Enforcement Training
CERT	Computer Emergency Response Team
CIFAS	Credit Industry Fraud Avoidance System
CNSA	Contact Network of Spam Authorities
CoE	Council of Europe
CPS	Crown Prosecution Service (UK)
CSEW	Crime Survey for England and Wales
CSI	Computer Studies Institute
CVC	card validation code
DBT	Department for Business and Trade (UK)
DCMS	Department for Culture, Media and Sport
DDoS	distributed denial of service
DHS	Department of Homeland Security (US)
DNS	domain name servers
DoJ	Department of Justice (US)
DTI	Department of Trade and Industry (UK)
EC	European Commission
ENISA	European Network and Information Security Agency
EPSRC	Engineering and Physical Sciences Research Council
ESRC	Economic and Social Research Council
EuroISPA	European Internet Service Providers Association
EUROPOL	European Union Agency for Law Enforcement Cooperation
FACT	Federation Against Copyright Theft (UK)

FBI	Federal Bureau of Investigation
FUD	Fear, Uncertainty and Doubt
GCHQ	Government Communications Headquarters
GUI	graphics user interface
HTCC	High-Tech Crime Consortium
HTTPS	Hypertext Transfer Protocol Secure
IC3	Internet Crime Complaint Center (US)
ICANN	Internet Corporation for Assigned Names and Numbers
ICMEC	International Centre for Missing and Exploited Children
ICO	Initial Coin Offering
INTERPOL	International Criminal Police Organization
IoT	Internet of Things
IP	internet protocol (also see TCP/IP)
IPR	intellectual property rights
IPTS	Institute for Prospective Technological Studies
IRC	internet relay chat
ISIPP	Institute for Spam and Internet Public Policy (UK)
ISP	internet service provider
IWF	Internet Watch Foundation
MPAA	Motion Picture Association of America
NCA	National Crime Agency (UK)
NCCU	National Cyber Crime Unit
NCIS	National Criminal Intelligence Service (UK)
NCSC	National Cybercrime Security Centre
NCVS	National Crime Victimization Survey
NFIB	National Fraud Intelligence Bureau
NFIC	National Fraud Information Center
NFT	non-fungible token
NHTCU	National Hi-Tech Crime Unit (UK)
NIM	National Intelligence Model (UK)
NIPC	National Infrastructure Protection Center (US)
NISCC	National Infrastructure Security Co-ordination Centre
NSA	National Security Agency (US)
NSPCC	National Society for the Prevention of Cruelty to Children
OCJS	Offending, Crime and Justice Survey
OECD	Organisation for Economic Co-operation and Development
Ofcom	Office of Communications (UK)
ONS	Office of National Statistics
P2P	peer-to-peer
PC	personal computer
POLCYB	Society for the Policing of Cyberspace
RaaS	ransomware as a service
RATware/RAT	remote administration trojans
RDP	Remote Desk Protocol
RIAA	Recording Industry Association of America
ROCU	Regional Organized Crime Unit (UK)
SAP	Sentencing Advisory Panel

SCADA   Supervisory Control and Data Acquisition
SDR   Software Defined Radio
SOCA   Serious Organized Crime Agency (UK)
SSL   secure sockets layer
TCP/IP transmission control protocol / internet protocol
TIA   terrorism information awareness
ToR   The Onion Router
UNIRAS Unified Incident Reporting and Alert Scheme
UNODC   United Nations Office on Drugs and Crime
VoIP   voice over internet protocol
VPN   Virtual Private Network
WWW   World Wide Web

1 Introduction

Chapter at a glance   *This introductory chapter describes the aim of this book, for whom the book is written, the principal research questions to be answered and how they feature in the chapter structure. It then outlines the questions which shape each chapter: What are cybercrimes? What do we know about them? How have networked technologies changed opportunities for criminal activity? What are those criminal opportunities? How is criminal activity continuing to change in the information age? How is cyberspace policed and by whom? How are cybercrimes to be regulated and prevented? Why are the answers to these questions so important? Finally in this introduction, some suggestions are made as to how this book can be used as a basis for teaching cybercrime.*

Introduction

I would like to think that the cover photographs of this and the previous edition of this book reflect changes in the cybercrime field in the eras they span. The first edition cover displayed a young woman sitting alone with her laptop in the corner of her favourite internet café. She had just pressed the send button and was looking nervously over her shoulder. Who was she? A victim, an offender, a passer-by? A decade or more ago, the answer was not clear at all as to who she was or what she was doing because the internet distorted conventional reference points, forcing us to challenge our (then) previously held assumptions, particularly about crime and the internet. But the answer to these questions is still not as clear today as we had hoped it would be, but at least we are further on than we were – the problem today is that there are a host of entirely new questions to answer. The prevailing moral concerns at the time of the first edition were largely centred around the threat of extreme materials, especially sexual content, and low-level frauds. Now, more than a decade and a half later, the climate has shifted to one where the major concerns are largely about the threats to society from economic cybercrimes and data theft. So, the cover for this edition is therefore more direct, illustrating how digital and network technologies have become much more invasive, pervasive, ubiquitous and automated in developing new crime opportunities – which is a recurring theme throughout the book. I suppose that if one were to be more accurate, one of the many hands in the cover photo should also be holding a mobile device or two, and another pointing in the direction of a bank or a nation-state conflict, but these could be themes for the next editions!

This book still remains an exploration of what is a relatively new and evolving field of criminal activity. This field is commonly referred to as 'cybercrime' because it arises from the bad side of the cyberspace imaginary, which is the way in which society reacts to the convergence of digital and networked technologies. Not only does cybercrime continually evolve, but it also keeps being reinvented as the cybersecurity landscape changes. Indeed, between the editions of this book a number of profound changes have occurred in it that are exposing us to an entirely new generation of data-fuelled cybercrime facilitated by cloud technologies, the Internet of Things (IoT), social media and cryptocurrencies, plus a number of terrestrial conflicts, which I have tried to capture in the text.

What has changed since the first edition?

Crudely put, this book deconstructs cybercrime for the reader. In so doing, it shows how the internet (digital and networked technology) has mechanized and industrialized a particular type of criminal behaviour online. If the first two decades of cybercrime, as represented in the first edition, showed how it enabled individuals to take control of and perform bulk cybercrimes by themselves on a global scale, then the next two decades chart how technology has further developed some of the key transformations (or technological affordances) that were only briefly outlined in the first edition: technologies which, in turn, have introduced social media networks and the Internet of Things into our lives. Digital and networked technologies have also created new market forces that have driven cybercrime opportunities which have caused cyber-offenders to become more organized in order to make cybercrime pay.

This recent period is when the early fears about cybercrime have actually become a reality. Yet many of the events that occurred in the period covered by the previous edition have shaped what happened after then. What this means for the reader is that part of the original analysis is repeated in this edition because these events shape how we view this later period.

The 2007 edition illustrated how the networked and digital technologies created entirely new opportunities for cybercrime, by effectively deskilling some pre-internet crime processes into their component parts and automating them. The reskilling (of the managing of) the automated processes allowed one person to commit online a complete crime that would otherwise have taken a group of individuals working closely together. Cybercrime in the mid-noughties was serious in terms of disruption and small-impact bulk victimizations, but not always as serious as predicted by the early cybersecurity industry, which had a vested interest in gloomy predictions.

Since the 2007 edition, there has been a marked shift in the cybersecurity land-scape. This is because offenders have had to adapt to circumstances and scale up their crime operations in order to reach their criminal objectives in terms of financial gain, disruption, destruction, stealing crucial data. To achieve their criminal goals, a supply chain emerged of skilled specialists that could be hired to facilitate cyber-crime. The market for these skills constitutes a cybercrime ecosystem which has expanded the cybercrime landscape and provided a foothold for organized crime groups. After many years of apocryphal warnings from the cybersecurity industry that 'the sky is falling in' – at the time it was rather like listening to a weather report from an umbrella manufacturer – the evidence now looks as though it is in danger of doing so! Nevertheless, it is important to underline this rather brash statement with the caveat that the cybersecurity industry and police, and various internet guardians, have also made some massive strides forward in understanding and counteracting cybercrime behaviour – which has meant offenders have to work harder to be successful.

The long-standing relationship between technology and crime continues

A simple reading of history shows that the relationship between crime and technol-ogy is by no means new and that the potential for creating harm never seems to be far away from any apparently beneficial new technological development. Although the hardware used to implement technological ideas may change across the span of time, many of the basic crime ideas remain familiar, particularly those which exploit chains of trust created and supported by technology. In the early nineteenth century, for example, the ingenuity of some of the wire frauds perpetrated by tapping into electric telegraph systems bears an uncanny resemblance to modern-day hacks. This long-standing, though 'uneasy', relationship between crime and technology also extends to ideas about crime prevention and security – the architects of the pyramids, for example, employed sophisticated security technologies to thwart tomb raiders – a few wrong or unexpected moves and . . . slam! . . . the tomb entrance was sealed forever – not so different in principle to the automated surveillant technologies installed at airports to detect potential terrorist actions by identifying abnormal pat-terns of movement. And on the subject of the electric telegraph, no sooner had it been invented than it was being used to catch criminals, as murderer John Tawell reflected upon in the moments before his execution in 1845. After killing his mistress and flee-ing to London by train, Tawell's physical description was telegraphed forward by police and he was arrested upon his arrival (Standage, 1998: 51).

Today, the technological cat-and-mouse game between offender and investiga-tor remains today much the same as in the past. Offenders still adaptively exploit new technologies while the investigators rush to catch up quickly, using those same technologies for investigation, apprehension and prevention. What has changed significantly in late modern times is, as indicated above, the increase in the scale of cybercrime due to the availability of personal and mobile computing across glo-balized communications networks. The time frame during which harmful behaviour occurs is substantively much shorter today because 'cloud technology' has speeded up networking. It is also particularly worrying that the length of time for a cybercrime opportunity to turn into a cybercrime wave is now measured in hours, minutes and even seconds, rather than days, months or years. As a consequence, digital and networked technology has become more than simply a 'force multiplier', because networks have globalized ideas about committing crimes. Ideas about commit-ting crime being carried out across globalized networks. Of course, they have also globalized ideas about its investigation and prevention, which, along with develop-ments in methods of technological detection, have contributed to offenders having to up their game. So fast has been the rate of change that this book has already been revised considerably during the course of writing and revision, which is living proof of Moore's proposal that one internet year is approximately equal to three months or less in real time (based upon Moore, 1965: 114).

Drawing upon almost three decades of multidisciplinary research and sources, this book explores the transformation of crime in the information age. Although it tends to focus upon high-end cybercrimes – those which are solely the product of networked technologies – it also seeks to explain the broader range of behaviours referred to as cybercrime. Moreover, it also addresses the various legal, academic, expert and popular constructions of cybercrime and explains the disparities between them. It is argued that not only have networked technologies changed the criminal process by creating new generations of hackers and crackers, fraudsters and pornographers and hate-mongers, but these have themselves now been superseded. The convergence of digital and networked technologies with other technology has arguably led to a third (and possibly fourth or fifth) generation of cybercrimes to augment, or even succeed, the first (computer-crime) and the second (hacking) generations that emerged in the first decade of the twenty-first century. It can now be argued, for example, that earlier concerns about the 'hacking' of individual systems by skilled individuals have become sidelined by new advanced attack methods whereby offender groups rent crimeware-as-a-service (CaaS) facilities to commit their crimes, almost as casually as if they were renting a film. These CaaS facilities are themselves chosen as if from a slot machine. Run from digital dashboards, they employ 'botnets' of many millions of 'zombie' computers infected by remote-administration malware and facilitated by cloud technologies and the Internet of Things. CaaS can now automate the hacking process, and also the process by which offenders engage with their victims. These facilities and the relationship between them are explained later in greater detail.

The challenges of responding to cybercrime remain considerable. On the one hand, sensationalized media coverage has raised public expectations of a high level of cybercrime. Yet, on the other hand, the reality is that many of those cybercrimes are not regarded by victims as being particularly serious, because either their impacts may be delayed, or they may be offset by the victim's banks or insurance policies. Police actions and prosecutions are also relatively low against reports of crime, as they are for most crime. But, culturally and historically, the police are not very well equipped to respond to cybercrimes, so they tend to take a tactical 'whack a mole' rather than strategic approach (Palmer, 2021). Politically, cybercrimes simply do not 'bang, bleed or shout' (BBC, 2019), which, as illustrated in chapter 8, does not make cybercrimes a primary policing priority. However, localized crime statistics also tend not to grasp the global picture because the true seriousness of cybercrimes often lies in their aggregate impact or subsequent knock-on cybercrime, as in the case of data theft. The first edition identified a world of low-impact, multiple-victim crimes where bank robbers no longer had to plan the high-risk thefts of millions of dollars because new technological capabilities meant that one person could commit millions of low-grade robberies of $1 each. In fact, recent cloud technologies increase data processing power and now mean that one person could technically commit billions of lower-grade robberies of $0.1 each: small (*de-minimis*) crimes that are practically impossible to investigate.

The main development since the 'early' period of cybercrime, however, is that, while many cybercrimes have relatively small impact, the scale has increased and so have the proceeds of cybercrime. This has meant that our understandings need to change to incorporate the bigger picture today. Many of the smaller and individual victimizations originate out of larger keystone crimes, typically corporate data breaches, which provide the essential data to set up the various components of the cybercrime ecosystem – for example, gaining access to victims' accounts or setting up botnets. Unless this is countered, we face the prospect of being faced with 'ubiquitous' and automated victimization.

The framing of this bigger picture in which offenders upscale their cybercrimes via a cybercrime ecosystem to make their crimes lucrative, is an important part of the narrative within this book. But so is the role of law and law enforcement in dealing with the conceptual fog of cybercrime trends and the recurring problems of 'de minimism' and jurisdictional boundaries. On the one hand, criminal justice systems that are used to one criminal per crime are still not geared up to deal with either multiple offending across different bodies of law or the aggregations of offences. Because of their enormity, cybercrimes can create many practical, technical and legal problems for investigation and prosecution. On the other hand, optimistically, the digital realism, of cybercrime is such that the more a behaviour is mediated by new technology, then the more it can be governed by that same technology. Laws, for example, could be and are starting to be written into the very codes that make software work. However, unless reduced, this trend could create the spectre of citizens being exposed to ubiquitous law enforcement and the potential problems it creates of acting on a 'pre-crime' prediction. This is where artificial intelligence analyses all available data about individuals and the surrounding circumstances to anticipate when a cybercrime is likely to occur, rather than when it actually does. Such an idea is very attractive to some sections of society but also contains drawbacks for various cherished personal freedoms.

Rather surprisingly, after a quarter of a century, both researching and teaching cybercrime still seem like an uphill struggle, as box 1.1 illustrates.

Box 1.1 Can't we just switch it off?

Exactly 25 years ago, I recall talking to a meeting of international security chiefs about the cybercrime threat. The head of a rather large international airport said in a somewhat incredulous tone, 'The answer is simple, let's just switch it off.' After being patiently told that you can't switch off the internet as it is designed to be resilient to attack, he exclaimed, 'Which idiot allowed that to happen!', to which a terse reply came from a senior US defence official: 'Well, we did, the internet was built by the US so that we could retain governmental and defence communications across the country if ever a nuclear attack occurred and wiped out a major communications hub.' After the penny dropped, the newly enlightened and now less incredulous security chief was far more understanding of the problem and contributed to the debates. For me, this vignette illustrated not only how quickly the internet had become embedded in everyone's lives, even if many, at the time, did not even realize it had done so. It also illustrated the wider extent to which governments did not fully appreciate or even understand the complexities and criminal implications of internet technologies, and how little of the cybercrime problem was understood by those responsible for protecting society against it. Finally, it illustrated how vulnerable they were at the time to what Ross Anderson has referred to as 'the siren call of the software salesman' (cited in Claburn, 2022). Cybersecurity had become big business and those in the industry were never going to be guilty of understating the problem.

Today, these themes and attitudes are reflected in many of the debates about social media-driven hate speech, and also recent concerns about artificial intelligence. And the message is the same, we can't just switch it off, delete materials; and there is no silver bullet that will magically resolve the issue. The world has changed and will continue to change, and criminals will continue to capitalize on this fact. Society, therefore, needs to adapt its responses accordingly!

The aim of this book

As indicated earlier, the primary aim of this second edition remains much the same as the first, which is to contribute to our knowledge and understanding of cybercrimes. It is not a manual of computer crimes nor the methods by which to resolve them – others do that far better. Rather, it seeks to obtain a critical understanding of the various transformations that have taken place in criminal activity and its regulation, as a result of digital and networked technologies. Central to the arguments made in the forthcoming chapters is a 'transformation thesis' which looks at the various ways in which cybercriminal behaviours are transformed by the informational, global and networked qualities of these technologies. Such an approach will reveal that there are actually a range of different types of cybercrime that are the product of digital technology that reduces objects such as images, documents, sounds into computer files, and networked technologies which send them (potentially) across the planet. In so doing, they have transformed the more traditional divisions of criminal labour to provide entirely new opportunities for, and indeed new forms of, crime that typically involve the acquisition or manipulation of information and its value across global networks. This notion of transformation is important because it offers the prospect of reconciling very different accounts of cybercrime by representing them as very different phases in the crime process. The transformation concept is also important because its flipside, as indicated earlier, is that the same technologies which create cybercrimes also provide unique opportunities for their regulation and policing. However, while this may provide a solution, it also stimulates an important debate about the framework for maintaining order and law enforcement on the internet.

Who is the book written for?

This book is primarily written for those who are interested in this field of study, my various cybercrime students, colleagues near and far, as well as the many policymakers and practitioners working in this field. I also must confess to writing it for myself as an aide-memoir after researching this field for over 30 years.

When the first edition was commissioned, there were few comprehensive cybercrime texts available. Now there are many available texts, but few are positioned between law, criminal justice and criminology, and this book fills that spot. It will be no surprise then, that the book's main academic reference point is the intersection between law and criminology, particularly as it relates to the 'law in action'. This is because many of the harmful internet behaviours that raise public concern do not necessarily fall neatly within the criminal or civil codes. Furthermore, how they are currently resolved is framed increasingly by the broader discourse over public safety, as well as specific law enforcement debates. Although the narrative is driven by a progressing thesis, it also maps out and contextualizes the range of cybercrimes, and in so doing the book contributes to ongoing academic debates. The book's intended audiences are advanced undergraduates and graduate students on a variety of programmes, as well as the professional communities involved in cybercrime-related policymaking or practice. It also complements some of the very good texts that emerged on the subject in what has now become quite a crowded field; see, for example, the seminal work of Grabosky and Smith (1998; Smith et al., 2004) and Grabosky (2016), followed by McQuade's (2006b) and Majid Yar's (2006; 4th edn, with Steinmetz, 2023) sociological treatise on cybercrime and society, and Fafinski's (2009) legal/regulatory debate; Maras's 2016 *Cybercriminology*, Steinmetz's (2016) analysis of hackers, Leukfeldt's (2016) study of cybercrime and organized crime; also Lusthaus (2019), Lavorgna (2020), Holt and Bossler (2015) and Holt et al. (2022) on digital forensics in cybercrime; and Button et al. (2022) on economic cybercrimes. And there are many other tomes that are too numerous to mention, yet, I must add, no less important!

Informed by my own empirical research and that of other colleagues in the field, the narrative has largely been constructed from a grounded analysis of events and draws upon a range of diverse and different sources. Theoretically, it owes debts to the narrative criminologies of Katz (1988) and colleagues, the grounded theories of Glaser and Strauss (1967), Gibson's 'Affordance Theory' (1966) and Cohen and Felson's routine activities theories (1979). It is also informed by, and sometimes opposes, the cultural cybercrime narratives mapped out in the 1980s cyberpunk literature (see later). The narrative is also shaped by the distributed (as opposed to centralized) organization of the internet and multiple flows of often conflicting information about cybercrime offending and victimization. A fact of life is that we (researchers) continually fight against the myth of available data about cybercrime, and the assumption that data streams exist, when in fact they do not exist in an easily usable form for social scientists. Furthermore, networked information has the tendency to flow quite freely in all directions and so evades the editorial verification and control of dissemination which characterized previous media technologies. Some of these information sources are the product of impartial and reliable news reporting, others are not. The latter may be the product of vested (usually commercial) interests, or the results of academic research, or surveys conducted by the many governmental and non-governmental agencies that have an interest in most things 'cyber'. As an example, consider the problem of when a cybercrime event actually takes place so that it can be recorded. Is it when a particular law is broken, or when the victim reports it, or an offender claims it (it does happen!), or a journalist or some other party exposes it? Event identification has been an age-old problem for criminology but becomes even more problematic when cybercrimes are involved. Wherever possible, original and independent sources of information have been drawn upon to ensure the reliability of information, in order either to confirm a particular trend in two or more independent data sets or to record the occurrence of an event. Since the first edition, this includes open-source databases on cybercrimes, ransomware victims and conflict groups assembled for various funded research projects.

Adopting such an approach has helped to counter simplistic or conventional wisdoms, often simplified by the media for public consumption. Particular care was taken to avoid following purely sensationalized news streams, where one article reporting a sensational news event would tend to spawn a chain of others. The resulting analysis therefore takes a multidisciplinary approach to respect the many voices of crime (Garland and Sparks, 2000). The digital realist perspective adopted here is not, however, to be confused with the artistic theory of pseudo-realism which carries the same name (see Surman, 2003: 11) or indeed debates about left-realism (Young, 1997). Rather, it originates more in the work of Lessig (1998a, 1998b, 2006) and Greenleaf (1998), but, as indicated earlier, also combining and adapting the work of criminological theorists, routine activities theory (Felson), affordance theory (Gibson), symbolic interactionalism (Matza) and cultural sociology (Katz) to understand and contextualize cybercrime. It is essentially a multiple discourse approach which recognizes that cybercrime, like ordinary crime, is a form of behaviour that is mediated as much by technology as by social and legal values, economic drivers and also opportunities. The interrelation between these influences not only shapes the digital architecture of criminal opportunity, but also provides directions for resolving the same harms.

What follows, then, is a systematic enquiry based upon available knowledge, literature and research findings, much of which is outlined in the next chapter. It is also informed by my own funded research projects into crime, criminal justice and the internet, conducted between 1999 and 2023 for a range of organizations and agencies.[1]

What are the principal research questions to be answered and how do they feature in the chapter structure?

In pursuit of the central aim of exploring the transformation of crime in the information age, which is simply defined as the time period after adoption of digital and networked technologies in the early 1990s when information, rather than things, became keys to progress (or not, as the case may be), this book seeks to answer six logical research questions that frame the discussion in each of the forthcoming chapters.

What are cybercrimes, what do we know about them and how do we make sense of them? Chapter 2 looks at the production of knowledge about cybercrime and the origins of the term. It then looks at the various discourses that give meaning to it, before exploring critically the tensions that exist between various ways in which knowledge about cybercrimes is produced. Analysis of 'the problem' provides a language with which to discuss it.

How have networked technologies changed opportunities for criminal activity? Chapter 3 discusses the emergence of networked society and the technologies that construct it. The chapter then explores the various ways in which their distinctive characteristics have transformed criminal behaviour and created new conduits for cyber-assisted, cyber-enabled and cyber-dependent criminal activities.

How has criminal activity changed in the information age? The following three chapters seek to answer this question by exploring the different focus, or modus operandi, of cybercrimes.

Chapter 4 looks at *cybercrimes against the machine* (which I have previously referred to as computer integrity crime (2007b) and cybertrespass (2001b)). It specifically outlines the various challenges to the integrity of computing systems, for example through hacking, to breach established boundaries to gain access to spaces over which ownership and control have already been established.

Chapter 5 explores *cybercrimes using the machine* (previously referred to as computer-assisted crime). Much of the discussion here focuses upon the various permutations of what is effectively cyber-theft or frauds – deceptive and acquisitive behaviour in cyberspace. But computer-mediated communications also increasingly fall under this banner because they seek to deceive.

Chapter 6 focuses upon *cybercrimes in the machine* (previously computer content crime) and considers these types of cybercrimes in the context of three key broad areas of concern: extreme pornography, hate speech, extreme political speech.

How is criminal activity and its organization continuing to change in the information age? Chapter 7 explores how the organization of cybercrime is becoming more sophisticated. Developments in malware are continuing to automate victimization, and social engineering has become more technically and psychologically sophisticated – both to the point that they are now the province of those selling their specialized skill sets as a service to would-be offenders. Not only is crime-as-a-service creating entirely new levels of cybercrime, but it also expands the scale of the offences and their impact upon victims. The chapter also contemplates some of the informational problematics that arise with regard to identifying offenders and their victims. In some contexts, the very concepts of offender and victim are challenged – both being central to the understanding of law and criminology.

How is cyberspace policed and by whom? Chapter 8 explores how cyberspace is policed. It plots the compliance framework that currently shapes the regulation of behaviour online to illustrate how order and law are currently maintained on the internet. It then identifies the challenges posed by cybercrimes for criminal and civil justice processes before positioning the 'public police' as gatekeepers to the criminal justice system, within that structure.

How are cybercrimes to be controlled, regulated and prevented? Given that we can't just switch the internet off when something goes wrong, chapter 9 looks at the regulatory challenges by focusing upon the processes that govern online behaviour and the roles played by law, technology and other influences in the regulation of cyberspace.

Why are the answers to these questions so important? Chapter 10 concludes by summarizing the findings of the preceding chapters and explaining how crime has become transformed by digital and networked technologies. Hopefully, the answers to the above questions will help you, the reader, to understand the different layers of phenomena colloquially known as cybercrimes. It will also help you to develop a language framework through which you can develop your own information about changing trends in cybercrime and communicate them with others.

Can this book be used for teaching?

Yes, the chapter structure can be easily adapted to create a cybercrime teaching module for students on third-level undergraduate degree programmes in criminology, criminal justice or law, or specific Master's degrees in cybercrime, cybersecurity, and terrorism and intelligence, even computer science. In the latter cases, it can help both to contextualize and to deconstruct cybercrime for the students. The introduction and conclusion and eight substantive chapters each provides insight into a different cybercrime issue and provides a set of thematic teaching or discussion points regarding the cybercrime issue which teachers can further develop. By following themes rather than a list of crimes, students can learn to grasp the varying implications of different cybercrimes; also, such a principle future-proofs the module as the threat landscape evolves. Often expressed as a question, the chapters' thematic component parts can be used to structure lectures and organize accompanying seminars around.

A suggested cybercrime teaching curriculum session structure based upon each chapter is:

- **Introduction to the cybercrime module** – About the module.
- **How is knowledge about cybercrime produced?** – Reflecting upon how we know how criminal behaviour has changed online.
- **How has criminal activity been transformed in cyberspace?** – How have networked technologies changed opportunities for criminal activity? The following three sections look at three different modus operandi of cybercrime and their respective bodies of law.
  - **Cybercrimes against the machine** (hacking, cracking and denial of service attacks) – How have crimes against the machine changed in the information age?
  - **Cybercrimes using the machine** (scams and thefts; virtual robberies; social media network crime; violent, offensive communications; large-scale privacy violations) – How have crimes using the machine changed in the information age?
  - **Cybercrimes in the machine** (extreme sexual imagery, hate speech and

    violent speech) – How have crimes in the machine changed in the information age?

- **How criminal activity is continuing to change in the information age** – Cybercrime futures: the (re)organization of the cybercrime supply chain as an ecosystem.
- **Maintaining order and law on the cyberbeat** – Policing cybercrime: how is cyberspace regulated and policed, and by whom?
- **How are cybercrimes to be regulated and prevented?** – Controlling and preventing cybercrime.
- **How has crime been transformed in the information age?** – Concluding session.

At the beginning of each chapter (as is the case with this chapter) is listed the chapter structure and the key points covered, followed by a 'Chapter at a glance' paragraph. At the end of each chapter are also listed some discussion points and questions, along with some ideas for further reading. These are useful for the reader to reflect on what they have read, or the ideas behind them could be later adapted for essay or seminar questions.

A more detailed breakdown of the teaching issues outlined above can be found in Appendix 1. Also see note in Appendix 1 about using the UNODC Cybercrime Module to help broaden the curriculum further if necessary.

Further Reading   At the end of each chapter, I have outlined some specific further reading that will enable students and researchers to take their studies further. Please note that not all of the sources are referenced directly in the text, but they are nevertheless influential. Students who wish to study the whole field further are recommended to start with the following texts: McGuire (2007); Holt and Bossler (2015); Maras (2016); Gillespie (2019); Lavorgna (2020); Yar and Steinmetz (2023). Not only are these, and the further readings mentioned at the end of each chapter, a source of different perspectives, but the references they draw upon will also provide another useful route of discovery. Please note that these should be available online or via your library, but please do note that, while some of the older versions may not be currently available in hard copy, they should still be available in an electronic format.

2 Producing Knowledge about Crime in Cyberspace

How do we know how criminal behaviour has changed online?

Chapter contents and key points

Producing knowledge about cybercrimes?

- Cyberpunk and the conceptual origins of cyberspace
- What, then, are cybercrimes?
- The origins of the terms 'cyberspace' and 'cybercrime' in social science fiction
- Academic literature on cybercrime
- Statistical sources: state and the cybersecurity industry

Tensions in the production of knowledge about cybercrimes?

- Over-dramatizing cybercrime: reporting bias and media construction
- Under-reporting cybercrimes
- The ongoing power struggle for control over cyberspace as a contested space
- Competing expert claims
- Conflicts and confusions between public and private sector interests
- The danger of confusing the rhetoric with reality
- Criminological theory and cybercrime

How has crime transformed criminal behaviour online and how do we know about it?

Chapter at a glance   *Chapter 2 seeks to look critically at how we understand what cybercrimes are and, importantly, the nature of problems and tensions that arise from the competing (inter-disciplinary) viewpoints that constitute the production of knowledge about them. It reconciles different versions of events with the narrative that frames cybercrime. The first part, therefore, looks at the cultural origins of the term 'cybercrime' and outlines the various sources of knowledge that inform our understanding of crime in the information age, in particular identifying various 'voices' that are present within the literature. The second part identifies the various tensions and competing views in the production of knowledge about cybercrimes and the culture of fear around cybercrime which can shape understandings of it.*

Introduction

Although few would deny that the internet has had a major impact upon criminal behaviour, there is much less consensus as to what that impact is. Even when commentators agree that cybercrimes are a problem, there appears to be little consensus about how to deal with them collectively (Goodman and Brenner, 2002: 89). To be blunt, after three decades of the internet, everyone still agrees that cybercrimes exist and are a problem to society, but fewer still seem to agree as to what they are! Sometimes the discussion is about hacking; at other times it is about frauds, obscene, hate or political materials. It is also often the case that claims about the prevalence of cybercrimes still lack clarification as to what it is that is particularly 'cyber' about them. Indeed, when so-called cases of cybercrime come to court, they often have the familiar ring of 'traditional' crime rather than 'cyber' about them. These offences typically comprise hacking, fraud, pornography, paedophilia and, to an extent, bullying, stalking, harassment and even fake news, which are already part of existing criminal justice regimes. Perhaps more confusing is the contrast between the many hundreds of thousands of incidents that are supposedly reported each year and the relatively small number of known prosecutions that take place. Is this a case of the absence of evidence not being evidence of its absence – what Donald Rumsfeld called the 'unknown-unknowns' (Barone, 2004)? Or should we be asking if there are actually such things as cybercrimes (Brenner, 2001: para. 1)? Authors including myself (from 1997), Jones (2003: 98), McGuire (2007), Yar (2006; Yar and Steinmetz, 2023) and many others since have questioned whether cybercrimes are actually categories of crime in need of new theorization, or whether they are understood better by adapting existing theories.

Indeed, important additional questions arise as to whether or not cybercrimes have changed substantively in recent years. Early attempts to understand them did not really foresee the upscale in cybercrime victimization caused by the industrial development of malware such as ransomware: malware which not only defrauds victims at a number of levels but also collects the money for the criminals. Nor did they foresee the expansion of offending behaviours related to social media networks that create new attack psyops (psychological operations) vectors which manipulate populations socially, emotionally and politically. What is clear, however, is that not only has the internet transformed social behaviour and crime online, but criminal activity online, referred to as cybercrime, has become so grounded in culture and common language that the term 'cybercrime' is here to stay. What remains uncertain is how we as researchers of cybercrime describe the phenomenon to others, so we need to develop a common language framework to express it.

While 'cybercrime' is best regarded as an umbrella term that describes a series of different offensive behaviours that use digital and networked technologies, it remains both a prickly and a contentious issue. The fact that there still exist contrasting viewpoints, over whether it is related to technology or the behaviour (gullibility) of victim groups, exposes a large gap in our comprehension of cybercrime and begs important questions about the quality of the production of knowledge about it, which structure this chapter.

The first group of questions relate to the partiality and reliability of primary information sources that mould opinion and shape the conceptual context of cybercrime.

How do we know cybercrime is a problem and, if it is, have we an accurate measure of it? Has the level of cybercrime been understated? All indications are that it is both under-reported and under-prosecuted. Why is it of such great concern? Has it been blown up out of all proportion? If so, how has this happened? Has, for example, the media news-gathering process effectively fabricated an apparent crime wave out of a few novel and dramatic events? Alternatively, are we experiencing a calcu-lated attempt by the self-interested, 'self-dramatizing and fear-mongering world of security pundits' (Schneier, 2003) – the cybersecurity industry – to peddle 'Fear, Uncertainty and Doubt' (FUD). Green claimed in 1999 that 'FUDmongering', as this process has become known, 'is a tactic often used by vendors within a monopoly market in order to propagate their monopoly', and it still is today, although with a greater degree of sophistication. Or are these early fears now being borne out in full in a world where the likes of ransomware and cyber-warfare have a real and tangible real-world effect?

The second group of questions relates to the significant disparities between the alleged high significance of cybercrimes and their apparent lack of impact upon everyday life and the relatively low number of prosecutions. These ques-tions challenge the conceptual basis upon which the basic information that shapes assumptions is gathered. Could it be, for example, that criminal justice processes are just woefully inefficient at bringing cybercrime wrongdoers to justice? This raises the question of whether we realistically expect criminal justice processes designed to counter the social effects of urban migration to respond to an entirely new set of glo-balized 'virtual' problems? Or could it be that we are simply failing to understand the epistemological differences between the various legal, academic, expert and popu-lar constructions of cybercrime? There is not enough room in this book to answer all these questions conclusively, if indeed they are mutually exclusive, but there is clearly the need to 'separate the air that chokes from the air upon which wings beat' (Barlow, 1996).

These groups of questions are as valid today as in the past because the cybercrime threat landscape continues to evolve. This chapter therefore seeks a critical under-standing of the issues that frame cybercrimes in order to explain how we understand them, and, importantly, identify the nature of tensions that arise from the competing viewpoints that constitute the production of knowledge about them. It seeks to rec-oncile views on cybercrime events with the narrative that frames them.

The first part, therefore, looks at the cultural origins of the term 'cybercrime' and identifies the various sources of knowledge that inform our understanding of cybercrime, especially the various 'voices' that are present within the literature. The second part locates the various tensions and competing views in the production of knowledge about cybercrimes and describes the culture of fear around cybercrime which can shape understandings of it.

Producing knowledge about cybercrimes?

Why call it 'cybercrime'? The cultural history of cybercrime implies that it is simply a crime that takes place in cyberspace, a statement which immediately raises questions about what cyberspace is. But, if it is simply a crime that takes place in cyberspace, then are intrusions into computer systems the same as frauds or pornographic imagery or hate speech, because each is classified as a cybercrime? The answer is to be found in the origins of cybercrime.

Cyberpunk and the conceptual origins of cyberspace

The conceptual origins of cyberspace can be traced back to the late 1970s and early 1980s cyberpunk social science fiction literature. Cyberpunk authors combined cybernetics with the sensibilities of the contemporary punk movement to form a genre of science fiction that thematically joined ideas about dystopic advances in science and information technology with their potential capability to break down the social order. As Person (1998) observes: 'Classic cyberpunk characters were marginalized, alienated loners who lived on the edge of society in generally dystopic futures where daily life was impacted by rapid technological change, a ubiquitous datasphere of computerized information, and invasive modification of the human body.' The early cyberpunk leitmotif was essentially a 'hi-tech, but low-life', aesthetic, and the 'Classic cyberpunk characters' described by Person eventually became a social blueprint for the hacker stereotype – a stereotype which has evolved into a post-cyberpunk world where they are no longer alienated loners, but often employed and integral members of society who live in futures that are not necessarily dystopic. Yet, their lives are traumatized 'by rapid technological change and an omnipresent computerized infrastructure' (Person, 1998).

Cyberspace is the imaginary space created by a social, psychological and cultural reaction to the scientific combination of digital and networked technologies. Scientifically, digitization converts information (pictures, documents, written thoughts, memes, etc.) into digital files, which can then be communicated instantly to all the nodes of a network. But it was the early cultural representation of these ideas in fiction and film which helped embed them into the human imagination to create an imaginary space that people could inhabit and map their way around.

The origins of the term 'cyberspace' lie in Gibson's (1982) highly influential short story 'Burning chrome' about the hacker group 'Cyberspace Seven'.[1] It quickly became a popular descriptor for the cyberspace imaginary within which networked computer activity takes place. Gibson's short story was published in *Omni Magazine* (1978–98) which was a science-fiction-meets-hard-science forum that promoted explorations into cyberpunk. Along with other science fiction forums, novels and films during the 1980s, *Omni* contributed to the progressive definition of 'cyberspace' as a contrast to real space, the physical environment (see Gibson, 1984). The linkage between cyberspace and crime quickly evolved because it made the narrative seem all the more daring and 'sexy'. Having said this, the linkage between the two has been confused by the evolution of two quite different visions of cyberspace that are usefully delineated by Jordan (1999: 23–58). Gibson's original symbolic vision of cyberspace sees individuals leaving their physical bodies behind and shifting their consciousness from their 'meatspace' into 'cyberspace' as, for example, in the movie, *The Matrix* (1999, dir. Wachowski and Wachowski). John Perry Barlow's hybrid (Barlovian) vision, on the other hand, joined the virtual with the real to combine Gibson's virtual concept with real-world experience (Jordan 1999: 56; Bell 2001: 21). The product was an environment that could be constitutionalized, over which order could prevail (Barlow, 1996). Albeit ambitious, Barlow's alternative vision of cyberspace is, after Sterling (1994: xi), a place that is neither inside the computer, nor inside the technology of communication, but set in the imaginations of networked individuals. Although imaginary, it is nevertheless real in the sense that things happen in that space which have real consequences for those participating within it. Hence, it is impossible to separate the two spaces as per the digital dualism argument: "the digital and physical are increasingly meshed" (Jurgenson, 2011), especially where cybercrimes are concerned.

What, then, are cybercrimes?

As stated earlier, 'cybercrimes' are simply the crimes that take place within cyberspace, but the term has come to symbolize insecurity and risk online more broadly. By itself, cybercrime is fairly meaningless because it tends to be used metaphorically and emotively rather than scientifically or legally, usually to signify the occurrence of harmful behaviour that is somehow related to the misuse of a networked computer system. Largely an invention of the media, 'cybercrime' originally had no specific reference point in law, especially in the UK or US.[2] The offending that did become associated with the term was a rather narrow legal construction based upon concerns about hacking, or pornography or fraud. In fact, many so-called cybercrimes that caused concern during the first decade of the internet were not necessarily crimes in criminal law at the time when the concerns were expressed. If we could turn the clock back to the 1980s, then perhaps the term 'cyberspace crime' would have been a more precise and accurate descriptor.

The precise origin of the term 'cybercrime', in contrast to 'cyberspace', is unclear. It seems to have emerged in the late 1980s in the later cyberpunk fiction and associated audiovisual media. Yet the linkage between cyberspace and crime was implicit in the early cyberpunk short stories by William Gibson, Bruce Sterling, Bruce Bethke and Neil Stephenson[3] and others. As indicated earlier, crime adds a thrilling aspect to the cyberspace narrative. The cyberspace-crime theme was subsequently taken to a wider audience in popular contemporary novels such as Gibson's 'Sprawl' trilogy of *Neuromancer* (1984), *Count Zero* (1986) and *Mona Lisa Overdrive* (1988), and also Stephenson's *Snowcrash* (1992). Cyberpunk effectively defined cybercrime as a harmful activity that takes place in virtual environments, and made the 'hi-tech low-life' hacker narrative a norm in the entertainment industry. It is interesting to note at this point that whilst social theorists were adopting the Barlovian model of cyberspace, it was the Gibsonian model that shaped the public imagination through the visual media.

Regardless of its descriptive merits and demerits, the term 'cybercrime' has entered the public parlance and we are stuck with it (Wall, 2005). It remains a normatively laden concept and simple mention of it invokes dramatic images of planes being driven from the skies, nuclear power stations in various states of meltdown, bank accounts haemorrhaging, evil paedophiles grooming innocents, etc., some of which are related to real events. Similarly, the very mention of the word 'cybercriminal' equally conjures up stereotypical and dramatic mental images of legions of (young and not so young) hackers – introverted and unshaven Russian males glued to their computers whilst hacking into the bank accounts of innocent Westerners at the behest of a bejewelled crime lord with vested interests in drugs, prostitution, people trafficking and child pornography. Indeed, the etymology of the term 'hacker' is also normatively laden as it initially described those who illicitly explored (hacked) forbidden physical spaces such as roofs and tunnels and was adopted by MIT computer scientists (Harvey, 1985). For decades now, readers only have to type the phrase 'hackers attack' into a search engine and the first pages of results are populated by stories which replay tired cold-war politics about mainly Eastern hackers (APT (Advanced Persistent Threat) groups from North Korea, China, Iran or Russia) attacking various Western states.

What is certain is that the hard imagery conjured up by the emotive terminology used in media reports sharply contrasts with the pictures of dejected, young, lone hackers being led away in handcuffs to jail by law enforcement officers – images that are usually accompanied by fairly mundane descriptions of their actions that never seem to match the drama of the initial media reportage of their exploits.

This is not to suggest that hacking is a fiction, for it certainly does take place with very serious damaging consequences for society and its infrastructure. Nor is it simply the predictable post-glasnost reconstruction of cold-war bogeymen from Russia, China or North Korea attacking the cherished icons of the West. Rather, the most striking observation from the contrast between the imagery and reality is the uncritical and unquestioning assuredness of commentators, policy-makers, law enforcement officers and all other actors involved in cybersecurity as to who the hackers are, and the seriousness of what they have done, even though the dogmatic headlines and some of the available evidence often place speculation above the facts.

Why, then, do these expectations exist as to who the hackers are, and why do we 'naturally' expect cybercrime to be dramatic, when both are not necessarily evidenced by fact? Indeed, it almost feels wrong to think otherwise, which begs the metaphorical question: does the (folk) devil actually drive a Lada (Wall, 2012)[4] or do we just think he does, and why do we assume that 'he' is a 'he'? It is very important to question these assumptions because they often obfuscate some very important distinctions between the crimes of the cybercriminals. Hackers are frequently classed in terms of their motivations. For example, ethical or 'white hat' hackers are driven by ethical motivations often relating to improving computing security and are usually contrasted against the unethical or 'black hat' hackers (initially called crackers) who are primarily driven by the prospect of financial or political gain. The problem with this contrast is that one person's ethics are another person's expression of resistance, especially when politically or morally motivated. This raises a bigger question about who decides who falls into the ethical and unethical categories, which in turn makes it harder to collect data about them. Indeed, it is wrong today to focus so much on hackers, since there are now a range of other offenders in the field who are more interested in attacking than hacking. It is perhaps better to view offenders in terms of their skill level rather than of more moralistic qualities which have bedevilled previous hacker profiles, which have fixed cybercrime with a hacker criminal stereotype that skews understanding? Offender groupings are discussed later.

In an ideal world, our knowledge of events such as cybercrime would be developed from a reliable source of relevant statistics surrounded by a body of literature. Yet, although the internet is now over three decades old and statistical sources are beginning to emerge, they still tend to vary according to national jurisdictional definitions.

In fact, there are a lot of available statistics, but they do not always tend to be compatible. In theory, statistics should replicate each other, but there is not currently an internationally agreed definition of cybercrime, nor a basis upon which statistics should be collected. Why this should be the case is relevant to this discussion because we need to understand the fluid and often abstract nature of the cybercrime concept. On the one hand, cybercrime has important cultural origins, yet on the other hand, it is a concept that has also important scientific antecedents in the literature over the past century or more. Cybercrime has both a cultural and scientific life as well as a legal and political one.

The origins of the terms 'cyberspace' and 'cybercrime' in social science fiction

Knowledge both about the internet and cybercrime was for many years largely dependent upon its powerful cultural antecedents in social science fiction.[5] Social science fiction is the branch of science fiction that explores forms of society that are the product of technological change. Its narratives tend to be informed by scientific facts relating to possibilities – see, for example, the works of William Gibson, Bruce Sterling, Neal Stephenson and Bruce Bethke (and others) mentioned earlier, all informed by theoretical and practical developments in science and technology. The mythologies emerge when proof of concept ideas become presented as reality – especially where fictional ideas frame concepts and become presented as truths that reinforce existing public anxieties and apprehensions. This is not to say that 'Cyberpunk writers made it all up'[6] – rather, the issue is that social science fiction begins to shape the public's imagination conceptually, especially when translated to movie narratives. They continue to be one of a number of cultural reference points that are relied upon when knowledge production lacks the critical objectivity of the actual facts or does not match expectations. Since the mid-2000s there have been many representations of hacker culture in various media; however, the earlier imagery shaped initial opinions and has echoed in subsequent interpretations. Although social science fiction has a fairly niche readership, it has played a broader role in the construction of contemporary imagery linking computers to crime which originates via a series of popular films dating back to the 1960s (some of which predate cyberpunk) which expressed the prevailing 'white heat of technology' theme. These include hacker and haxploitation movies.

Although cyberpunk literature was popular with social science fiction readers during the 1980s, the audience was relatively small. Cyberpunk entered mainstream popular culture through the cultural fusion of cyberspace and crime and five generations of hacker movies into which some of the cyberpunk ideas gradually dripped. Common to the five generations of hacker movies is 'haxploitation' which exploits the public fear of hackers or attackers for entertainment purposes (my definition). The dramatic exploitation of this fear can, in situations where there is little counterfactual information, increase levels of public fear about cybercrime.

The first generation of hacker movies became defined by contemporary technologies and crimes committed within discrete computing systems. It conceptually predated cyberpunk but demonstrated to a wider audience the dramatic potential harm of the computer 'hack'. The first generation of movies included the *Billion Dollar Brain* (1967, dir. Russell), *Hot Millions* (1968, dir. Till), *The* [original] *Italian Job*

(1969, dir. Collinson), *Superman III* (1983, dir. Lester) and *Bellman and True* (1988, dir. Loncraine) and others. In these movies, the 'hackers' tended to be portrayed as male, fairly old and somewhat comically eccentric. See, for example, Benny Hill as Professor Peach in *The Italian Job*, Richard Pryor as Gus Gorman in *Superman III*, or Peter Ustinov as Marcus Pendleton in *Hot Millions*; and in *Lawnmower Man* (1992, dir. Leonard), Jeff Fahey as Jobe, an educationally challenged gardener who is given super-capabilities by computer technology.

The second generation of hacker movies were defined by early network technology, typically using dial-up modems to enable computers to communicate with each other (Wall, 2007a: 45). In contrast to the first-generation movies, they were clearly influenced by cyberpunk ideas and focused upon the hacker mentality rather than the hack. The earlier second-generation films romanticized the guile of the hacker as a penetrator of inter-connected computer systems while also celebrating a broader set of ethical values. These early second-generation movies consolidated the 'hacker' stereotype which endures to this day: of a disenfranchised, misunderstood genius teenage male who uses technology to put wrongs right whilst having a 'coming of age' experience and also some fun. Such films included *War Games* (1983, dir. Badham), *Electric Dreams* (1984, Barron), *Real Genius* (1985, dir. Coolidge), *Weird Science* (1985, dir. Hughes) and *Ferris Bueller's Day Off* (1986, dir. Hughes). The later second-generation films continued this theme but were a little more sophisticated because the narrative shifted from portraying hacks across (dial-up) communication networks to hacks using the broadband internet, or an imaginative sci-fi equivalent. The later second-generation films notably include *Die Hard* (1988, dir. McTiernan), *Sneakers* (1992, dir. Robinson), *Goldeneye* (1995, dir. Campbell), *Hackers* (1995, dir. Softley), *The Net* (1995, dir. I. Winkler) and *Net 2.0* (2006, dir. C. Winkler), *Johnny Mnemonic* (1995, dir. Longo), *Independence Day* (1996, dir. Emmerich), *Enemy of the State* (1998, dir. Scott), *Takedown* (2000, dir. Chappelle), *AntiTrust* (2001, dir. Howitt), *Swordfish* (2001, dir. Sena) and *The* [newer] *Italian Job* (2003, dir. Gray), plus many others. In this later second generation, hackers were still young(ish), but not as predominantly male as previously. Strong female characters include Angela Bennett in *The Net*, Winkler), Trinity in *The Matrix* trilogy and the Lisbeth Salander character in Stieg Larsson's trilogy: *The Girl with the Dragon Tattoo* (2009,dir. Opley); *The Girl who Played with Fire* (2009, dir. Alfredson); and *The Girl who Kicked the Hornets' Nest* (2009, dir. Alfredson). And yet Gordon (2010) found that only seven (12 per cent) of the sixty film hackers studied in his analysis were female. Hackers in this generation of movies were also less likely to adopt the moral high ground as in earlier films, and their ethical motivations were driven by the ends justifying the 'technological' means, rather than the opposite.

The third generation of hacker movies depict both hacker and the hack within a virtual environment, or blurring the boundary between the virtual and physicality. They are epitomized by *The Matrix* and its later derivatives, but also *TRON* (1982, dir. Lisberger) and *TRON: Legacy* (2010, dir. Kosinski). Underlying *The Matrix* narrative, and also *TRON*, is an articulation of the Gibsonian linkage between cyberspace and meatspace via the avatar, set within the conceptual framework of French social philosophy. Jean Baudrillard's (1994) ideas about 'hyper-reality' (the inability to differentiate fantasy from reality) greatly inspired the Wachowskis who wrote and produced *The Matrix*. Indeed, so strongly did the idea of hyper-reality shape the construction of the film's narrative that Baudrillard's *Simulacra and Simulation* (Baudrillard, 1994) was allegedly set as required reading for the film's principal cast and crew (McLemee, 2007). However, true to Baudrillard's critical personality, when asked for his view on this application of his work, he is reported to have bluntly retorted that he thought the producers and writers had misunderstood it (Longworth, 2007). An interesting micro-detail related to *The Matrix* is that observant viewers of the 'follow the white rabbit' scene will notice that Neo stores his computer disks in a hollowed-out hardback copy of Baudrillard's *Simulacra and Simulation*.

As the World Wide Web has become more embedded in our everyday lives and virtual reality becomes our 'reality', then the third generation of hacker movies is giving way to a new, fourth generation. The fourth generation has emerged to exploit potentially dystopic relationships between online and real-world environments experienced by 'digital natives'. It derives/derived its (usually crime-based) drama from the ways in which online relationships can have real-world effects. In the fourth-generation movies, there is a noticeable shift away from the traditional hack narrative that emphasized the hacker's often humiliating power over the vessels of state and society towards an exploitation of the fears and risks associated with the technologies of today, especially interoperable converged networked technologies and social networking sites – see, for example, *Hard Candy* (2005, dir. Slade). It is anticipated that the new fourth-generation haxploitation narrative will continue to erode the now traditional relationship between the outlawed individual hacker and the state to re-express the latter's dominant norms. Moreover, in the new narrative, there is often a clear reversal of the roles so that, in select examples, the state, or the victim corporate organization, develops a strategic alliance with the hackers in order to protect itself or further its own goals. In movies such as *Die Hard 4.0* (2007, dir. Wiseman), for example, the state hits back against a rogue element within it with help from a previously outlawed hacker. Alternatively, in *Enemy of the State*, rogue elements in the state apparatus hack the individual. This is similarly the case in *23* (1998, dir. Schmid); *eXistenZ* (1999, dir. Cronenberg); *In the Realm of the Hackers* (2003, dir. Anderson); *Source Code* (2011, dir. Jones and Ripley); *Reboot* (2012, dir. Kawasaki); *Who Am I* (2014, dir. bo Odar); *Cyberbully* (2015, dir. Chanan); *Blackhat* (2015, dir. Mann); and *Mr Robot* (2015–19, dir. Esmail), to name a few.

Where the fourth-generation movies differ from their predecessors is that the battle lines are not so clearly drawn as before in the cyber-arms race between the adaptive capacities of hackers and law enforcers. As a consequence, today's 'hacker' equivalent is no longer the reclusive male seen in the second-generation movies. They may still be as active online as the early hackers were, but the information exchanged largely relates to social as well as technical activities. Curiously, the term 'hacker' is also used colloquially to describe someone who invades a friend's or enemy's social network account and changes it to poke fun at, or humiliate, the victim in front of their friends. Consequently, a new social network hacker is evolving as a much more social individual, though the old ethical and unethical hacker types still remain on the sidelines.

The fifth generation of hacker movies are mainly docufilms about actual hackers themselves, hacking events or the internet. See, for example, *The KGB, the Computer and Me* (1990 TV movie, dir. Bates) about Clifford Stoll's takedown of a hacker; *Home Page* (1998, dir. Block) about Justin Hall, one of the first bloggers (not a hacker);

Takedown (2000) and *Freedom Downtime* (2001) about hacker Kevin Mitnick; *The Social Network* (2010, Fincher) about Mark Zuckerberg; *War for the Web* (2015, dir. Brueckner) about the infrastructure of the internet; *Deep Web* (2015, dir. Winter) about darkmarkets; *Snowden* (2016, dir. Stone) about Edward Snowden; *Hacker* (2016) about the Anonymous hacktivist group; and others. These fifth-generation movies tend to apply movie values to real-life situations. They are where art and reality can simultaneously imitate each other.

The cultural impact of these hacker movies is significant as factional[7] hacker narratives skilfully combine fact with fiction to crystallize the 'super-hacker' offender stereotype as the archetypal 'cybercriminal' (Wall, 2007a: 16). The combination of the image of the independent 'outsider' with an expression of the power that they can yield against individuals, corporations and the state configures the hacker as a potential folk devil, which is precisely what the image of the hacker has become (Nissenbaum, 2004).

It is fairly unlikely that there will be a distinctive sixth generation of hacker movies, because the hacker role has become so ubiquitous and diffused by variation that it has ceased to be the spectacle that it once was. Perhaps the spectacle around which future movies are framed might be the absence of new technologies, rather than their presence, but only time will tell. The sixth generation is more likely to be defined by the fact that hackers have become synonymous with criminal entrepreneurs, as the later chapter on the cybercrime ecosystem explains. They have made cybercrime their career choice!

What makes these various 'hack'-related sources of visual and textual imagery significant is that 'contemporary movie and media imagery subconsciously ordered the line between fact and fiction' (Furedi, 2006; Wall, 2007a: 16), so much so that Burrows (1997) argued that not only has the Gibsonian concept of cyberspace transmuted into a tangible reality, but Gibson's technological vision has also fed back into the theory and design of computer and information systems. Furthermore, despite the contradictions between the different visions of cyberspace, Gibson's fictional perspectives on cultural, economic and social phenomena have also begun to find their way into social and cultural analyses as viable characterizations of our contemporary world (Burrows, 1997). Yet, as outlined earlier, it was the hybrid Barlovian model of cyberspace, rather than the pure Gibsonian vision, that has actually found greater purchase with social theorists, especially in thinking about cybercrime. This is because, if cyberspace is also a space in which criminal intent can be expressed as action, then the extent to which harmful acts are mediated by networked technologies therefore becomes a useful measure of whether or not an act is a true cybercrime or not – which is a conversation we return to in the next chapter.

Before moving on to the next section, it must be noted that the science fiction hacker narrative itself echoes the character of the savant who appears in a number of Victorian science fiction novels and is a prototype for the hacker. The savant constructs or appropriates technological inventions in order to give them extra-human power to wield control over others. It is as popular a theme in modern science fiction as it was a century or so ago in the novels of H. G. Wells[8] and his contemporaries. These early novels were written during a time of great social upheaval caused by technological innovation, and described worlds that had been transformed, but also threatened, by new and potentially oppressive technologies. The savant tradition continued throughout the twentieth century to the cyberpunk of the present day via the works of Brian Aldiss, Aldous Huxley and many others. It is the power that the savant can independently wield by using technology (for good or evil) that makes them so attractive as a science fictional character and sets the narrative scene for the later construction of the hacker.

Not only does contemporary movie and media imagery subconsciously order the line between fact and fiction (Furedi, 2006) as stated earlier, but it also framed 'the hacker' as the predominant offender stereotype. It was, and still is, a powerful image characterized by introverted youth utilizing technological might to ubiquitously subordinate 'the system' and indiscriminately victimize its subjects.

Academic literature on cybercrime

It is too simplistic to pin the current conceptualizations of cyberspace and cybercrime solely on social science fiction, although the cyberpunk authors deserve immense credit – I am a fan. This is because cyberpunk concepts of cyberspace were also augmented by a century of discourse within the academic literature that also informs our general understanding of the impacts of technology upon society and the way they relate to crime.

Indeed, Castells (2000a) explicitly observes that the contemporary networked society, often attributed to the internet, actually predated it by a number of decades. The most notable academic discourses on the social impact of technology focused upon longstanding concerns expressed in the volumes on industrial sociology from Karl Marx through to Harry Braverman (1976), and the Frankfurt School through to today. Technology's function in this literature, with caveats, was perceived primarily as a means of rationalizing the power of capital by specializing the division of labour to reduce the cost of the production process. Building upon this tradition is an equally long-standing debate over the technologies of social control, which ranges from Bentham and Foucault through to Gary Marx (2001) and others. Attending these concerns are socio-legal discourses of freedom of expression, privacy and human rights (Rotenberg, 2001; Kerr, 2003; Balkin, 2004; Kozlovski, 2004; Lessig, 2006; Solove, 2008; Koops et al., 2013), often informed by the various theories of information society (Castells, 1997b, 2000b, 2000c; Bell, 2001; Webster, 2002). As a meta-narrative to these classics are a range of broader discourses about late, high or post-modernity (Giddens, 1990; Bauman, 1998), but also governance and risk (Miller and Rose, 1990; Rhodes, 1996; O'Malley, 1999; Garland, 2001; Simon, 2007). A key driver of each is the need to identify what is normal (and abnormal) behaviour in a rapidly technologizing society, to locate the step-change. Moving closer to cybercrimes are various debates in criminology over deviance and society, and also the governance of deviance (see Braithwaite, 1992; Furedi, 2002; Crawford, 2003; Stenson and Edwards, 2003; Shearing, 2004). These are followed by theories of crime science and prevention (Clarke and Felson, 1993; Felson, 2000; Hughes et al., 2001; Yar, 2005b: 407); debates about policing society (Reiner, 2000; Stenning, 2000; Loader and Walker, 2001; Jones and Newburn, 2002; Crawford and Lister, 2004) and policing the risk society (Beck, 1992, 1999; Ericson and Haggerty, 1997).

Focusing the lens upon the network technology and crime axis reveals specific discourses about the governance of online behaviour. Some authors address the physics of digital law (Geer, 2004), while others address the architecture created by the codes that constitute the internet (Lessig, 1998b, 2006; Post, 2000; Katyal, 2001, 2003). Accompanying these debates are texts which outline and debate the intricacies of specific computer crime legislation (Akdeniz, 1996, 1997; Akdeniz et al., 2000; Wasik, 2000; Reed and Angel, 2003; Walden, 2003, 2016; Carr, 2004; Lastowka and Hunter, 2005; Fafinski, 2009). Finally, there is the literature that addresses the issue of cybercrimes more generally (Grabosky and Smith, 1998; Denning, 2000; Loader and Thomas, 2000; Brenner, 2001, 2002; Grabosky et al., 2001; Wall, 2001b, 2003, 2004, 2005; Jewkes, 2003, 2006; Moitra, 2003; Newman and Clarke, 2003; Barrett, 2004; Morris, 2004; Smith et al., 2004; Broadhurst and Grabosky, 2005; Furnell, 2005; Pattavina, 2005; Yar, 2005a, 2005b, 2006, 2013; McQuade, 2006a, 2006b; Jewkes and Yar, 2009; Grabosky, 2016; Maras, 2016; Steinmetz, 2016; Holt and Bossler, 2015; Lusthaus, 2019; Yar and Steinmetz, 2023; Lavorgna, 2020). Other literature addresses specific aspects of cybercrime, such as policing and law enforcement (Goodman, 1997; Brenner, 2001; Shinder and Tittel, 2002; Wall, 2002a, 2007b, 2017, 2021; Britz, 2003; Barrett, 2004; Sommer, 2004; Jewkes and Andrews, 2005; McQuade, 2006a). The more topic-specific cybercrime literature is discussed in later chapters.

Finally, there is the non-fiction cybercrime literature, such as that by Sterling (1994); Menn (2010); Glenny (2012); Goodman (2016), plus the memoirs and biographies of former hackers (e.g., Poulsen, by Littman, 1997; Mitnick and Simon, 2012, etc.), which provide competent journalistic, albeit sensational, accounts of specific types of cybercrime, but often lack a broader theoretical context.

Box 2.1 Give me the data and I'll tell you what the crimes are!

A personal vignette sums up this disparity in academic discourse. Some colleagues and I discussed setting up an interdisciplinary cybercrime project and we pondered upon what sort of data we would need to work on. Coming from social science, I immediately thought of a policy-based issue and obtaining empirical data relating to it. A computer science colleague, however, saw it differently. He said: 'If you can give us the data, then we can tell you when the crime has occurred.' Not only did we see the issue from completely different methodological perspectives, but also different interpretations of the terminology. I saw a crime as something defined by law and about four or five sets of governmental criteria relating to its reporting, recording, seriousness, public interest in prosecution, weight of evidence, etc. My colleague, on the other hand, saw each 'crime' as essentially a series of breaches of scientific rules. If only things were so straightforward!

The rich vein of literature identified above tends to fall into four main discourses, which collectively exhibit a wealth of knowledge about the content of cybercrime and its attendant issues. The legislative/administrative discourse about cybercrimes defines or debates the rules that set the boundaries of acceptable and unacceptable behaviour as its primary concern. The academic discourse, on the other hand, seeks out criminological, socio-legal, sociological, social policy, computer science, software engineering, information management, economic and/or technological understandings of what has actually happened.

The expert discourse, often driven by the cybersecurity sector, explores and understands trends in cybercrimes in order to provide explanations and inform solutions. Finally, there is the popular, emotional or layperson's discourse, reflecting the person on the street's understanding of cybercrime, which also has a bearing on the market, social values, the security response and eventually the law. The claims made about the extent, breadth or number of cybercrimes are, however, often contradictory because of their respective epistemologies. Very often, there simply is not a police code to record the crime, as was the case with ransomware, but these claims are more often at odds with the public or lay discourse about cybercrimes as expressed in the popular media. Whereas the legal, academic and expert discourses are typically driven by rational considerations, the latter are predominantly journalistic and emotive in construction (Wall, 2008). This dissonance does not assist the acquisition of a broader understanding of the nature of the problem(s) and the subsequent formation of good public policy.

Statistical sources: state and the cybersecurity industry

A body of statistical sources has emerged since the first edition. The cybersecurity industry continues regularly to produce statistics from data returned via their products. The quality of this data has improved greatly and very often the methodologies are explained. Various government agencies now collate and publish statistics on cybercrimes. In the UK, for example, Action Fraud receives and collates information from victims reporting cybercrimes. The Home Office, via the Office of National Statistics, publishes summaries of various cybercrimes that have been reported and recorded in the criminal justice system. In the US, the Internet Crime Complaint Center (IC3), an equivalent of Action Fraud, publishes statistics of victim reports. A number of other countries, mainly with common-law systems, also generate such official statistics.

In addition to these are various regular victim surveys, the Annual Crime Survey of England and Wales, for example, asks questions about cybercrime victimization. This is augmented by a range of official and industry-commissioned business surveys. In addition, there are now a range of open-source databases that can be accessed by researchers in the field – see, for example, Hackmageddon's useful timelines of reported cybercrime events.[9] Various academic institutions now collect and provide data. The Cambridge Cybercrime Centre[10] provides research data on various cybercrime themes, including known prosecutions. Indeed, some of the research included in this book is informed by open-source databases on cybercrime and also ransomware.[11] In the case of the latter, key data is provided by the offending groups themselves who publish the names and details of their victims to evidence the hack to discomfort and shame them enough for them to pay the ransom. This process is part of the offenders' criminal business model, which has to compete in a competitive market. It therefore depends (like all businesses) upon its strong reputation to 'do business'. So the offenders' published data relating to attacks tends to be accurate, although the true impact of the victimization is not always known until reported by other media.

These multiple sources of information are a leap forward from the early 2000s, but they, nevertheless, raise a number of questions about what is meaningful data and, importantly, how we can judge which of the available information or data is dependable? Is, for example, our understanding of cybercrime based upon verifiable 'reliable data' or are we forced into 'condensing facts from the vapour of nuance' (Stephenson, 1992: 56). We need reliable information about criminal trends not only to make sense of 'the problem', but also to act as a key driver of criminal justice policy reform and resource allocation within relevant agencies. This is important because information policy, which frames criminal policy, is arguably becoming the new social policy in that it includes, excludes and stratifies before invoking a political debate (Wall, 2012). Various tensions currently exist in the production of knowledge about cybercrimes.

Box 2.2 What constitutes a ransomware attack for recording purposes?

There remains an important question to be answered about what constitutes a ransomware attack for recording purposes. Is it when the victim reports it, when the offender reports it, when the media identifies it? Bear in mind:

(a) that, for victims, there exist commercial disincentives to report and share data (embarrassing to reputation, takes company time, main concern is to get back in business). Develop an autonomous reporting system for giving data anonymously (perhaps to a third party owned by a business sector, like the UK payments model), rather than take a 'responsibilizing victims' approach.
(b) that offenders are over-eager to name and shame – but can they be believed? They have to be convincing as they seek to develop a commercial relationship with the victims – they present victims as clients with security problems.
(c) that media are over-sensitized towards ransomware and can over-report examples, especially when they think the victim has tried to deny the attack. Cybercrime is newsworthy, and so is any denied reporting of data loss.
(d) what happens when an attack is declared by the ransomware group, and the victim: (i) denies it; (ii) mitigates it; (iii) is not actually affected by it.
(e) What and when should victims report? (i) Simply the 'initial access' only? (ii) Lateral movement within the system? (iii) The identification and exfiltration of key data? (iv) The encryption of data or locking of the operating system? (v) The lost data? (vi) Lost money? (vii) (i)–(v) + the successful return of data and deletion of copies upon payment of a ransom? And what happens when the ransom is paid? The victim becomes a participant. It is harder to prosecute.

An agreed scripted approach is needed to collect and share data. This is more than just victim self-reports.

Tensions in the production of knowledge about cybercrimes?

There is no simple answer to the question of how to judge the quality of information sources, online or otherwise, because, as Mike Levi opined over two decades ago: 'the normal disciplines by which we evaluate the plausibility of threat levels are absent' (Levi, 2001: 50) – they still are absent. It is a situation, he states, which is also found in the risk assessments of other non-traditional types of crime, such as economic crime. It is therefore important to take a critical view of the production of knowledge about crime in the information age in order to understand the tensions which researchers, policy-makers, practitioners and other interested parties must eventually reconcile. The main tensions explored here are the over-dramatizing and under-reporting of cybercrimes. In addition, there exists a power struggle for control over cyberspace as a contested space, including competing expert claims, and conflicts and confusions between public and private sector interests, which combine to confuse rhetoric with reality.

Over-dramatizing cybercrime: reporting bias and media construction

Perhaps the conflicting viewpoints about cybercrime are simply indicative of the way in which we now 'consume crime' as just another sensationalized news item in contemporary consumer society. Baudrillard argued in 1970 that: '[w]hat characterises consumer society is the universality of the news item [le fait divers] in mass communication. All political, historical and cultural information is received in the same – at once anodyne and miraculous – form of the news item' (1998: 33). In this respect, little has since changed. Far more than ever, the news item nowadays is reduced to its signs, the symbols to which individuals emotionally react. After being spectacularly dramatized, the news is then consumed by readers or viewers who may not have any personal experience of the issue. Baudrillard's point is that mass communications do not give us reality; rather they give us what he calls 'the dizzying whirl of reality [le vertige de la realité]' (1998: 34) – what he later called the 'precession of simulacra' (2009). Most cases of crime reporting are now so distanced from the consumer that only the fact that the crime event has taken place has any meaning. This observation adds weight to Garland's (2001) 'crime complex' argument, whereby public anxiety about crime has become the norm and now frames our everyday lives.

Currently, activities involving the internet are still so newsworthy that a single dramatic incident of cybercrime has the power to shape public opinion and fuel anxiety, frequently resulting in (political) demands for 'instant' and simple solutions to what are very complex situations. This situation reflects a broader shift in the reorganization of news dissemination in the information age. The news business was initially built upon its singular ability to control the distribution of news information, but this power has become weakened by the internet because unlimited information can now be made available on a range of different devices and from a multitude of sources. Sambrook (2006) has argued that '[t]hanks to the internet, the role of media gatekeeper has gone. Information has broken free and top-down control is slipping inexorably away.' Sambrook further argues that the news business no longer controls what the public know, and that the internet has led to 'a major restructuring of the relationship between public and media'. This disintermediation of news is affecting politics and policy because the public can now access the politicians and the political process directly, or they can address, even mobilize, other members of the public with similar views (Sambrook, 2006). In short, an important layer of 'guardianship' for regulating rational behaviour has been removed from the governance framework.

Once voiced, demands for governmental and agency responses cannot simply be ignored, precisely because of the fear of the political consequences of not responding. This leads to a further twist to the tale of cybercrime in that the advent of social media technologies in the late 2010s arguably led to a further disintermediation of the news process and a further step towards what Baudrillard (1994) has termed 'hyper-reality'. This is a state in which individuals are unable to consciously distinguish reality from simulations of reality, and the truth of an issue becomes less important than the fact that it is being talked about. It is a situation which results in mythologies prevailing over reality – thus tempting the arbiters of news values to chase the story at the expense of the truth behind it.

Changes in the news process: churnalism   One of the principal reasons why internet myths can persist is that contradictions exist in the ways in which knowledge about cybercrimes is produced. These ultimately need to be resolved through knowledge-producing cybercrime research strategies (see further Wall, 2007a: 13; 2008). We find, for example, that there are conflicting discourses simultaneously talking about cybercrime. Lawyers, administrators, police, criminologists, diverse academic disciplines, security experts, computer scientists, information officers and the lay person all have a slightly different view on cybercrime reflected in their version of events. The most notable is the epistemological disparity between scientific and social science knowledge, between what could happen (proof of concept) and what actually does happen. Both are valuable viewpoints but can also be confusing when one is represented as the other. Furthermore, the way in which news is generally disseminated has changed because of networked technologies. There are now so many different networked news sources that it has become disintermediated (see Sambrook, 2006). Editors do not exercise the overall level of editorial control over the news process that they once did so that information sources are arguably no longer subjected to the same balances and checks.

Drawing upon the findings of specially commissioned research to analyse the content of two weeks' news output (covering over 2,000 stories) from 'the quality newspapers', *Guardian* journalist Nick Davies argued that only about 12% of newspaper stories are the product of journalists' own initiative and are thoroughly checked for integrity (Davies, 2008; HOC, 2009: Ev126, Q402). The purpose of Davies's research, also reported in detail by the researchers in Lewis et al. (2008), was to identify how many stories were based upon a central factual statement and whether or not the evidence for that statement had been thoroughly checked. Rather disturbingly, the bulk (72%) of the remaining 88% were found to have been either directly copied or adapted from wire copy mainly drawn from the PA (Press Association) or other news agencies, or directly taken from PR outputs and press releases. Yet, in nearly all cases (99%), these stories were attributed to a by-lined reporter or 'independent journalist', with little acknowledgement of the original sources (Lewis et al., 2008: 29).

BBC journalist Waseem Zakir has described this new type of journalism as 'churnalism', arguing that it is a form of modern instant journalism that results from the impact of the twin pressures of time and money. It does not follow the traditional journalistic practice of confirming the integrity of a news story by seeking two or more independent sources of information:

> 'Ten or 15 years ago you would go out and find your own stories and it was proactive journalism', he explained. 'It's become reactive now. You get copy coming in on the wires and reporters churn it out, processing stuff and maybe adding the odd local quote. It's affecting every newsroom in the country and reporters are becoming churnalists.' (Waseem Zakir interview in Harcup, 2008)

Davies (2008, 2010) has further argued that the process of the internet has led to a situation where 'An industry whose task should be to filter out falsehood has become a conduit for propaganda and second-hand news.' The core function of churnalists is, then, to utilize 'information subsidies' in the form of press releases, wire stories and other forms of pre-packaged material (see Gandy, 1982) to create articles in newspapers and other news media without undertaking further research or checking. When this 'churnalism' combines with blogging, it becomes a central component of viral information flows, further disintermediating news sources.

Box 2.3 The Illinois water pump hack

A leaked intelligence memo sensationally claimed that Russian hackers had remotely destroyed a water pump at an Illinois utility. It produced a flurry of sensationalized stories alleging that it was evidence of the 'first-ever destruction of U.S. infrastructure by a hacker'. A subsequent analysis found a Russian IP address in the SCADA (Supervisory Control and Data Acquisition) system used to control the water plant. An assumption made by various authorities was that a contractor's computer had been hacked and his credentials used to access the plant by a Russian state agency. The truth was quite different. Whilst on holiday in Russia, the contractor had accessed the water plant remotely to resolve a problem. As the information passed from one agency to another, the story was not corroborated and grew in seriousness, which led to the false and subsequently embarrassing conclusions (see Zetter, 2011). The story became stronger than the truth.

In much the same way, but for different reasons, statistics about cybercrime (outlined earlier) are also disintermediated. Because there are no longer any central and formalized points of collection (e.g., police), there are fewer commonly applied standards and fewer checks on information quality – which can result in misinformation. Yet this disintermediation of the news process runs counter to the construction of the imagery surrounding cybercrime, which originates in the days prior to the internet when the mass media was organized more centrally. Before news media became transformed by contemporary networked technology, understandings of crime were mediated at source by state agencies associated with the criminal justice processes, for example through UK Home Office crime statistics. They were therefore shaped by the more traditional (Peelian) notion of dangerousness and of the need to protect the public at large (Wall, 1998: 23; Reiner, 2000: ch. 2). Indeed, media accounts of cybercrimes frequently invoked the dramatic imagery of an 'Electronic Pearl Harbor' (Smith, 1998; Taylor, 2001: 69) or a 'Cyber-Tsunami' (Wall, 2001b: 2) where a vulnerable society is brought to its knees by forces beyond its control.

Such an observation is hardly surprising because early thinking about the application of networked technologies was closely entwined with science fiction media. The now defunct *Omni* magazine, which was published between 1978 and 1998, was one of a range of contemporary publications that combined articles on science fact with short works of science fiction to form popular technology-related narratives. It was, coincidentally, in the pages of *Omni* magazine that William Gibson first coined the word 'cyberspace' (1982). These are themes and memes that are still surprisingly alive in the approaches of the hacker groups Anonymous and Lulzsec.

The phrase 'Electronic Pearl Harbor' combines both the historical World War II outrage with a 'Future Shock' to conjure a stark image of helplessness and anomie. It not only contributes to the propagation of a culture of fear (Furedi, 2002; Wall, 2008), but also serves to heighten levels of public anxiety while also moulding public expectations about desirable legal and regulatory responses. Ironically, these same anxieties enhance the apparent dangerousness of the cybercriminal (Ohm's super user, 2007) and provide regulatory bodies with an implied mandate for taking action to protect the public. Moreover, a pervasive 'culture of fear' assumes that individuals are naturally fearful of the absence of any broadly recognized measure of the actual risk of cybercrimes. Therefore, public anxiety becomes intensified by the tendency of journalists, pressure groups and policy-makers – and also academics – to fail to differentiate between the 'potential' and 'actual' risks and associated harms. It is easy to fall back on the old adage 'Don't let the truth get in the way of a good story', but the implications of doing so are fairly serious. Once risk assessments are con-fused with reality, then the only perceivable way to satisfy heightened public anxiety about cybercrime is to introduce additional legislation and stringent technological countermeasures. See, for example, the later discussion about the reassurance gap in policing the internet whereby police and government cannot meet the public's demand for security against cybercrime. This 'ideology of regulation' shifts the debate towards the needs of the state and corporate interests, and away from impor-tant principles such as liberty and freedom of expression. The main way to counter the effects of ideology, and indeed erroneous media constructions, is through the presentation of reliable empirical data.

The lack of reliable statistics   The most conventionally accepted 'reliable' data are statistics; however, the distributed environment in which cybercrime thrives under-mines conventional centralized methodologies for collecting data. This is because information about reported victimizations does not flow through a single portal such as the police in the same way as does, say, the reporting of street and related crime. In this, cybercrime is little different to other invisible or hidden crimes such as white-collar or organized crime (see Croall, 2001; Davies et al., 2015). There exist reports and surveys that purport to estimate the extent of cybercrime, typically covering network abuse and commercial crime (see Ryan and Jefferson, 2003), but very few 'official' sources. This point was raised by the UK All Party Internet Group in May 2004 when it reviewed the Computer Misuse Act 1990, and it has been raised many times since.

One problem is that successive governments have not expressed much aware-ness of how deep a problem cybercrime is, and not because of the methodological problems mentioned here. A practical explanation is more probable as each part of the government saw (and sees) cybercrime in terms of its own subject area and not as a whole. Whilst in the UK the Office of National Statistics (ONS) now has a much stronger overview of this issue and publishes statistics of computer misuse, and online fraud reported crime statistics, as part of its annual estimation of crime in England and Wales (ONS, 2022: Table F8). For many years, cybercrime figures were not audited by the National Audit Office which means there was less (bureaucratic) pressure to deal with the issue. As Derek Wyatt, the APIG (All Party Internet Group) chairman, stated in 2004: 'The first thing we have to do is find out the extent of the problem. We won't win the battle of resourcing the police if we don't get the crimes recorded' (cited by Broersma, 2004). Scholars have criticized the idea of attempting to evaluate the costs of cybercrime statistically (Anderson et al., 2013).

Even today, there are problems in evaluating the impact of ransomware, which is both a crime of extortion and one of computer misuse. This means that ransomware is often included under the statistics for both offences. To complicate matters further, depending on jurisdiction, operationally, responsibility can fall between the police forces responsible for economic crimes and for cybercrimes. Even if it was possible to collate more accurate 'official' statistics, there still remains the additional problem of not being able to apply standardized conceptualizations of 'crime' to systematic reporting and recording methodologies. A consequence of this is that statistics are hard, if not impossible, to replicate. In 2003, for example, computer intrusion statistics published online by the Computer Emergency Response Team (CERT) at Carnegie Mellon University were regarded as a barometer of cybercrime activity. Yet the number of reported intrusions rose from 6 in 1988 to 137, 529 in 2003, and confusion arose because these were mainly low-level and automated reports of intrusions, with few representing actual crimes. Thus, because it was impossible to assess the scope and impact of attacks, CERT discontinued in 2003 publishing the number of incidents reported.[12]

An indication of the inexact science of cybercrime estimation arose in October 2005 when John Leyden deconstructed claims by an anti-spyware firm about the level of infections caused by spyware (Leyden, 2005e). The data upon which the statistics were based were collected by Webroot's Phileas automatic web crawler, which proactively sought out data about active spyware (Webroot, 2005: 13).[13] The findings were dramatic and revealed high levels of spurious infections. Leyden, however, subsequently found that the methods used to calculate the statistics clumped together benign 'cookies' with much more malicious spyware such as trojans and keylogger programs. Once the cookies were removed from the calculation, the average number of spyware infections on each PC fell from 18 to 4.5 (Leyden, 2005e). While still relatively high, the revised calculations radically change the meaning of the statistics and any conclusions that can be drawn from them. These examples graphically highlight the need to understand first the methodological assumptions underlying the compilation of statistics.

Today, there exists a greater reliance upon victim self-reports and victim surveys to identify patterns of victimization that inflict harm. Not only can victim surveys more reliably capture their experience and perspective, but the victims themselves tend to determine which offences demand action. There are a number of such surveys. As stated earlier, some are self-reporting; others seek out and canvass information from specific respondent groups. Self-reporting victimization surveys are (or have been) run by organizations such as the US National White-Collar Crime Center and the National Fraud Information Center (NFIC) and mainly focus upon the business and financial sector. Currently one of the most frequently cited information sources in the USA is the Computer Studies Institute[14] survey, which regularly canvasses US businesses about their experience of victimization. Similarly, companies such as Experian, KPMG and others produce occasional (rigorous) victim surveys. In the UK, various surveys were conducted historically by different government departments (e.g. NHTCU, 2002; NCIS, 2003; DTI, 2004), but the *Cyber Security Breaches Survey* (see DCMS, 2021) is widely regarded as a current indicator of business victimization.

When using business victimization surveys, it is important to note that most businesses are more likely to become victims of crime simply because of the risks they are exposed to in the course of their day-to-day operations, both online and off. Yet they are often reluctant to formally report their victimization, for commercial reasons relating to loss of business reputation. They are more likely to report victimization under a cloak of anonymity.

Individual victimizations online show different dynamics to those of organizations because of the personal nature of the impacts. The main crime victimization surveys in the UK and US have incorporated questions about online victimization. Since 2003, for example, the British Crime Survey (now the Crime Survey of England and Wales) has incorporated a small number of questions about individual internet victimizations.[15] The Crime Survey of England and Wales canvasses a sample of approximately 13,500 households about their experience of victimization.

The victimization surveys indicate, as they have done for almost two decades, that cybercrimes may not always be individually as serious or impactful as many industry (technical) estimations of cybercrime have claimed. The seriousness of most cybercrimes against individuals mainly lies in their globalized aggregation. Crimes against business, however, have become more serious as cybercriminals have scaled up their attacks with sophisticated malware such as ransomware, as explored in chapter 7.

While victimization surveys are beginning to build up a cumulative picture of victims of cybercrime which establishes who the victims are and the manner of their victimization, they can also help to calculate the amount of relevant policing resources that should be allocated to the problem. However, when the different patterns of victimization are not explained fully, the 'statistics' can fuel sensational news stories that subsequently depict the internet as ungovernable and criminogenic, when, in fact, information such as that related to online frauds suggests that the internet is increasingly secure for personal online transactions and that the main risk lies in the vulnerability of input and output procedures.

Under-reporting cybercrimes

Although statistics about cybercrimes have greatly improved during the past fifteen years, there are a number of factors that continue to vex the construction of victim profiles. This is because not only can they vary from individuals to social groups to businesses, but also the harms done to them can range from the actual to the perceived. With types of offending, such as cyber-stalking, the theft of cyber-cash or fraud, the victimization nearly always focuses upon the individual. However, with other patterns of offending, such as cyber-piracy or cyber-spying/terrorism, the impact of victimization is usually directed towards corporate or governmental bodies. Similarly, the focus of hate crimes tends to be upon minority groups. Moreover, as found with the reporting of white-collar crimes, it is likely that primary or secondary victims of cybercrimes, individuals and organizations, may be unwilling to acknowledge that they have been victimized, or at least it may take some time for them to realize it.

At an individual level, reluctance to report offences may arise because of embarrassment, ignorance of what to do, or just simply 'putting it down to experience'. Alternatively, where victimization has been implied by a third party upon the basis of an ideological, political, moral or commercial assessment of risk, the victim or victim group may simply be unaware, or may not believe, that they have been victimized, as is the case in some of the debates over pornography (extreme sexual materials) on the internet. At a corporate level, victims are disincentivized from reporting their victimizations because of the fear of damage to reputation and loss of consumer confidence from adverse publicity. Corporate victims are fearful that publicizing corporate vulnerabilities might encourage attackers, damage the business and compound workforce concerns about their job security (Cashell et al., 2004: 13). Both sets of factors greatly reduce corporate willingness to report their victimization to the police.

Research by Kemp et al. (2021) into business cybercrime victimization reporting behaviours found that trends in reporting increase when the victimization causes major impacts. However, also important in making the decision to report is the priority which the organization places upon on its own cybersecurity. The research also found that businesses tended not to report victimization to public authorities when their cybersecurity management was outsourced, but that in-house cybersecurity teams were more inclined to report to public authorities (Kemp et al., 2021).

Evidence of the impacts of disincentives in reporting can be illustrated by comparing fraud victimization survey findings with the relatively low incidence of internet-related frauds reported by the public to the police (Wall, 2003: 132). Low levels of reporting, for whatever reason, lead to low levels of police action, fewer prosecutions, fewer statistics, reducing the amount of available knowledge about offenders and ultimately hampering the development of a criminology of virtual offenders.

The ongoing power struggle for control over cyberspace as a contested space

The increasing political and commercial power of the internet is forging new power relationships that are gradually shaping and reshaping what is and what is not a cybercrime. This political economy of information capital is marked by an ongoing power play, or 'intellectual land grab', for market control and protection (see Boyle, 1996). Consequently, definitions of acceptable and deviant cyber-behaviour are being shaped by the interests of the 'new' powerful – those who gain a commercial and legal hold on the upper ground. The rising intolerance of the new powerful towards 'risk groups' they perceive as a threat to their own interests is causing concern, especially when 'the problem', as it becomes regarded, is reconstructed within a criminal, rather than civil, law discourse that contrasts competing interests in an adversarial good guys / bad guys binary. See, for example, the debates over the downloading of music and film and also the threats of prosecution, typically 'letters before action', speculative invoicing and actual prosecutions brought by the Recording Industry Association of America (RIAA), the British Phonographic Industry (BPI) (see Carey and Wall, 2001: 36; Marshall, 2002: 1; David, 2010; Wall, 2015a) and the Motion Picture Association.

It would be wrong, however, simply to assume that the construction of online deviance is one-sided. Even if definitions of crime and deviance are originated by the social activity of elites or powerful groups, they have to be embedded in the lives and understandings of ordinary members of society as well as offenders themselves for them to translate into social action. On this, Melossi has observed that 'the struggle around the definition of crime and deviance is located within the field of action that is constituted by plural and even conflicting efforts at producing control' (1994: 205). The key issue here is therefore about whether reliable information flows freely to form reliable viewpoints.

Competing expert claims

Very influential in the production of knowledge about cybercrimes and in shaping public and governmental opinion are the claims of 'experts' who possess superior knowledge of a situation. Without reliable knowledge, especially recognized metrics, it is not only hard to validate expert claims, especially when they compete, but also difficult to counter inaccurate claims with factual information. The cybersecurity industry, which comprises security consultants and aspects of private and public law enforcement agencies, has an economic interest in cybercrime that can shape the focus of any claims made. While media claims may be grounded in good information, industry members often present views that favour their own particular interests. There has, for example, been a historical tendency to overestimate the extent of crime on the internet by inflating the importance of low-level automated intrusion statistics.

Levi argues that this is systemic and that the potential impacts of cybercrime may simply be 'talked up' by 'experts', who may deliberately or paranoically inflate the threat, conflating 'experience of with theoretical risk from computer crime' (Levi, 2001: 50) for their own gain, particularly when competing for government resources. Levi has argued that the conflation of experience with theoretical risk is part of the broader 'intelligence threat-assessment mental set' that is perpetuated by 'the self-serving PR of security consultants whose income depends on shocking . . . or . . . "creating awareness among" . . . senior executives and government agencies who complacently fail to spend "enough" money on security' (Levi, 2001: 50). The same PR also feeds the media's current lust for internet-related news and subsequently shapes public knowledge about, and attitudes towards, the internet and drives the resulting debate over crime, providing the regulatory bodies with a mandate for taking action (Wall, 2002a: 190). It is alleged, for example, that the hacking exploits of Richard Pryce and Matthew Bevan (aka Datastream Cowboy and Kuji) were deliberately overblown by experts in order to secure funding for government agencies. During the course of a Congressional hearing, Pryce and Bevan were allegedly described as 'possibly the single biggest threat to world peace since Adolf Hitler' (Power, 2000: ch. 6; Bevan, 2001). Yet both defendants were very young: Pryce was still at school (Ungoed-Thomas, 1998: 1). Despite the serious allegations against them, the case against Bevan was dropped because there was no evidence. Bevan explained that the 'Crown Prosecution Service (CPS) held that it was not in the public interest to prosecute me' (Bevan, 2001). Pryce was subsequently found guilty by a Magistrates Court and fined £1,200. While Bevan openly states that he was a hacker, with the benefit of hindsight he feels that he became part of a larger agenda:

> Looking back, I now believe that my case was not about hacking, but an exercise in propaganda. In the same year that a handful of hackers were caught, there was an estimated 250,000 attacks on computers in the US, Department of Defence. It was a

prime target. I believe it was no coincidence that when the Senate was being asked for money to fund protection against Information Warfare, a case study appearing to prove their point fell in their laps. (Bevan, 2001)

This is a view also held by journalist Duncan Campbell (1997: 2): 'The collapse of Bevan's trial has exposed the US infowarriors. On the back of overblown rhetoric and oversold threats, they have won lavish funding from Congress for new military and intelligence infowar units, and recently sold their security services to private corporations.' The irony here is that Bevan is now an expert himself. Echoes of the Datastream Cowboy and Kuji affair were heard a decade later in the case of Gary McKinnon, the 'Pentagon Hacker', and a further decade later with British hacker Lauri Love.

Accused of being a threat to US national security following what was alleged to be 'the biggest military computer hack of all time' (Ronson, 2005), McKinnon faced extradition to the US from the UK in 2006 to face charges that could lead to up to seventy years in prison (BBC, 2006g). McKinnon claimed to have explored the Pentagon website out of curiosity, looking for evidence of the existence of extra-terrestrial technology, but finding, instead, unsecured areas containing highly confidential information. His supporters argue that the prosecution was purely politically motivated, and that McKinnon actually exposed expert failings and showed 'the shortcomings of security policies on US military networks' (McKinnon's defence: BBC, 2006g, 2006h). Lauri Love was also accused of similar activities (McGoogan, 2016) but subsequently won his extradition appeal on the grounds that it would be 'oppressive by reason of his physical and mental condition' and could be tried in the UK courts (*Lauri Love* v. *The Government of the USA*, 2018).

The point of this section is not to denigrate the value of the expert – indeed, most expert claims are well informed – but to emphasize that expert sources are not 'value' free. It also highlights that an objective view must incorporate a range of perspectives, not one. This observation also applies to the claims of another expert group, the hackers themselves, who tend to exaggerate claims of their technical prowess and proficiency. Hackers (usually those driven by less ethical motivations), may 'fake' the methodology of their crime to hide the fact that they actually used social engineering, or deception, to trick people into giving out personal information such as passwords to secure systems by exploiting their weaknesses, rather than using technological skills to obtain key access information. This fact was revealed by the notorious hacker Kevin Mitnick, himself now an 'expert' (see Mitnick and Simon, 2002).

Conflicts and confusions between public and private sector interests

A recurring theme of this discussion is the tension between the public and private sectors in seeking forms of justice that represent different interests. The relatively low levels of prosecutions for breaches of computer security and low levels of recorded internet-related fraud are poignant examples of this tension (see chapter 5). They suggest that most breaches of security tend to be dealt with by victims rather than the police, highlighting the preference of corporate victims to seek private justice solutions instead of invoking the public criminal justice process that might expose their weaknesses to commercial competitors (Wall, 2001b: 174). The model of criminal justice offered to corporate victims by the police and other public law enforcement agencies is not generally conducive to their business interests (Goodman, 1997: 486). As mentioned earlier, organizations under-report crimes against them, preferring to sort out their own problems by using their own resources in ways that are more likely to meet their own ends. Even where there is a clear case for prosecuting an offender, corporate bodies will usually tend to favour civil recoveries rather than criminal prosecutions. This is partly because a lesser burden of proof is required, but also because they feel they can maintain a greater control over the justice process. In other cases, they may take no specific action and simply pass on the costs of victimization directly to their customers or claim their losses through insurance.

With regard to the latter, however, Cashell et al. were critical in 2004 that many businesses tended not to include cyber-attacks in their insurance policies. Yet, almost two decades later, following an increase in ransomware attacks, on the one hand, cyber-insurance appears to be encouraging cybercrime (because offenders know that their ransom will likely be paid!) (Lindsey, 2019), and yet, on the other hand, although necessary to mitigate risks, the basic business model of cyber-insurance is becoming limited (MacColl et al., 2021: 53).

The danger of confusing the rhetoric with reality

What this chapter has illustrated is that cybercrime victimization is not a given, incontrovertible fact. Our understandings of it have been constructed over the past two decades from various countervailing discourses and their attendant epistemologies. Hence the earlier emphasis upon understanding it in terms of narrative criminology. Some groups of commentators are concerned with risk assessment (what ought), others with reality (what is). In acknowledging the respective strengths and weaknesses of these discourses, we increase our understanding of cybercrimes. To ignore their origins lays us open to confusing risk assessment with reality and its accompanying dangers, particularly the way that it can 'corrupt systems' by creating mindsets in which the only way to combat cybercrimes is thought to be an increase in resources for the enforcement of law and/or introducing stringent technological countermeasures. This confusion can be further compounded by the over-reliance by the various media on contestable statistical 'guesstimates' produced by the cybersecurity industry (see above, Leyden, 2005e) and the media's dependence upon so-called 'experts' for confirmation. This sometimes results in what Rosenberger (2003) has termed 'false authority syndrome'. On top of all this, the internet allows both good and bad ideas to proliferate quickly and so is a fertile ground for myths (Rosenberger, 2003) and conspiracy theories: '[m]ore than anything, the Web encourages viewers to make links and trace the hidden connections . . . so conspiracy theory on the Web provides surfers with a substitute sense of empowerment of being an active participant in the process of discovery and detection' (Knight, 2000: 211).

Together, these self-confirming sources can quickly create panic and prejudice rational solutions and explanations, but they can also become self-fulfilling by announcing system flaws and potential opportunities for offending. 'Hotspot paranoia', for example, has long been a concern, along with pharming and phlooding (see below, and Glossary), with no clear evidence of any large-scale occurrence. It was thought that 'evil twin' sites might be set up to spoof established sites to harvest usernames, passwords and any other useful information that could subsequently be used in criminal activity. As Kewney (2005) argues, this is perfectly feasible: 'yes I could sit down at a public hotspot, give my PC the ability to act as a hotspot . . . properly done . . . I could even make the logon screen look exactly like a Starbucks logon screen, which is where most T-Mobile hotspots are. And if you logged on with your credit card, I could get your details. And if you logged into your bank to do some financial work, I might get your password.' However, he argues that the flaw in the 'evil twin' argument against wi-fi hotspots is why anyone would go to the trouble when broadband internet-based exploits are a much easier and more effective means of obtaining passwords and accompanying information. Therefore, while there is a risk, the chance of victimization from hotspots is likely to be small. 'So, yes: there will be hackers setting up "evil twin" access points, but your chance of meeting one is pretty slim – they'll be students trying to prove they could do it. They'll have useful careers ahead of them, and middle-class aspirations, and after a couple of experiments, they'll either get caught or, get bored' (Kewney, 2005).

Another long-standing concern has been 'pharming' or 'cache poisoning', which is a more automated version of 'phishing' (fraudulently obtaining personal information) that does not rely upon social engineering to trick the recipient into clicking onto a bogus site because it automatically redirects them to it (Jackson, 2005; Lemos, 2005; Leyden, 2005a). Examples of pharming have related mainly to drug sales and redirection to online pharmacies – hence 'pharming' – but redirections to banking sites increased in number during the mid-2000s (Jackson, 2005). In the case of pharming, the headlines acted as the 'determining agent of reality' and preceded the offending, thereby creating the danger of the 'self-fulfilling prophecy . . . the coming to pass of the myth' (Baudrillard, 1998: 128). So, confusing the myth with reality is a problem that has to be addressed by critically questioning sources.

The above exploration of the production of knowledge illustrates how crucial it is to consider the quality of all news sources, and not only those relating to cybercrime. It also suggests that many of the more spurious sources found in the early 2000s are now more reliable today, especially those providing statistics and commentaries. Not only have commentators more collective experience in evaluating sources and analysing them, but the market for information is much more competitive today, which also introduces a potentially influential new guardian to improve the quality of data. However, the same phenomenon is also a breeding ground for misinformation. At the end of the day, the production of knowledge about cybercrime can only improve if sources are viewed with a critical eye and the various tensions that exist are acknowledged.

Criminological theory and cybercrime

Finally, although academic literature was mentioned earlier as a source, there was little discussion of its value for understanding the subject. We begin this final part of the discussion with an assessment of the value of criminological theory in producing higher knowledge about cybercrimes. The small amount of factual knowledge currently available about cybercrime and offenders comes from the findings of a relatively few research projects, such as Smith et al. (2004), and also reported cases and offender surveys, such as the UK-based OCJS (Offending, Crime and Justice Survey) (Allen et al., 2005; Wilson et al., 2006), and more recently via the work of Hutchings and Holt (2015, 2018), Brewer et al. (2019), Leukfeldt and Holt (2021), and also occasional intelligence briefings such as from the National Crime Agency (NCA, 2017).[16]

These sources confirm that offender profiles are like those of most offenders – young and male – but possess rather different, often opposing, characteristics to those found in the criminology of street criminals. They are more likely to be introverted, and more likely to share a much broader range of social characteristics. Perhaps more significant is that their use of the internet enables them to commit crimes at a distance, and also crimes that would previously have been beyond their means. Consequently, when combined with the offenders' relative isolation from others, these characteristics reduce the amount of available criminal intelligence about them and make the law enforcement job harder.

The generalizability of the above observations will, of course, vary further according to the types of crime involved and the available opportunities to offend. Such is the view of the situational crime prevention theorists (see Newman and Clarke, 2003). However, while this may easily explain computer-mediated thefts, it sits less comfortably with computer integrity and computer content crimes. McQuade (2006b: 113–35) gives a very useful overview of offender profiles but acknowledges the problems in so doing because: '[i]n reality, cybercriminals carry out different types and combinations of illicit actions in the course of committing abuse, attacks and/or crimes, thus underscoring the difficulty and limitations of categorising offenders' (p. 133).

If the construction of offender profiles is problematic, so too is the ability to isolate offender motivations. Normally in criminology, we may turn to the more complex theories of criminalization for guidance. McQuade (2006b: 179), for example, applied six criminological theories to cybercrimes, which each outline different motivational factors. They are classical choice theories, based upon rational decision-making; trait theories, which focus upon psychological imperfections in the individual; social process theories, which explore how individuals learn criminal behaviour; social structure theories, which consider the individual's social and economic position in society; conflict theories, based upon non-consensual, pluralistic and conflict views of social organization. He also observed a sixth, integrated theories, which combine aspects of the previous five. The problem McQuade identifies is that criminologists have long tended not to consider the impacts of technology in the commission of crime. Furthermore, the field of study is currently unfolding – especially where an act of cybercrime comprises various forms of offending behaviour. So, one solution to improve understanding of cybercrimes and criminal behaviour online is to combine relevant criminological theories.

Rational choice theory has been criticized for being overly positivistic but becomes useful in understanding cybercrimes by explaining how people visually perceive the nuances of the environment, which shapes what is rational and what is not. Cybercrimes do not just happen. On the one hand, they are products of an 'affordance', a possibility for rational action created by an object or technology (Gibson, 1979: 119–37). An 'affordance' could be a computer program, a discussion forum, social media network, almost anything related to digital and networked technologies. On the other hand, cybercrimes also require an underlying will that inspires the criminal imagination to the affordance. For this, we can turn to the early cultural criminology of Matza (1964) and Katz (1988), which also emphasizes the importance of offending being 'fun' and providing a 'sneaky thrill', ultimately combining to create various seductions which lure offenders into cybercrime (Goldsmith and Wall, 2022).

Presdee's 'carnival of crime' thesis describes two states of imagination that can further explain how the offenders 'drift' into cybercrime (also see Goldsmith and Brewer, 2015). Although not directly addressing cyberspace, Presdee expressed a broader concern about the criminalization of everyday life, in which: 'everyday responses to modern, highly commodified society become themselves defined as criminal' (Presdee, 2000: 15). He argued that much of the crime occurring in society, especially that relating to social disorder, is a product of the fact the existing relationships of production encourage us to live two lives. Our 'first life' is our official life characterized by work and imposed order, which sustains our physical existence. In contrast, our 'second life' is where we live out our fantasies and obtain emotional fulfilment (not to be confused with the website of the same name). It runs counter to the alienation caused by the 'rhythms of production' in the 'first life', by working to restore some meaning to our lives and control over our existence (Presdee, 2000: 62). During the course of living out this 'second life', which Presdee calls our 'carnival of leisure', the boundaries of order are frequently crossed. We, in effect, consume crime, not just through our diet of entertainment, but also when the 'commodification of excitement' that characterizes our leisure is taken one step further – into the 'sneaky thrill'. Presdee's main concern is that the 'bulk of crime is created, through the criminalisation and policing of social behaviour as against dishonest behaviour and that it is a crime to be many things including poor, young, disadvantaged, to fail and even at times to be creative' (Presdee, 2000: 162).

This explanation of second-life fulfilment can go a long way to explaining much of the internet's broader popularity, but also offending and victimization. The internet has become a 'safe site' of the second life of the people (Presdee, 2000: 54) and it certainly does provide an environment 'where we can enjoy in private immoral acts and emotions' (Presdee, 2000: 64). But he is also right when he states that the days when the consumption of crime, as he puts it, was 'a blissful state of "non-responsibility", a sort of never-ending "moral holiday", are long gone, if they ever existed, especially on the internet'.

There is, it is argued here, no single theory of cybercrime, but, by combining rational action theory with affordance theory and cultural criminology, we can explain how the technologies and the cultural environment create and facilitate cybercrimes. Especially as they are, broadly speaking, relatively anonymous and can be carried out across physical boundaries, they are also not subject to guardians (direct governance), yet they are risky, but can yield illicit returns. Adapting Goldsmith and Wall (2022), the technological opportunity (affordance) invokes a social or emotional response which creates a 'perception' (of low risk, thrill/fun, gain) that drives offenders' rational action and transforms criminal behaviour.

Conclusions: how has crime transformed criminal behaviour online and how do we know about it?

Understandings of cybercrime continue to be distorted by various popular mythologies which perpetuate myths about super-hackers (Ohm, 2007), the rise of internet mafias, nation state involvement, the apocalyptic digital pandemic and so on. Each of these is based upon part-truths and usually framed by fictional narratives against a backdrop of contemporary real-world events. They further increase the drama and culture of fear around 'cybercrime' during a time when society is becoming more and more digitalized and networked. Yet, while the young bedroom-dwelling hacker is clearly still part of the cybercrime landscape in the 2020s, it will be argued in chapters 3 and 7 that a new sophisticated cybercrime ecosystem has emerged to facilitate the commission of cybercrime. It is more professionalized than previously and also displays elements of organized crime activities, but new types of organization which contradict some of the earlier cybercrime myths still echo from the past.

Reliable information about cybercrime informs policy, practice and the public view. It helps to prevent information sources over-representing their own interests and reconciles the needs of the state and corporate interests, rather than dividing them. It also upholds important principles, such as liberty and freedom of expression. But just as important as the constitutional need for truth is the requirement to obtain reliable information in order to create realistic public expectations. This helps to mitigate the existing tensions within the production of knowledge about cybercrimes between the actual shock of the 'Future Shock' and the expectation that we will be shocked by the 'Future Shock'. This needs a little further explanation. 'Future Shock' is what Toffler (1970) describes as the anxiety, stress and disorientation that arises from too much change in too short a time. But Standage argues that, because of the '[t]he hype, scepticism and bewilderment associated with the Internet – concerns about new forms of crime, adjustments in social mores, and redefinition of business practices', the 'shock' is 'only to be expected [as] the direct consequences of human nature, rather than technology' (Standage, 1998: 199). We find here a strong resonance with Garland's 'crime complex' (2000: 367), which he describes as a symptom of late modernity where order is 'brittle' and public anxiety towards crime has become the norm. In the case of cybercrime, there is the culture of fear around it, we are shocked by cybercrime, but also expect to be shocked by it because we expect it to be there, but – confusingly – we appear to be shocked if we are not shocked (if we don't find it)! So, if information about cybercrime broadly distorts public expectations, then it is all the more important that the information should be reliable.

But how feasible is it to create reliable data streams in distributed systems where the activities are so heterogeneous? Indeed, is it possible to create such data in the same way as we do for non-cybercrime? For practical reasons, it may not be possible to gain an overall picture of the prevalence of cybercrime because of the dark figure, but this is the problem with all crimes. Yet it is still important to know why this may not be achievable and whether the information, statistics and data that are currently available have value. Do they display common trends? The distributed nature of information flows means that, at best, one can do little more than draw together many sources to build up a composite picture of cybercrime as social action. To maximize use of these resources, it is essential to understand the range of dynamics outlined above that shape the production of criminological knowledge about cybercrimes to understand what cybercrime is.

Some discussion questions based upon this chapter

How would you explain cybercrime to someone who does not know what it is?

Is cybercrime really different to offline criminal behaviour, or is it an invention of the cybersecurity industry or a cultural construction?

How do you know that cybercrime exists? How would you classify cybercrime for data-recording purposes? Where would the data come from?

Further Reading   While the internet creates the crime dystopias that this book focuses upon, the same technology also assists researchers in the field. To this end, a number of commentators have developed academic ideas, methods and even methodologies about how to conduct such research. Students and researchers who wish to study this area further are recommended to follow their work: Yar (2018); Bossler and Berenblum (2019); Lavorgna and Holt (2021); Dupont and Holt (2023).

3 Cyberspace and the Transformation of Criminal Activity

How have networked technologies changed opportunities for cybercrime?

Chapter contents and key points

The internet and the birth of the information society
- The transformative impacts of cyberspace upon criminal activity
- Networking and the convergence of digital and networked technologies
- Informational transfer and value
- Globalization

Changes in the organization of crime and the division of criminal labour
- Greater control over the criminal process by the individual
- New forms of criminal organization online through collaborations between different skill sets
- Deskilling criminal labour online
- Reskilling criminal labour online: automation and facilitation – the rise of the cybercrime ecosystem

Changes in the scope of criminal opportunity online
- Cyber-assisted crimes using computers to assist traditional offending
- Cyber-enabled opportunities for crimes across a global span of networks
- Cyber-dependent cybercrimes wholly mediated by technologies

Changes in the type of criminal opportunity online (modus operandi)
- Cybercrimes against the machine (computer integrity crimes)
- Cybercrimes using the machine (computer-enabled – or computer-related – crimes)
- Cybercrimes in the machine (computer content crimes)

Changes in the focus of criminal opportunity online: individual victims, organizational victims, nation state victims

Chapter at a glance *This chapter explains the transformative impacts of cyberspace upon criminal activity before looking at the changes in the organization of criminal behaviour online. It then explores changes in the modus operandi of criminal behaviour online – specifically changes in the organization, scope, types and focus of such criminal activity.*

Introduction

One of the main reasons why there is such little agreement about what cybercrimes are is the tendency for commentators to conceptualize them as an absolute, rather than a relative, concept (Wall, 2019). This is not a new observation; Howard Becker (citing Lemert (1951), Tannenbaum (1951[1938]) and Kitsuse (1962)) wrote in 1963 that 'deviance is not a quality of the act the person commits, but rather a consequence of the application by others of rules or sanctions to an offender' (Becker, 1963: 9). By seeking to explore the more relativist and even ontological aspects of cybercrime (see Donalds and Osei-Bryson, 2019), questions arise about how networked and digital technologies have transformed criminal behaviour. This chapter will explain how the internet has created new opportunities for criminal activity online. It starts by exploring the emergence of the information society before attempting to identify the transformative impacts of digital and networked technologies upon criminal behaviour. It then goes on to explore the ways in which those impacts have helped to create new conduits for criminal activity, mapping out changes in the modus oper- andi of criminal behaviour online in terms of organization, scope, types and focus of criminal activity online. In so doing, it not only identifies what is distinctive about cybercrime in terms of substantive areas of criminal behaviour, but also suggests a structure and language (framework) to explain the different types of cybercrime.

The origins of the internet through its associated information technologies are well documented from its military origins through to its educational, commercial and, later, social use (Rheingold, 1994; Castells, 1997b, 2000a; Jordan, 1999; Bell, 2001; Webster, 2002). From this literature comes the clear message that the internet has radically changed aspects of our lives, but how has it and by how much? Some commentators argue that it has only had a marginal effect, while others, mostly postmodernists and post-structuralists, believe that the information society has con- tributed to the rupturing of traditional links across time and space and has caused the demise of modernity.[1] Yet, authors such as Castells (1997b: 7) and Giddens (1990) steadfastly maintained that the shift towards post-, late or high modernity (depend- ing upon the author) was already occurring well before the popularization of the internet in the early 1990s. Indeed, Standage (1998) ambitiously traced the internet's historical links back to what he calls the 'Victorian internet', the nineteenth-century information networks created by the electric telegraph system.

The internet and the birth of the information society

A simple keyword search on Amazon.com reveals many academic commentar- ies on the subject of the internet, the 'information age' and 'information society', yet the most significant academic thinker in this field for this discussion is Manuel Castells. Castells's influential trilogy of work was published under the series title *The Information Age: Economy, Society and Culture* (Castells, 1997b, 2000a, 2000b, 2000c). He claims that the information age has transformed the relationships of pro- duction/consumption, power and experience (2000c: 5). He specifically argues that one of the hallmarks of the information age, the network society, was the product of the historical convergence of three independent processes during the late twentieth century: the constitution of the information technology revolution in the 1970s; the

restructuring of capitalism and statism in the 1980s; and the sociocultural movements of the 1960s and their 1970s aftermath, particularly feminism and ecologism
(1997a: 7). Consequently, Castells believes that, although the information technology
revolution (the internet) did not create the network society, the latter would not exist
in its present form without it. Although Castells's explanation is much contested (see,
for example, Van Dijk, 1999), he nevertheless explains why some of the characteristics
commonly associated with the internet today actually predate it – such as globalization or even late modernity. He also shows that the internet has accelerated change
and accentuated the qualities that have come to characterize late modernity, particularly the 'discontinuities' highlighted by Giddens (1990: 6) that separate modern and
traditional social orders. The social orders which bind time and space have become
disembedded and distanciated: 'lifted out of local contexts of interaction and restructured across indefinite spans of time–space' (Giddens, 1990: 14; Bottoms and Wiles,
1996). One major resulting social transformation has been a change in the meaning
of the individual because, Castells (2013: 10–11) states, modern (network) society
is constructed around personal and organizational networks that are powered by
powerful digital and networked technologies. Castells argues that, because these
networks are global, they do not know any boundaries, so not only is network society
globalized, but also the social structure it creates is historically different from previous individual societies. Moreover, it has given rise to major sociocultural changes,
not least 'the rise of the Me-centered society, or, in sociological terms, the process of
individuation' (Castells, 2013: 10). Individuation is 'the reconstruction of social relationships, including strong cultural and personal ties that could be considered a form
of community, on the basis of individual interests, values, and projects' (Castells,
2013: 11). Castells also identifies that whilst individuation signifies the decline of
community as has previously been understood, it is not the end of community or
the end of 'place-based interaction'. Individuation has been materially produced by
both new forms of organizing economic activities and changes in social and political
life outlined in his trilogy on the Information Age (Castells 1996–2003): 'But individuation does not mean isolation, or even less the end of community. Sociability
is reconstructed as networked individualism and community through a quest for
like-minded individuals in a process that combines online interaction with offline
interaction, cyberspace and the local space' (Castells, 2013: 11). Castells emphasizes
that: 'Individuation is the key process in constituting subjects (individual or collective), networking is the organizational form constructed by these subjects; this is the
network society, and the form of sociability is what Rainie and Wellman (2012) conceptualized as networked individualism' (Castells, 2013: 11).

Continuing to draw upon Castells, he observes that a new information economy
has emerged which possesses three distinct characteristics (2000c: 10) that provide a
conceptual starting point for analysing changes in criminal behaviour. First, the information economy is based upon informational productivity which has 'the capacity
of generating knowledge and processing and managing information'. Second, it is
global. Its 'core, strategic activities, have the capacity to work as a unit on a planetary
scale in real time or chosen time'. Third, it is networked. These three characteristics
have created a new era of economic organization, or networked enterprises, that are
composed of networks of organizations (or parts thereof), including social media.
Therefore, the main unit of production has shifted from the organizational unit to

the 'project'. Castells contends that, while the organization remains the legal unit of capital accumulation, it is nevertheless just one node in a global network of financial flows (Castells, 2000c: 10; see also the discussion in Mendelson and Pillai, 1999). Cyberspace is a virtual environment in which economic value is attached to ideas and their virtual expression rather than physical property (Barlow, 1994). In short, the information age argument is based upon a shift in values from more tangible to fewer tangible forms of wealth; from things to ideas expressed in informational sources. If the organization remains the legal unit of capital accumulation, as Castells predicts, then the global networked informational economy and its valuable content will become attractive to criminals.

The full social and economic impact of cyberspace upon the individual has become clear over the past two decades. In principle, individuals are freer than probably at any other time in history to develop social relations commensurate with their own interests and lifestyles – relations which are potentially more meaningful than they could previously have been (see Rheingold, 1994). Some individuals, for example, regularly work outside the traditional workplace, doing office work at a distance without the office politics (or commute!). They can work where their abilities can be best utilized and their pay and conditions maximized, thus reducing many of the alienating aspects of work. They can also maintain essential personal and familial connections whilst experiencing a broader personal fulfilment through participation in internet-based activities (see the 'second life' theory, in chapter 2). The realities are, however, more pragmatic, being much less ideological or romantic in outlook.

While the internet is not a serious substitute for face-to-face interactions, it is the case that in a society where 'the personality' transcends politics (Sennett, 1992: 238), individuals are no longer accustomed to doing things together or performing public roles and are therefore unable to find community and the intimacy it gives. Community, in its satisfying and organic form, is not to be found, so culturally reinforced expectations of community, often embedded in policy, result in what Sennett calls destructive *Gemeinschaft* (Sennett, 1992: 238). The virtual relationships within online communities contain neither the full panoply of social relationships nor the cohesive or organic expectations of *Gemeinschaft* (community relationships), an argument also to be found in Presdee's (2000) 'carnival of leisure' (see chapter 2). Instead, individuals experience a form of *Gesellschaft*-based community, which encourages the social deskilling[2] of the individual through the specialization and compartmentalization of interactions. It can certainly be argued that the internet has been successful in supporting the subsequent growth of new social networks which Licklider and Taylor described in their ground-breaking 1968 paper as the 'network of networks' (1990[1968]: 38). And yes, individuals can lock into networks that give the illusion of satisfying emotional or informational needs, but these networks are nevertheless restricted experiences and, despite expectations to the contrary, networked individuals do not experience holistic community experience.

As access to the internet becomes more widely available through decreasing network charges (often subsidized), hardware costs and public access policies, major divisions in society are, and will continue, to arise through inequalities in access to information rather than because of conventional socio-economic inequalities. Those individuals who do not engage with the information revolution face informational exclusion. Consequently, a new networked order is emerging in the information society, as described by Castells (2000a, 2000c) and others. One visible expression of this new order has been an increase in the privatization of information and ideas. Overall numbers of registrations for trademarks and patents have increased, combined with a new aggression in the application of intellectual property laws to protect properties and the expression of ideas. This suggests that information, some of which was previously in the public domain, is routinely becoming commodified as intellectual property. This encourages not only the growth of a new political economy of information capital and new power relationships (see Boyle, 1996; Wall, 2004; David, 2010), but also new forms of deviant behaviour in a bid to appropriate the value of informational content. In this way, cyberspace today not only challenges our conventional understanding of ownership and control, but also blurs the traditional boundaries between criminal and civil activities, along with some of the principles upon which our conventional understandings of criminal harm and justice are based. A good example here is the reduced ability of prosecutors to prove an offender's intention to permanently deprive another person of their digital informational property (as would be required under section 1 of the UK Theft Act 1968). Consequently, important questions have emerged as to what cybercrimes are and to what extent they differ from other activities that we currently recognize as crime.

The transformative impacts of cyberspace upon criminal activity

Because the defining characteristic of cybercrime is its mediation by networked technologies, the test of a cybercrime must rest upon what is left if those same networked technologies are removed from the activity. This I call the 'transformation test'.[3] It is not intended to be applied in a scientific manner; rather, it is a heuristic device, a rule of thumb which simply enables us to understand how the internet has become a conduit for criminal activity. The particular transformations that affect the digital architecture of criminal opportunity are, after Castells (2000c: 10), the growth in networking through the convergence of technologies, the importance of informational transfer and brokering (acquisition of information but also dataveillance through data mining), and globalization. These transformations are not simply the product of technology, nor are they necessarily mutually exclusive; rather, they signify the hybrid nature of cyberspace where actions there can have real impacts outside it. These broader processes provide useful focal points for further discussion.

Networking and the convergence of digital and networked technologies

Reduced to its basic form, the internet is essentially a set of agreed informational protocols that enable personal computers to communicate with each other across networks. It represents the successful convergence of computing and communications technologies into a consumable and easy-to-use product. The process of convergence is therefore an important key to understanding how criminal opportunity began to change in the information age, and can be defined in simple terms as the ability of different (networked) technology platforms, such as consumer devices (telephone, television and personal computers), to deliver similar kinds of services (European Commission, 1997b: 1). A decade on from the early debates over digital convergence, the definition has not really changed, but the extent of convergence may now surprise the early commentators. We can, for example, now make phone calls (voice over internet protocol – VoIP) from computers to mobile phones, we can send text messages to mobile phones, we can send emails to computers from mobile phones and then use those same phones to change the interactive TV channel (TVs that we have purchased using our computers) to be played on our phones or computers (computers we may also have bought using other computers). Interfunctionality, new permutations and function creep caused by convergence are increasing, particularly since the advent of (wireless) ambient (AMI) technologies, identification (biometric) technologies and technologies of location through affordable satellite linkage (IPTS, 2003). Although still unproven, Software Defined Radio (SDR) (BBC, 2006j) could be a particularly significant convergence development in years to come. Sometimes known as 'Tower of Babel' technology because of its ability to read and understand different kinds of radio waves, SDR has the ability to link a range of different technologies and communications systems thus creating many new opportunities for linking individuals to each other, and also their homes and workplaces – assuming that the two will remain separate in the years to come.

The significance of convergence is that it creates a new value-added – the information network – which had not been envisaged when each individual technology was invented, being outside their individual capabilities. The subsequent convergence of newer communications technologies to make them inter-functional has refined and extended our ability to construct new social networks across a global, social and cultural span. Perhaps the most graphic illustration of the growing sophistication of networks has been the emergence of distributed and decentralized peer-to-peer (P2P) networks, or grid technologies,[4] that rely upon user participation and generate new forms of decentralized commercial and informational relationships between individuals. Other examples are networks that have grown up in virtual worlds – virtual environments in which participants are represented by avatars, or visual representations of users as they would like to be seen – or through discussion groups and blogsites (see below). The relationships that emerge can enhance citizenship and democratic participation, while also facilitating e-commerce and improving the overall quality of life. But, as illustrated earlier, there are some limits to the claims that can be made about these.

Informational transfer and value

If the internet is little more than a set of agreed informational protocols, then at its core is the process of information transfer to trade access protocols or content. Simply switching on a networked computer begins a process of information brokering, but once computers have exchanged their network protocols, the procedure for gaining access to a particular network is invoked. During this procedure, an individual's access codes (personal information) are compared with data already held by the computer system to verify his or her access rights and identity. This data doubling is an act of surveillance that all computer users experience. Once access to a particular network has been obtained, informational content can be exchanged, usually at a price, as we shall see below.

Value in cyberspace is attached mainly to the expression of informational ideas rather than things. The aim of cybercrime, therefore, is to acquire information in order to extract its value. Activities that we understand as cybercrime include the illegal acquisition of access codes to closed systems, access to sources of finance, and the manipulation or destruction of intellectual property in the form of copyrighted or trademarked materials, information and data. They also include new aspects of pornography in the form of distributed extreme sexual materials and video nasties, information warfare, economic espionage and many other activities.

Interestingly, the ability of networked technologies to create and retain informational data records of all internet transactions, usually for billing, advertising or even explicitly for law enforcement purposes, means that the intensity of informational surveillance increases to the point that it is now becoming impossible to escape from the electronic gaze. These data, or 'mouse droppings' as they are sometimes known, are primarily designed to make the system work by ensuring security and assisting the user. A subsequent analysis of the data trail (dataveillance) can also assist law enforcement. Data records can be recalled either to prove or disprove that a user had undertaken a transaction, or they can be monitored in real time to identify abnormal patterns of behaviour that may be criminal in much the same way that financial institutions currently monitor transactions to identify money laundering, payment card fraud and other areas of illegal activity (Levi and Maguire, 2004: 397). We begin to experience what Haggerty and Ericson have described as the 'disappearance of disappearance' (Haggerty and Ericson, 2000: 619). This, of course, poses a potential threat to the maintenance of privacy and human rights and has engendered a further debate that is touched upon later.

Globalization

The internet, as an information network, has contributed to the acceleration of globalization by collapsing traditional geographies of distance to the point that 'in the networked world, no island is an island' (McConnell International, 2000: 8; Goodman and Brenner, 2002: 83). It is, for example, as quick to communicate by email halfway across the planet as it is within a locality. While 'equidistance' can have immense benefits in terms of information dispersal, democratic participation in society and commerce, it can also bring risk that much closer. Within the specific context of crime, globalization has created informational crime opportunities across cultures and jurisdictions by extending the reach of criminals globally. Dan Geer has rather dramatically observed that everyone moves that little bit nearer on the internet with the consequence that 'every sociopath in your neighbourhood is now living next to you, and there are no good neighbourhoods' (Geer, 2004).

But globalization should not simply be interpreted as an extension of technological reach; rather, it is a social process that configures and reconfigures 'relationships between multiple entities – from individuals to international agencies – which are widely distributed in space' (Cain, 2002). These relationships are neither innocent nor power free because they are based upon the exchange of informational value – and not always a fair exchange. Swift has argued that globalization 'is the product of a kind of turbo-capitalism that utilizes technologies to project itself through trade, investment and speculation at ever-faster speeds to ever-farther horizons' (2002). As a consequence, globalized information flows have broadened the imagination of criminals beyond traditional cultures and geographical boundaries, and disparities between the local and the global have created new criminogenic scenarios. Cybercrime is, then, more than a globalized phenomenon that can be committed anywhere on the internet, from anywhere, at any time, but it is built on ideas that transcend cultural and geographical boundaries. Theoretically, at least, changes in one place should also be found in another.

At some point, however, the 'local' enters into the equation, first via the offender, because the crime has to be committed somewhere, and second, via the victim, because they are victimized somewhere. A third intrusion of the 'local' comes via the investigation, which has to take place somewhere – usually, though not necessarily, where the offending or victimization took place. It is important to note here that this is a different 'local' from that found in the analysis of street crime, because it is a 'local' that is transformed by the global. Bauman (1998) conceptualizes this 'glocalization' as an intrinsic linkage between global and local processes which, he points out, are not 'trans-' or 'inter'-national – rather, they are 'glocalized'. The internet may, for example, introduce entirely new types of victimization into a locality. So, from a law enforcement point of view, globalization not only impacts upon local criminal practices, but also changes the relationship between the global and the local (Robertson, 1995; Findlay, 1999), thus shaping local enforcement and policing cultures. Of course, the local can also shape the global in that local events can generate broader criminal opportunities – for example, the prohibition or excessive taxation of goods in one jurisdiction may immediately create criminal business opportunities elsewhere, and the internet provides the global links through which those opportunities can be exploited.

Although concepts such as 'globalization' and 'glocalization' are highly contestable, they nevertheless provide a language for understanding change. One certainty is that cybercrimes will proliferate and become increasingly more global. Visible examples of this trend are already to be found in the criminal opportunities that exploit the convergence of different information technologies, for example email spams and viruses, or the convergence of communications technologies with linked databases that contain very private information about us or our patterns of consumption and lifestyles. The upshot of the transformations in networking, informational transfer and globalization is that networked information technology creates quite dissimilar and novel information flows that join participants together in different ways and in different time frames. Information of interest can flow by 'word of mouse' (email) very quickly and the information flows can be almost viral in the way that they are distributed, travelling quickly from node to node across networks (see the discussion about videos in Geist, 2006). This use of the term 'viral' is not to be confused with malicious software, although there is an indirect link in terms of the escalation of distribution. Rather, it is about the way that relationships are organized across the internet, along which information can flow, particularly following the rise in popularity of the virtual social spaces created by the interaction of email, webmail, social networking websites, blogging sites, chat rooms and instant messenger services. These viral information flows create the possibility of asymmetric *Gesellschaft*, or transactional relationships with other individuals, in place of symmetric face-to-face relationships. Just as one individual can be in touch with many others simultaneously during the course of routine communications, the same technology can also engender asymmetric relationships between offender and victim, with the result that one individual can simultaneously victimize a number of individuals, either synchronously in real time, or asynchronously in chosen time (Morris and Ogan, 1996: 42–3). To use a fishing analogy to describe this phenomenon, offenders can place many hooks in the water simultaneously with many different baits so that victimization can take place either immediately or sometime after the initial communication. A useful example of asymmetry and asynchronicity in viral information flows is found in the computer-mediated offender–victim relationship caused by malicious phishing (spams). Together, these transformations in networking, informational transfer and globalization have contributed to radical changes in the organization of crime and the division of criminal labour and also the scope, type and victim focus of criminal opportunity online.

Changes in the organization of crime online and the division of criminal labour

Each of the above transformations now gives individuals greater control over the criminal process across a global span and facilitates new forms of criminal organization.

Greater control over the criminal process by the individual

Perhaps the most profound transformation has been the power that the internet places in the hands of a single person, often referred to as the 'empowered single or small agent' (see Rathmell, 1998: 2; Pease, 2001: 22; Artosi, 2002). These are lone offenders who exploit networked technology to carry out incredibly complex and far-reaching tasks that can be repeated countless times globally. Tempered only by technological limitations such as bandwidth and language, they are now able to commit crimes previously beyond their financial and organizational means. The changes in the dynamics of the return on investment now make offending more cost-effective and represent a significant step-change in criminality. On the one hand, offenders can commit smaller-impact, bulk victimizations across a broad geographical span, while, on the other hand, they do not have to have many successes before they break even. Furthermore, because they tend to work alone and remotely, their chances of getting caught are reduced by the fact that there is little criminal intelligence circulating about them (in comparison, to, say, a bank robbery, the organization of which involves a comparatively large number of individuals). The knock-on effects of this change in the organization of criminal activity for the justice process are considerable. This is particularly true where the principle of *de minimis non curat lex* (the law does not concern itself with trifles) begins to apply: the problem of small or low-impact multiple victimizations distributed across many jurisdictions collectively constitutes a significant criminal activity yet individually does not justify the expenditure of resources in investigation or prosecution (see chapter 8).

New forms of criminal organization online through collaborations between different skill sets

The second most profound effect of the transformations is the new genre of collaborations between different offending groups: hackers, virus writers and spammers. Initial concerns about the transfer of organized crime to the internet were largely dispelled by Brenner. She predicted that organized criminal activity would likely manifest itself online in 'transient, lateral and fluid' forms, as networks of criminals (2002: 1), rather than replicate the two principal models of organized criminal activity found in the 'real world': the 'gang' model and the hierarchical American 'Mafia'. This is mainly because the latter evolved largely in response to real-world opportunities and constraints that are largely absent in cyberspace. Brenner anticipates that 'online criminal activity will almost certainly emphasize lateral relationships, networks instead of hierarchies . . . [a] "swarming" model, in which individuals coalesce for a limited period of time in order to conduct a specifically defined task or set of tasks and having succeeded, go their separate ways' (Brenner, 2002: 50). Individuals with different skill sets are more likely to join in ephemeral relationships to commit a common act, or to reproduce their skills and knowledge. These predictions are largely borne out by contemporary evidence – see, for example, Mann and Sutton's research into the operation of cracker[5] news groups (1998), and Wall (2000). The important questions here are: why should this be the case, and will the pattern continue?

Although an entire (cyber-) criminal process can be perpetrated by very few people, the division of labour has become very specialized, and an array of specialized components needs to be drawn together to make it work. While virus writing, for example, can be part-automated, the higher specifications of sophisticated malicious software today require increasingly specialist skills in their construction, as the later discussion about botnets and zombie (see Glossary) computers illustrates. But to give a brief illustration, in 2004, German Magazine *C'T* found that virus writers had been selling the internet protocol (IP) addresses of computers infected with their remote administration trojans to spammers (*C'T*, 2004). Not only do these infected computers, or 'zombies', enable spammers to use the infected systems to illegally distribute spams without the knowledge of the computer owners, but the 'botnet' network of installed trojans (see Glossary) forms a powerful tool which the distributors of the viruses can use, among other things, to launch distributed denial of service (DDoS) attacks (BBC, 2003a; *C'T*, 2004; Libbenga, 2004; McQuade, 2006b: 99; see chapters 4 and 7).

Behind this collaboration of skill sets and the rise in malware attacks from botnets are concerns that 'organized crime' interests are now exploiting this 'new generation' of cybercrime. In June 2005, the UK NISCC (National Infrastructure Security Co-ordination Centre)[6] warned of the practices of 'a highly sophisticated high-tech gang' reputed to be located in the Far East using various means to infect sensitive computer systems in order to steal government and business secrets (NISCC, 2005; Warren, 2005). The warning provided details of forms of criminal organization that not only are unique, but also depart from traditional thinking on organized crime, although it is thought that high-level organized crime may be involved. The attacks 'demonstrate a high level of expertise . . . coupled with the use of . . . social engineering to obtain email addresses and names of targets' (Warren, 2005). The warning confirmed the suspicions of security analysts who stated that they believed the attacks, about three per day, had been launched over a period of up to a year (see Naraine, 2005).

The attacks described above were distinctive for a number of reasons. The first was that they did not demonstrate the patterns of behaviour that hackers have tradition-ally displayed and they did not 'appear to have the incentives that organized crime is after in terms of a fast financial return' (Warren, 2005). What was more certain, according to Warren, was that those involved were 'one of a number of organized groups that are spreading around the world in a high-tech crime wave'. The second reason was that the pattern of the attack was more like a phishing expedition than a premeditated assault on one or more organizations. The gang was believed to be composed of a dozen or so individuals who attacked systems using information that had been returned randomly from infected computers within the network. For example, it was not simply targeted at corporations, because governmental organi-zations and agencies were also found to have been caught out (Leyden, 2005c). The third reason was that the information returned would then be used to identify quickly key individuals in the target organization about whom further information would be sought, often with a turn-around of as little as two hours. The 'personal' informa-tion contained in subsequent emails sent out in a targeted attack would 'engineer' the individual to open an attachment. In so doing, their computer would become infected by sophisticated trojans, which have the ability to change themselves regu-larly to evade detection by anti-virus and spyware software. The trojans would then seek out and return to the gang corporate and personal information that may be passed on to a competitor or be used to compromise the target organization (Leyden, 2005c; Lueck, 2005; Warren, 2005). Initially, it was thought that only time would tell whether these 'gangs' come to constitute a 'new internet mafia' (Berinato, 2006). The issue is possibly more profound two decades later. As stated in the preceding chap-ter, while the young bedroom-dwelling hacker is clearly still part of the cybercrime landscape, a new sophisticated ecosystem has emerged to facilitate cybercrime. It is run along more professional lines than previously and displays elements of organized crime activity, but it is flat in structure and not hierarchical. Moreover, this transna-tional ecosystem is based upon sound business models (Musotto and Wall, 2022) and not only lacks the drama invoked by the cybercrime mafia-themed mythologies, but is quite boring by comparison (Collier et al., 2021).

Deskilling criminal labour online

A useful way of understanding the impacts of networked technology is to explore them in terms of the 'deskilling effect' (Braverman, 1976). The deskilling hypothesis draws upon Marxist theory to argue that the main rationale behind the develop-ment and utilization of technology is to increase the efficiency of human labour and actions to maximize investment in capital. Central to this operation is the process of rationalizing and 'degrading' labour by breaking it down into essential tasks and then automating each of those tasks to make them more efficient and economical to carry out. Examples can be found in most occupations, notably in the factory where legions of manual assembly-line workers have now been replaced by machines. The deskilling effect is by no means restricted to the production process – for example, in most clerical and managerial occupations, typing is now a generic skill, along with using computers, whereas not too long ago both typing and computing were carried out by specialists. While the critics of technology have been quick to highlight the negative effects of the deskilling effect upon labour (e.g., unemployment), they have largely ignored the inevitable and simultaneous reskilling process that also occurs when workers (albeit fewer of them) take control of more complete, but automated, production processes.

These deskilling and reskilling arguments can equally be applied to the organization of criminal labour – as can be seen, for example, in the increasing use of networked computers to automate offending. With digital and networked technologies, one person can use a computer to control a complete set of processes to commit a crime. At a basic level, computers were, and still are, a sophisticated tool that can be used to commit offences, such as the 'hack', a theft, etc. Originally performed manually by hackers trained as programmers, hacking subsequently became enhanced by the use of 'scripts' – as in the first and second generations[7] of cybercrimes (described later). It was, however, the automation of these processes, using web-based 'point and click' tools that enabled malicious software and code to be more easily and effectively compiled en masse (BBC, 2005e) and made available. Interesting evidence of the deskilling and reskilling of online criminal labour is to be found in the demise of the once popular hacking magazine *Phrack*. For over two decades, *Phrack* 'spanned the evolution of hacking from the days of bulletin boards to 3G mobiles with a knowledgeable, politically aware and frequently controversial take on information security' (Leyden, 2005d). Its last editor (Ollie) complained that 'the basic skill level hackers need to build up was rising all the time. It's much harder to get to a point where you can actually do stuff . . . [y]ou have to learn much more and read many more books. But, although the increased complexity of the cybercrime process has meant that the entry-level of skills has been raised' (Ward, 2005), yet, on the other hand, the business dynamics of technology and also hacking (in its many forms) mean that the deskilling and automation process continues; please read on.

Reskilling criminal labour online: automation and facilitation – the rise of the cybercrime ecosystem

While it is still feasible that a suitably skilled offender could singly perform each of the functions of a cybercrime, the expertise required for success is of a high level and the various tasks time consuming. Moreover, the risks of being detected are high and the financial rewards are comparatively low. To reduce the risk of being caught and increase the proceeds from crime, offender groups have identified gaps in the market for specialized services – aided by the dark web. Specialized services are linked to the special skills needed for the different stages of an attack. These groups benefit from such an inter-dependent relationship because it can help to offset criminal liability at each stage as some of the skills lie in the grey area between the legal and illegal activity. As will be explained more fully in chapter 7, there are plenty of specializations in the cybercrime underworld. Briefly, there are spammers who hire out spamware-as-a-service software that phishers, scammers and fraudsters use to steal people's credentials. Databrokers then trade these stolen details on the dark web. These details might be purchased by 'initial access brokers', who specialize in gaining initial entry to computer systems before selling on those access details to would-be attackers, as is the case with ransomware. These attackers often engage with crimeware-as-a-service brokers, who hire out malware (for example ransomware) software as well as other services, for example DDoS stressers (Musotto and Wall, 2022). To coordinate these groups, darkmarketeers provide online markets where criminals can openly sell or trade services, such as code writing, or cybercrime advice services (consultancies), usually via the ToR network on the dark web. Monetizers can also be engaged to launder cryptocurrency and turn it into fiat currency, while negotiators, representing both victim and offender, can be hired to settle the ransom amount. This ecosystem is constantly evolving as the recent emergence of cybercrime consultants illustrates: they collect their fee for advising offenders at key stages of an attack, just like a business consultant. As with the demise of manual labour, the components to commit a cybercrime can be obtained online.

The internet clearly provides a new conduit for criminal and harmful behaviour. The transformative impacts change the traditional spatial and temporal relationships between offender, victim and the state by creating entirely new opportunities for harmful or criminal behaviours, for example by widening the offender's reach of opportunity globally, enabling offenders to engage victims in new ways and providing new means for the organization of criminal behaviours.

So, although the fundamental nature of the victimization may be familiar – for example, deception or theft – when the behaviour has been transformed by the internet, it is referred to as a cybercrime. But what actually is a cybercrime? Without a systematic clarification of the nature of cybercrimes, dystopian and often inapt concerns about them can result in misplaced or exaggerated public demands for policy responses from criminal justice and other agencies.

Changes in the scope of criminal opportunity online

The origins of cybercrime can be traced back to the interception of semaphore signals in the eighteenth century, or, as indicated earlier, the wiretap in the nineteenth and early twentieth centuries (Standage, 1998). In both cases, valuable information which could be used to defraud and monetized was intercepted as it was being transmitted across hitherto unparalleled spans of time and space, and then sold. However, the true genesis of cybercrimes originates in early computer crimes prior to their subsequent transformation by networking over two further generations. The notion of 'generation' is traditionally used to infer the passage of time, but here it is used to invoke the state of technology at a particular time. Importantly, each distinct generation is conceptually different but can either run concurrently or overlap with the others, as shown in Figure 3.1, which describes contemporary differences currently found within the scope of criminal opportunity.

Cyber-assisted crimes using computers to assist traditional offending

The first generation of cybercrime describes computer technologies that assist traditional criminal behaviour. Initially, these behaviours took place within discrete computing systems and were characterized by the criminal exploitation of mainframe computers and their discrete operating systems. Focused mainly upon the acquisition of money or the destruction or appropriation of restricted information,

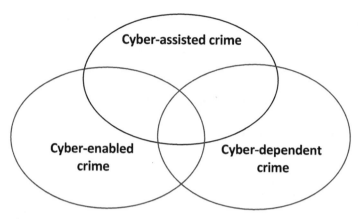

Figure 3.1 The different impacts of technology upon cybercrimes.

this first generation marked a departure from conventional criminal opportunity because of the scope and volume of activity that could be brought into effect. See, for example, the 'Salami fraud' (Kabay, 2002; Singleton, 2002: 39) committed by Gus Gorman in the film *Superman III* where he corralled the surplus half cents from banking transactions into his monthly pay cheque. The opportunity was created by inconsistencies in the computing system relating to 'rounding up' fractions less than the lowest denomination of money. In this way, even though the crime appeared to be completely mediated by technology, the offending was localized by the limitations of the mainframe computing system. Although this first generation of cybercrime involved, and still involves, the use of computers, networked or otherwise, the behaviours, frequently referred to as cybercrimes, are in fact 'traditional' (Wall, 2001b) or 'ordinary' (McQuade, 2006a, 2006b). They are 'low end' cybercrimes, a distinction adapted from Brodeur's (1983) work on policing.

Cyber-assisted crime is where computers are primarily used during the preparation stage of a crime, either as a tool of communication or to gather preparatory information (for example, 'how to kill someone' or 'how to manufacture drugs or weapons'). Here, existing patterns of harmful activity are sustained by networked technologies – but if they are removed, these activities will still persist by other means. Drug dealers, for example, will use whatever convenient and less risky forms of communications and information technology are available. It is similarly the case with information about weapons and other harms, even manuals on how to commit crimes, which existed before the internet. Long before the advent of the internet, for example, radical book retailer Loompanics, specialized in selling books that illustrate technologies and techniques that can result in potentially harmful and illegal actions – protected by freedom of expression laws. So, radical information was previously available, but not as instantly or conveniently. Thinking back to *Superman III*, even Gus Gorman's 'Salami fraud' could still have been committed by a subtle misuse of the internal banking orders.

Cyber-enabled opportunities for crimes across a global span of networks

The second generation of cybercrimes are those committed across networks. Mainly driven by hackers and crackers, they were originally the product of a marriage between the skills of the early computer operators and the communications skills of the phone phreakers who imaginatively 'cracked' telephone systems to make free telephone calls. The phone phreaker was epitomized by the legendary exploits of Cap'n Crunch (aka John Draper), so named because he used a toy whistle obtained from a box of Cap'n Crunch cereal to access AT&T's audio-based dial-up system by whistling its long-distance dial tone. The marriage gave birth to 'hackers', who were driven by a combination of the phreakers' ethical belief in their moral right to hack into systems, the civil libertarian culture of 1970s post-Vietnam US and a growing culture of suspicion of government and large corporations amongst US youth. Hackers would use their knowledge of telephone systems in conjunction with their computing and 'social engineering' skills to 'talk' information out of the owner and access discrete but linked computing systems. For the uninitiated, hackers claimed to be driven by ethical principles, whereas crackers did not. The term 'cracker' was originally adopted by the cybersecurity community to avoid the misuse of the word 'hacker' by the media; however, today the term 'cracker' has become largely redundant because it does not resonate well with contemporary debates about diversity within the tech industry.[8] The term 'cracker' predates computers and has a historical use as a racial slur against poor white people in the southern states of the US (Foreman, 2013). Useful histories of cybercrime can be found in Shinder and Tittel (2002: 49–92), Britz (2003) and McQuade (2006b).

The first personal computers became available to the public in the late 1970s and early 1980s and could be connected by phone-in Local Area Networks (LANs). The early hackers tested these systems and shared their philosophies and knowledge of 'hacks' on bulletin board services (BBS). Those same BBS systems developed into early virtual trading posts from where information services and goods were sold, thus creating opportunities for theft and the acquisition of goods and services. They were the predecessors of today's darkmarkets on the ToR network. This second generation of cybercrime was given a boost when the internet opened up for general commercial use and TCP/IP (Transmission Control Protocol / Internet Protocol) was accepted as the standard. Prior to the mid-1980s, the internet had been the preserve of the military who originally conceived it as an attack-proof communications system. It was subsequently released for governmental and academic purposes before being opened up for general usage. The internet's massive potential for both good and bad purposes was realized in the early 1990s following the commercial popularity of the graphics user interface (GUI) and the development of the WWW.

The second generation of cybercrimes are mostly 'hybrid' or 'adaptive' (Wall, 2001b; McQuade, 2006a, 2006b). The internet's transnational environment has spawned entirely new globalized opportunities for harmful activities that are currently the subject of existing criminal or civil law. Examples of these activities include illegal internet trading (see Newman and Clarke, 2003: 94). Such trading was initially confined to the (searchable) clear web but then became popular with the advent of the deep or dark web.[9] Such trading included sexually explicit materials (including images of child sexual abuse or exploitation), scams / fraudulent activity (see

Grabosky et al., 2001: 30; Levi, 2001: 44), narcotics, pharmaceuticals, malicious software, criminal services, even people trafficking! (See chapter 5.)

Networked environments, especially the chat forums, also contribute to the circulation of criminal ideas. They have, for example, long circulated information about 'chipping', which is how to bypass the security devices in mobile telephones or digital television decoders (Mann and Sutton, 1998; Wall, 2000). They also provide information on how to manufacture and distribute synthetic drugs (Schneider, 2003: 374). More recently, chat forums have expanded in scope to circulate information, assessments and advice on the many services, skill sets and goods available to hire or purchase on the darkmarket. Take away the internet from these activities and the opportunities for offending with such ease over great distances reduce considerably, if not totally. Yet the behaviour often continues by other means, but on a more limited and localized scale.

As a consequence, cyber-enabled (hybrid or adaptive) cybercrimes are examples of the 'modernization of modernity' (Beck, 1992; Finnemann, 2002: 36). Furthermore, there tends to be both a common understanding of this type of offending and a commonly held view as to which agencies are responsible for policing the offending behaviours. Indeed, their subject matters are covered not only by law but also by the public policing mandates of most countries, in so far as there tends to be clear public support for policing agencies to intervene. The main policing problems arising with cyber-enabled crimes tend to be related to matters of trans-jurisdictional procedure rather than substantive law (see chapter 8). This contrasts with the cyber-dependent crimes, where the legal and social responsibilities are not always so clearly cut.

Cyber-dependent cybercrimes wholly mediated by technologies

The third generation of cybercrimes are wholly dependent upon digital and networked technologies. They are characterized by the internet's distributed and automated nature and were ushered in by the replacement of dial-up modem access with broadband around the turn of the twenty-first century. Originally, online offender–victim engagement took place via spammed emails (phishing) which encouraged recipients to respond directly or to click onto websites. More recently, spam email has converged with virus attachments and 'www' links. When opened, these attachments or links further automate cybercrime. A particularly potent example of the latter is the multifunctionality of the 'blended threat', which submits control of the infected computer to the infector while also gathering and passing on personal information from the same computer (see the later example of ransomware). The two actions were previously considered parallel threats, but they now have one source. They are almost wholly mediated by networked technologies and rely less and less on social engineering once access to the system has been obtained. Most importantly, they illustrate a step-change in the transformation of cybercrime itself insofar as traditional hackers, 'by and large, are becoming an amusing diversion [and no longer] an opportunity to dust down 20-year-old clichés about teenage geniuses' (Sommer, 2004: 10). This is not, of course, to imply that the seriousness of 'hacking' or hackers has in any way diminished – rather the opposite, in fact. See, for example, the Ohio children's hospital hack which exposed 230,000 files to identity thieves (Leyden, 2006d) and the many other subsequent data hacks. Rather, as mentioned earlier, it indicates that the overall level entry for hacking has risen, but also that the hacking process has been 'rationalized' and automated into component services that can now be hired. The stakes have also changed.

Between the mid-2000s and today, there has been a massive explosion in the volume of data theft as data have become valuable commodities in and of themselves. Data are now the focus of many modern cybercrimes (Wall, 2018; Porcedda and Wall, 2021). In 2020, for example, it was estimated that 37 billion personal records had been exposed in 2020 by hackers (Afifi-Sabet, 2020). Although the actual number of breaches seems to have fallen when compared to previous years, hackers are now targeting the databases of larger corporations, so the sheer volume of stolen data has increased. In 2022, it was estimated that 2 data breaches potentially exposed the records of 22 million Australians, or 76 per cent of the population (Wadhwani, 2022). Not only has the cybercrime agenda changed, but also the culture of fear that once surrounded hacking has transferred to the fear that our personal information, given in good faith, can now be used against us.

Cyber-dependent crimes exist at the high end of the continuum. They are the spawn of the internet and therefore embody all of its parent's transformative characteristics, breaking the temporality of geo-social relationships by distanciating (distancing and estranging) them across a global span. Since they are solely the product of opportunities created by the internet, they can only be perpetrated within cyberspace, even if some of their effects may fall outside it. They are therefore *sui generis* (of their own kind). At the far extreme of cyber-dependent crimes lie the more controversial harms, particularly 'cyber-rape' (MacKinnon, 1997), cyber-bullying (Cowie, 2013), cyber-hate (Williams et al., 2020) and the 'virtual vandalism' of virtual worlds (Williams, 2006). In addition, there has been an increase in the appropriation of intellectual properties, which tend to fall outside the jurisdiction and experience of the criminal justice process, as exemplified by the ongoing battle between the music and movie industries and downloaders (Carey and Wall, 2001; Marshall, 2002: 1; David, 2010, Wall, 2015a).

Spamming (phishing) was and is a particularly poignant example of a cyber-dependent crime because it initially stood outside the law, and became an illegal behaviour in its own right in both US and EU law and also in many other jurisdictions in the early 2000s. Some twenty years later, phishing in the 2020s is still regarded as a major cyber-threat. In their predictions for 2022 and 2023, Cyber Security Hub found that three-quarters of the cybersecurity professionals they polled placed phishing and social engineering in the top category of threat (Powell, 2022). This is because it enables offenders to engage with potential victims at a number of different levels and can lay victims open to various subsequent or secondary types of cybercrime (such as fraud), both as an individual or as part of an organization. The key characteristic of cyber-dependent crimes is that if you take away the internet, then they disappear completely.

Although not discussed here in detail because the technologies are still in the development phase, it is anticipated that a fourth generation of cybercrimes will eventually emerge from criminal opportunities generated by cloud technologies, the Internet of Things and also ambient intelligent networks being created by the convergence of wireless, including Software Defined Radio, and networked technologies (briefly mentioned earlier) (IPTS, 2003). The increased data flows arising from these ambient technologies lend themselves to being managed by artificial intelligence technologies. Although still in a relative state of infancy, research is already being conducted into using artificial intelligence to predict legal, regulatory and techno-logical safeguards that will be required in a world of ambient intelligence (see further Friedewald et al., 2006).

By placing cybercrimes within a framework of time rather than space, we can understand them as successive generations defined by different states of technologi-cal development, with each transforming criminal opportunity. This approach also helps us to quickly differentiate the technological differences between crimes, and to position the subject area within criminology and its associated discourses. It helps to avoid any confusion caused by simply applying the term to all crimes involving computers. For example, where digital evidence is involved, or even where comput-ers and their components are stolen, '[t]his is misleading at best, and self-serving, at worst' (Britz, 2003: 4). More specifically, the 'transformation test', mentioned earlier, proves a simple but useful way of categorizing the different types of online offending behaviour currently being referred to as cybercrime, for example in distinguishing between those which have a familiar ring to them and those which appear to jump straight out of the pages of a science fiction novel. But the *scope* of criminal opportu-nity discussed above does not say much about the *type* of crime.

Changes in the type of criminal opportunity online (modus operandi)

Online offending tends to fall into one of three basic types of crime, each invoking a different body of law and requiring different legal and criminological understandings. These groups are crimes against the machine, or offending relating to the integrity of the computer system; crimes that use the machine, or offending assisted by comput-ers (not to be confused with the earlier typology); and crimes in the machine, where the offending focuses upon the content of computers. Each of these illustrates specific discourses of public debate and experiences within the broader criminal justice pro-cesses.[10] The three types of impact on substantive areas of criminal behaviour serve as the basis for the next three chapters, although it is admittedly becoming harder to disaggregate the three within the new generation of automated cybercrime. In prac-tice, there will be some blurring across boundaries because the true cybercrimes will appear to involve combinations of two or more types. Phishing is a good example of this 'blending' of crime because offenders engage their victims through spam (integ-rity), and steal their personal information (computer-assisted) by deceiving victims into logging on to a bogus website (content) which they think belongs to their bank. Phishers then assault the integrity of the victim's own financial system to perpetrate a fraud. However, in only one of the three types (crimes using the machine) will the motivation to steal money be the primary driver behind the crime. Hence, some of these newer mediated forms of offending will appear across a number of chapters in different guises, and (unfortunately) with a degree of repetition.

The above discussion not only defines the modus operandi (motivation) but also indicates the different crimes and the main bodies of law that cover them. These fall into three categories, cybercrimes against the machine, cybercrimes that use the machine, and cybercrimes in the machine.

Cybercrimes against the machine (computer integrity crimes)

Cybercrimes against machines (computer integrity crimes) are an unauthorized breach of computer access controls to gain access to and trespass upon networks and spaces where rights of ownership or title have already been established. Once they get into a system, offenders move laterally across it to increase their privileges to access more remote areas where information of value is stored – rather like a burglar breaking into a house. Alternatively, depending upon whether the motive is economic, vengeful or political, offenders might try to steal or wipe data, or simply block others from gaining access, as in the case of ransomware or DDoS attacks. Mostly, crimes against the machine prepare the ground for a range of further crimes which are either enabled by the machine or in the machine and informational. They can include fraud, stealing data, vandalism, spying, denial of service, the planting and use of viruses and trojans (see further Gordon and Chess, 1999). Those involved range from principled hackers who seek to release information in the public interest to unprincipled hackers who seek personal, financial or political gain. Many jurisdictions now have legislation, such as the UK's Computer Misuse Act 1990, to protect against unauthorized access to computer material, unauthorized access with intent to commit further offences, and unauthorized modification of computer material.

Cybercrimes using the machine (computer-enabled – or computer-related – crimes)

Cybercrimes using machines are very different to crimes against the machine. The issue here is not how that individual got into the system, but how the system is subsequently used to exploit victims to the offender's advantage through fraud, theft, deception, extortion, and so on. Crimes using the machine are mainly economic crimes to acquire money, goods or services dishonestly. Most jurisdictions now have theft acts and legal procedures for the recovery of lost assets, along with intellectual property laws to protect citizens against the illicit acquisition of the expression of ideas.

Cybercrimes in the machine (computer content crimes)

Cybercrimes in the machine are related mainly to the contents of the computing systems – the informational content which lies within the computer, including data, and which can be copied ad infinitum. There are three main broad areas of crime that fall within this category: extreme sexual materials and content, violent materials (including hate speech) and extreme radical materials (terrorism). Each of the latter has been further facilitated since the mid-2000s by social media networks, which have given billions of citizens an internet platform. Often this informational content illustrates evidence of wrongdoing and sometimes possession of it is evidence in and of itself, as in the case of extreme sexual or radical political materials. Most jurisdictions have variants of obscenity laws, and laws which prohibit incitement, although their legislative strength can vary where internet content is also protected by legislation that guarantees freedoms of speech and expression.

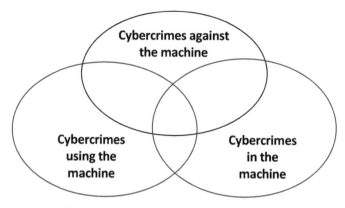

Figure 3.2 The three types of cybercrime modus operandi.

The above categories not only illustrate the development and diversity of cybercrimes, but also provide practical demarcations for analysis. They are ideal types, and when displayed together (figure 3.2) illustrate the considerable areas of overlap.

They can, for example, be used to identify the different resourcing implications for investigation and enforcement, or for choosing methodologies when designing research to further our knowledge of cybercrime. They are individually the subjects of the next three chapters.

Changes in the focus of criminal opportunity online: individual, organizational and nation-state victims

An important and rare consideration when seeking to understand cybercrime is the issue of who the victim groups are in terms of their wealth, power and position, each of which is a factor that can motivate offenders. Victim groups therefore differ according to whether offenders are targeting individual citizens, organizations and businesses – or whether offenders have a bigger political picture in mind and seek to victimize nation states via their economies or infrastructures. Figure 3.3 illustrates the many areas of overlap between these levels of victimization.

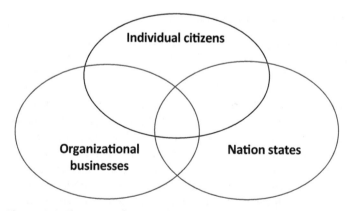

Figure 3.3 The areas of overlap between levels of victimization.

Individual citizens are typically affected by frauds, scams and extortion, but also political, sexual and religious hate speech. In contrast, organizations and businesses tend to fall victim to larger-scale frauds, ransomware or data kidnap, which are often highly publicized by the offender to increase the victim's reputational damage and get them to pay the attackers. Nation states fall victim to attacks that are tactically designed to alter the political status quo. These are usually direct attacks on infrastructure, which can inconvenience citizens and embarrass governments who may be prevented from delivering key services; or they can be more indirect such as orchestrating misinformation (fake news) campaigns, designed to shape and change citizens' views in a particular direction; or by 'nibbling' at businesses and economies to create a broader economic distress.

Conclusions

Together, these various impacts of cybercrime provide a conceptual language frame that helps to explain the variations of cybercrime more accurately – not least, the ways in which internet technologies have effects on a crime ('assisted', 'enabled' or 'dependent'), but also what the intentions are (against the machine, using it or in it) and who the crimes are levelled against (individuals, organizations or nations). This frame helps to explain the component parts of the cybercrime in greater detail, as will be demonstrated in the next chapter. Remember that cybercrime is a big field – see, for example, the offences covered by the FBI's Internet Crime Report 2020 (published March 2021), which lists a wide range of internet-related activities reported by victims to the IC3 (FBI, 2021). These offences range from phishing attacks to hacktivism. In between are a number of offences that range from being cyber-assisted to cyber-enabled to cyber-dependent. Some are offences that facilitate cybercrime (e.g. phishing), whereas others are the cybercrimes themselves (e.g. using ransomware). What is clear from the previous section is that cybercrimes are temporally complex events and cannot be neatly slotted into any one category, not least because, as will be explained later, offenders are extremely adaptive. It is also the case that some cybercrimes are actually more 'cyber' than others. Importantly, the terminology of the language frame provides a basis for explaining the complexities.

To summarize, new networked and digital technologies impact upon criminal behaviour by increasing the scalability of crime online in three distinct ways. Firstly, they massively increase the speed by which crime can be committed. Secondly, they expand the distance over which it can be committed. Thirdly, they increase not only the overall scalability of the crime but also the volume of crime that can be committed. This is what is referred to as the 'cyber-lift', or difference in terms of new behaviours and also new opportunities for crime that are over and above the normal evolution of crime due to technology. This increase in 'scalability' is ever increasing along with advances in technical capabilities, as illustrated by the metaphor of Moore's Law, which argued (in 1970) that computer power will double every two years.

Today, computing ability is being increased by new cloud technologies which expand further computing power and storage space whilst also reducing relative computing costs. Moreover, these developments in technology have also facilitated an increase in the functionality of devices that, on the one hand, greatly increase the quality of our lives but, on the other, create information flows that can be exploited in one way or another. The Internet of Things, as it is called, expands the spread and scope of online criminal opportunities and thus further increases the overall scalability of cybercrime (Wall, 2017).

The transformative impacts of the internet, working either in isolation or in combination, support the argument that the internet provides a new conduit for committing criminal and harmful behaviours. They change the more long-term and traditional relationships between offenders, victims and the state. By widening the offenders' reach of opportunity to a global scale, enabling offenders to engage victims in new ways and providing new means for the organization of criminal behaviours, they create entirely new opportunities for harmful or criminal behaviours. They also allow a wider access to the technologies, which means that almost anyone can commit crimes that were once the domain of the privileged. In short, the internet has democratized crime, anyone can now commit it!

So, although the fundamental nature of online victimization might remain familiar in terms of theft, deception, exploitation, the scale and ways in which victimization takes place via internet technologies differ considerably from the past, and herein lies a basis for delineating between cybercrime and non-cybercrime. The simple principle for understanding the difference between the two is to apply the 'transformation test' (Wall, 2007a: 34) – in other words, by asking what would happen to these crimes if the networked and digital technologies were taken away?

In his analysis of the Victorian electric telegraph, Standage observed broadly that '[g]iven a new invention, there will always be some people who see only its potential to do good, while others see new opportunities to commit crime or make money. We can expect exactly the same reactions to whatever new inventions appear in the twenty-first century' (Standage, 1998: 199). The above analysis shows that the particular characteristics of the internet – informational activity, networking and globalization – have transformed criminal behaviour by creating new opportunities for old crimes and, importantly, also new opportunities for new crimes. It also explains how the present cybercrime debate often confuses traditional patterns of offending using computers with the forms of cybercrime that are solely the product of the internet. The next three chapters look in greater detail at the transformations taking place within substantive areas of criminal activity.

Some discussion questions based upon this chapter

What has caused criminal behaviour to change online?

How has the organization of crime online changed?

How have the scope, modus operandi and victim focus of criminal behaviour changed online?

Further Reading   To take the study of the impact of cyberspace upon criminal activity further, students and researchers are recommended to look at the following texts, which each address the issue from slightly different perspectives: McGuire (2007); Holt et al. (2015); Yar and Steinmetz (2023); Maras (2016).

4 Cybercrimes against the Machine (Computer Integrity Crime): Hacking, Cracking and Denial of Service

How have crimes against the machine changed in the information age?

Chapter contents and key points

Hacking and hackers

- Ethical hackers
- Unethical hackers
- Cyber-conflict and espionage actors
- Cyber-terrorists and information warfare

Hacker tactics to compromise the integrity of networked computers

- Social engineering
- Inserting malicious software and code
- Using spyware and surveillance software
- Attacking services used by victims

Motivations and attractions for offending

- Criminal gain or commercial advantage
- Revenge
- Curiosity and the intellectual challenge
- To get 'sneaky thrills'
- The need for peer respect
- To show off skills and impress potential employers
- Politically motivated protest

Chapter at a glance   *This chapter explores cybercrimes against the machine: cybercrimes which are intended to attack computer systems and networks, sometimes as crimes in their own right – for example, to prevent users from gaining access, or at other times to gain entry to a system with a view to stealing content or holding the content to ransom. The first part looks at the different types and variations of hackers. The second part discusses the tactics used by hackers to attack machines. The third part explores the different motivations and attractions for this type of cybercrime offending.*

Introduction

This chapter will explore the changing role of the hacker over the years, and it will outline the various types of cybercrimes against the machine[1] before looking at the various motivations and tactics used for compromising the integrity of computers. Without trust in the integrity of a computer network, everything that it represents, including its services to users, becomes compromised. A major problem, therefore, in assessing the impact of a trespass or hack is to be able to accurately ascertain whether or not the attack is the end in its own right, or a precursor to other crimes – which is a useful principle when distinguishing between different types of hackers. With this important distinction in mind, this chapter will focus upon criminal attacks upon the integrity of networked computers. The first section will look at the variations of attacks involving hacking; the second discusses the tactics employed to breach the integrity of systems; and the third identifies the different motivations for offending.

Hacking and hackers

Hacking is a colloquial expression to describe deliberate and unauthorized attempts to access digital spaces that belong to others. The primary aim of hacking is to breach the security of a networked computer system, either illegally or legally, by assaulting its integrity. The term 'trespass' would probably be more descriptive of the broader range of attacks upon system integrity because it does not carry the emotional and ideological baggage that comes with the term 'hacking'. The term 'cracking' was popular in the early days of the internet to differentiate between good and bad hackers, but the term has ceased to be of descriptive use in the twenty-first century. The use of the terms 'hacking' and 'hackers', like 'cybercrime', is now embedded in everyday language.

It is no great surprise that hacking has generated public and corporate concerns. For many years, surveys from both sides of the Atlantic consistently indicated high numbers of security breaches against both individuals and organizations. In 2002, for example, the Information Security Breaches (Victim) Survey of the UK Department of Trade and Industry (DTI) found that '44% of UK businesses suffered at least one malicious security breach in the past year, nearly twice as many as in the 2000 survey' (DTI, 2002: 1). Such a relatively high level of victimization also reflected the experience in the US. During 2002, the CERT at Carnegie Mellon University recorded about 100,000 incidents of security breaching. Twenty years later, the statistics from the UK *Cyber Security Breaches Survey* 2022 (DCMS, 2022) found the percentage of businesses experiencing breaches much the same (2017, 46%; 2018, 43%; 2019, 32%; 2020, 46%; 2021, 39%; 2022, 39%), although the impacts and costs to businesses were much more severe than previously. Organizations (and individuals) today, for example, have a much higher level of digital exposure than twenty years ago. The *Cyber Security Breaches Survey*[2] found that over 'nine in ten businesses (92%) and eight in ten charities (80%)' used either banking or payment systems online (DCMS, 2022). There has also been more than a hundredfold increase in data theft. The US Identity Theft Resource Center (ITRC, 2023) reports 1,802 breaches compromising 400 million victims, compared with about 160 breaches twenty years ago. Many organizations are reluctant to report cybercrime victimization, usually to prevent

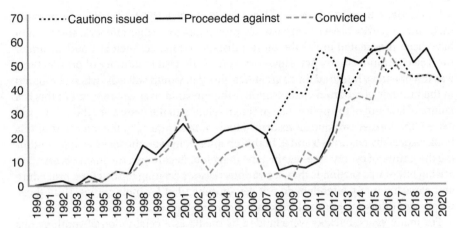

Figure 4.1 The number of prosecutions and convictions in England and Wales under the Computer Misuse Act 1990.
Source: a compilation of various ONS sources.[3]

losing their business reputation and to resolve the victimization in their own, rather than the public, interest.

Similarly, individuals now put more investment in digital and networked technologies than they did twenty years ago in terms of their purchasing, finance and leisure and pleasure pursuits. With some fluctuations, the findings of the Crime Survey for England and Wales (CSEW) (a victim survey), which annually interviews 30,000 adults, estimate that about 1 million computer misuse offences are committed each year in the UK. About half involve a 'computer virus' (Corfield, 2019). Numerically, computer misuse victimizations are about a tenth of the number of frauds; in 2022, only 14 recorded incidents per 1,000 adults were for computer misuse,[4] compared with 145 incidents per 1,000 adults for fraud (ONS, 2023: Table F8).

This apparently high level of victimization (and therefore offending) is not reflected in the prosecution statistics. Figure 4.1 is compiled from various ONS and government sources and shows how the number of cases annually prosecuted progressively increased in the late 1990s and fell in the early 2000s before rising over the past decade.

The number of prosecutions reflects developments in the UK national policing capacity to address cybercrime. The numbers, about 40–60 prosecutions per year are nevertheless small when compared with the reported incidents. One explanation for this disparity is that so few cybercrime incidents are passed on to police forces by Action Fraud, which receives reports and triages them for evidence (Corfield, 2019). Another reason is that many computer misuse offences also involve frauds and are dropped in order to focus the investigation resources upon the latter.[5]

In England and Wales, security breaches fall under the Computer Misuse Act 1990 which protects victims against unauthorized access to computer material (s. 1); unauthorized access with intent to commit or facilitate commission of further offences (s. 2); and unauthorized modification of computer material (s. 3). During the first decade following its introduction (1991–2000), 53 offenders were cautioned under the Act, and a further 88 prosecuted. Of the latter, 68 (77 per cent) were convicted: 15 under

s. 1, 11 under s. 2, and 42 under s. 3 (*Hansard*, 2002; Wall, 2003: 131). It is very possible that, since security breaches are usually precursors to further offences, some might have been prosecuted under the more substantive offence, such as fraud, or under the Telecommunications Act. However, even if the visible number of prosecutions was ten or even a hundred times greater, a shortfall would still exist when compared to the number of reported victimisations. The question over whether or not this is a failure of law and of the police, or a problem relating to the nature of cybercrime, still exists? The former two questions drive much of the enquiry in the later part of this book, especially chapters 8 and 9. In this chapter, however, the focus is upon outlining the nature of cybercrimes against the machine. Regardless, the main observation arising out of this section is that, for various reasons relating to structure, procedure and capacity, many offenders do not get apprehended for their crimes. Until these issues are addressed, criminal hacking remains viable.

For many years, hackers were lauded by media as a celebration of youth genius and the pioneering spirit of America, but they have subsequently become demonized (see Ross, 1990: para. 4; Sterling, 1994; Chandler, 1996: 229; Duff and Gardiner, 1996; P. Taylor, 1999; Wall, 2008; Steinmetz, 2016). Today, there is a clear distinction between 'white hat hackers', who celebrate the original ethical hacking traditions, and 'black hat hackers', who are driven by unethical, criminal motivations such as financial gain or revenge. Although there remains some regard for the public service / civil liberties ethics of the ethical hacker, the skills and beliefs of both types of hackers have arguably become so co-mingled that both are now distrusted and regarded as a threat, and are outlawed by most computer misuse laws. More specifically, hacking has developed far beyond the idealistic first-generation system hacks to reveal a broad array of activities and motivations. On the one hand, the legitimate hackers have now defined themselves as ethical hackers and train for qualifications – for example, as penetration testers. On the other hand, the illegitimate hackers represent a spectrum of qualitatively different types of transgressive behaviours, from intellectually motivated acts to political actions to criminally motivated activities.

In its least invasive form, hacking is considered – mainly by the hackers themselves – to be an intellectual challenge resulting in a fairly harmless trespass intended to test security systems, release information or advertise the intruder's hacking abilities, rather than to purposefully cause any serious and lasting damage, and hackers even advertise their work as improving security procedures and processes. At its worst, hacking can cause considerable damage to the infrastructure and also to information, leading to financial and physical losses. Plus, there is also the damage caused by secondary or knock-on impacts of hacking, in the form of loss of trust in systems, loss of business, and reduced participation in networks. Since 'hacking' is now largely the accepted term, it is appropriate to talk of the distinction between ethical and unethical hackers, but the proliferation of hacking has meant that each category now has a number of different variants often denoted in the cybersecurity media by their 'hat' colour: white, black, grey, green, blue, red and even yellow. Please note that the use of colours to describe the various status of hackers can be controversial and not always consistent. I have tried to cut across the literature; for a useful brief description of the basic differences, see Shea (2019). You have to make up your own mind up about whether to use these categories or not.

Ethical hackers

Ethical hackers, as the name suggests, possess a high level of ethical standards which they express through specialized knowledge combined with a belief in the ethics of freedom of access to public information. From the early days of communications technologies, hackers played a crucial role in the development of the internet (see Ross, 1990: para. 4; Sterling, 1994; Chandler, 1996; Duff and Gardiner, 1996). They tested systems and forced code writers to achieve higher standards of quality, while also lending their skills and imagination to shape the internet. Written in 1986 and published in the now defunct *Phrack* magazine, the 'Hacker's Manifesto' encapsulates these ethical values: 'Yes, I am a criminal. My crime is that of curiosity. My crime is that of judging people by what they say and think, not what they look like. My crime is that of outsmarting you, something that you will never forgive me for' (The Mentor, 1986).

Ethical hacking has, during the past two decades, developed a set of consistent practices that guide the curriculum for training and form the basis of qualifications. The ethical hacker's role is not to attack the integrity of networks, but to find vulnerabilities in systems and networks which could be exploited by criminals, and therefore to strengthen their security. Through brute force (sometimes called Black-Box) testing, they work with IT departments to identify weaknesses and then review systems and help to develop policies and procedures to make systems safe. As such, they have become a significant part of the cybersecurity industry which has emerged to protect systems. But there are some nuanced differences between the different types, which the terminology of different hat colours denotes.

White hat hackers tend to be trained security specialists who are hired to find vulnerabilities in software and hardware before the black hat hackers find and exploit them. Blue hat hackers are much like white hat hackers in that they are employed by an organization to find security holes and vulnerabilities in new products before they are released for sale. Red hat hackers prefer to deal out their own form of justice outside the law. Whereas a white hat hacker would report the black hats to the police, red hat hackers act as vigilantes (sometimes acting on behalf of governments) to attack and destroy black hats' computer systems in revenge for their hacks. Purple hat hackers seek to improve and test their skills, but only on their own systems rather than those belonging to others. Finally, grey hat hackers are a fusion of the white and black hat hackers and may use illegal methods to find flaws. What I call 'light grey hats' are very often reforming black hat hackers in a move towards becoming white hat. They can be distinguished from 'dark grey hats' who use illegal methods to find vulnerabilities which they sell to the highest bidder.

Unethical hackers

Unethical or black hat hackers maliciously and illegally search for vulnerabilities in systems, to exploit for their own gain. They are driven by a range of motivations, from financial or political gain to revenge or simply to show how skilled they are to attract peer respect. In practice, unethical hackers usually fall somewhere between white and black hat depending upon the level of maliciousness and harm inflicted. The grey hat – and especially 'dark grey hat' – hackers described above use illegal methods to find vulnerabilities which they sell to the highest bidder, and occupy a space where they are unclear as to what is good or bad behaviour, seeking only to achieve their desired goals. Hacktivists are a variant of the dark grey hat hackers who combine hacking with activism and, often controversially, use hacking to promote political ideas to effect social change. Often appearing to exist in the 'grey area' where it is hard to ascertain what is right or wrong in achieving their ideals, their actions can often be malicious and destructive (Shantz and Tomblin, 2014).

Young (1995: 10) distinguished between utopians who naively believe that they are contributing to society by demonstrating its vulnerabilities – a self-justification rather than a conviction – and cyberpunks who are aggressively anti-establishment and intentionally cause harm to the target. Both, of course, tend to create disruption through their unauthorized presence at a particular site. It is often fairly hard to distinguish between the two in practice and further demarcations may be made in terms of experience. Green hat hackers, or 'script kiddies', 'wannabes' or 'lamers', are junior and inexperienced hackers who are curious and eager to learn black hacking skills. They have low levels of competency and frequently solicit help from specialist chat forums. Here they are schooled by 'Gurus', who are the experts with long-term knowledge and experience; 'Wizards', who are renowned for the depth of their knowledge; and 'Samurai', who have practical experience in carrying out hacking tasks. 'Script kiddies' tend to be inexperienced and unskilled hackers who try to infiltrate or disrupt systems by running pre-made tools. They 'vandalize websites both for the thrill of it and to increase their reputation among their peers' (Mead et al., 2005). Lemos has referred to them as 'ankle-biters' (2000). Although denigrated for their lack of IT skills, they can nevertheless send out strong messages. Since their primary motivation is to command peer respect for their skills or their sheer audacity, script kiddie achievements (evidence of audacious hacks) are often displayed on one or more of a number of sites. One such site, 2600: The Hacker Quarterly, has an archive of 'hacked' sites (www.2600.com). Once they become experienced, script kiddies can graduate into black hat hackers.

Yellow hat hackers focus on illegally hacking social media accounts to take them over or distort content to gain revenge on a person, idol or particular commercial brand. They are sometimes known as social media hackers, but effectively act with the same levels of skill and ruthlessness as black hat hackers.

Cyber-conflict and espionage actors

Whereas most hackers want to be noticed for their skills, even if they do not want to be caught, cyber-spies, who seek to conduct political or industrial espionage, in contrast, do not. They want to enter and exit sites discreetly, avoiding detection[6] in order to obtain restricted information such as government or trade secrets, which might, for example, enable the possessor to gain a marketplace, or political, advantage over their competitors. The internet can assist the act of cyber-espionage in a number of distinct ways. Aside from the obvious advantages of signals intelligence used by the security services, cyber-espionage can be used by others to exploit a number of other internet advantages. The first is that it enables disgruntled insiders, who are a prime source of information, to seek revenge or gain by abusing their system access rights to obtain information electronically and send it outside the organizational boundaries. A second is to exploit 'well-meaning' insiders who have the interests of their organization at heart but override the security system to achieve their own professional goals – typically, by extracting documents to work on in their own time (Wall, 2013). The third way is for insiders to provide outsiders with unauthorized access to closed systems to obtain information. This may be achieved by getting an insider to install spyware or back doors into a system to allow remote access, or by 'socially engineering' an insider to reveal the access codes (see Mitnick and Simon, 2002). The fourth way is to discreetly probe a system looking for default system usernames and passwords – for example, where both are the same, such as 'guest',[7] or an email address is used as username and 12345 as password, or even the word 'password' as the password. Such practice is less common today than in past years because of training, warnings and log-in rules, but these messages do not always get through. The fifth way is much less dramatic and not necessarily illegal. The surveillant capacity of the internet enables outsiders to observe the intelligence radiated by organizations via their own websites. By pulling together many minor pieces of information, a fairly complete picture of the organization's structure, ambitions and plans can often be assembled.

Cyber-spying (for want of a better description) has long been a concern because of the ease with which it can take place. In theory, there exist four main groupings of cyber-spy. The first are cyber-warriors, who are specialized black hat hackers who act like 'guns for hire' and sell their skills to the highest bidder. Second are the industrial spies, who focus upon enterprises and are money driven and sufficiently skilled in their work to seamlessly infiltrate and exfiltrate organizations. The third are government agents, who are highly trained, skilled, and seek to achieve political goals. Finally, the fourth group are the military hackers, who serve in the military and seek to achieve military goals. In practice, as is often the case with things cyber, the reality is that the various groups or actors tend to occupy the same space. But the reality of cyber-espionage is that the boundaries between the actors are not so clear cut. Lindsay has argued that hackers (and cyber-conflict actors) exploit vulnerabilities caused by 'constitutive inefficiencies (market and regulatory failure) and incomplete contracts (generative features and unintended flaws)'. So, cyber-conflict is, effectively, 'a form of cheating within the rules, rather than an anarchic struggle'. It is 'more like an intelligence–counterintelligence contest than traditional war' (Lindsay, 2017). As a consequence, the serious damage predicted in the dominant threat narratives over the past years has not appeared, although the consequences are nevertheless being felt downstream as activities such as data theft and service disruption impact upon victims (Wall, 2008; Lindsay, 2017).

During the past decade, cyber-conflict has become an increasing concern and also more of a reality as the overall number of cyber-conflict groups and activities has increased, especially since Russia's 'special operation' in the Ukraine in 2014 and latterly in 2022. The conflict groups allied to both sides comprise sympathetic non-nation-state and nation-state actors, indicating some significant state involvement in government-promoted cyber activities. Like many online groupings (see chapter 7), these cyber-conflict groups are very fluid and ephemeral, regularly breaking up and reforming because of internal disagreements or counter actions, or deliberately to evade law enforcement. Importantly, some non-nation-state actors (mainly criminal offenders) draw some credibility from geopolitical affiliation to hide their criminality, especially economic crime. Meanwhile, nation-state actors also exploit the economic criminals to hide their own strategic goals, not least the damage caused to the 'enemy' by cyber-campaigns and the intelligence obtained from any stolen data. However, the declared allegiance to Russia by ransomware group Conti resulted in a civil war between its members allied to the Ukraine and to Russia, which led to its collapse (Goldsmith and Wall, forthcoming).

Cyber-terrorists and information warfare

Beyond crimes, new digital network technologies and their cyberspace arguably constitute a 'new battlefield' in which to wage war against adversaries, invoking the term 'cyber-warfare'. This concept involves discussion about cyber-attacks, the management of communications information and robotics, of which the latter is not discussed here.

Cyber-terrorism has been a long-standing media trope, and although concerns about it predated September 11, 2001 (see Denning, 2000), it has since become a very emotive topic and remains so to this day. This is partly because of the real threat to infrastructure, but also because of the dramatic imagery that it invokes. The purpose of cyber-terrorism is to use computers to attack the physical infrastructure to generate mass fear and anxiety and, in theory, manipulate the political agenda. Writing in the early 1990s, Sterling warned that 'hackers in Amtrak computers or in air-traffic controller computers, will kill somebody someday' (Sterling, 1994: 185). In February 1998, the vulnerability of the US military computers was exposed when it was discovered that hackers had entered the Pentagon's system via a way-station computer in the United Arab Emirates. The implications of the attack were played down by the Pentagon, which, in contrast to its previous experience of intrusion, suggested that the break-ins were the result of a contest perpetrated by a small group of amateurs (Dolinar, 1998: A03). In this case, what is not known is whether the hackers left themselves trap doors: 'the digital equivalent of the key under the welcome mat to use next time' (Dolinar, 1998: A03). There have been a number of similar examples in the twenty-five years since.

The main weakness with the concept of cyber-terrorism is that, although anticipated, it is hard to ascertain when it has taken place. There are, in fact, few examples of it taking place as an event which impacts sufficiently upon a population to have a political outcome. On the one hand, it is certainly possible that key public computer systems, networks, services and utilities could be disrupted or disabled through malicious intrusion. However, since most key state and corporate critical infrastructures have been protected since September 11 – and many before that date – by protection and enforcement policies supported by the necessary financial and human resources, the likelihood of a successful cyber-terrorist attack will have been considerably reduced. Indeed, without understating the potential threat, this strength may well explain why the earlier doomsday predictions about cyber-terrorism have yet to materialize.

More likely to occur is a variant of what is commonly referred to as information warfare (Szafranski, 1995: 56), much like some of the nuanced attacks which have been carried out by conflict and related actors since the Russia/Ukraine conflict situation emerged. There have been a number of examples, for instance, of ransomware attacks by Russian-speaking threat groups upon businesses that provide part of the US infrastructure. The attack on the Colonial Pipeline in mid-2021, for example, crippled fuel supplies to the east coast of the USA (Goldsmith and Wall, unpublished). Whilst this had the effect of dramatically impacting upon the population, the actors appear to have been primarily motivated by money, as a ransom demand was paid (Newman, 2021). Yet it arguably helped nation-state actors achieve their goals.

Information warfare becomes more possible in the information age. The emergence of social media networks and talk radio has, as indicated in the previous chapter, effectively disintermediated the media to allow a voice to a much broader audience. One of the outcomes of this is that at the margins of the media, to paraphrase Baudrillard, the truth is no longer important – just what is being talked about is important (Baudrillard, 1994). There have been a number of significant examples in US (and UK) politics during the past decade.

Interestingly, the older accounts of information warfare define it as the military use of information as a tool of warfare against national information systems. Information warfare has long been used to weaken the resistance of 'the enemy' and examples can be found centuries before the internet came into being. It can take the form of using propaganda to persuade the enemy to surrender, or of feeding disinformation or propaganda to one's own population to persuade them to rally to the cause. As old as information warfare may be, networked technologies provide new possibilities for conducting it effectively and efficiently, and especially for undermining an enemy's data and information systems. So great is the concern within military circles about the potential for using networked technology for information warfare that military strategists regularly prepare counter information warfare strategies to be effected by formally constituted Information Warfare Units (Berger, 1996; Rathmell, 2001).

Contemporary definitions of information warfare tend to view it less militaristically, and rather as the manipulation of information to obtain a competitive advantage over an opponent, corporate or otherwise. But it is important not to downplay the potential impact of information warfare just because the attack may use information or focus upon information systems. An attack on key government informational data, such as tax codes or social security numbers, could have serious long-term impacts on political and societal stability. It is important to note here that the main threats from information warfare are more likely to take the form of viral information flows, which are often of individual minor significance, but which have a greater aggregate impact. Indeed, Berkowitz and Hahn (2003) and Francisco (2003) have concluded that the main threat from information warfare is not the economic damage resulting from a single large-scale attack, but the damage caused by a few small, well-publicized attacks that undermine public confidence in the systems being attacked.

Hacker tactics to compromise the integrity of networked computers

A common myth about hackers, perpetuated by hacker movies and fictional literature, is that they possess the superhuman ability to break into computer systems and map their way around them. This mythology assumes that the expert knowledge and skills of 'super-hackers' give them 'access to all areas' once their moral bind has eroded and they go over to the dark side and become a danger to society. Ohm (2007) has observed that the cybercrime expert discourse is replete with the construction of super-hackers (or superusers). These mythical super-hackers appear to be immune from technical constraints and are greatly feared by policymakers – policymakers who, Ohm argues, exaggerate the super-hacker's powers. This tendency often leads to over-reaction and the passing of overbroad, ambiguous laws intended to ensnare the superuser, but which are used instead against transgressive ordinary users (Ohm, 2007: 1). The reality of hacking today, as indicated earlier, is quite different from in previous decades because hackers – or, more accurately, attackers – tend to buy in services to facilitate their crimes from a range of experts with computing skills and advanced knowledge about communications systems and networks. These facilitating services comprise the cybercrime ecosystem and are described in greater detail in chapter 7, although a snapshot illustrates the complexity of a modern cybercrime.

This ecosystem is most easily explained by looking at the nine distinct stages of a ransomware attack, which each requires a specific and specialized set of hacking skills to complete. First, reconnaissance is required to identify potential victims and their network access points. Second, initial access has to be gained to a target system, using login credentials. These are obtained by 'phishers' after tricking the owners out of their information, which will subsequently be collated into pre-assembled credential data and bought on the dark web by an 'initial access broker'. Alternatively, rather than use the selective social engineering approach, the phishers (or initial access brokers) may use either a brute-force or a credential-stuffing[8] attack to gain entry just to see if the credential sets are still live for further use. Both procedures use high powered 'bots'[9] to run routines to gain access and achieve the required scalability. Brute-force attacks rely upon users using simple guessable passwords, and the 'bot' tries to guess the passwords using frequently used passwords, common words or phrases found in dictionaries, or random strings of letters. Credential stuffing uses potential credential data from one of the many databases of known breach credentials that are available free, or at a cost for the more reliable sets. Collections #1–5, for example, was a database freely circulated on the dark web which contained an 'unprecedented collection of 2.2 billion unique usernames and associated passwords' (Greenberg, 2019). This data was a collection of leaks from Dropbox and LinkedIn and many other companies over a period of years. Although old, the databases still contain useable data because users have either not updated their password, or used the same password for another application (Greenberg, 2019).

Third, once initial access has been gained, attackers then seek to escalate their access privileges and move laterally across the organization. This allows them to search for key organizational data which will cause the victim the most pain when they are deprived of its use. Which is why hospitals, educational institutions and governmental records, alongside corporate client information, are so often the target of ransomware attacks. Fourth, before any encrypting ransomware is installed and activated, however, the key data is identified and extracted, and saved by the criminals. Fifth, after the ransomware has been installed and deployed – very often when the organization is at its weakest, such as during a public holiday – the first sign that the victim has been attacked is when its key data has been locked and the victim cannot operate. Sixth, the victim's name is then published on the ransomware operators' dark-web leak site to shame them publicly. The naming statement may also feature threats to share or auction stolen sensitive data to further frighten the victim into paying the ransom demand. Seventh, successful ransomware attacks require the ransom to be paid in cryptocurrency, which can be difficult to trace.

Eighth, once the payment has been received, the cryptocurrency is then monetized. It is laundered, then converted into fiat currency. Ninth, after paying off their debts for the facilitating services, the attackers often invest the proceeds of their crimes in the legitimate economy, although some clearly invest in researching and preparing their campaign of attacks (Wall, 2021).

What the above analysis of the ransomware attack illustrates is the range of skills required to achieve a successful operation. As indicated earlier, a sassy hacker could achieve each of the functions, but not with the degree of expertise and organization required to achieve the scale of operation at low risk which makes it viable. Spammers hire out spamware-as-a-service software that phishers, scammers and fraudsters use to steal people's credentials, and databrokers trade these stolen details on the dark web. This data may be purchased by initial access brokers, who specialize in gaining initial entry to computer systems before selling on those access details to would-be ransomware attackers. These attackers often engage with crimeware-as-a-service brokers, who hire out ransomware-as-a-service software as well as other malicious malware. To coordinate these groups, darkmarketeers provide online markets where criminals can openly sell or trade their services, usually via the ToR network on the dark web. Monetizers are employed to launder cryptocurrency and turn it into fiat currency, while negotiators, representing both victim and offender, are hired to settle the ransom amount. The ecosystem around ransomware is constantly evolving and a recent development has been the emergence of the 'ransomware consultant', who collects a fee for advising offenders on key stages of an attack such as potential victims, sourcing initial-access credentials and those with skill sets to carry the attack through.

What the above reveals is that modern cybercrimes are complex cybercrime operations which, aside from some business acumen, require the application of social, as well as technical, hacking skills.

Social engineering

Social engineering, or people hacking, implies the various techniques employed to get the victim to do something they do not want to do, usually by deception or trickery. The object of social engineering is to obtain information about a victim in order to acquire personal information that can be used against them or to obtain access codes to their computer or employer's network. Or the objective may be to trick victims to insert some malicious code onto their computer that leaves them or their organization vulnerable to attack.

Social engineering is understated within, and runs counter to, the hacker mythology. Although social engineering has now become an adopted practice, few early hackers would admit to using it, preferring instead to have the outside world believe that their technical skills were at the forefront of their prowess. Although the term had a prior history in Skinnerian behavioural psychology, the expression became popularized by Kevin Mitnick in *The Art of Deception* (Mitnick and Simon, 2002), in which he explained that many of his hacks were achieved by exploiting the weakest link in the security chain, the people who have access to systems, rather than directly attacking the systems themselves. He described how the hackers' success lies in their ability to combine expert knowledge of communications and computing systems with their capacity to build trust relationships with individuals who have access to systems, in order to 'socially engineer' passwords and pass codes out of them. The secret, according to Mitnick, lies in not making the target suspicious: '[t]he more a social engineer can make his contact seem like business as usual, the more he allays suspicion. When people don't have a reason to be suspicious, it's easy for a social engineer to gain their trust' (Mitnick and Simon, 2002: 41).

Social engineers tend to use their knowledge of systems to make themselves appear credible to staff (usually administrative or secretarial) who have access to the system they are trying to enter. They will adopt the language of the organization, using first names, often referring to work colleagues using intimate terms. Once the credibility of the 'engineer' has been established, then access information will be sought from the victim. This activity does not usually take place in isolation. Other tactics may support or inform the practice of social engineering. If access information cannot be talked out of victims, then personal information may be sought from discarded documents retrieved from waste disposal. This personal information may be used to give the illusion of credibility in subsequent conversations with them. Of course, it may be that the operatives' paper waste could even directly provide the desired access information. Other more sophisticated techniques of social engineering, designed to trick individuals into parting with access information, may include impersonating staff by using credible documentation such as fake organizational identity cards. A further trick sometimes used is reverse social engineering where the hacker causes a technical problem within a system and then positions himself or herself to be commissioned to fix it, thereby gaining access (see Mitnick and Simon, 2002: 60).

The modern social engineer's tactic is the phishing campaign. Phishing for credentials involves tricking users into revealing their network access credentials or giving data that can be used to develop an access profile. Phishing tends to take place at both lower and higher levels. At the lower level, phishing starts off as a general data hunt, an indiscriminate cyber-dependent crime to get individuals to respond to an email. At worst, a cold reply shows that the email account is live and still being used; at best, it also contains contact information about the victim and maybe even a website containing more information about them. This data is either sold to potential attackers to gain low-level initial access to an organization, or it may be further developed to increase its value. The information from those who respond to phishing attempts will be filtered by data specialists and classified in terms of their usability to provide system access credentials which are then sold online as off-the-shelf live access credentials. Initial access can enable attackers to enter a system, for example, to encourage a target victim within to allow the attacker into the network via RDP (Remote Desk Protocol) methods. Or they may be used as the basis for a 'big game hunt' (or spear phishing) to target a key manager or officer within an organization, to steal or deceive them out of their privileged access login credentials. Group-IB (2021) found that in 2020 incidents of phishing had been overtaken as the main means of breaking into networks by RDP credentials, followed by phishing and then exploiting public-facing applications such as Citrix, WebLogic, VPN servers or Microsoft Exchange (Group-IB, 2021).

Inserting malicious software and code

Once the victim has been socially engineered into some form of compliance by persuading them to open an email attachment, clicking on a URL or downloading a malicious file (often pretending to be an update), this malware (in a number of different ways) enables the attackers to gain remote control over the victim's computer and then move laterally across its network. In some cases of advanced social engineering, for example where the attackers claim to be from a software company or even the police, victims are persuaded to disable their network security and even allow attackers direct remote access to their computers by RDP.

During the past decade, the increasingly specialized division of criminal labour and growth in strategic collaborations between hackers and virus writers and spammers, along with advances in hacking tools technology, have led to an arsenal of different types of malware and the software tools to install them. Whereas these tools used to include key loggers or RATs (remote administration trojans), a range of sophisticated software suites are employed today to enter networks and move laterally across them. Some of these tools have been stolen from government agencies. The 2017 Wannacry and not-Petya ransomware attacks, for example, were facilitated by combining 'DoublePulsar', a backdoor implant, with 'EternalBlue', a software routine which exploits a vulnerability in unpatched computers. Ironically, both routines were originally developed by the US National Security Agency (NSA), from where they were stolen by the ShadowBrokers hacker group (Goodin, 2017).

Box 4.1 The Wannacry cryptoworm ransomware attack

The May 2017 WannaCry ransomware attack illustrates a number of main themes in this chapter, not least the collaborations between different cybercrime groups and the use of cybercrime to inflame conflict situations. Launched by the Lazarus Group, which allegedly has links with North Korea, the Wannacry ransomware cryptoworm hit many organization networks globally infecting a quarter of a million computers and causing millions of dollars of damage. The ransomware requested a relatively small payment of $300 in Bitcoin (BTC) for a decryptor. The attack caused havoc, for a day or so, mainly because those infected were unaware of its seriousness and so immediately closed their systems down preventing business from taking place.

Wannacry targeted an unpatched version of early MS Windows systems, using a combination of the EternalBlue exploit which enables the DoublePulsar backdoor implant tool to be installed and a ransomware encryptor inserted. Both routines were stolen from different parts of the US NSA by a hacker/hacktivist group calling themselves 'the Shadowbrokers', who allegedly have links with Russia. The attack was fairly quickly foiled by UK security researcher Marcus Hutchins, who found a weakness in its construction, registered a kill switch and prevented it from spreading and encrypting infected computers (Greenberg, 2017; Newman, 2017a, 2017b).

Variants of Wannacry attacked the Taiwan Semiconductor Manufacturing Company in August 2018, and the EternalBlue and DoublePulsar combinations were later used in the not-Petya attack in June 2017. Not-Petya (a variant of Petya) was allegedly used by Russian government agencies to attack mainly Ukrainian organizations.

Using spyware and surveillance software

Another 'hacking' tactic is to use clandestine spyware and surveillance software to observe victims to obtain information about them, including access to their various networks. Keylog programs are directly employed to record passwords and steal information, and today a number of variants of spyware are employed with each displaying different levels of insidiousness. Moving from the seemingly inoffensive through to the invasive, 'cookies' assist interactions between web browsers and websites. They can also be used for low-level mass surveillance by reporting back to a third-party low-level information about the user's browsing and purchasing preferences, for example as used by advertising analysts such as DoubleClick (see *In re Doubleclick Inc.*, 2001).

Then there is password-sniffing technology that can be used to interrogate the access files of operating systems to identify passwords, and a 'traffic movement logger' which records the communications made by users but not the content, followed by the 'key-stroke logger' (mentioned above) which records what the users actually type. Finally, there is 'content spyware' which conveys the entire actions of users on a specific computer, including the content of any communications they may send or receive.

Over the past twenty years, the surveillance debate has changed from primarily using bespoke software for finding out data about individuals to mass surveillance programmes using 'apps' developed for social media networks. In 2018, the Cambridge Analytica scandal broke to reveal that the company had developed a personality-profiling 'app' called 'This is your digital life', which 270,000 Facebook users adopted. Behind the scenes, the 'app' surreptitiously collected data about the users' networks of contacts and harvested the personal information of 97 million Facebook users, who did not give their permission for it to be used. Although the information was claimed to be for academic purposes, it was used for more nefarious reasons. The app developer was subsequently found guilty of breaching Facebook's terms of service by passing on the data to Cambridge Analytica, who had a complaint filed against them by the US Federal Trade Commission for data misuse. In the UK, concerns were raised about the political use of the data and a 3-year-long inquiry by the Information Commissioner's Office found there was no evidence of Russian involvement in the Brexit campaign (BBC, 2020b). The US government, however, found that sensitive US election and polling data had been passed on to the Russian intelligence services by a Cambridge Analytica contractor (Siegelman, 2021).

Attacking services used by victims

A final hacking tactic is the man-in-the-middle attacks where attackers secrete themselves between the user and the service they are trying to access in order to intercept communications. Whilst the victim believes they are communicating directly with the service provider, they are also providing information to the attacker, who can then 'steal login credentials or personal information, spy on victims, sabotage communications, or corrupt data' (Swinhoe, 2022). Alternatively, the attacker can alter the information given to the user by the service or upload malicious code.

There are two basic types of man-in-the-middle attacks which give attackers control over communications between user and service provider. The first type are those which attack the encryption layers – for example, HTTPS spoofing, SSL hijacking and SSL stripping. The second type actually intercepts the communications via IP spoofing; ARP (Address Resolution Protocol) spoofing; Automatic Proxy Discovery Attack; DNS spoofing; or BGP (Border Gateway Patrol) misdirection (Savvy Security, 2021). Although they are not especially prevalent when compared to incidents of ransomware and other cybercrimes, there has been a surge in cases in recent years. Moreover, their impact upon the victims can be devastating.

DDoS/cyber-barrage

DDoS attacks have constituted a real threat to network and computer integrity since the 1990s. In direct contrast to hacking, the primary goal of cyber-barrage is to prevent legitimate users from gaining access to networks and computer systems by bombarding access gateways with a barrage of data, often login.

DDoS attacks have evolved over time. Originally, they were 'socially engineered' group actions in which large numbers of individuals gain access to a particular system within a short time period, usually assisted by scripted software, to overload its access gateways and achieve a political or ethically motivated objective. This fusion of ethical motivation and the use of computer technique is the basis of 'hacktivism' (Taylor, 2001: 59). In the 1990s, the Electronic Civil Disobedience Theatre successfully orchestrated high-profile hacktivist attacks aided by Floodnet, a Java applet that reloads the target web page every few seconds to flood the host server with requests for access, and eventually disrupts the operation of the targeted website. A less computer-intensive variant of this type of hacktivism has been the deliberate spreading of damaging rumours, for example about a system's insecurity or about the owner's ethical practices to discourage usage of a network or system.

DDoS tools have, over the past two decades, become immensely powerful, especially when powered by cloud computing technologies. They have increasingly been used to attack a range of systems with significant effect. They have also been used to augment other cyber-tactics, such as ransomware, to increase victim discomfort whilst they are deciding whether to pay the ransom. At the softer end of this attack spectrum, some DDoS attacks are simply intended to irritate or to test system security, or offenders are interested more in trying to impress friends or colleagues with their expertise than in causing serious damage. At the hard end of the spectrum, however, some attacks are clearly designed to seriously damage victim organizations, as in the alleged cases of cyber-warfare.

While cybersecurity professionals develop resilience measures which try to decrease the potential disruption from DDoS attacks by installing larger servers to support heavier levels of traffic, or creating honeypot traps, or slowing down and identifying DDoS attacks and malware entering a system network, DDoS developers are adaptive in their research and development to develop stronger malware to overcome resilience measures by scaling up the volume and intensity of DDoS attacks (Krupp et al., 2016). Morales (2018) illustrated this growth and found that, in 2007, the peak DDoS attack sizes were 24 megabytes. A decade later, in the first quarter of 2018, the peak attack sizes had grown to 1.7 terabytes, almost a thousandfold increase

(Morales, 2018). As the demand for DDoS tools has increased, new facilitating actors (DDoS brokers) have emerged to supply DDoS tools. 'Stressers' are DDoS-for-hire services, a form of crimeware-as-a-service, usually sold via darkmarkets to economic cyber actors, pranksters or hacktivists wanting to prevent access to specific websites. DDoS attacks are among the most rapidly proliferating cybercrimes as they achieve a range of outcomes for offenders, although offender motivations and victims vary considerably (Musotto and Wall, 2022).

In the future, it is likely that the motivations behind DDoS attacks will further replicate those of hacking and shift DDoS use from ethics or politics towards criminal gain, as has happened with ransomware. There exist examples of such a shift, with DDoS being launched to extort a ransom payment to get it to stop (Wakefield, 2005). In 2021, a major Fortune Global 500 company was targeted using DDoS attacks as part of an extortion attempt to overload their network whilst the cybersecurity professionals were trying to recover from a ransomware attack (Spadafora, 2021). Having said that, DDoS has had a resurgence in use for political purposes in the recent Russia/ Ukraine conflict. Many of the cyber-conflict groups that have emerged to support the warring parties have used DDoS attacks to frustrate their opponents and their backers. In March 2022, for example, the KillNet group, expressing allegiance to Russia, launched an attack on a US airport because the airport was believed to be linked to the supply of material to the Ukraine defenders: 'when the supply of weapons to Ukraine stops, attacks on the information structure of your country will stop' (Strozewski, 2022; Goldsmith and Wall, unpublished). Of the known conflict groups (222), the two main cyber-tactics were DDoS (38%) and hacking (37%), followed by psyops (10%), dataleaks (7%), ransomware/wipers (6%), botnets (2%) and defacement (1%) (Goldsmith and Wall, unpublished).

Motivations and attractions for offending

Relatively little is known about offender motivations, other than what can be gleaned from literature, known offences and the small amount of information that we have on the relatively few offenders who have been prosecuted. This is because of the tendency of victims to under-report instances of cybercrime for all the reasons mentioned earlier. Relatively little is also known about the offenders beyond their offending (see Wall, 2001a: 8–9). Furthermore, the more that cybercrimes are resolved in the private interests of corporate victims, the less information is known. But, over the past thirty years, the body of knowledge about offending online has grown. From what we do know, cybercrime offenders' motivations are not so far removed from those in traditional patterns of offending, particularly with regard to white-collar crimes (see Leyden, 2004b). However, the informational, networked and global qualities of the offending suggest some fundamental differences in the ways in which offenders broker information and culturally reproduce themselves online.

A 2017 NCA (National Crime Agency) study of arrested offenders in the UK found that the average age of hackers was 17 and that some were as young as 12, compared with the previous years when the average age was 24. One reason for this drop was the small number of cases and the arrest of some very young offenders, which caused the average to fall (NCA, 2017). More broadly, HackerOne found in their 2016 survey of 617 (mainly white hat) hackers that they were typically male and under the age of

34. The survey also revealed that 72 per cent hacked for money, but 70 per cent also agreed they did it for fun, while 66 per cent said that they thrived on the challenge (Newcomb, 2016). What the surveys do indicate is that offenders are young, predominantly male and motivated by fun and the thrill of the challenge (the sneaky thrills mentioned in an earlier chapter) as much as by financial gain.

The literature on digital drift (see Goldsmith and Brewer, 2015; Goldsmith and Wall, 2022) argues that young people are seduced into cybercrime and then 'drift' through the various levels of seriousness. This seductive drift, therefore, needs to be understood in terms of the 'possibilities for action' ('affordances') that the internet presents and the 'irresistible' pull of its persuasive technologies. The internet becomes seductive because it enables and provokes transgressions, sustaining the drift into cybercrime and making it very difficult to reverse. This is especially the case for adolescents, because of the way it combines human and computer agency to produce what are in effect 'cyborg crimes', which are often neither visible nor predictable and exhibit a 'technological unconscious'. Consequently, in interactions between individuals and social media platforms, human foresight of outcomes is limited by the unpredictable composition, structure and operation of the internet's architecture (Goldsmith and Wall, 2022). Digital drift, for many people (especially the young), becomes very easy. The technologies of digital seduction offer new levels of accessibility, affordability, anonymity, but also the online qualities of abundance, ambivalence, arousal and asymmetry (see Goldsmith and Wall, 2022).

Not only does the internet seduce potential offenders, but the digital and networked technologies create an environment (or cyberspace) in which some advantages or affordances lead the offender to crime. As mentioned previously, these affordances (possibilities for action) include the ability to complete a crime operation remotely by themselves or working with others, whom they may only know online. The offenders are free of face-to-face social interaction when planning a crime. The same technologies also enable them to distance themselves from their victims. A convicted offender, interviewed for this book about conducting an internet fraud, claimed that it was the lack of direct contact with the victim that became the attraction for him: '[f]or me the internet made it, it was anonymous; you just tapped your details into the page'. When probed further, it became apparent that the real appeal was the anonymity afforded by the mechanized encounter that distanced the offender from the victim. The offender was quite clear that, had the encounter been 'face to face, which is what the [credit card] transaction was designed for, then no way. It was a specific opportunity that arose.' In a twist to this distancing, online fraudsters are alleged to favour easy-to-set-up webmail accounts (website-based email) when conducting online frauds because they can hide, or obscure, their true identities and any trails they leave (Leyden, 2006c).

Another affordance is that 'hacking' skills can be reproduced online in the chat forums, again at a distance. The process of more experienced hackers, gurus, wizards and samurai tutoring and schooling young newbies was mentioned earlier. At the core of the forum are the established hackers, the gurus, who provide the knowledge base; around them are the protégés (newbies or cluebies) who are learning the arts. On the periphery of this network are the newbies who, being new to the list, are not yet trusted by the members. They have yet to prove themselves and eagerly seek to perform simple tasks under supervision, for the personal satisfaction of having achieved the task and praise from the seniors (see Wall, 2007b: 65–8). This practice of training newbies is similar to that documented by Mann and Sutton (1998) in their study of 'net crime', and the cyberworlds community observed by Williams (2006). Of course, online training such as this may become rarer as the entry-level skills for hacking rise (Ward, 2005) or as key hacking routines become automated.

In addition to these affordances, and also drawing more generally from the literature, which covers the various generations of cybercrime, seven main groups of motivations for offending can be identified.

Criminal gain or commercial advantage

A popular motivation driving economic crimes is the lure of easy financial gain – if not directly through fraud, then through extortion or blackmail by threatening businesses with a DDoS attack unless a ransom demand is paid. Online bookmakers appear to be particularly vulnerable to DDoS threats: 'Criminals are pricing extortion rates at under the cost of preventing attacks. It's cheaper to pay up even if this encourages them [the crooks] even more' (Overton cited by Leyden, 2005f). In addition to the threat of DDoS attacks there are ransom viruses (Ransomware) that are designed to be neutralized by a code provided by the blackmailer once a ransom has been paid. An early example occurred in the late 1980s when organizations all over the world received sets of free floppy disks purporting to be AIDS training packages. When activated by installation, the program contained on the disks locked the target's system and could only be disabled by a code released to victims once they had sent a sum of money to a specified address in the US (Chandler, 1996: 241). Alternatively, the blackmailer may require credit card or restricted information (BBC, 2003b, 2003c, 2004a; Britz, 2003; Biever, 2004). During the first three months of 2006, Gostev et al. discovered an increase in cases of cyber-blackmail whereby data was illicitly encrypted and money extorted from its owners in exchange for the encryption key (Gostev et al., 2006). In May 2006, a computer user fell foul of the Archiveus trojan and found that her files had been encrypted with complex passwords. She was instructed by the blackmailers not to contact the police but to buy some drugs from an online pharmacy where she would discover the password (Oates, 2006). The files were quickly unencrypted, and the password was then published on the internet so that no other victims would have to pay up (BBC, 2006c).

Revenge

Revenge often motivates offending, especially with regard to disgruntled insiders in organizations (Britz, 2003). Revenge attack tactics vary, though offenders usually seek to redress some form of injustice felt to have been inflicted upon them by the organization or an individual within it. Where the intent is to cause damage, grievance worms or logic bombs are often used. They are set to go off at a specific time, usually after the employee has resigned from (or been fired from) the organization.

Curiosity and the intellectual challenge

Britz found that cyber-criminals were often in pursuit of 'an intellectual challenge' (2003: 65). Some, such as the 'informational voyeurs', were motivated either by curiosity or by boredom, or took part just for the thrill of it – the fun and enjoyment!

Others involved in the more serious forms of offending, such as stalking and harassment, tended to be motivated by the need for sexual gratification (2003: 65). Weaver et al. (2003) observed that worm designers often 'express an experimental curiosity'.

To get 'sneaky thrills'

The seductive features and affordances of the internet, combined with risk, create what Katz (1988) has called 'sneaky thrills'. In the internet's exciting and seemingly boundless environment, 'normally' perceived boundaries are blurred to cause 'normally' non-deviant (especially young) people to become deviant (Goldsmith and Wall, 2022). These 'sneaky thrills' not only draw potential offenders into the hacking world, but also drive subsequent offending – the argument being that progressively more sneaky thrills are sought each time an offence is committed.

The need for peer respect

Many accounts of hacking, cracking and virus/worm writing suggest that the offenders' behaviour is motivated by the need to obtain respect from peers by demonstrating their ability to show contempt for the system, or by displaying their ability and superior knowledge of how to inflict harm on others. If they are not looking to bolster self-pride, they may feel a sense of empowerment from the respect they receive.

To show off skills and impress potential employers

There exist a number of examples of past hackers being subsequently employed as security consultants. A fairly rare, but emerging, motivation of virus writers (VXers) in recent years has been to write viruses in order to prove their skills competencies to potential employers. One of the suspects in the 'Love Bug case', Michael Buen, created a macro virus and named it after himself (W97M/Michael-B) (Hayes, 2005). Buen designed his virus so that, if opened on a Friday after the 23rd of each month, it would interrupt any pending print jobs and print out Buen's own CV instead. The printed message allegedly ends with the following threat: '[i]f I don't get a safe job till the end of this month, i will send a third virus, that will delete every directory on the main HDD . . .'[10] In another example, the author of the MyDoom.V hid inside the worm's code in the message: 'We searching 4 work in AV industry' (Leyden, 2004d).

Politically motivated protest

Politically motivated protests aim to disrupt the political order and/or favourably influence the political process. Such protest can take the form of hacktivism or information warfare / information terrorism by targeting critical infrastructure.

Conclusions

This chapter has explored how criminal activity has changed in the information age with regard to cybercrimes against the machine, which mostly involve computer misuse. It has looked at the changing role of the hacker and the distinct types of cybercrimes against the machine, and at the activities and tactics adopted to compromise the integrity of computers.

There is a regular tendency in the literature to depict the hackers as 'criminal others' and describe them in terms of their 'dangerousness'. But the evidence about known hackers indicates that they are not the burly street criminals that police regularly meet. Rather, they tend to have opposite characteristics, being reserved and distancing themselves from their victims and shunning face-to-face contact. This is an important observation when profiling both the individual and their crimes. Importantly, because of this need for social distance, they tend to be schooled online. Despite purges against forums, many survive that are devoted to enabling networking and the brokering of information about offending activities. Not only do they support criminal activity through information exchange, but they also reproduce skill sets and criminal cultures.

During the past decade or so, the commercial popularity and mass usage of the internet have raised the financial stakes and introduced a generation of new players, representing new entrepreneurial interests that they wish vigorously to protect. During this period, the once ethical art of hacking has become corrupted by less ethical motivations, simply because of the raised stakes. Also, during this period, hacking has become automated, and has been deskilled through the scripting of routines to enter systems, move laterally across them, hire malicious software such as ransomware or DDoS, launch the attack, and monetize it if successful. But it has also become reskilled as skill sets have emerged to run these new processes successfully and deliver them as a service. What this means is that the traditional, skilled and ethical hacker, as was, is now largely a historical artefact, and hacking, or cracking, has morphed into something quite different, presenting a range of new threats and exposing network users to a range of new risks.

Some discussion questions based upon this chapter

Is it morally possible to have an 'ethical' hacker?

In what ways do hackers achieve their hacking goals?

Why do hackers hack? What are their motivations?

Further Reading As you can see from the above discussion, the world of hacking is complex in terms of its breadth, scale and also usage of the term as a description of action. Those wishing to take their study forward in the field of cybercrimes against the machine are recommended to look at the following sources, which include in-depth studies of hackers and also more general comments on the differences between them. See, further, Steinmetz, 2016; Grimes, 2017; Hutchings and Holt, 2018; Leukfeldt and Holt, 2021).

5 Cybercrimes Using the Machine (Computer-Enabled Crime): Virtual Robberies, Frauds and Thefts

How have crimes using the machine changed in the information age?

Chapter contents and key points

Virtual bank robbery: identity theft and exploiting online financial and billing systems

- Electronic input frauds
- Input fraud (identity theft)
- Identity theft through phishing
- Identity theft through DNS cache poisoning (pharming)
- Identity theft using surveillance software (spyware)
- Output frauds
- Card-not-present and other payment frauds (output frauds)

Virtual stings, online deceptions, frauds and extortion

- Business email compromise (BEC)
- Authorized push payments (APP) scams
- Online gambling scams
- Internet advertising frauds (click frauds)
- Premium line switching frauds
- 'Short-firm' frauds
- Ransomware and data extortion

Virtual scams

- Scareware scams
- Arbitrage / grey market exploitation
- Pyramid selling scams online
- Direct investment scams
- Loans, credit options or the repair of credit ratings
- Website domain name scams
- Deceptive advertisements for products and services
- Entrapment marketing scams
- Internet auction frauds
- Advance-fee frauds (419 scams and romance fraud)
- Online ticket scams
- Drug sales / health cures / snake-oil remedies
- Cryptocurrency scams

Virtual theft (digital burglary) and cyber-piracy
- Cyber-piracy

Chapter at a glance *This chapter explores cybercrimes in which offenders use 'the machine' to commit virtual robbery, fraud and theft by exploiting the internet's scalable and globalizing qualities.[1] These cybercrimes differ from crimes against the machine, such as hacking (see chapter 4) and those where the cyber-crime is in the machine, such as content crimes (see chapter 6). To illustrate this point, the chapter will look at virtual bank robbery (cybercrimes against financial and billing systems online); virtual stings (deceptions, frauds and extortion); virtual scams (which are mainly deceptions); and virtual theft and digital burglary (cyber-piracy and 'stealing' informational intangibles).*

Introduction

If 'Slick' Willie Sutton, the much-quoted 1930s gentleman bank robber, was embarking on his criminal career today, he would contemplate using the internet to commit his robberies. There is a long-standing assumption that Sutton, like all bank robbers, was purely motivated by money – bolstered by a reply, when interviewed about why he kept robbing banks, in which he allegedly said 'Because that's where the money is!' This phrase made him famous and also became the basis for Sutton's law;[2] however, Sutton denied ever saying this, stating that the reporter focused on one phrase because it made for a stronger story. Rather, he actually emphasized that he robbed banks because he enjoyed the thrill of being in a bank whilst undertaking a robbery because it made him feel more alive than at any other time in his life (Sutton and Linn, 1976: 160). So, although Sutton is not with us anymore to confirm or deny whether he would use the internet, it is clear that he enjoyed the sneaky thrill of transgression rather than just the mechanical act of theft, although he did imply that the money was also a motivator.

These motivations for financial crime do not seem to have changed much during the past century (see chapter 2); however, the difference between then and now is that Willie Sutton or his colleagues would no longer be planning arduous and dangerous million-dollar bank robberies because, as outlined earlier, networked technologies now enable him to commit millions of micro-robberies[3] with much less personal risk and providing the same 'sneaky thrill'. Significantly, and from a criminological perspective, network technologies have effectively democratized financial crimes. Once they were a 'crime of the powerful', committed by offenders who abused their privileged position in society (Sutherland, 1949; Pearce, 1976; Weisburd et al., 1991; Tombs and Whyte, 2003); today, many financial crimes can now be committed by anyone who has the will and access to the internet (Wall, 2010a).

Also unchanged is that crime today, as in the past, still tends to follow opportunity (Grabosky and Smith, 1998: 1), but those opportunities have changed in scope and scale. In 2007, for example, approximately one-third (32 per cent) of UK adults used internet banking; however, by 2022, the percentage had risen to over 90 per cent (Statista, 2023). Globally, Statista estimates that, by 2024, there will be about 2.5 billion active online banking users worldwide (Statista, 2023), approximately one-third of the planet. On the one hand, this is great news for the financial services sector, but on the other, it is bad news for society because of the rise in losses through theft, frauds and extortion resulting from the increase in criminal opportunities afforded by the technological change.

Such change takes place because of the maturity and convenience of online payment systems, in addition to, or as variants of, online banking. Mondex, for example, pioneered an early (stored value) smart card that enabled direct peer-to-peer (cashless) money transfers that did not require prior authorization. It was a forerunner to the modern mobile payments system. Similarly, intermediaries such as Paypal and Applepay (and others) act as trusted third parties to ensure payment security for both vendor and vendee. Following these trailblazing systems, many other new payments systems are either being trialled or introduced. More novel cryptocurrency-based value exchange systems are being trialled, with various levels of success and teething problems, which of course each bring with them new criminal opportunities.

This chapter addresses the different ways in which offenders use networked computers to assist them to inflict deceptive and acquisitive harms upon individual or corporate victims for informational or pecuniary advantage. These types of digital malfeasance are not to be confused with those discussed in the previous chapter on cybercrimes against the machine, or those in the next chapter which focus upon informational content (cybercrimes in the machine). However, as observed earlier, information and identity theft, and copyright piracy, are becoming major precursors to online economic crimes. In fact, it is increasingly hard in practice to identify the boundaries between the three but, as is the case elsewhere in this book, the aim is to map out the range and variety of risk behaviour that fall under each specific theme. Rather than simply list the different forms of offending, an attempt has been made here to order them into four distinct groups of cybercrimes that use machines. The first part explores virtual bank robbery, which exploits financial management systems online, mainly banking and billing. This crime is usually enabled online to produce proceeds offline. That is, until cryptocurrency came along, which meant that some of the proceeds remain online until cashed out. The second part looks at virtual stings, where the victim is deliberately targeted, and the context often framed to deceive the victim. The stings tend to target individuals' bank holdings, or use them to access organizations; they are enabled online and ultimately take place offline. The third part explores virtual scams, which are designed to tempt anybody who is exposed to them. They are enabled online, although the defrauding ultimately takes place offline. They illustrate the ways in which the internet can be used to deceive and defraud individuals and commercial enterprises. The fourth part outlines virtual theft or digital burglary. Virtual thefts are the stealing of a virtual object of value. They are enabled online, and the criminal gain ultimately takes place online. They typically involve the theft of a virtual tangible in the form of data or intellectual property, and central to each activity is a form of information that has an exchange value. In contrast to the virtual robberies, much of this crime stays online.

Virtual bank robbery: identity theft and exploiting online financial and billing systems

As the internet became a popular means for managing financial affairs, then financial systems and their users became the targets of criminal opportunity – recall from above the (almost) two-thirds increase in online banking between 2007 and 2022. The term 'virtual bank robbery' is used here to bring together online crimes that relate to stealing from banking and financial systems either directly or via users' accounts. A virtual robbery ultimately targets online financial payment and management systems, mainly banking and billing. These are mainly input frauds that focus upon obtaining user credentials to access banking systems, and are enabled online and ultimately go offline to cash out.

Financial criminals have for some time used the Internet to defraud banks, building false identities, opening accounts and then running them to build up credit ratings to obtain personal loans that are subsequently defaulted upon, or used to launder money and turn 'dirty money' into clean money by obscuring its origins through quick transfer from one bank to another and across jurisdictions. Although easy to carry out in theory, it is nevertheless quite hard in practice to deceive banking security checks, and offenders will weigh up the opportunities against the risks of being caught or prevented from carrying out a theft. Nevertheless, 'criminals will go to wherever the easiest target is' (Cards International, 2003), so they will seek out system weaknesses, which tend to lie at both the input and output stages. Although not always easy to separate in practice, *input frauds* are where fraudsters obtain personal or financial information that can give them illegal access to financial systems, as in identity theft (see Finch, 2002; Finch and Fafinski, 2010). *Output frauds*, in contrast, are where access to credit cards and payment systems is used to fraudulently obtain goods, services or money. The emphasis here is mainly upon the process of identity theft because, in one way or another, the identity data drives the cybercrime chain (see Porcedda and Wall, 2019, 2021).

The internet's expanding virtual shop window offers many opportunities for payment (or output) fraud. Goods and services can be obtained deceptively by using genuine credit cards or payment schemes to which access has been obtained illegitimately with fraudulent information, for example via identity theft or account take-over. Alternatively, they can be obtained by using counterfeit credentials created from stolen information bought off the internet, or by using the information directly in less secure jurisdictions, although this route is closing as finance security becomes more globalized.

Electronic input frauds

It used to be possible for offenders to generate counterfeit card details through software such as CreditMaster 4.0 and other similar programs which were readily available from internet vendors. For a number of years, they were used to generate strings of valid credit card numbers for use in transactions, most often for the purchase of mobile phone airtime (Kravetz, 2002). Important to note here is that, while the counterfeit numbers were generated by downloaded programs obtained online, the internet was not usually the means by which the transaction took place. The counterfeit card transactions tended to take place using mobile phone systems which required only the card number. The introduction of card validation codes (CVC2), the three-digit number on the back of credit cards, dramatically reduced the value of card number generators and has rendered them useless today. Even where CVC codes were available, illegal 'carding websites' that once existed to provide cloned credit cards, such as 'carderplanet' and 'shadowcrew' (BBC, 2005a), are no longer in existence and their replacements are not as prevalent.

Input fraud (identity theft)

From the earliest days of e-commerce, online retailers fell victim to fraudsters who obtained goods by deception, either by supplying false payment details or by using a false address to have goods sent to. During the early days of e-commerce, personal cheques and bank drafts were the focus of online frauds simply because they were the preferred methods of payment at the time, but they were quickly superseded by credit cards and other online credit card payment facilities. Credit cards are still popular, however, because of the issuing banks' guarantee, although third-party escrowed internet payment systems such as PayPal, Mondex and Applepay are expanding as intermediaries. Most payments today are made by cashless transfers.

Identity theft (input fraud) is the precursor to output fraud and other financial crimes because it is the stage at which criminals obtain personal information from victims and acquire credit facilities by fraudulent means.[4] Although identity theft leads to further crime, it is not a recordable offence in the UK. Nevertheless, Action Fraud recommend that victims report it to them.[5] Since the mid-1990s, the term 'identity theft' has, arguably, been misused to suggest that it is less important than output frauds, which can be more easily measured. Bruce Schneier (the well-known security technologist) argued that the emphasis upon identity theft 'is a misnomer which is hurting the fight against fraud'; identity theft would be better conceptualized as a type of 'fraud due to impersonation' (Leyden, 2005b). Basically, he is suggested that placing more emphasis upon identify theft would mean less cases of output fraud (see later).

Here, the discussion about identity theft is purely within the context of input fraud, which includes fraudulently obtaining information to apply for credit facilities, including making illicit credit card or payment system applications[6] or using stolen credentials to take over the owner's accounts. After a decline in credit card fraud numbers during the 2010s, CIFAS (the UK's main fraud prevention service) predicted a surge in identity fraud cases resulting from identity theft as the economy recovered from the pandemic. In support of this observation, the National Fraud Database revealed an 11 per cent increase in reports during the first six months of 2021 (CIFAS, 2021). In 2022, a year later, identity fraud had increased by nearly a quarter (23 per cent) to represent 68 per cent of all cases on the National Fraud Database (CIFAS, 2023).

There are currently four main ways by which personal financial information can be obtained: through phishing, pharming, tabnapping and use of spyware.

Identity theft through phishing

The first way is identity theft through phishing. Initially, personal information was obtained by trashing or 'dumpster diving', which is the practice of going through rubbish bags to obtain discarded documents and then using the information to apply for credit facilities. Another conventional method of fraud has been the use of trust obtained through family bonds or friendship in order to steal or hijack a victim's identity with a view to defrauding them (see Javelin, 2009). Both are labour intensive, local and fairly low yield. The growth of criminal opportunities from electronic banking and payment systems has increased the demand to intensify phishing, to a level which, it could be argued, has become industrialized.

An adaptation of fishing, phishing is the pursuit of personal financial information that is subsequently used to defraud the victim and relies upon the recipient's inability to distinguish a fake email, website or phone call from a real one (see Toyne, 2003). The now traditional 'phishing expedition' is characterized by the indiscriminate mailing of millions of emails purporting to be from the recipient's bank, payment system or the provider of any other familiar form of financial transaction they use, such as digital marketplaces such as eBay, Amazon or Etsy.[7] The emails typically ask recipients – with a sense of urgency, and often exaggerated by an alleged security breach – to log onto the URL given in the email and confirm their personal information details (Oates, 2004a). Many of these phishing emails are 'spray and pray' in approach, and involve a generic email being sent out in the hope that someone somewhere will respond. The evidence is that not many do. To increase the 'yield', phishers have adopted a more focused 'prey and slay' approach called 'spear phishing', where the intended victim, usually a specific organization or individual, is exposed to a 'highly targeted and co-ordinated attack designed to extract critical data' (Leyden, 2006a). A variation of spear phishing is 'whale phishing', where a senior executive of an organization is targeted along with colleagues, with a linked narrative being fed to each, with the intention of getting the target to authorize a false payment.

The targets of spear or whale phishing will often be identified from stolen data that has been subsequently processed to locate the email addresses and information on a specific identifying characteristic, such as a specific profession or sport, trait, passion, sexual preference. The targeted phishing email will send a message which the target can relate to – for example, to lawyers, about accreditation in a new field or a legal conference. Some bank-related 'spear phishing' attacks target online bank customers by offering them a cash reward for completing a 'bogus' survey in which they disclose their critical personal information (Leyden, 2006b). Generally speaking, the email will have the look and feel of a genuine communication and appear to come from a legitimate source with appropriate logos whom the recipient will identify and trust. When read through quickly, an appropriately framed email with interesting content might appear plausible to the unsuspecting recipient, causing them to respond or act on the instructions. Such emails rely upon the victim's inability to distinguish the bogus email from a real one (see Toyne, 2003). By targeting profiled groups with tailored emails, Phishers deliberately prey upon their victim's desires for goods or services; pressurizing them to make decisions quickly so that victims cannot reliably check the sender's identity, the validity of a web page or the software they are downloading. FireEye conducted research into the spear phishers' tactics and found them to be very tactical in terms of exploiting current concerns (FireEye, 2012; Leyden, 2012). Such spear phishing attacks display an increasing psychological and emotional, in addition to technological, sophistication (Wall, 2010a; RSA, 2011; Stajano and Wilson, 2011).

Although the email message (targeted or not) may mean little to those who do not use the services purporting to send it, such as eBay, Amazon, Etsy or similar platforms, the message may mean something to the millions who do use the service, particularly with phrases such as 'Please Note – If you choose to ignore our request, you leave us no choice but to temporally suspend your account' (*sic*). However, closer examination usually reveals inaccuracies, typically an author's misuse of grammar and syntax that is not up to the standards of the service it purports to be from. Not only are there often grammatical mistakes, but there are often strange placings of, for example, capitalized letters and punctuation marks: '*Please do not respond to this e-mail as your reply will not be received Respectfully,' (*sic*).[8]

What is distinctive about phishing is the speed with which new variations on the theme emerge, especially when generative AI is used to compose new messages. One of the crucial advantages that offenders have over their victims is the, albeit narrowing, window of opportunity between the identification of a vulnerability in a system, the onset of an attack and the production of a technological fix to solve the problem. Therefore, as soon as major financial institutions find ways to counter phishing attacks, the 'attackers' change their approach. One notable example of the adaptability of the phishers, following adverse publicity about their activities, has been their ability to deliberately play upon recipient's concerns about phishing and mould the email message hook to entrap victims as a warning message to avoid phishing.

Figure 5.1 illustrates the sevenfold increase in phishing attacks between 2014 and 2022, illustrating the criminal interest in and resilience of identity thefts, as well as the advanced technical capacity to send spam emails and the rise in spam as a service. Research by Group-IB estimated that a Russian-based spam-as-a-service operation

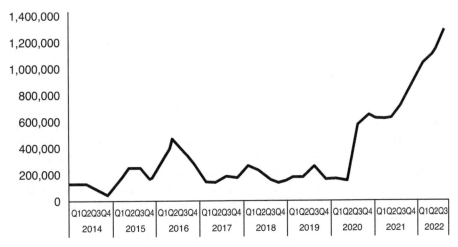

Figure 5.1 Quarterly number of reported phishing attacks 2014–2022.
Source: compiled from the APWG Phishing Activity Trends Reports 2014–22.

codenamed 'Classiscam' helped forty groups of scammers to steal an estimated $6.5 million from victims across the US, Europe and former Soviet states in 2020 (Cimpanu, 2021). The trendline also imitates the ransomware trendline which is often initiated by a response to a phishing email, although a precise statistical link is hard to establish. When the number of known ransomware attacks (RWdb[9]) are plotted against the Anti-Phishing Working Group's (APWG's) statistics, the success rate is about 0.07 per cent, but this rate is probably understated because of the dynamics of reporting. APWG estimated in September 2022 that almost a quarter (23.2 per cent) of phishing attacks were against the financial sector, and that BEC (business email compromise) was the most troublesome and had increased in volume by three-fifths (59 per cent) (APWG, 2022).

In addition to email phishing campaigns, there has been a rise in social media network phishing, 'smishing' and 'vishing'. As social media networks have become more ubiquitous during the past fifteen years, so has their potential as a medium for sending out phishing expeditions, especially as the platforms can have billions of accounts. Instagram, LinkedIn, Facebook, Twitter and Telegram and other social media network platforms reach a large volume of people and can be used by phishers to steal personal data or even access their social media accounts.[10] The phishing pattern is very similar to that with email but, as indicated earlier, phishers adapt their practices to the distinctive characteristics of each platform. With Instagram, for example, phishers often undertake a 'browser-in-the-middle attack' (see later) by creating a fake Instagram login page to harvest the victim's credentials, which redirects the user to the real login page. In the case of LinkedIn, phishers send out emails which purport to come from the LinkedIn administration (which has a number of different email formats). Phishers use Facebook, which specifically seeks to connect family and friends, by sending out fake Facebook messages via Facebook posts or its messenger service asking for recipients to confirm their details. Phishers use Twitter and Telegram in much the same way, although the recipients can be anybody, but phishers send out fake Twitter or Telegram admin messages seeking to confirm login credentials and personal financial information. Telegram uses algorithms to suggest messages, so users have even less control over what they receive. In addition to sending messages, phishers also sell phishing kits via the platforms, which they allege will increase the user's circulation. The harvested credentials from social media phishing expeditions will, like those from the other media, either be used directly against the victims or be collected and sold on the dark-web markets.

Smishing is the sending of SMS text messages to potential victims, which contain more or less the same message as in the original phishing emails. In the same vein as phishing emails, they ask victims to reconfirm their 'important security information' immediately by return SMS message, or via a www site. Alternatively, the smishing attack may be a technical support scam in which the caller claims to be from a major operating system to say that they have detected a problem in the user's interface and offer a technical support service to remedy the problem, for a fee. Or they may seek to get the user to give them remote access to their computer so that they can solve the problem, whilst installing a remote administration trojan.

Vishing exploits VoIP in much the same way as the phishing and smishing, but by voice. The size of the problem was outlined by Ofcom, the UK telecommunications watchdog, which found that 45 million people (82 per cent of users) had received a suspicious phone call and 71 per cent a suspicious text message, with half saying that they received them regularly.[11]

Victims are tricked into responding to questions or ringing back the number given, which may also switch them to a premium rate, or they may be asked to log onto a web address given in the message, which could download various types of malware. Such malware could join the victim to a botnet, further increasing the agony by making them subject to more repeat calls or even using the victim's device to relay messages (and act as a force multiplier). Once established, botnets (as a service) are managed like a commodity for offenders to hire. Some, such as 'Pushdo', have incredible resilience and have survived numerous attempts to take them down (see Leyden, 2013). Alternatively, malware, such as Zeus,[12] contains a number of 'attack' functions including infecting other computers, clandestinely searching for users' security information, account numbers, user ID, passwords and additional security information, then sending the information to the identity thief. This is information that may provide direct access to the victim's bank account, therefore dispensing with the need to perpetrate an application fraud.

Identity theft through DNS cache poisoning (pharming).

Pharming, or DNS (domain name server) cache poisoning (or 'spoofing'), as per a typical phishing attack, contains seemingly 'relevant' information in the sender and subject lines that tricks individuals into opening the email. Once opened, code in the email automatically directs recipients to the phisher's bogus www site. Unlike phishing, pharming does not rely upon 'social engineering' to trick the recipient into clicking onto a www site. Instead, it deceives the domain name server into automatically accepting incorrect, or forged, access data. The effect of pharming is to increase the 'hit' rate of the spoof website, which has the look and feel of the victim's own bank site. But, as with phishing, the use of recognized symbols of trust 'socially engineer', or trick, the recipient into disclosing their financial information.

A variation of pharming has evolved in form of the website-based man-in-the-middle attack.[13] In the 'man-in-the-middle' (or 'browser-in-the-middle') attack, a sophisticated piece of malware is placed between the computer and the browser, usually following infection of the victim's computer by a drive-by-download to enable the man-in-the-middle attack to take place. They are typically, though not exclusively, used in banking attacks. When victims log onto their banking www sites, a fake bank page opens over the original with additional information slots to receive the user's normal access data and other more personal information. The pages look as they always do and as users would expect to find them. Once all of the user's data are entered, they are sent to the phishers' database and the browser in the middle is closed down, and the correct data are then sent to the bank www site which moves to the next page as the victim expects it to. Since the operation took place in seconds, the victim is unaware that they have been deceived. The information from such attacks has great market value because it is verified access data to financial systems. Also significant with this development is that it demonstrates a shift in the visibility of phishing patterns from overt to stealthy (see Wall, 2010b).

Identity theft through 'tabnapping'

Tabnapping is a computer exploit which literally kidnaps inactive tabs so that when the user reactivates them the page has been redirected. It exploits the user's trust in the website's reputation and their inattention to detail by impersonating well-known websites and convincing users to submit their login details and passwords once they reactivate the tabs (Claburn, 2010).

Identity theft using surveillance software (spyware)

Identity theft has also evolved through the increased use of illegal spyware. Illegally and sometimes legally installed spyware either keeps a log of the victim's keystrokes (including passwords, etc.) or it may actively seek out key financial information stored on the hard drive. In both cases, the information is subsequently relayed back to the infector. Zeus – mentioned earlier – for example, is a professionally crafted piece of malware that enters computers via spammed emails or a 'drive-by-download' after visiting an infected www site. At first glance, it looks benign, but it infects insecure computers to steal the bank login information from individuals and businesses and also to launch malware. Furthermore, Zeus, like many of its type, has a built-in capacity to evade detection. It has evolved through a number of iterations.

Output frauds

Output frauds are where stolen identity details (credentials) are used to access credit cards and banking payment systems to fraudulently obtain goods, services or money. They are often referred to as identity frauds. Offenders may open bank accounts; obtain credit, loans or benefits; buy goods using the stolen victim credentials; take over the victim's bank accounts; take out mobile phone contracts or acquire documents such as passports or driving licences in the victim's name (see the earlier Action Fraud note). A number of examples of output fraud are given elsewhere in previous chapters. Many are traditional economic crimes that are made easier through the internet, on a larger scale than previously possible.

The most recent significant form of virtual bank robbery is the cryptocurrency exchange robbery – many are thefts that are not identity-related frauds but stings or scams, e.g. Mt Gox, OneCoin, Poly Network, Bitfinex (see next section), but there have been an increasing number of exchange robberies during the past decade where hackers have used stolen credentials to take over accounts or create them under false names. Lane (2022) notes that email phishing, investment scams and romance scams are most 'commonly observed in the cryptocurrency space'. Each seeks to persuade, or socially engineer, victims either to give credentials or to open accounts (crypto-wallets) and transfer money.

Card-not-present and other payment frauds (output frauds)

As touchless payments and online transactions increase, card-not-present transactions have become the mainstay of ecommerce-based retail operations. Not surprisingly, card-not-present frauds are scams where the offender makes a transaction with credit details relating to a card they do not have in their possession or own. There has been a considerable increase in all losses incurred through card-not-present frauds, to the point that it has been described as a threat to national security (Corera, 2021). Card-not-present frauds originated outside the technology of the banking systems in changes made to the banking rules that allow retailers (initially in phone transactions) to take credit card details without the credit card being present. These changes in policy arguably took the credit card beyond its original purpose and opened the door to new types of fraud: 'The Internet has taken the credit card schemes further than they were ever intended for. It was never meant to be used for card-not-present transactions over the WWW.' From the fraudster's point of view, '[t]he actual process of putting the card details into the website is something that anybody could do when you place the order'. The key to the payment fraud was to get 'an address that is not your own and then have someone who is there to receive the goods and sign for them'.[14]

Virtual stings, deceptions, frauds and extortion

Clinging tightly onto the coat tails of technological innovation, fraudsters exploit the new opportunities for e-commerce to find new victims via virtual stings. A virtual sting is a targeted deception: the victim is deliberately targeted and the context of a connection (e.g., the email) often framed to deceive the victim. Virtual stings are therefore the range of online techniques used by offenders to exploit legal and financial system deficiencies in order to defraud individuals and organizations. They are enabled online but usually try to move the location of the fraud offline. Most virtual stings, like those offline, revolve around some form of deception via social engineering. They focus upon obtaining money from businesses and are enabled online and go offline as the offender cashes out. Although they exploit new changes, history reminds us that the principles and practices of deception remain similar.

Business email compromise (BEC)

BEC is one of the most prevalent and costly cybercrimes.[15] It is a form of 'spear' or 'whale' phishing where the offender impersonates a trusted person and uses email or social media communications to deceive victims into revealing confidential business information or sending money to the offender. BEC was identified (see earlier) as the most troublesome form of phishing, with a 59 per cent increase in 2022 (APWG, 2022). This is reflected in the UK business losses to BEC of £140 million announced by the UK's National Economic Crime Centre (Muncaster, 2021). Similarly, in the US, the FBI-run IC3) received 21,832 complaints regarding BEC in 2022 with losses to victims in the region of $2.7 billion (IC3, 2022: 11). Because of the considerable losses to industry, BEC has become a major law enforcement priority for the FBI, INTERPOL and the NCA. In 2019, 281 individuals were arrested in 'Operation Rewired', a coordinated law enforcement operation (USDOJ, 2019). It followed a previous 'Operation WireWire' in 2018 which led to 74 arrests (FBI, 2019). BEC scams are associated with and frequently connected to romance, employment opportunity, fraudulent online vehicle sales, rental and lottery scams. The difference between them and other scams is that the targets are high-level business executives.

Authorized push payments (APP) scams

A recent example of output fraud that has emerged from networked banking system technologies is the authorized push payment (APP) scam. This is where the offender targets and socially engineers the victim into agreeing to making a 'legitimate' push payment from their own account into the fraudster's account. The scam can be initiated by targeted phishing emails saying that it is important to get in touch with the bank on the number given. Or it can be initiated by direct phone calls (vishing) purporting to be from the bank asking victims to change money into a new account. Or, more insidiously, victims may be persuaded by relatives or friends to transfer money to pay a bill or buy goods or services, often through social media. While these may be new, they are variations on an old theme, just on a smaller scale.

Online gambling scams

Online gambling scams grow with the popularity of the industry in various jurisdictions, especially those which hold negative legal and moral attitudes towards gambling. The size of the online gambling industry is illustrated by statistics released by GamCare, a UK-based charity addressing the social impact of gambling. GamCare estimates that there are approximately 1,700 gambling websites on the internet (GamCare.co.uk). Further, Merrill Lynch found that the online gambling market had a turnover of $6.3 billion in 2003 (Leyden, 2004c). A decade and a half later, a 2020 Gambling Commission survey found that online gambling has stabilized and is a £5.5 billion industry comprising 40 per cent of the overall market. Although mobile phones were the most popular device used, especially amongst young people, the survey found that networked devices such as laptops and PCs are becoming more prevalent, along with networked smart TVs (Gambling Commission, 2021), each expanding the fraud attack surface.

The debate over online gambling has predictably focused upon its legality and morality, particularly in the US, 'which has both a puritanical streak running right through the national psyche and a thriving, and powerful, home-grown gaming sector' (Fay, 2005). So, the main thrust of this debate has understandably been about increasing US jurisdictional control over the inter-jurisdictional aspects of running illegal gambling operations in and from other countries (Goss, 2001: 32). In 2023, online gambling is allowed in approximately twenty-five US states, however – but each state also has laws that restrict the topics that can be legally gambled on in relation to charitable causes, lotteries, racetracks (onsite) and sports betting. But, as Legal Betting Online advises: 'if they don't [allow it], you can still wager legally and safely using online overseas operators' (Legal Betting Online, 2023).

One thing that is certain about online gambling is its popularity, which arises from the desire of punters to beat the system either within, or by, its own rules (not dealt with here), or outside them by defrauding gambling operations. With regard to the latter, in 2002, Europay, MasterCard's partner in mainland Europe, claimed that one fifth of losses due to online fraud were related to gambling (Leyden, 2002). The revision of acceptable use policies by electronic payment providers, such as PayPal, to no longer allow customers to subscribe to online gambling sites, combined with new security technology, will likely lessen incidents of online gambling fraud.[16]

Internet advertising frauds (click frauds)

Click fraud occurs where a pay-per-click online advertisement is deliberately accessed to inflate an advertising bill. It illustrates how new commercial opportunities online quickly become the focus of fraud. Internet sites that display adverts receive a small fee from the advertiser each time the advertisement is viewed. Individually, these are minute payments, but they aggregate within a high-volume environment. As a consequence, they have given rise to 'Click fraud', or 'bogus click syndrome' (Liedtke, 2005; Modine, 2009), which defrauds the internet advertising billing systems. Unscrupulous website owners employ individuals to bulk click advertisements, sometimes outsourcing to third-world countries where labour is cheap. Here, 'factories' of low-wage workers will click manually on web ads, often in circumstances where the boundary between wage labour and coercion is vague. More common, however, is the use of bespoke software, such as 'Google Clique' which effects computer-scripted clicking to perform the same task (USDOJ, 2004). Another related example is 'link spamming' which also exploits the burgeoning internet advertising industry. The aim of 'link spamming' is to link a keyword, such as 'pornography', with a particular www site. Although it is not necessarily illegal (depending upon jurisdiction), it does often flout fair trade practice rules. Link spammers, or search engine optimizers as they often describe themselves, regularly spam websites and personal web-blogs with blocks of text that contain key words to inflate the search engine rankings of websites that offer 'PPC – pills, porn and casinos' (Arthur, 2005). A recent development on link spamming is the blog spam (or spamdexing), which is a series of comments or phrases whose purpose is to entice people to go to another site, thus boosting its rankings (Abou-Assaleh and Das, 2008).

Premium line switching frauds

Before broadband replaced the dial-up modem, a fairly common form of telephone billing fraud was premium line switching. Here visitors to unscrupulous www sites, usually pornography-related, would, during the course of their browsing, unknowingly become the victim of a 'drive-by download'. They would find themselves infected with a virus, a 'rogue dialler', that would automatically and discreetly transfer their existing telephone service from the normal domestic rate to a premium line service and defraud them (Richardson, 2005). New variations of the premium line switching frauds are beginning to exploit mobile phone services rather than landlines.

'Short-firm' frauds

Short-firm frauds exploit online auction reputation management systems (see Wall, 2010a). Introduced to protect users of auction houses such as eBay, and Amazon and others, reputation management systems enable purchasers to rate vendors on their conduct during previous sales prior to doing business with them. A knock-on effect of reputation management systems is the emergence of 'the short-firm fraud' which is the virtual equivalent of the long-firm fraud where trust is artificially built up, at a cost, by selling off some quality articles below their true value. Once a good vendor rating is acquired, then a very expensive item is sold, often offline to a runner-up in the bidding war, and the vendor disappears once the money has been received. In a short-firm fraud, fraudulent vendors build up profiles based upon their customer feedback and past sales performance, which enables potential purchasers to vet them before making bids. Good reputations are highly valued and maintaining them discourages dishonest behaviour by vendors and bidders.

Virtual scams

Whereas virtual stings tend to focus upon the business community, virtual scams are primarily aimed at victimizing individual users. A virtual scam, in contrast to a virtual sting, is designed to tempt anybody who is exposed to it. It is enabled online and ultimately takes place offline. Virtual scams bait victims with attractive hooks such as cut-price goods or services far below the market value, 'better than normal' returns on investments, or some other advantage, such as alternative cures to serious illness or rare drugs not available in the jurisdiction (Hall, 2005). From an analytical point of view, it is often hard to discern between enthusiastic, even aggressive marketing, bad business and wilfully criminal deceptions. What we can do, however, is outline the spectrum of deceptive behaviours related to e-commerce that are causing concern; they are mainly spam-driven. Particularly prevalent on the margins of e-commerce are the scams that sit on the border between aggressive entrapment marketing and deception, such as get-rich-quick schemes which tempt internet users to invest in financial products that, they think, will yield a substantial return. The potential for scamming is often fairly clear, if not obvious, and the US IC3 and UK Action Fraud, UK Payments (formerly APACS) and BIS (Department for Business Innovation and Skills, formerly DTI and then BERR) and many other sources of victimization statistics clearly show that even normally risk-averse internet users can fall victim. Virtual scams focus upon obtaining money from individuals and are enabled online, and then go offline, moving into physical space as the offender cashes out.

Scareware scams

Scareware scams have plagued the internet for many years and seem to be a recurring theme (BBC, 2009; USDOJ, 2018). Scareware is an aggressive sales technique through which the scare(soft)ware inundates computer users with misleading messages that emulate Windows security messages. Usually (though not always) delivered by Windows Messenger, these messages are designed to convince recipients through scare or shock tactics that their personal computer has been infected by malicious software and therefore requires fixing. Of course, the message recommends buying the 'scaremongers' own brand of software (see 'entrapment marketing' below). Scareware signifies a move towards the true cybercrime because the software both conducts the scam and sends the fraudulent gains to the offender. More recent versions of scareware are deliberately stealthy with the 'look and feel' and authority of common operating systems. Consequently, victims do not always know that they have been scammed (see Wall, 2010a). In 2018, a Latvian national pleaded guilty in the USA to providing bulletproof hosting services, giving technical support to a scareware scheme directing visitors to the website of the *Minneapolis Star Tribune*. The scareware scheme caused the *Tribune*'s computers to infect the site's users with malvertising software that operated a scareware antivirus scam (USDOJ, 2018).

In a variant of the scareware scam, victims would receive a message purporting to be from a police force or authority via an email, text or telephone call. The message would say that they have been found guilty of committing a crime and fined – for example, because of downloading pornography, speeding, parking in the wrong place or some other offence. They are told to pay the fine immediately, or else further penalties will be levied. In one scam, victims were told that their negligence had caused their computer to be infected with ransomware and that they had to pay a fine or pay for a service to clean their computer. During the mid-2010s, such scams were more prevalent than today because of recent advances in counter-phishing technology.

Arbitrage / grey market exploitation

The global reach of the internet enables the exploitation of 'grey markets' created by price differentials across jurisdictions (see Granovsky, 2002), especially with regard to currencies and commodities. The speed and span of the internet enable arbitrage by circumventing pricing control mechanisms imposed by manufacturers, producers or government-authorized channels for the distribution of goods. In this way, any price differentials caused by local differences in the costs of producing basic commodities, or in currency exchange rates, or taxation (VAT or import tax) can be exploited. Needless to say, arbitrage is a long-standing sting but results in illicit cross-border trade in portable items such as cigarettes, alcohol, consumer durables, pharmaceuticals, even fuel, but also exotic rare animals and their skins and furs (BBC, 2005b; IFAW, 2005). In addition to price differentials, there is legal arbitrage – legal differentials – where goods that are illicit or restricted in one jurisdiction can be purchased from jurisdictions where they are legal; such is the case with prescription medicines, sexual services, rare stones, antiquities, rare animal skins (again) and even human body parts. Of course, many of these goods and services are non-existent.

Pyramid selling scams online

Pyramid selling schemes and their variants have been successful scamming tactics for many hundreds of years and predate the internet. The scam exploits various friendship, personal or other trusted networks. Like other lucrative scams, pyramid selling found its way on to the internet in many ingenious disguises; they are also sometimes called Ponzi scams, after Charles Ponzi, an Italian immigrant who ran such schemes in the US in the 1920s. Pyramid selling is an elaborate confidence trick which recruits victims with the promise of a good return on investment. The secret of the schemes' success is that early investors are paid from money invested by later investors and confidence builds quickly to encourage further investors. New recruits are encouraged by – often genuine – claims from early investors that they can recoup their initial investment by introducing new recruits to the scheme. It is basically a numbers game and, because returns are based upon new recruitment numbers rather than profit from product sales, as is the case with legitimate multi-level marketing practices, the pyramid selling schemes are mathematically doomed to fail. They merely redistribute income towards the initiators and the many losers pay for the few winners. The internet versions of pyramid schemes, usually (though not exclusively) communicated by email, reflect the terrestrial versions, although the internet gives the scammer access to a larger number of potential recruits and the stakes are therefore higher.

Direct investment scams

Direct investment scams on the internet are rife. Some focus on businesses, whilst others upon individuals. Some may be genuine, though misguided, attempts to stimulate business by providing recipients with a genuine investment service. Others are less genuine and seek to persuade interested recipients to part with money before, and without, receiving any service in return. Alternatively, they offer investors the opportunity to earn large incomes whilst working at home. In the latter case, victims are encouraged to send off a fee for a package of information that explains the scheme. If, indeed, they do receive anything at all, usually what subscribers receive is worthless, impractical or may even involve them participating in a nefarious activity. Particularly vulnerable to these scams are the less mobile or the unemployed, or those who are housebound, such as single parents or carers.

Beyond the work-at-home schemes are the more harmful scams perpetrated by those purporting to be legitimate investment brokers, who, upon sign-up – for which they usually require a joining fee – produce free investment reports to customers that subsequently trick them into investing their funds in dubious stocks and shares, if indeed these actually exist (see the case of OneCoin below). Along similar lines, 'pump and dump' scams deceive investors playing the stock market by circulating misinformation on the internet about real stock. This information artificially drives up the price of the stock (the pump), which is then sold off at inflated prices (the dump). Research by Frieder and Zittrain in 2006 found that respondents to 'pump and dump' emails can lose up to 8 per cent of their investment within two days, whereas 'the spammers who buy low-priced stock before sending the e-mails, typically see a return of between 4.9% and 6% when they sell' (BBC, 2006i; Frieder and Zittrain, 2006).

Loans, credit options or the repair of credit ratings

A particularly insidious group of financial scams committed via the internet are those which prey upon the poor and financially excluded sections of society with promises to repair their credit ratings, provide credit options or credit facilities, credit cards with zero or very low interest, or instant and unlimited loans without credit checks or security. Such offers, if followed up, tend to come at high cost to victims in terms of inflated interest rates or entrapping them into a nexus from which it is hard to escape. Even worse, the entrapment may lead to the victim becoming embroiled in a wider range of criminal activity to pay off the original debt.

Website domain name scams

Website domain name scams cluster a range of activities, of which two are most prevalent. The first is where a business is sent a letter that appears to be a renewal notice for a domain name. As in invoice frauds, the business listed may be different to the business which originally registered the domain name. The second is where a scammer directly contacts a business to give them first refusal on a domain name, stating that it is either available or coming out of registration, and that another party wishes to purchase it – sometimes the name may belong to the target.

Deceptive advertisements for products and services

Deceptive advertisements sell goods at greatly reduced prices to hook victims. Some advertisements simply fail to deliver, whereas others sell substandard goods (e.g., reconditioned), and others exploit grey markets (see earlier). Deceptive office-supply advertisements online target business managers responsible for purchasing office, medical or other supplies and who might be attracted by the prospects of low costs. Typically, the office-supply advertisements offer specially priced print cartridges or greatly discounted computing and, in some cases, expensive equipment. They often offer the lure of 'incentives' to purchasers. Other deceptive advertisements online are aimed at the individual and offer a range of consumer durables, other branded goods or services at greatly discounted prices. They may also offer fake educational qualifications, or other desirables. One of the more pernicious scams is the appeal for money – usually by fake charities linked to obscure religions – or organizations soliciting donations to help victims of disasters such as the events of 11 September 2001, the 2004 Boxing Day tsunami, the 2005 London bombings (7/7 and 21/7), Hurricane Katrina, the Pakistan earthquake and Asian bird-flu, through to the 2009 swine flu epidemic, the 2010 Haiti earthquake, the 2011 Fukushima nuclear disaster in Japan, 2014 Malaysian plane crash, 2017 Hurricane Harvey, the 2019 New Zealand shooting and the 2020 COVID-19 pandemic (see Dodt, 2020). Even the death of celebrities such as Patrick Swayse and Michael Jackson (and others) were used as bait to seek donations to non-existent charities. All are inspired attempts to exploit public sympathy and extort money by deception or to deceive recipients into opening infected attachments.

Within a few hours of the first London bombings on 7 July 2005, for example, the spam message in box 5.1 was circulated.

Box 5.1 Scam email

From: breakingnews@cnnonline.com
Subject: TERROR HITS LONDON
Filename: 'London Terror Moovie.avi <124 spaces> Checked By
Norton Antivirus.exe'
'See attachments for unique amateur video shots'

The purpose of these scam emails is not always to directly elicit money. Sometimes the purpose is to encourage recipients to click on a link to infect the recipient's computer in order to render it receptive to remote administration as a zombie. Robot networks (botnets) of zombie computers are themselves very valuable commodities. In 2006, during Slobodan Milošević's trial for war crimes at The Hague, for example, spam emails were circulated claiming that he had been murdered. The emails listed various www sites and their addresses where early news footage and photographs of the alleged murder were posted. Once the web addresses were accessed, the computers of the curious were infected by a malicious trojan (Dropper-FB) which rendered them susceptible to remote administration (Leyden, 2006c).

Entrapment marketing scams

Entrapment is the stage beyond deception because it locks the victim into a situation from which they cannot easily extricate themselves and may become repeat victims. Entrapment can occur upon being deceived into participating in some of the activities mentioned earlier, or by falling victim to one of the many entrapment marketing scams. The classic, often legal, entrapment marketing scam is whereby individuals are enticed to sign up for a free trial subscription to a service. This may range from prepared meals by post, through to entertainment streaming channels. To sign up and get the deal, users have to give their financial details in case they wish to keep the service, but have the option to cancel the subscription at the end of the trial period. This is now a common and legitimate business practice, but more unscrupulous vendors will offer a free trial, for example, of access to sites containing sexually explicit materials, or being given free lines of credit in new trial gambling www sites. The key to the scam, assuming the content is legal, is to place the onus of responsibility upon the applicant to notify the vendor of the cancellation, which keeps many scams on the right side of the law. To withdraw from the service, free trial subscribers often have to give a prescribed period of advance notice and usually in writing – facts that may be obscured in rather lengthy terms and conditions. Because of this, subscribers can end up paying an additional monthly subscription.

Internet auction frauds

The popularity of online auction sites attracts fraudsters because bidders base their judgement on descriptions and photographs and not the real object. Although auction sites advertise rigorous security procedures to build consumer trust, fraudsters still exploit them. The fraudsters' key objective is to lure the bidder outside the well-protected online auction environment. In 2005, three fraudsters were jailed for defrauding eBay customers out of £300,000. They placed advertisements for items ranging from concert tickets to cars, some of which were genuine, others not. After the auction concluded, the fraudsters got in touch with unsuccessful bidders to give them a second chance to buy the goods, which they would be encouraged to pay for using money transfers. The bidders did not subsequently receive the goods (BBC, 2005c). The England and Wales crime statistics for 2021 and 2022 showed that online shopping and auction fraud constitutes about three-fifths (60 per cent) of consumer and retail fraud (ONS, 2023).

Box 5.2 Ebay's scam warning

Ebay's eBay Security Center[17] warns users of the site of a range of scams against both the seller and the bidder (adapted from Bischoff, 2021).

Against bidders

- *The non-delivery scam*. For some items, the seller can accept direct payment.
- *Incorrect labels*. Goods sent with an incorrect label after the transaction is completed. The buyer thinks they have received someone else's parcel and returns it. The seller gets the product back and keeps the payment.
- *The empty box scam*. Buyers pursue a desired item and quickly buy it only to find it is an empty box.
- *Counterfeit goods*. Scammers offer desired brand-name items for sale at a very attractive price which are counterfeit or 'knock-offs'.
- *Payment outside of eBay*. Illegitimate sellers offer an item for sale and request that the payment is sent outside of the platform.
- *Fake customer service*. Fraudsters place a fake customer service number on their profile or product page. Victims call the number when their order is wrong or not delivered and gets the scammer pretending to be customer service and who gets the victim to pay or give sensitive information such as a bank account to process a refund.
- *Gift card scam*. Gift card scammers call victims and offer a limited-time discount and ask for a gift card number to use as payment and then disappear with the gift card balance.

Against sellers

- *Private deals offered outside eBay*. Buyers may offer to pay for an item privately rather than using eBay's official payment channels to avoid paying the transaction fee. The seller closes the listing and sends the item, but buyers either do not pay, or dispute the transaction with eBay claiming the item was broken or the listing fake.
- *Overpayment offers*. A potential buyer may contact the seller and offer to pay more than the asking price. An offer that is hard to refuse, but the buyer pays with a fraudulent cheque and item is sent promptly, then the cheque bounces.
- *Changed address*. A buyer offers to purchase an item and sends a larger payment than asked for, claiming it is to cover additional shipping costs because they want it to be sent to a foreign country. The scammers also ask for the seller's PayPal email address which is contacted by fraudsters pretending to be from PayPal, asking for postal tracking numbers and stating that the payment will be released to the seller once they have proven that the goods have been sent. Trusting vendors send the item in good faith.
- *Empty box claim*. The buyer pays quickly and the item is sent without concern. The buyer receives the item but claims they only received an empty box accusing the sender of fraud; eBay demands a return and the buyer sends the empty box back to the sender, keeping the item.
- *Buyer claims the item wasn't received*. Sellers must ordinarily provide signatory proof of item delivery, but if the item cost less than $750 then only an email or text

delivery notification is adequate proof. Experienced scammers take advantage of the loophole and claim the item was not received and demand a refund.

- *Broken replica scam.* A buyer purchases an item which is shipped to them. The buyer then accuses the seller of sending a damaged item and provides photos. The photos are of a replica of the items sent and the buyer reports the item as damaged to eBay and asks for a refund.

- *Unwarranted chargeback.* After a successful transaction is completed, the buyer (scammer) pays with a credit card or PayPal, then they contact the provider to cancel the transaction. The money will be recovered from the seller and an additional chargeback fee is charged ($20 for PayPal and various charges for credit cards). The scammer only needs to say to the intermediary (the selling site) that they suspect something was wrong and most will chargeback immediately, regardless of whether or not they have the item.

- *Feedback extortion.* Building an online reputation on eBay is important. Bad feedback is bad for business, so scammers will buy from a seller and then demand additional money be sent privately to ensure that negative feedback will not be left on the seller's account. It is a type of blackmail because completed feedback cannot be disputed.

Other examples of online auction-related frauds include the overpayment scam, whereby the scammer (the bidder this time) intentionally pays more than the agreed sum. The payment cheque clears the banking system after a few days and the seller sends off the goods (to a different location from that registered for the bank account) and refunds the overpayment. The fact that the cheque is counterfeit is usually not discovered until a few weeks later, leaving the victim liable for both losses. In a variant of this scam, the buyer agrees to collect goods bought over the internet, such as a car, and overpays the seller using a counterfeit cheque. The overpayment is then refunded by the seller before the cheque clears, but the goods are not collected – the seller retains the goods but loses the value of the overpayment (Rupnow, 2003).

Advance-fee frauds (419 scams and romance fraud)

At the hard end of entrapment scams are the advance-fee frauds – sometimes called 419 frauds because they originated in Nigeria and contravene Code 419 of the Nigerian Penal Code. Advance-fee fraudsters have bilked money from individuals and companies for many years, but concerns have intensified because of the increasing use of emails to contact potential victims. Prior to the popularization of email as a key means of communication, advance-fee frauds were mainly conducted by official-looking letters purporting to be from the relative of a former senior government official, who, prior to their death, accrued a large amount of money currently being held in an overseas bank account. The sender invites the recipient to assist with the removal of the money by channelling it through their own bank account. In return for collaborating, the recipient is offered a percentage of the money (say, $12m, 20 per cent of the $60m money – see Wall, 2007a: 91) to be transferred. When the recipient responds to the sender, an advance fee is sought from them to pay for banking fees and currency exchange, etc. But the experience drawn from many cases shows that as the victim becomes more embroiled in the advance-fee fraud and pays out their money, then it becomes harder for them to withdraw. Needless to say, the majority, if not all, of these invitations are bogus and are designed to defraud the respondents, sometimes for considerable amounts of money.

The link between the massive increases in emailed advance-fee scams and the numbers of actual victimizations resulting from them is inconclusive – that is, as opposed to those arising from the more persuasive hard-copy invitations. Research conducted in 2001 by the UK National Crime Intelligence Service (NCIS, now NCA) found no direct link between the number of emailed requests and increase in victimizations (Wall, 2007a: 92) – the main reason being that individuals tend to be fairly risk-averse to most of the email 'invitations' because of their lack of plausibility due to poor written English and bad narrative. The hard-copy invitations tended to have been more thoroughly researched and personal. However, there are a number of conflicting forces at play here. On the one hand, it must also be recognized that there are additional reporting disincentives in play here because many victims will usually destroy the letter or email that drew them into the fraud so that they are not subsequently accused of being involved in a conspiracy. On the other hand, having said this, the incentives to report do nevertheless tend to increase as the loss escalates, or, even worse, if victims feel a threat to their well-being. Furthermore, the consequences of falling victim to an advance-fee fraud can be catastrophic in one of two ways.

The first consequence is financial. The US National Internet Fraud Information Center's internet fraud report of 2005 shows that 8 per cent, or 985 out of 12,315 fraud complaints, were about 'Nigerian' money offers, with an average loss of about $7,000. Seventeen years later, in 2022, the IC3 found that advance-fee complaints were 1.6 per cent,[18] or 13,020 out of 800,944 complaints, with an average loss of $8,012 (IC3, 2022). An analysis of advance fee frauds in the UK found that average losses per case were lower than those in the US, at $3,493[19] (Andrews, 2023). The personal losses were arguably not particularly large in overall fraud terms, but they could be catastrophic to personal finances, especially of vulnerable people.

The second consequence is the increase in personal risk, especially when individuals are lured abroad, or have tried to confront the fraudsters in an attempt to recover their money (Reuters, 2005). A few individuals who have travelled abroad in an attempt to do so have subsequently been kidnapped, and a few have reportedly been murdered (BBC, 2001). The numbers are small but real.

Box 5.3 Example of a 419 advance-fee fraud: excerpt from email

During the time my father was in the government with the late General Sani Abacha as the head of state, they were both involved in several deals that yielded Billions of Dollars . . .

During this period my father was able to make some good money for himself and kept in his private bank accounts . . . Right now, my father has been arrested and detained for interrogation. As the eldest son of my Father, I believe that I owe the entire family an obligation to ensure that the $60M is successfully transferred abroad for investment purposes. With the present situation, I cannot do it all by myself. . . .

I have done a thorough homework and fine-tuned the best way to create you as the beneficiary to the funds and effect the transfer accordingly. Is rest assured that the modalities I have resolved to finalize the entire project guarantees our safety and the successful transfer of the funds. So, you will be absolutely right when you say that this project is risk free and viable. If you are capable and willing to assist, contact me at once via email for more details.

Believe me, there is no one else we can trust again. All my fathers' friends have deserted us after exploiting us on the pretence of trying to help my father. As it is said, 'it is at the time of problems that you know your true friends'. So long as you keep everything to yourself, we would definitely have no problems. For your assistance, I am ready to give you as much as 20% of the total funds after transfer and invest a reasonable percentage into any viable business you may suggest.

Please, I need your assistance to make this happen and please; do not undermine it because it will also be a source of up liftment to you also. You have absolutely nothing to lose in assisting us instead, you have so much to gain.

Source: email (verbatim) received by author, 8 March 2001 (with similar ones on many subsequent occasions)

The jury is still out on the actual impact of 419 fraud victimization by email because the trusted symbols of letterhead and signature are absent, but a number of interesting variations of the advance-fee theme have been found in emailed letters requesting loans rather than fees. In other examples of advance-fee frauds, in which there are many 'lures', relationships may be deliberately struck up on online dating services and then flight costs and other expenses are requested in advance by the recipient to visit the person advertising on the dating services – leaving love-struck victims waiting for loved ones, who never arrive. Romance scams are a variation of advance fee fraud. They are deceptions engineered online through false romantic intentions directed towards victims. Romance frauds are by no means new, but the creation of Facebook, Instagram and other more niche networking sites has both facilitated and enabled them, especially across borders. Research by the bank TSB found 7,000 victims from 2020 to 2022, and that losses through romance frauds increased almost threefold in three years (Goodman, 2023). The romantic encounter generates goodwill, then trust, which inevitably results in the victim sending money to the fraudster or giving them access to their personal information and even bank accounts.

Frequent themes are: asking for financial help to pay bills, needing money for medical help or cash for home improvements. The TSB research found that these constituted 60% of cases recorded by the bank, and another 21% of losses resulted from victims paying the fraudsters' travel costs after they claimed that they were stuck abroad and 8% from money to book a trip for the victim, which never materialized. A further 4% of cases where losses were incurred saw the victims being blackmailed by the fraudster who threatened to share personal information or intimate images. Other cases involve the victim also taking out loans to pay fraudsters. Although victims tended to be from all age groups, the greatest losses (46%) were found amongst victims aged 51–65. Annual losses in the UK are thought to be about £65 million (Goodman, 2023). Individual losses can be considerable. One victim was reported to have lost £320,000 to a romance fraudster (BBC, 2020b). UK Finance (2022b) found in their survey that two in five people (38%) who dated someone online and had never met them were asked for money and just over half (57%) gave or lent it. The scammers are very experienced at getting money and information from victims, and there is evidence that organized criminal gangs are behind them.

Alternatively, users may receive an email telling them that they have won a lottery prize or that they have been entered into a prize pot in a promotions exercise. They are directed by the email to a www site which supposedly will provide the information that will release their prize. At this site they will be asked for their personal information and also, because the money comes from overseas, a small fee to pay for bank or administration charges. All variants of advance-fee frauds are designed to elicit money in advance of any action.

Online ticket scams

As the sale of tickets for entertainment has moved online, the numbers of ticket scams have also increased. The typical ticket sales scam offers victims the chance to buy tickets to a popular event from a website, often promoted on social media sites. The hook to catch the victim is that the event is near to, or actually, sold out, or the tickets have yet to go on sale but are likely to sell out immediately. The victim pays for the tickets and then a number of scenarios arise. Either the tickets do not arrive, or purchasers may be told to meet a customer representative at the venue on the day and nobody turns up. Or the tickets may arrive, but are fake and purchasers are denied entry.[20] Action Fraud found that ticket scams in the UK are increasing and cost victims over £6.7 million in 2022 (Action Fraud, 2023).

Drug sales / health cures / snake-oil remedies

The sale of narcotics has been boosted by the internet. At a local level, street dealers began selling drugs via social media. Research commissioned by advocacy group Volteface and polling 2,006 16- to 24-year-olds found that a quarter of young people had seen illegal drugs being advertised on social media (White, 2019). At a transnational level, the emergence of darkmarkets hosted on the Tor network appears to be satisfying a resilient global market in drug sales. Almost a decade after Silk Road, the first darkmarket, ceased trading, and despite continuous intervention by law enforcement, new replacement markets have emerged and drug sales on the dark web are still thriving. Martin and Barratt surveyed thirteen vendors to see why the dark web is attractive to consumers of drugs, but also to vendors. They found that it was ideal for those 'who are averse to confrontation, and who are sufficiently tech-savvy . . . [it] offers an alternative to the risk and violence of dealing drugs offline' (Martin and Barratt, 2020). Darkmarkets run along the same lines as the established commercial concerns on the clear web, such as Amazon. They operate reputational management systems to help to guide consumers in a competitive marketplace. Basically, the offenders ensure that customers get the best quality and, rather ironically, they police the quality themselves.

The sale of prescription drugs through internet sites has become commonplace and part of the regular health regimes today. Prescription drugs are, however, mostly administered under supervision of trained personnel but there is still a clandestine market for them. This market provokes concerns because of the potential dangers that can arise from the circulation of unregulated, or even fake, drugs. Promises of quality goods, value for money, availability and also convenience of access would appear to be frequently shattered by broken promises and fraud. A poignant example was the booming international trade in the early 2000s for Viagra, the anti-impotence drug (Cialis) (Satchwell, 2004: 44; Humble, 2005). The more plausible adverts for selling pharmaceuticals, which usually provide a trading address and some other credible business credentials, often lead to drugs being legally transported across borders to circumnavigate local prescription restrictions or exploit pricing differentials. Similar markets are also found trading steroids and other body-enhancing drugs, such as slimming pills (Satchwell, 2004: 44). The growing use of the internet to sell counterfeit drugs is worrying for drug regulators as it makes global an already booming business (Satchwell, 2004). The World Health Organization (WHO) has estimated that about 8–10 per cent of all medicines available globally are counterfeit. Of particular concern are stories that indicate that, for example, over 60 per cent of drugs sold in Nigeria were found to be counterfeit, some sold via the internet. Such examples provoke demands for international regulation to verify the quality and legality of manufacture and also to authorize their purchase (WHO, 2004). The two primary concerns about internet drug sales relate to mass sales and to the regulation of private selling to individuals – which is much harder to control. Two decades later, controlling these concerns is proving hard to achieve: '[a] 2021 survey by the Global Alliance for Safe Online Pharmacies found that 95% of online pharmacies are operating illegally' (Dumais, 2022). This finding is especially problematic following the COVID-19 pandemic, which increased the demand for online pharmacies.

Alongside the sales of pharmaceuticals is a robust market for alternative health cures and snake-oil remedies which attempt to persuade buyers/victims that the product or service is to be trusted. Unlike the entrapment scams, however, which hook potential victims through their greed-driven gullibility, the snake-oil scams play upon personal insecurities, or even the individual's ill health. It is, of course, no surprise that individuals should seek longevity and the classical literature is full of tales about the quest to restore youth and to achieve immortality. Indeed, these tales go back 4,000 years to the Epic of Gilgamesh set in ancient Mesopotamia (Sandars, 1972: 97). Miracle cures became popular on the stalls of the mediaeval English fairs, and in the nineteenth century became the basis for the American medicine show (Anderson, 2000). It is therefore also of no surprise that the internet has become the site of the 21st-century virtual medicine show feeding the same old personal insecurities and peddling miracle cures and snake oil, but on a global scale. Commonly found in email inboxes are offers to maintain and enhance vitality, youthfulness, health and longevity; miracle diets and potions; body enhancement lotions or operations to reduce body fat; lotions and creams to enlarge breasts or penises, or to chisel body muscles (typically abs and pecs). At the very bottom of the (moral) barrel are the bold claims of cures for cancer and other serious illnesses.

Cryptocurrency scams

In addition to being a common exchange medium in frauds and extortions, cryptocurrency has itself become a popular target for scammers (as well as hackers – see earlier), especially as the currency is stored in a digital wallet rather than a bank account and uses a blockchain for verification and authorization. Scammers use relatively tried-and-tested methods to scam users and, of these, cryptocurrency investment schemes are probably the most frequent cryptocurrency scam. Scammers contact potential investors claiming to be experts in investment management. They assume that victims will already be aware of the massive rises in the value of crypto-currency, especially Bitcoin, which piques their curiosity, greed and ultimately exposes their own vulnerability to fraud. Posing as fake investment managers, the scammers ask for upfront fees and also personal information, which subsequently can give the scammer access to the victim's accounts. Scammers may also use fake celebrity endorsements to give the appearance that the celebrity has made a large financial gain from the investment (Osborne, 2020; Hetler, 2022). On the one hand, they impress investors with their apparent successes, whilst, on the other hand, rail-roading them into making investments.

Fake initial coin offerings are a popular technique. The basis of the scam is an effort to raise upfront investments to launch a cryptocurrency. Much of the media hype in 2017 about cryptocurrencies meant that, in 2018, around 1,000 ICOs (Initial Coin Offerings) failed, losing the backers in the region of $100 million. Kshetri observes that many of the ICOs did not have any original ideas, and more than 15 per cent of them were copied from other cryptocurrency projects (Kshetri, 2019). OneCoin is probably the most famous of these (see box 7.1). Despite claiming to be the 'Bitcoin Killer' and attracting billions of dollars in investments globally between 2014 and 2016, OneCoin was a complete scam as OneCoin never existed in a viable form. It had no blockchain and was purposefully designed to steal money from investors. It is estimated that investors lost approximately $3.8 billion, and the scammers made $2.5 billion profits. The scam was eventually exposed and the main organizer, Dr Ruja Ignatova, the self-titled 'CryptoQueen', disappeared, along with the money (BBC, 2019).

Other investment scams are directly imported from fiat currency. Arbitrage traders impressed investors with their specialist market knowledge, claiming to capitalize on knowing price differences between cryptocurrency exchanges (Kshetri, 2019). CryptoCallz was a chatroom on Telegram which advertised itself as a cryptocurrency pump group which claimed to 'skyrocket' the value of cryptocoins for six hours at a time (Mac, 2018). CryptoCallz is one of a number of such ventures on Telegram. They claim to be legal because, while pump and dump is 'fraudulent in the securities industry', the regulations have not yet been introduced (at the time of writing) for the cryptocurrency field (Mac, 2018). At the heart of the cryptocurrency investment scams is the greedy lure of quick profit on the part of both offenders and victims and the absence of a reliable guardian, a banking system or other party to inform custom-ers of the threat.

Cryptocurrency, combined with social media platforms, is also a target (a perfect storm) for 'trading bots' which, despite the promises of large returns, tend to be thinly disguised Ponzi schemes (see 'Pyramid selling scams online' above). The Global Trading bot offered a 'different level of sophistication' and unique selling point by exploiting arbitrage, buying Bitcoins from the US and trading them on a South Korean exchange (Mac, 2018). Investors were told to send some cryptocurrency to a wallet where it was held for one to three months, after which time investors could withdraw the money. A Telegram-based 'bot' would keep investors informed of the progress of their investment every four hours and also provide links to be shared with family and friends (Mac, 2018).

Virtual theft (digital burglary) and cyber-piracy

A virtual theft is the act of illegally taking a virtual object of value that has been conceived, constructed and delivered online. Virtual theft is enabled online, and the crime stays online.[21] In this sense, virtual thefts are cyber-dependent crimes, and yet the term 'virtual theft' is a misnomer because 'theft' legally implies permanently depriving[22] the owner of the use of the object under criminal law. This contrasts with the fact that digital artefacts are simulacra, as they have no original that can be 'owned' (Baudrillard, 1994). Virtual theft does, however, dilute[23] the object's value and any exclusivity of ownership that may be enjoyed over it, as it can with more physical objects, and so has financial and emotional consequences. Thus, the verification of rights of ownership has become crucial in allowing access not only to virtual environments, but also to exchange transactions that take place within them. 'Digital burglary' may be a better term for this act because virtual theft often requires the offender to break into a system to 'steal' the artefact, especially where data rather than intellectual property theft is concerned (see chapter 6), but, as has been so often the case in this field, 'virtual theft' has become part of the colloquial language.

As indicated earlier, internet technologies perfectly lend themselves to digitizing previously physical intellectual property which the networks enabled to be distributed. Thus, intellectual property in the form of merchandized trademarks and copyrighted imagery has become the real estate of cyberspace, especially where the IP is also linked to the architecture of the internet (e.g., domain names, etc.). Thus, cyberspace has become a virtual terrain marked by the struggle for control over its 'intellectual' real estate, of which property the value increases in proportion to the strength of the legal and technological control that exists over its dissemination. The downside is that this control makes it all the more desirable as something to be acquired, for use or to be sold on.

On the above note, there is increasing interest in 'non-fungible tokens' (NFTs) that transcend currency and intellectual property and may indicate a new hunting ground for fraudsters in the future. Non-fungible tokens are individual digital assets that carry rights of ownership, and they can neither be copied, substituted nor divided. Like cryptocurrency, the asset is recorded on a blockchain which certifies its authenticity and ownership.

Box 5.4 Donald Trump and his NFT digital trading cards

In December 2022, Donald Trump released a series of $99 digital trading cards (NFTs), which showed Trump as 'various characters including as a superhero, a cowboy and an astronaut' (Kaonga, 2023). They were popular with his followers and sold out quickly, allegedly netting him $1 million in the cryptocurrency Ethereum. In April 2023, Trump announced a second series of digital trading cards, which also sold out. The trading price of the first series soared with the speculation that Trump was to be indicted in New York, then it slumped when the arrest did not take place. Although Trump was mocked for his NFT venture, he defended his decision to release them in the interests of art and not money: 'I'm looking at this stuff and I'm saying "Wow, that's sorta cute, that might sell, that might sell." They thought it would sell in six months; it sold in six hours' (Trump quoted by Kaonga, 2023).

The additional problem for intellectual property right-holders and for the law is that the internet also facilitates new types of participatory consumption (prosumption) of informational properties. While prosuming a product or service, consumers increasingly take part in the production of what they consume, and not only demand what they want to consume but also demand how they want to consume it – a process which blurs the line between the producer and consumer of intellectual ideas that the creative industry has long preserved (Ritzer and Jurgenson, 2010). For example, prosumption started by people buying individual tracks rather than complete albums (Stanley, 2013), or with karaoke, but internet technologies have enabled regular consumers to add their own creativity in quite sophisticated ways to music, photography, film and written texts in ways not previously imagined. Not least, consumers can actually rework music by inputting their own creativity – thus disrupting long-standing power relations between the cultural industries and the public. So the motivation for appropriating intellectual property may be driven by broader creative reasons. Such reasons may include libertarian,[24] artistic, moral, even educational goals, and not necessarily the prospect of financial gain. See, for example, the culturally different, yet significant, examples of the protection of intellectual property rights by the owners of Elvis Presley's imagery, the Tellytubby trademark, the pop group Oasis's copyright, Marvin Gaye's sound, and many other examples. Although not explored in detail here, these and many more examples nevertheless demonstrate the gravity which owners of IPR (intellectual property rights) attach to threats to their interests. They also illustrate the dilemmas that IPR holders face with regard to the paradox of circulation and restriction in an environment of participatory consumption (prosumption), which requires them to balance carefully their need to restrict the unauthorized circulation of their informational property to maintain income streams, while also allowing sufficient circulation of the intellectual property to allow the market to consume it as culture in the broadest sense, and enabling it to reach new markets (Wall, 2004: 35).

Cyber-piracy

The ability of networked technologies to disseminate, share or trade informational (intellectual) property in the form of text, images, music, film and TV through information services has been one of the more significant developments of the internet. This 'intellectual property' is informational, networked and also globalized, and its authors or their licensees have a right of ownership or control over it, including the right to receive payment for access to the content. Both the informational property and the means to access content delivery services have a market value which simultaneously creates opportunities and motivations for what has become known as cyber-piracy. Although cyber-piracy follows the *mens rea* (guilty mind: intent) and *actus reus* (guilty act) of traditional piracy, the globalized and networked qualities of the internet give piracy a new scope and scale never imagined before. Examples of cyber-piracy now include illegally providing access to streaming services that deliver music, films, informational services, television, software, gaming and virtual artefacts (online IP), and online social spaces. Streaming was made viable by developments in communications technologies and vastly increased download speeds, and expansions in bandwidth.

The most popular way of stealing information services is to pay by using stolen (cloned, counterfeit or stolen) credit card details. Alternatively, information services can be accessed via account takeover using stolen or borrowed credentials. In circumstances where the technology permits, a legitimate subscription may even be taken out and the access details then shared by a number of contributing individuals. The various streaming media providers usually restrict the number of logins in a particular account. The main way of obtaining illegal access is, however, via a broker who provides illegal access to a service via a parallel service or decoder, usually for a fee, but one which is less than that charged by the legitimate providers.

At the heart of the cyber-piracy debate is a broader debate over the morals of intellectual property and the internet – not least, the ability of those who have legitimate control over the rights to digital intellectual property to both legally and practically maintain that control in their own interests. The problem is largely one of policing its usage, because digital property, whether in written, musical, or video form, has the unique characteristic of being stored as code and therefore being produced in its original form each time the file is run. As stated earlier, there is often no original, and digital copies are identical, which creates new problems for controlling their dissemination in ways that preserve income streams. They are very different in nature to physically based intellectual property which has been reproduced by analogue technology, such as vinyl records or film, which degrade in quality with each generation of copy. This characteristic emphasizes the value of the original artefact, but also installs an informal policing mechanism into the process. Without adequate controls in place, the value of digital property can be lost very quickly, as can the rights of control. Consequently, running in parallel to the growth of the internet has been a growth in the number and complexity of intellectual property laws relating to trademarks, copyright and patents (see, for example, the debates over the changes in privacy and publicity laws in the US; Madow, 1993; Boyle, 1996).

The growth in these laws and the controversy surrounding some of the IP claims – for example, where the IP has become generic or co-created – have intensified the debates over piracy. The intersection of the cyberspace and more restrictive intellectual property laws has become quite a potent combination, especially at a time when, as Baudrillard observes, economic activity has become the outcome rather than the cause of cultural values and norms (Baudrillard, 1988, 1998). Hence, much of the legal debate focuses upon the economic rather than cultural aspects of the IP, and yet often uses the latter to justify the former. Importantly, the fact that productive ideas can now be put into place without the need for expensive mechanical manufacturing processes means that the monetary value of those ideas is further enhanced.[25]

Intellectual property piracy follows the centuries-old practice of counterfeiting products by making copies of the original and then passing them off as originals. The trademark was introduced as a trusted sign to counter piracy by indicating to the purchaser that the product is genuine and produced by quality manufacturers (see Sherman and Bently, 1999). In the age of mass consumption, the trademark has itself acquired its own status and value as a brand, independent of the quality of the goods or services provided under the name. For goods carrying trademarks, the internet has become a natural marketplace,[26] especially with the increasing popularity of e-commerce, digital marketplaces and internet auction sites. These market sites can also be used to sell counterfeit branded hard goods, like Rolex watches, designer clothes and accessories, but also counterfeit branded soft goods that have been copied and packaged or made available to download.[27]

The first practical IP copyright challenges created by the internet were the illegal downloading of music and films via the MP3 (see David, 2010) and MP4 formats. The industry outcry against the change was championed by FACT (Federation Against Copyright Theft) and MIA (Music Industry Association) in the UK, and the Recording Industry Association of America (RIAA) and the Motion Picture Association of America (MPAA) in the USA, which are the largest industry organizations. Their ferocious anti-piracy projects sought to deter users from downloading illegal MP3 and MP4 files and included FACT's 2007 'Knock-off Nigel' television campaign, which outlined both the financial and social implications of illegal downloading. One of the outcomes of some of these campaigns was the practice of identifying downloaders and invoicing them for their use. This had mixed results (see box 5.5) because, on the one hand, it illustrated the issues and told the public that the practice was wrong, but, on the other hand, it corrupted some of the lawyers, the very people who helped to police IP rights. Today, technological developments have made entertainment streaming big business and, as streaming services now have rights to circulate the contents, the focus has shifted from the individual item of IP (song, album, film) to the service itself.

Box 5.5 Policing downloading via speculative invoicing

An interesting twist in the cyber-piracy/cybercrime debate occurred in the 2010s when some lawyers acting on behalf of the creative industries became corrupted by the process of identifying and prosecuting illegal downloaders. Ordinarily, lawyers (solicitors) are instructed by their clients (IP rights owners) and apply to the courts to obtain lists of IP infringers from the internet service providers. They then send invoices to them charging for the services they 'stole'. Any returns from the invoices would be sent to the IP rights holders minus the lawyer's fee. If the infringers declined to pay, then cases would be taken to court, and the courts usually decided for the IP rights holder. Some lawyers, however, developed a practice of acting before instructions from the IP holders, by applying to the courts for lists of infringers and sending out bulk 'speculative invoices' to infringers with dire threats of court action if they did not pay. They would then inform the IP rights holders and send them a percentage of the returns. The practice of 'speculative invoicing' generated so much bad publicity for the music IP rights holders that they turned their back on the practice. The lawyers shifted their focus and migrated to the adult entertainment industry to use the same process against the downloaders of pornographic films. The outcry over speculative invoicing eventually led to a number of cases being brought against the offending lawyers. In the USA and Canada, there were cases of *Canipre* (Canadian Intellectual Property Rights Enforcement), *Prenda Law* and *Malibu* and others. In the UK, the case of *ACS Law* has become renowned (see further Wall, 2015a). ACS Law not only was found to have bullied alleged infringers, but also used bullying tactics to protect itself by acting against its critics (Masnick, 2010a, 2010b). Not only was the speculative invoicing model largely based upon untruths, but in cases such as ACS Law hardly any conclusive evidence was provided to justify the damages calculated upon loss of sales that were the subject of the invoices. It also established the practice of outsourcing litigation and perversely incentivized (and corrupted) the lawyers involved. It was found that 'speculative invoicing' not only contradicts the legal profession's code of conduct, but also quickly became 'copyright trolling' and a form of harassment, even extortion, which is a long way from the intended aim of regulating copyright infringement (Wall, 2015a). It corrupted the 'guardians' of intellectual property rights.

Most anti-piracy campaigns today are directed towards the uploaders who are the brokers providing illegal services, especially music and film streaming services. There are, however, some anti-piracy campaigns against downloaders – for example, West Mercia Police targeted 1,000 people who illegally streamed sports channels into their homes (ITV, 2023). Hern has argued that piracy has become easier than ever today, even though streaming was intended to stop it: '[w]hen there are things to pay for, there will always be people looking for ways to get them for nothing" (FACT in Hern, 2021). Spotify, the music streaming service, arguably provides 'instant access and a better user experience than piracy', with music streaming providing a large part of music revenues, which are the highest since 2003 (Hern, 2021). The problem is keeping services up to date with trends in consumption. Hern has observed that 'after just a few years of streaming, we now have streaming fatigue' – there are now too many different services because each wants to develop its own exclusivity, but not enough time to access them all (Hern, 2021). Piracy will be an ongoing problem for IP rights holders.

Conclusions

This chapter has illustrated how inventive, reflexive and responsive cybercriminals using computers can be, and also how close the crimes sit alongside legitimate business opportunities. It shows how the virtual bank robbery, virtual stings, virtual scams and virtual thefts are areas of harmful and criminal activity that are rapidly evolving in step with technological developments. As they evolve, they create new challenges for law enforcement. For example, in the UK, the law is based on the understanding that machines cannot be deceived, only the people who use them; data cannot be stolen; fraud and deception are yet to be fully established as specific crimes; and trade secret theft is still not an offence (only the way that the information was obtained). But is law the most effective local solution to what has become a global problem? The example of MP3 and MP4 file-sharing is a graphic illustration of where private corporate interests compete with the public interest and capture the crime agenda.

The bulk of this chapter has focused upon fraudulent behaviour driven by the desire for economic or informational gain. This profile will gradually broaden as new opportunities for offending are created by the even greater convergence of networked technologies in the home, work and leisure with those managing identity and location. Importantly, this new world of convergence will be characterized more and more by information brokering, and 'information capital' will become increasingly more valuable. As a consequence, we shall probably see a further rise in the extent and breadth of information theft. Future debates on cybercrimes using machines will therefore focus increasingly upon the rights relating to the protection of information, and also the restoration of information and reputation once compromised.

Some discussion questions based upon this chapter

How dangerous are input frauds and should they be treated the same as output frauds?

Should virtual robberies, stings and scams be classed as cybercrime or as fraud?

Should virtual theft (e.g., of digital art or non-fungible tokens) be treated as theft, or some other crime?

Further Reading   The volume of cybercrimes using the machine is continuing to grow rapidly, especially as (amongst other developments) AI is being deployed to develop new methods to engage offenders with their potential victims. Student and researchers who wish to take this topic of study further are recommended to explore the following sources, which represent quite different views on the subject. See, further: Button and Cross, 2017; Button et al., 2022; Levi et al., 2017; Hanoch and Wood, 2021).

6 Cybercrimes in the Machine (Computer Content Crime): Extreme Pornography, Hate and Violent Speech

How have crimes in the machine changed in the information age?

Chapter contents and key points

Illegal content that is *obscene or immoral*
- Sexually explicit and obscene materials online
- Extreme pornography
- Child sexual imagery and the internet

Illegal content that is *violent, hateful or harmful* online
- Terror materials
- Violent imagery / murder video nasties / curiosity viewing
- Hate speech, including racism and radical politics
- Using websites to circulate information used in the organization of harmful action
- Circulating information about making drugs and weapons

Content that contributes to wrongdoing
- Circulating misinformation and misleading information online
- Offensive communications: emails, chatrooms and blogging
- Chatroom and discussion group communications (stalking and grooming)
- Blogging and blogsites
- Cyber-bullying

Content that is the focus of cybercrime (stealing data, computer content and intellectual property)

Can content (words and imagery) actually cause harm by turning thoughts into actions?

Chapter at a glance   *This chapter explores cybercrimes within the machine, or content crime. These crimes typically involve some form of informational materials or data held on a computer or device which are either illegal to possess, constitute evidence of wrongdoing or whose contents are the focus of cybercrime. The structure of this chapter represents these aspects of cybercrimes in the machine.*

Introduction

Internet content can be socially, culturally, educationally, politically beneficial, but if the content and context of use are poorly or maliciously designed, then the outcomes can be very different and even harmful (Rauterberg, 2004: 51). Such an observation is not surprising and confirms what has long been assumed, but the question remains about what content is harmful and why? There are currently three substantive areas of concern about how informational computer content can harm people through words and imagery. The first section discusses the problem of materials that are obscene or immoral being held on computers, such as extreme sexual imagery, especially including child images. The second section considers illegal content that is violent, hateful or harmful online, which includes terrorist materials, hate speech, racist speech, or images of violence and other prohibited content. The third section looks at the holding of materials that contribute to wrongdoing and cause harm, but that can also be evidence of that harm, such as cyber-bullying, violent or harmful content, offensive communications, evidence of grooming. The fourth section explores contents that are the focus of cybercrime such as data theft, and also what the data represents, as with intellectual property. The fifth and final section discusses the effect of harmful content upon conduct (social action) and explores the boundary between harmful thoughts and harmful actions and between words and conduct and the tension between offensive content and freedom of expression.

Illegal content that is *obscene or immoral*

The first part of this chapter will look at materials whose possession is morally or legally prohibited: they include online sexual materials, terror materials and violent imagery.

> STRONG WORD OF WARNING. While pornography and the other content crimes may be interesting subjects and legitimate topics for intellectual study, you must be careful to search the internet ethically for information. Be aware that search engines can include images that you may not want to see and may not be able to unsee later, especially if you are of a 'nervous' disposition. ALSO make sure your family or institution is aware of your plans for study and keep to words and discussion and away from any imagery – remember that viewing some imagery and content may be illegal in your country even if you have not downloaded it.

Sexually explicit and obscene materials online

The sale and trading of sexually explicit materials, colloquially known as pornography, have been a morally contentious issue and have become the subject of many laws. When photographs are digitized or taken with digital cameras and then distributed globally via the internet, the sale and trading of the materials become even more contentious, especially when they are sold and 'commodified'. Novelist Irving Welsh's anti-hero character in *Trainspotting*, 'Sick Boy', succinctly outlines the relationship between the consumer society and pornography. He argues that society needs pornography:

because we're consumers. Because those are things we like, things we intrinsically feel or have been conned into believing will give us value, release, satisfaction. We value them so we need to at least have the illusion of their availability. For [pornography] read coke, crisps, speedboats, cars, houses, computers, designer labels, replica shorts. That's why advertising and pornography are similar; they sell the illusion of availability and the non-consequence of consumption. (Welsh, 2002: 450)

Sick Boy's last point, 'the illusion of availability and the non-consequence of consumption' is poignant here because it begins to explain the attraction of the internet as a medium for both distributing and consuming pornography. Pornography and technological development have had a curious and contradictory long-term relationship, one which has involved the internet since the early 1990s (Johnson, 1996: 217). A commonly held belief during the mid-1990s was that pornographic materials could be accessed with impunity, and it was this that drew many people to the internet. Interest was fuelled by the availability of new types of media delivery, such as the voyeuristic soft-core cam-girl sites such as Jennifer Ringley's JenniCAM.com.[1] The cam-girl sites were made possible by the (then) unique ability of the internet to converge textual and visual media in both real and chosen time, and at relatively low cost. The cam-girl sites represented, if not facilitated, a shift in the politics of self-representation to enable women to express themselves on their own terms (Turner, 2004: 64), giving women a stake in the internet while further expanding the market for it. JenniCAM, states Jimroglou (1999), was a cyborg subject which, with other cam-girl sites, exposes 'more than just flesh' – they reveal cultural tensions surrounding epistemological conceptions of vision, gender and identity (Jimroglou, 1999). While JenniCAM may have retained its initial values during its lifecycle, many other cam-girl sites were quickly absorbed into the burgeoning online hardcore pornography industry brought together by 'cyber-pimps', or financiers who resourced their web-pages and linked them to cam-girl networks, sex portals and maintained their high positions in search engine rankings. Until 1999, the word 'pornography' was the number one target for internet search engines, a position which it held for almost a decade until it was eclipsed by 'MP3' (Carey and Wall, 2001: 35). By 2005, both had been superseded by 'Paris Hilton' (Wordtracker, 2005) as the most popular search phrase.

The high level of demand for sexually explicit materials online and the business it created encouraged the advancement of the technology that delivered it. During the formative years of the internet, the virtual sex-trade quickly became an electronic sexual information service (imagery, stories, etc.) which, controversially, not only pioneered the virtual transaction but also demonstrated the commercial potential of the internet to businesses and the criminal community. And it was the fear of vulnerable members of society becoming depraved by the content, and the thought of criminals driving unrestrained access to sexually explicit or pornographic materials that initially triggered public concern about the internet. This level of concern has been maintained as social media became popular. These fears are discussed later.

Today, the 'porn'[2] industry has become commercialized and professionalized and so large that the level of consumption is impossible to numerate. An indication, however, of consumer use can be found in figure 6.1, which illustrates the spikes in access to the 'porn' site Pornhub,[3] a video-sharing website, following the March 2020 lockdown during the global pandemic (COVID-19). The spikes are particularly large where lockdown was rapidly instituted, and they also illustrate the overall changes in

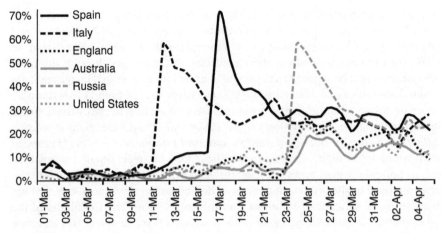

Figure 6.1 Percentage increase in user access to Pornhub during March 2020 following the COVID-19 pandemic lockdown.
Source: Wall (2021).

internet behaviour, which possibly include an appetite for riskier-than-normal activities. Such behaviour change is also relevant to other chapters in this book because it can render unsecured personal computers open to infection from various types of malware, plus it increases the attack surface if those same computers were used for working at home (Wall, 2021). While Pornhub itself appears to maintain good cybersecurity to protect its customers, and the site endeavours to ensure both that the materials shared are legal and the acts portrayed consensual, it is not the only such site available and many are less secure.

It is important to emphasize that sexually explicit materials that arouse the viewer are not necessarily illegal in many countries when the content involves consenting adults. The cyber-pornography/obscenity debate and the identification of obscene materials online, however, has been complicated by a latticework of moral and legal issues which differ from culture to culture and jurisdiction to jurisdiction, and yet the internet is a global phenomenon.

There are two fundamental problems in identifying obscene materials online. The first links with human rights, and is where to locate the boundary between the individual's right to freedom of expression and the right of the state to protect its own cultures and values. To this effect, Article 10(1) of the European Convention on Human Rights (Council of Europe) reflects Article 19 of the United Nations Universal Declaration of Human Rights and empowers EU citizens with the freedom 'to hold opinions and to receive and impart information and ideas without interference by public authority and regardless of frontiers'. But Article 10(2) clearly explains that the oversight and regulation of these freedoms, duties and responsibilities are prescribed by law and 'are necessary in a democratic society, in the interests of national security, territorial integrity or public safety, for the prevention of disorder or crime, for the protection of health or morals, for the protection of the reputation or rights of others' (see *R.* v. *Handyside* v. *United Kingdom*, 1976; *Paris Adult Theater I* v. *Slaton*, 1973 – the state should protect the morals of society).

The second problem is how to reconcile the considerable legal and moral differences when deciding which criteria should be applied to establish obscenity and depravation (see Chatterjee, 2001: 78) in a global medium such as the internet. In the UK, for example, individuals daily consume risqué images through the mass media which might be regarded as obscene in other cultures. Sexual images that are permitted after the 9 p.m. watershed on UK television, may be found on daytime TV in more permissive countries, and never in others. In seeking to clarify the defining criteria, the European Commission's *Green Paper and Action Plan on the Protection of Minors and Human Dignity in Audio-visual and Information Services* (European Commission, 1996) made the important distinction between situations in which children potentially gain access to legal websites with sexual (pornographic) content as opposed to sites containing material depicting illegal, obscene acts that are subject to penal sanctions (European Commission, 1997a). The usefulness of the legal distinction is that it identifies the point at which self-regulation ceases and state intervention starts, particularly where moral and political agendas drive public opinions. However, it is complicated by the broadly held view that while the pornographic content of websites may not necessarily be illegal, it may nevertheless still be judged to be harmful to children's development (European Commission, 1996: ch. 1).

The emotionally charged nature of the debate over the regulation of obscene materials on the World Wide Web has taken it in a number of different directions. In the early days of the internet, Rimm's Carnegie Mellon survey (1995), for example, alleged that the consumption of pornography constituted as much as half of all internet traffic, mostly through 'usenet' discussion groups. Rimm claimed to have identified '917,410 images, descriptions, short stories, and animation downloaded 8.5 million times by consumers in over 2,000 cities in forty countries, provinces, and territories' (Rimm, 1995: 1849). The public reaction to this influential survey contributed to the mid-1990s moral panic over the use of the internet, which persisted long after inconsistencies in the survey's methodology were exposed. Rimm's methodology was indeed deeply flawed as he had greatly overestimated the level of internet traffic in sexual materials by concentrating his data collection upon newsgroups and bulletin boards. In fact, when all forms of internet traffic were considered, it was later found that the overall percentage was less than 1 per cent, in contrast to the 83.5 per cent Rimm had claimed (Wallace and Mangan, 1996). Yet, despite the contradiction, Rimm's survey findings made a lasting impact upon the debate over early internet regulation and they were instrumental in setting the emotional climate in the lead-up to the passage of the Communications Decency Act 1996 (47 USC s. 223) in the US, which was later partly overturned (*ACLU et al.* v. *Reno* (1997); Heins, 2001b). Rimm's findings appeared to give strong empirical support to the anti-pornography lobby, who argued that pornography degraded women (MacKinnon, 1993) and was an assault on the moral fabric of society. For a while, the findings eclipsed the arguments of the pro-pornography lobby, who claimed that the availability of sexual materials on the internet would reduce sex crimes (Diamond and Uchiyama, 1999: 1, 18); of civil libertarians who defended the pornographers' right to freedom of expression; and of the advocates of laissez-faire, who believed that free market demand should determine the course of events. Although the moral panic has since subsided, it still lurks in the background and flares up occasionally.

The different moral and political perspectives on pornography highlight the need to differentiate the types of pornographic content found on websites in terms of their risk to viewers. The majority of internet-based pornography is adult consensual pornography, whether it is soft-core sexual imagery or even hard-core imagery depicting penetration and other sexual acts. Although subject to moral strictures, its consensual nature leaves it largely non-contentious within most Western jurisdictions, and, with some caveats, within the boundaries of law. Even 'extreme' pornographic materials depicting acts that appear to step over the borders of consensual behaviours are unlikely to be prosecuted so long as the acts can be proved to be consensual (*R. v. Brown*, 1993, 1994; *R. v Wilson*, 1996). It is only when there is clear evidence of violence against one or more of the parties by the other that an investigation may take place, and then usually only after a formal complaint has been made to the police. To illustrate this point, the UK's Crown Prosecution Service (CPS), which prosecutes on behalf of the Crown, argues that it is impossible to define all of the obscene activities that can be prosecuted, but it nevertheless began to list the most common categories. Yet the listing became contentious and unworkable following the passing of Extreme Pornography laws and the CPS eventually revised its guidance.

Extreme pornography

Perhaps the most heated issue relates to what has come to be known as 'extreme pornography'. This includes the extent to which adults, and especially children, should be protected from viewing extreme obscene imagery. The test for obscenity in the UK and other jurisdictions is whether or not materials deprave and corrupt the viewer: 'an article shall be deemed to be obscene if its effect or (where the article comprises two or more distinct items) the effect of any one of its items is, if taken as a whole, such as to tend to deprave and corrupt persons who are likely, having regard to all relevant circumstances, to read, see or hear the matter contained or embodied in it' (s.1(1), Obscene Publications Act 1959 (UK)).

In 2008, the UK introduced legislation against Extreme Pornography (Criminal Justice and Immigration Act 2008, Pt 5), which added further offences in addition to obscene materials to clarify and to legislate against some of the digital imagery being circulated on the internet. It sought to criminalize the possession of an 'extreme pornographic image' to protect those individuals who participate in creating sexual material that contains violence, cruelty or degradation who may notionally or consensually take part (CPS, 2019). It also sought to protect society as a whole, especially children, from exposure to extreme pornographic material to which access cannot be reliably controlled through legislation and whose viewing may encourage interest 'in violent or aberrant sexual activity' (CPS, 2019).

Under the 2008 Act,[4] extreme pornography had to be:

- Pornographic ('of such a nature that it must reasonably be assumed to have been produced solely or principally for the purpose of sexual arousal'), and
- Grossly offensive, disgusting or otherwise of an obscene character, and
- Portrays in an explicit and realistic way any of the following:
  - An act which threatens a person's life, or

- An act which results, or is likely to result, in serious injury to a person's anus, breasts or genitals, or
- An act which involves sexual interference with a human corpse (necrophilia), or
- A person performing an act of intercourse or oral sex with an animal (whether dead or alive) (bestiality), or
- An act which involves the non-consensual penetration of a person's vagina, anus or mouth by another with the other person's penis or part of the other person's body or anything else (rape or assault by penetration)

and

- A reasonable person looking at the image would think that the persons or animals were real.

In 2019, the CPS recognized the shortcomings of the Extreme Pornography rules and revised them by removing some of the troublesome examples and also emphasizing that those owning or producing pornographic material are unlikely to be prosecuted if:

- it features consenting adults, where the provision of consent is made clear where consent may not be easily determined from the material itself
- no serious harm is caused, whether physical or otherwise
- it is not otherwise linked with other criminality
- the likely audience is not under 18. (CPS, 2019)

In order to clarify the law relating to adult pornographic videos, the 2014 Audiovisual Media Services Regulations[5] brought 'professional pornography', that which is made commercially and sold online or in licensed adult stores, under British Board of Film Classification (BBFC) Rating 18: suitable only for adults. In 2019, the regulations were brought into line with Pt 5 of the Criminal Justice and Immigration Act 2008 to legalize filming sexual acts between consenting adults.

In deciding whether or not to prosecute complaints, the CPS considers whether the allegedly obscene presentation is in written or visual form, because the former is deemed to have a lesser impact than the latter. They also consider whether the presentation is personal or commercial; whether it could have been viewed by a child or vulnerable adult; whether it could be readily seen by the general public in a public place or shop; whether or not the defendant has a similar previous conviction. The final consideration concerns the degree of participation by the suspect and the level of his or her knowledge of the contents of the material (s. 2(5) Obscene Publications Act 1959). Of crucial importance to the prosecution process is that the publication is produced and disseminated within the country in question, which is a key problem when policing obscene materials on the internet. The Extreme Pornography laws made it an offence to possess images depicting scenes of serious sexual violence and other obscene materials that are illegal to publish in the UK under the Obscene Publications Act 1959 but accessible from abroad via the internet (Home Office, 2005, 2006).

Child sexual imagery and the internet

The most contentious type of online pornography is that which contains 'sexualised or sexual pictures involving children' (M. Taylor, 1999). Colloquially called 'child pornography', the terms 'child abuse imagery' or 'child sexual abuse materials' are often preferred and used. The Internet Watch Foundation (IWF), which analyses reports taken from the public of extreme sexual imagery (one of fifty such portals in countries all over the world), clearly states on the matter:

> We use the term 'child sexual abuse' to reflect the gravity of the images and videos we work with. 'Child pornography', 'child porn' and 'kiddie porn' are not acceptable descriptions. A child cannot consent to their own abuse.[6]

Child abuse imagery is addressed at international and national legal levels. In its 9th (2019) review of child sexual abuse material legislation in 196 countries, the ICMEC (International Centre for Missing and Exploited Children), which seeks to calibrate international legislation, reported that significant advances had been made in international legislative efforts but with mixed outcomes. Since the ICMEC project began in 2006, 150 countries have either refined or implemented new legislation against child sexual abuse materials. They also found that 140 countries made possession of simple child sexual abuse materials illegal, 125 countries defined it, but only 32 countries required Internet Service Providers to report suspected materials (ICMEC, 2019). This illustrates the common international concern over the issue which is significantly due to the existence of Council of Europe (CoE) and United Nation treaties covering it.

The CoE Convention on the Protection of Children against Sexual Exploitation and Sexual Abuse (CETS No. 201) became active in 2006. The CoE convention requires member states and signatories to criminalize 'all aspects of child pornography' (CoE, 2006). By 2023, it had 48 accessions or ratifications, which represented all of the 46 member states, plus the Russian Federation and Tunisia.[7] The other major treaty is the Convention on the Rights of the Child, Article 34, which requires all signatories to take appropriate measures to make illegal the exploitative use of children in pornographic performances and materials (UN, 1989). The UN treaty also has an optional protocol which requires its signatories to criminalize 'producing, distributing, disseminating, importing, exporting, offering, selling or possessing' child pornography. Of the 197 possible signatories, 178 have ratified it, 7 have signed it with the intention of ratifying it and 12 have taken no action yet (as of 23 Feb. 2023).[8]

In the UK, the legislative development path reflects that of most jurisdictions with regard to child sexual abuse materials. The Protection of Children Act 1978 currently defines four offences involving indecent photographs or pseudo-photographs of children (Sentencing Advisory Panel, 2002: 2).[9]

Under section 1(1) of the 1978 Act, it is an offence for a person:

(a) to take, or permit to be taken, or to make any indecent photograph or pseudo-photograph of a child; or

(b) to distribute or show such indecent photographs or pseudo-photographs; or

(c) to have in his possession such indecent photographs or pseudo-photographs, with a view to their being distributed or shown by himself or others; or

(d) to publish or cause to be published any advertisement likely to be understood as conveying that the advertiser distributes or shows such indecent photographs or pseudo-photographs or intends to do so.

The possession of indecent digital photographs of children in the UK was made an offence under section 160 of the Criminal Justice Act 1988. Section 62 of the Coroners and Justice Act 2009 defined which types of images of children it is prohibited to possess. To bring the legislation up to date with advances in digital technologies, Section 84(4) of the Criminal Justice and Public Order Act 1994 included possession of 'pseudo-photographs' (Akdeniz, 1997). The existence of 'pseudo-photographs' had previously weakened the case for the prosecution because of reliance on the fact that a child had been abused in the construction of the picture (see, further, *R. v. Jonathan Bowden*, 2000). The possession of an indecent photograph or pseudo-photograph of a child is a triable either-way offence (depending upon the evidence) that could be tried in either the (lower) Magistrates' Courts or (upper) Crown Courts, with a maximum penalty of five years' imprisonment upon conviction (Home Office, 2015).

Other legal jurisdictions have adopted legal considerations similar to those outlined in the UK; however, the constitutional protection of freedom of expression in the US and other countries has meant that, while the production and possession of child pornography are illegal, there are possible defences. Much of the debate therefore revolves around the definition of child sexual imagery. In the US, it is found under the Children's Internet Protection Act (18 USC 2256(8) (A–D)), (following the case of *Ashcroft v. Free Speech Coalition* in 2002; Landau, 2002):

(8) 'child pornography' means any visual depiction, including any photograph, film, video, picture, or computer or computer-generated image or picture, whether made or produced by electronic, mechanical, or other means, of sexually explicit conduct, where—

(A) the production of such visual depiction involves the use of a minor engaging in sexually explicit conduct.

(B) such visual depiction is, or appears to be, of a minor engaging in sexually explicit conduct.

(C) such visual depiction has been created, adapted, or modified to appear that an identifiable minor is engaging in sexually explicit conduct; or

(D) such visual depiction is advertised, promoted, presented, described, or distributed in such a manner that conveys the impression that the material is or contains a visual depiction of a minor engaging in sexually explicit conduct.

At the core of public and legal concerns about child sexual exploitation is the ability of investigators and prosecutors to determine when imagery contravenes the law. In order to standardize classifications that enable the assessment of images in both the investigation and the court process, the UK Sentencing Advisory Panel (2002) collapsed the University of Cork's COPINE ten-point classification for describing the range of exploitative images of children down to five levels (the Sentencing Advisory Panel or SAP scale) to make it more applicable. In 2014, the SAP scale was replaced by the Sentencing Council's Sexual Offences Definitive Guidelines (on sexual images) (Sentencing Council, 2013: 34) – see box 6.1.

Box 6.1 Sexual Offences Definitive Guidelines

Category A   Images involving penetrative sexual activity and/or images involving
             sexual activity with an animal or sadism
Category B   Images involving non-penetrative sexual activity
Category C   Other indecent images not falling within categories A or B

Source: Sentencing Council (2013: 34)

While these UK classifications have found support in the international law enforcement and legal communities and overlap with the tests applied in the US, they also display some fundamental differences. In the US, a key factor in determining whether or not child sexual imagery is obscene is whether or not it displays 'lascivious exhibition'. Many US courts apply the six-part 'Dost test' (box 6.2) from *United States* v. *Dost* (1986) to determine whether a picture constitutes a 'lascivious exhibition' (Adler, 2001: 262).

Box 6.2 The Dost test for lascivious exhibition

[I]n determining whether a visual depiction of a minor constitutes a

'lascivious exhibition of the genitals or pubic area' under [18 USC] S 2255(2) (E), the trier of fact should look to the following factors, among any others that may be relevant in the particular case:

(1) whether the focal point of the visual depiction is on the child's genitalia or pubic area;
(2) whether the setting of the visual depiction is sexually suggestive, i.e. in a place or pose generally associated with sexual activity;
(3) whether the child is depicted in an unnatural pose, or in inappropriate attire, considering the age of the child;
(4) whether the child is fully or partially clothed, or nude;
(5) whether the visual depiction suggests sexual coyness or a willingness to engage in sexual activity;
(6) whether the visual depiction is intended or designed to elicit a sexual response in the viewer.

Source: United States v. *Dost* (1986: 832).

Whereas the UK Sentencing Council's classifications tend to deal primarily with matters of fact, the 'Dost test' requires some degree of interpretation, which is not particularly useful when the meanings of what constitutes child sexual exploitation are 'not always quite so clear' (M. Taylor, 1999). What makes the pictures attractive to those with a sexual interest in children is only partly their content; the most important factor is the sexual fantasy and personal meaning that the content invokes. While the law can define the boundaries of behaviour, for example, possession of sexualized child images, including morphed imagery, is illegal in the UK and leaves much room for interpretation, especially with regard to where the public interest lies in terms of risk. In other words, where does the danger lie? It is therefore important to understand more about why child sexual material is produced, collected and consumed, and all indications are that this task will require us to think beyond the legal definition of child sexual exploitation and abuse imagery (Taylor and Quayle, 2003; Krone, 2004: 1).

Child sexual abuse imagery is by no means a product of the internet – it has been a problem for many years and there is much historical evidence to indicate that adult sexual interest in children dates back to ancient times. Within the context of this discussion, however, it is important to ascertain whether or not the internet has had a transformative impact on child sexual imagery, and if so, how. Taylor and Quayle (2003) drew upon the COPINE research to demonstrate how the internet creates the social, individual and technological circumstances (the affordances) that enable an individual with an interest in child sexual imagery to feel safe in expressing their sexual fantasies and, in some cases, realities. First, networking technologies (including social media) create a socially self-justifying online community for consumers of child sexual imagery in which otherwise deviant values are shared or even encouraged. Second, the networking technologies also allow individuals to gain access to pornographic material and to communicate with others from the privacy of their own home, giving them a feeling of security and also a sense of control over the medium, plus the choice over whether or not their involvement is going to be passive or active (M. Taylor, 1999). This illusory distance between participants and their perceived non-consequences of consumption, particularly through the possibility of anonymity by using false or fantasy identities or encryption, are further stimulated by the fantasies invoked by the imagery: 'the 50-year-old can present himself as a teenager . . . the weak as strong' (M. Taylor, 1999). The concern here is that these fantasies may eventually be acted out in online interactions with children or even in person, following meetings arranged online (Krone, 2004: 3). This game can, of course, be played both ways because the same media also enables police officers to pose as children in 'sting' operations.

Third, perhaps the main impact of networked technology on child sexual exploitation has been to provide new and increasingly effective methods of distributing child sexual imagery. Particularly significant was the increase in bandwidth following the transition from dial-up BBS (bulletin board services) to broadband, and then faster fibre-optic broadband. This development helped develop P2P (peer-to-peer) networks and facilitated the rapid dissemination of imagery, while simultaneously enabling those with an interest in such images, or a more general sexual interest in children, to organize themselves more effectively. Crucial to the effectiveness of this organization is the P2P network's dependency upon its participants to allow uploads from their public folders, combined with the membership requirement of many closed child sexual exploitation networks to submit a pre-specified number of images and demonstrate a willingness to exchange them. Fulfilling this condition not only makes all those involved in the network complicit in the act, further tying them in to the network while also encouraging the collecting of images as an end in its own right.

Some idea of the scale of the early demand for child sexual materials and also of the organization of its distribution can be gleaned from the yield of policing operations against the consumers of online child sexual imagery. 'Operation Ore' was the UK police response following supply by the FBI of the details of 7,200 British suspects who had subscribed to a Texan subscription portal. Landslide, the portal's name, gave subscribers access to 300 child sexual abuse image sites for about £21 per month (Sherriff, 2004). The UK side of the operation resulted in 3,744 arrests, with 1,848 people being charged, of whom 1,451 were convicted. A further 493 were cautioned and a total of 879 investigations were undertaken. In all, 109 children were rescued from abusive homes (Cowan, 2005).[10] Rather controversially, approximately 35 of those investigated have since committed suicide (Howie, 2006), and Leppard (2005) and Campbell (2005a, 2005b) have subsequently highlighted flaws in the evidence process. However, the sheer size of the whole Landslide subscription database, which contained the names and credit card subscription details of 390,000 subscribers across 60 countries, illustrates the globalized scale of the problem (Jewkes and Andrews, 2005: 49), and 'Operation Ore' was by no means the first such police operation. In 1998, 'Operation Cathedral' was launched against a paedophile ring called the Wonderland Club (after Alice in Wonderland) and 750,000 child sexual images were seized (Creighton, 2003: 3). In the subsequent analysis of these images, it was found that more than 1,200 different children were involved; however, only 18 were identified and discovered – 3 in the UK (Downey, 2002). This illustrates the complexity and resource intensity of the policing operation.

At one of the largest hotlines for reporting child sexual abuse imagery, the IWF's 70 staff assessed 375,230 reports in 2022 (a 4% increase on 2021). They found that 375,153 of these were reports of webpages and 77 reports of news groups. Of these reports, 255,571 webpages (6%) and 17 news groups (22%) were confirmed to have contained child sexual abuse imagery, or had links to imagery, or advertised it (IWF, 2023). The IWF also found that each webpage (URL) could also contain 'one, tens, hundreds or even thousands of individual child sexual abuse images or videos' (IWF, 2023). The IWF is a not-for-profit organization and works closely with police agencies, governments and NGOs on a global scale. They report evidence of child abuse imagery to the relevant police agencies.

The number of Child Abuse Image offences which involve possessing, taking, making and distributing child abuse material is roughly about 10% of all known cases, mainly because fewer of the webpages or offenders were hosted in the UK. Figure 6.2 lists the annual number of child abuse image offences between 2008 and 2020. Please note that these statistics are compiled from CPS and National Society for the Prevention of Cruelty to Children (NSPCC) sources and so are primarily illustrative. They comprise three different offence groups, whose proportions are fairly consistent within a couple of percentages each year. The three groups are: the sexual exploitation of children through photographs (making, distributing, showing, advertising) (77%); possession of an indecent photograph (21%); prohibited image of a child (1%). Note the slight increase in offences following the COVID-19 lockdown in 2020/1.

It is therefore interesting, and of some concern, that, despite the potentially serious nature of the offences, Edwards (2000) found that only a small number of cases of possession of illegal images were eventually proceeded with in the courts, especially the Crown Court. This same finding is reflected two decades later. In 2020/1, 3,025 child abuse offences were proceeded against in court with an average conviction rate of 85 per cent. Of these numbers, child sexual abuse imagery offences represent 1 of 12 child abuse offence groups, so the number of imagery cases is much lower.

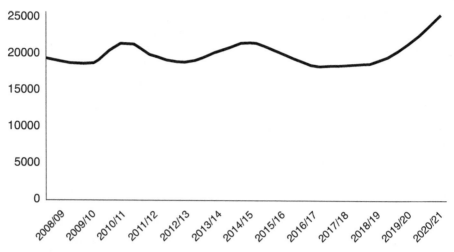

Figure 6.2 Child Abuse Image offences 2008–2020 (possessing, taking, making and distributing child abuse material).[11]
Source: adapted from CPS (2016) and NSPCC (2021) statistics.

Moreover, the 2020/1 numbers reflected half of the 6,394 proceeded against in 2016/17, and convictions also fell by 45 per cent from 4,751 to 2,595 (NSPCC, 2022).[12] Furthermore, the time taken for child cases to reach court and be completed has increased by 5 months in the 3 years between 2018/19 and 2020/1 – averaging 1 year and 10 months (NSPCC, 2022). The drop in numbers proceeded against and increase in the length of time to court can probably be explained by the restrictions on the criminal justice system by the COVID-19 pandemic. However, the fact of the matter is that the number of cases is still relatively small.

Edwards found that only the more serious offences of possession with intent to distribute and taking an indecent photograph were tried in either the Magistrates' Court or Crown Court (Edwards, 2000: 19). But another reason for the apparent shortfall in the prosecution of child sexual abuse imagery offences is that networked technology and a proliferation of different platforms (including social media) allow relatively few individuals, but the more serious offenders, to simultaneously control large databases across a number of illicit operations. This gives the impression that the offender population is more numerous. This latter point further emphasizes the need to differentiate between the different levels of risk posed by individuals so that resources into the investigation of offending can be efficiently allocated.

Drawing upon COPINE's research into collections of child sexual imagery traded online, M. Taylor (1999) found three main types of sexual material relating to children. The first consists of erotica, pictures of children in the form of personal snapshots, or advertisements for children's clothes. They are not necessarily sexual and not necessarily illegal, but the format of the collection may reveal the compiler's sexual interest in children. The second type depicts images of child nudity. Some will be collections of pictures taken covertly, or pictures posed in sexual positions (soft pornography); others will be drawn from naturist and artistic publications. As is the case with erotica, these may not individually be illegal, but are nevertheless indicative of a sexual interest in children. The third category is explicit sexual materials and those classed as obscene. While this is a very useful classification for imagery, it says little about the risk from offenders. Krone's (2004: 3) typology of online child sexual abuse imagery offending, outlined in box 6.3, specifically seeks to achieve this further goal. Particularly useful is his delineation between individuals whose sexual interest in children is confined to fantasies and those who actually abuse children. Krone takes into consideration the type and nature of the individual's involvement, the level of networking, the immediate security risk to children and the nature of the abuse.

What Krone usefully shows is that there are quite distinct groups among consumers of child pornography, each of which displays different levels of risk to the community. The first three groups – browsers, fantasists and trawlers – display very low levels of networking, and it is likely that much of their activity will remain internet-based, distanced and private, in thoughts, rather than actions. Furthermore, they are likely to be of less immediate risk to children. The others, however – the collectors, groomers, abusers, producers and distributors – are clearly prepared to put their thoughts into action and therefore pose a greater risk to children because of their willingness to become involved in networks of like-minded individuals.

Box 6.3 Krone's typology of online child sexual abuse materials offending

1 Browsers respond to spam or accidentally fall upon suspected sites. They knowingly save material. Browsers tend to be lone operators and do not network.
2 Private fantasists consciously create online text or digital images for their own use. They tend to be lone operators and do not network.
3 Trawlers actively seek child sexual imagery through openly available browsers. Trawlers tend to be fairly lone operators but may engage in low-level networking.
4 Non-secure collectors actively seek material through peer-to-peer networks. They are high-level networkers, but do not tend to engage any security measures in so doing.
5 Secure collectors actively seek material, but only through secure networks and engage high levels of security to avoid being detected. They are high-level networkers and are willing to exchange collections to gain access to new sources.
6 Groomers cultivate online relationships with one or more children, but they may or may not seek material as in 1–5 above. They are more likely to use pornography to facilitate abuse.
7 Physical abusers abuse children who they may have been introduced to online. As with the groomers, they may or may not seek material in any of the above ways. They are more likely to use pornography to facilitate abuse.
8 Producers record their own abuse of a child, or that of others. Or they may induce children to submit images of themselves.
9 Distributors may distribute imagery at any one of the above levels.

Source: based on Krone (2004: 4 (table 3)).

Making such distinctions is important for efficient resourcing of responses, but this is understandably an issue that also scares people. Public emotions run very high when it is felt that children have been abused. As a consequence, there is a high level of media sensitization that subsequently politicizes the policing of child sexual exploitation and paedophiles. Hewson believes that viewing child sexual imagery has become equated in the public eye with criminal responsibility for rape, which has worrying implications for liberty and also law. Of principal concern is that the current tendency towards wholesale condemnation of offenders is chilling critical debate about its actual impacts, while the strict measures being imposed are actually fuelling interest in the very thing that they are seeking to suppress (Hewson, 2003). It also raises the much broader and extremely contentious philosophical issue identified by Adler, though not discussed in this book, that: '[c]hildren and sex become inextricably linked, all while we proclaim the child's innocence'. The main problem for Adler is that 'sexuality prohibited becomes the sexuality produced' (Adler, 2001: 273).

Much further work is required to understand whether or not an individual's continued involvement as a browser or fantasizer will simply satisfy his or her curiosity (see Diamond and Uchiyama, 1999), or whether it erodes the browser's moral bind, gradually releasing them from the moral constraints of conventional order (Matza, 1964). Proponents of this widely prevailing 'drift theory' predict that the paedophilic *Weltanschauung* would progress the individual's lusts and sexual appetite up the scale of deviance. Yet, this 'ideology of paedophilia', which has emerged as a public moral response that automatically labels and demonizes all offenders, can cloud the understanding, investigation and resolution of the problem. This is particularly so in regard to understanding where the line is to be drawn between thoughts and actions, and raises the all-important question: are those whose sexual interest in children does not go beyond fantasizing a different group of individuals from those who actually abuse children? The answer has profound implications for the effective targeting of finite resources at the people who pose the greater risk to children via computer content. Such understanding is crucial in an area so emotionally charged because it is arguable that the former may need help, whereas the latter may deserve prison. Finally, on the topic of the point at which thoughts turn into actions, consider the example outlined in box 6.4, where behaviours that have changed because of new technologies become misunderstood by (old) law.

Box 6.4 Snapchat and 'sexting'

This case study was reported by the BBC (2015) and involved a 14-year-old boy sending a naked photograph of himself via the smartphone application Snapchat to a girl at his school. Snapchat deletes pictures after 10 seconds, but the recipient managed to save the picture within that period and sent it on to her school friends. The picture was brought to the attention of the school liaison officer and, although no charges were brought, it was officially recorded as a crime and the details of both the sender and recipient placed on a police intelligence database. They could be stored for up to 10 years and disclosed in a criminal records check. If the original sender of the image had been over 18 years of age, the boy would have been the victim of 'revenge porn' and the girl who distributed the image prosecuted. Interviewed by the press, the boy's mother said that her son has been 'humiliated' for being 'at best naive' and, at worst, just being 'a teenager'. What the case identified was that many young people now take part in so-called 'sexting' as a form of flirting

(BBC, 2015). It is a form of behaviour that has become part of 'a new normal' and which requires much more understanding by the older generation and the authorities (Wall, 2017).

Illegal content that is violent, hateful or harmful online

Informational content can violate individuals and social groupings by singling them out as a target for hate and then reinforcing that hate through threats and implied violence. While such activities do not necessarily have an immediate and direct physical manifestation, the victims can, nevertheless, feel the violence of the act and can bear long-term psychological scars as a consequence. Violent content can be expressed directly through hate websites: peddling violent imagery; providing information about the manufacture of drugs, bombs and weapons; offensive email communications through blogsites; and cyber-stalking/grooming in 'public' chat rooms. The use of violent content by offenders is discussed in the next section, and the different ways in which words and images impact upon individuals are discussed later.

Terror materials

As was the case with online sexual materials, digital and networked technologies provide the perfect storm for terrorism. Not only does the technology enable materials to be digitized and accessed or communicated across networks, but by enabling user-driven content it effectively democratizes communications, a quality that is not lost on those who wish to circulate terrorist materials. The internet has emerged as an important tool for terrorists because of the advantages it provides, not least the ability of a few people to influence mass media coverage worldwide. Terrorists can spread messages that intimidate, radicalize, recruit, and can eventually facilitate the carrying out of terrorist attacks – hence, the need to prohibit terrorist materials as computer content to prevent such activities. The more active components of terrorism are discussed later. The advantages of using the internet are that it provides easy access without much, if any, regulation or censorship, because governmental control is usually minimal. Any risk from restrictions that do exist is usually offset against the potentially global audiences, a degree of anonymity and instantaneity during communications for relatively low costs (see Weimann, 2006). As with other forms of illegal materials, the main controversy surrounding the banning of internet content is that it can restrict the freedom of expression of those posting the materials. Such controversy is particularly large where the right to freedom of expression is enshrined in the constitution of a particular country. The issue of prohibiting what are deemed as terrorist materials is especially sensitive because today's terrorists may become tomorrow's political leaders.

Walker and Conway (2015) usefully outline the range of state responses to online terrorism, which include taking down, and place the tactic of removing terror content within the frame of a broader range of counter-terror sanctions. They note that state countermeasures seek to reduce the impact of extreme ideologies via a combination of various tactics. On the one hand, 'positive' measures employ digital engagement and education and provide counter-narratives. On the other hand, 'negative' measures delete or restrict violent extremist online content and legally sanction both its online purveyors and users. They also note that other discretionary state sanctions employed include warning or counselling vulnerable individuals. Alternatively, they may use disruptive countermeasures to ban identified individuals from giving lectures, or even prohibit them from entering the UK and take down extremist websites. Finally, Walker and Conway note that when other softer sanctions fail, offenders can be prosecuted for collecting materials or information downloaded from the internet, or for sending messages, which directly or indirectly incite others into terrorism (Walker and Conway, 2015).

Most jurisdictions have passed some form of legislation prohibiting terrorist materials. Of course, the definition of terrorism can vary, and therefore the content. As was the case with online sexual materials, restrictions on terrorist materials fall under international and national laws.

The European Commission has introduced a series of voluntary and legislative measures and initiatives to help to mitigate the terrorist threat. Working on the EU definition of terrorist content as material that 'solicits someone to commit or to contribute to terrorist offences, or to participate in activities of a terrorist group, incites or advocates terrorist offences, such as by glorification of terrorist acts' (EC, 2021). The 'Regulation to address the dissemination of terrorist content online' built upon previous initiatives[13] and came into effect in June 2022. To strengthen the regulation, the EU Internet Referral Unit in EUROPOL identifies and refers terrorist content to over 300 platforms to take down offensive materials, and it also engages with companies to increase resilience against terrorist propaganda (EC, 2021).

In the UK, the Regulation of Investigatory Powers Act 2000 prohibits terrorist materials. Although terrorism and child sexual abuse materials are already prohibited by law, the UK government is also seeking to strengthen it by bringing the Online Safety Bill into law. The new law extends the list of criminal content to be removed as a priority to include online drug and weapons dealing, people smuggling, revenge porn, fraud, promoting suicide and inciting or controlling prostitution for gain.

Violent imagery / murder video nasties / curiosity viewing

The UK Obscene Publications Acts are not solely restricted to sexually explicit materials and can include materials that represent extreme violence, though cases of non-sexual obscene materials are few in number and may also be dealt with under legislation such as the Video Recordings Act 1984. Networked technology easily lends itself to the distribution of extremely violent imagery, especially in video format. Concerns were voiced during the 1990s about the online distribution of 'snuff movies' – films that purport to depict, sensationally and for the gratification of others, actual deaths, usually of women while performing a sexual act (Harding, 2001).[14] Initially sold illegally as complete movies in video format and later reduced to web video clips, snuff movies are designed to convince viewers that 'they are privy to something rare and exclusive'. FBI investigations in the mid-1990s concluded that snuff movies were likely to be bogus and that the murders depicted in them were staged, a conclusion that is now the conventional wisdom on the subject: 'I've not found one single documented case of a snuff film anywhere in the world. I've been searching for 20 years, talked to hundreds of people. There's plenty of once-removed sightings, but I've never found a credible personality who personally saw one' (Ken

Lanning, FBI Training Academy, cited by McDowell, 1994; also cited in Harding, 2001).

Concerns about violent pornography persisted following the death of a British teacher, Jane Longhurst, in 2003 at the hands of a man who was allegedly obsessed with violent sexual imagery. The case brought the issue to the fore, and in 2006 the UK government announced that it would seek to make the viewing of violent pornography illegal (Home Office, 2006). Following this announcement, a study of violent pornography available online conducted by the BBC concluded that, although the material viewed was extremely convincing, it mainly appeared to be faked (Oliver, 2006), thus opening up the controversy about the impact upon individuals who view violent sexual imagery.

An insight into the impact of non-sexual violent imagery online can be obtained by examining the emergence since the 2003 'Gulf War' of a chilling genre of 'execution' videos that depict the murder of foreign nationals, such as British citizen Ken Bigley in April 2005, who had been kidnapped by Islamic groups based in the Middle East. The recordings were made available through various websites and show the victims being forced to make a humiliating public plea for their lives before being executed in cold blood. Unlike the snuff movies, which were designed to be sold, these execution videos are primarily instruments of cyber-terror because they are intended to further the maker's political agenda, spreading fear and outrage across the victims' communities, while also galvanizing their own supporters. In addition, the recordings subsequently became widely circulated by net users on the internet as a spectacle and a curio.

In his short article, Walker (2004) briefly summarizes the popularity of murder videos as being primarily due to viewers' curiosity: '[a] lot of it's to do with the taboo of seeing stuff we're not supposed to'. This curiosity is excited by the cold and calculating quality of the act and has stirred the rantings of the conspiracy theorists who claim that the videos are faked to serve anti-Muslim interests. So, people watch just to see if it is real (Illuminati News, 2004)! The motivations of the host sites to show these recordings vary. Some use the viewers' curiosity to increase the volume of visitors to their site, while others may further a moral or political agenda either in support of the action or against it. Korean pro-liberation groups, for example, have released video footage of public executions in North Korea to demonstrate the barbarity of the incumbent regime and promote their own cause (CNN, 2005). Alternatively, other sites containing gruesome imagery may actively seek to uphold their right to freedom of expression, especially those located within the US.

Hate speech, including racism and radical politics

There is a degree of academic controversy about the precise meaning of 'hate speech' because of the different actions that it involves, such as hate, bigotry, prejudice, exclusion (see O'Connor, 2003: 62). However, a definition derived from various commonly cited sources is that it is a form of speech that is uttered intentionally to degrade, exclude, intimidate or incite violence or prejudicial action against another person based on their race, ethnicity, national origin, religion, sexual orientation or disability. Online hate speech expresses much the same characteristics, but is exercised online and is therefore informational, networked and global. The explosion of social media outlets has further amplified the spread of misinformation and also the process of individuation (see chapter 3; also Castells (2013) and Rainie and Wellman (2012)). Of key importance to the criminological debate over online hate speech is the point at which the informational content crosses the line between thoughts and action, and when the words become actual threats (Rothman, 2001: 1). This is discussed later.

The internet is host to some very disturbing hate speech, and responses to it vary across jurisdictions. Perhaps one of the most dramatic examples is holocaust denial, as illustrated in the case of *R. v. Zundel* (1992). Zundel, a Canadian, attempted to rewrite Jewish history by denying that the persecution of the Jewish people by the Nazis had ever taken place. Zundel was originally prosecuted in 1988 for 'publishing false news', but his conviction was later overturned on appeal because the false news law was subsequently judged to have contravened the Canadian Charter of Rights. He subsequently moved the offending website to a server in the US, where it came under the protection of stronger freedom of expression laws. Zundel is not alone, and other websites are also devoted to the issue of holocaust denial (see Greenberg, 1997: 673), along with many more directed towards hate speech. In January 2003, a protocol against racism and xenophobic material on the internet was added to the CoE's Convention on Cybercrime (CoE, 2003). Although the US ratified the Convention on Cybercrime in 2006, it is unlikely that this additional protocol will be signed in the near future because it is inconsistent with the US constitutional right to free speech.

Using websites to circulate information used in the organization of harmful action

Websites can be used to organize harmful actions by, for example, announcing details of meetings and gatherings or even identifying specific targets towards which hate should be directed. In the organization of such activities, a range of bodies of law are contravened: notably, public order or conspiracy. Where physical harm occurs, laws protecting the person are invoked. Sometimes referred to as cyber-thuggery,[15] specific examples include the following.

Nuremberg Files   The American Coalition of Life Activists (ACLA), a pro-life group, collected personal information about both doctors who performed abortions and their supporters. It passed this information to an anti-abortionist, Neal Horsley, who loaded it onto his website called 'The Nuremberg Files'. Some of these 'named' individuals were subsequently attacked in a brutal manner and after each attack the authors of the website struck through the names of the dead and highlighted the names of the wounded (Gey, 2000: 541; Maynard, 2001: 41;). In the subsequent court case, *Planned Parenthood v. ACLA* (2001), the issue of thought versus action featured prominently. The court concluded that the tone of the website's language made it easier for the abortion providers to be identified, to the point that it could be seen to encourage the attacks. However, this was not judged to be sufficient to warrant conviction because the actual statements on the website did not mention violence; nor did they specifically threaten the doctors with harm. The statements were judged to be part of a public discourse and therefore not considered to have constituted a threat (Maynard, 2001: 42).

Racist websites (organizational)   Websites may host racist content and also be used to organize groups by recruiting and disseminating information about events. They mostly comprise political and religious extremist groups.

Flash-mobbing and protest groups   Flash-mobbing uses networked communications technologies to organize people spontaneously. It began as a series of fairly surreal, even pointless, stunts to gather people together, such as congregating in a toy store. However, flash-mobbing has since been utilized by those with political agendas to organize spontaneous protest – for example, in some (but not all) of the anti-G8 protests. Although flash-mobbing and protest may have some protection under freedom of expression laws, it is frequently treated with hostility by those with the responsibility for maintaining order.

Criminal gang organization   Criminal gangs are known to use the internet to circulate information about themselves and also to publicize their symbols and achievements. The websites can also be used to organize physical or online gatherings, with the details often deeply hidden within the servers to all but members. In some cases, the information might be hidden by encryption, although such action is more likely to arouse outside interest. The groups involved may include paedophile gangs (Hayward, 1997), software piracy gangs (see 'DrinkorDie'[16] cases: Shenon, 2001; USDOJ, 2002; BBC, 2005d), gangs of football supporters (BBC, 1999b), street gangs (Chicago Crime Commission, 2000)[17] and organized crime gangs (Computing, 2005).

Circulating information about making drugs and weapons

Discussion about crime, its commission and the technology required to achieve it occurs in news groups, internet relay chat forums and blogsites. The topics vary considerably and their potential for influencing individual action is even more contentious than that relating to obscene or violent content. At one end of the spectrum is the circulation of information outlining sophisticated technologies designed to circumnavigate existing infrastructural frameworks.[18] For example, Pryce, the hacker mentioned earlier, stated that he used bulletin boards to get software and gain access to hardware:

> 'I used to get software off the bulletin boards and from one of them I got a "bluebox", which could recreate the various frequencies to get free phone calls', he said. 'I would phone South America and this software would make noises which would make the operator think I had hung up. I could then make calls anywhere in the world for free.' (Ungoed-Thomas, 1998: 1)

At the other end of the spectrum is bomb-talk, which ranges from the circulation of instructions on how to make a bomb or other weaponry to the deliberate targeting of groups with a view to committing a violent act (see Wallace and Mangan, 1996: 153). Perhaps the most vivid example of the latter was the supposed use of the internet by members of various militias in the planning of the Oklahoma bombing (Deflem, 1997: 5) and, more recently, by Richard Reid, the 'shoe bomber' (BBC, 2002). Similarly, the manufacturers of the devices used in the London bombings of 7 July and 21 July 2005 are alleged to have got the recipe for the acetone peroxide-based explosive from the internet. There is, however, some controversy about this claim because, while the formula may be available, the extremely volatile nature of the substance requires specialist expertise in the manufacturing process to stabilize it and prevent a premature explosion. As one of the correspondents to Bruce Schneier's security weblog soberly commented: '[t]rying to make explosives from instructions downloaded from the internet is pretty stupid. Explosives are something you don't generally want to try to make (or even handle) without proper training' (posted 5 August 2005, 9.36 a.m.).[19]

Making weapons from online plans   In 2012, following the advent of the 3D printer, Cody Wilson and Defense Distributed crowd-funded and designed the first viable internet printable firearm – a 'wiki weapon' called 'The Liberator' – and published the plans online. Wilson and colleagues wanted to turn a CAD design into 'an operational gun capable of firing a standard .22 caliber bullet, all in the privacy of their own garage'. Their ambition was primarily proof of concept and they wanted to show it was possible.

> 'We want to show this principle: That a handgun is printable,' says Wilson, a 24-year-old second-year law student at the University of Texas. 'Yo' don't need to be able to put 200 rounds through it . . . It only has to fire once. But even if the design is a little unworkable, it doesn't matter, as long as it has that guarantee of lethality.' (Greenberg, 2012)

The project created considerable media coverage and much public concern over the possibility of a rise in gun crime and the possibility of terrorists smuggling home-made weapons into public places, alongside underage or disqualified owners getting their hands on them. Wilson's gun fired the shot, but not very effectively or reliably, and the concerns died down, mainly because of the ready supply of real weapons in the US (Greenberg, 2012). A decade later, the issue re-emerged. A BBC report found that, while the early printed guns were unreliable single-shot weapons, newer versions are 'credible and viable'. Advances in 3D printing could now make 80 to 90 per cent of the weapon, although the other 10–20 per cent – the barrel and other essential parts – would still have to be made from metal (Vallance, 2022). Yet police are seizing greater numbers of 3D printed weapons, although the numbers are small compared to those for conventional weapons. One of the reasons given for the rise in seizure of printed weapons since 2020 is that difficulties in transporting weapons across borders during the coronavirus pandemic may have contributed to criminals' interest in printed guns. But perhaps more significant is that, 'even if some of the "plastic-type" guns . . . remain relatively unreliable, they still have the power to intimidate; guns . . . are only fired in about 20% of gun crimes' (Squires, quoted by Vallance, 2022).

This reveals once again the need to be able to differentiate between thoughts and actions, and truths and untruths, in assessing risks – a dialectic that characterizes just about all things internet and crime. Also relevant here is the fact that because talk about crime is regarded as speech, it is often given freedom of expression protections, for example under the US Constitution and Canadian Charter of Rights,[20] even though the intent behind the harmful speech might conflict with criminal codes.

Content that contributes to wrongdoing

In contrast to computer content that is a crime to possess, computer content can also contribute to wrongdoing. Such content usually involves circulating misleading information or misinformation online and, as the terms indicate, they respectively mislead and misinform the recipients. They are applied broadly here to describe behaviours that either are crimes, such as stalking, bullying or grooming, or are precursor actions and frame a range of subsequent crimes, such as the frauds, deceptions or extortions outlined in chapter 5 – or, even worse, for example, they help offenders to commit technological domestic abuse, gendered trolling or harassment, doxing,[21] or justify pro-rape groups, etc., or human trafficking, as is the issue in the Andrew Tate case in box 6.5.

Box 6.5 The Andrew Tate case – online misogyny

The case of Andrew Tate illustrates how content can contribute to wrongdoing – more specifically, how the increasing power of the social media influencer can be abused with potential broader societal impacts. Tate is a former kickboxer and social media influencer who became an internet celebrity after being removed from the reality show *Big Brother* after a video was circulated of him hitting a woman with a belt. He subsequently promoted his ultra-masculine, ultra-luxurious (toxic machismo) lifestyle via misogynistic posts on social media – views which are alleged to promote an ideology that has infiltrated British schools and is exerting a toxic influence on male school children (Weale, 2023).

Tate gained many millions of followers, but was suspended by various platforms, a practice which appears to have further stimulated interest in him and his views. Tate was investigated by the UK Crown Prosecution Service between 2015 and 2019, but the CPS declined to prosecute because they considered that there was 'no realistic prospect of a conviction'. In December 2022, he, his brother and others were arrested by Romanian police on suspicion of human trafficking and forming an organized crime group. The group were alleged to have coerced victims into creating pornographic imagery in their webcam studio for sale via pornography social media. They were subsequently charged in June 2023 with rape, human trafficking and forming an organized crime group to sexually exploit women. What is of interest is that the impacts of these technology-driven offences would be felt offline. On the one hand, Tate has promoted misogynistic and generally offensive views; on the other hand, he is alleged to have committed offline crimes which create the imagery that supports that offending. Readers may wish to follow this case and its outcomes.

Circulating misinformation and misleading information online

In a world that relies heavily upon information, misinformation can have a very powerful impact upon opinion and action, especially when it is deliberately used to mislead populations in order to change agendas. The growth of social media and advances in the speed of internet technologies have expanded the reach of those who seek to deliberately misinform others. They have also accelerated the process of 'individuation' outlined by Castells (2013) (explained in chapter 3) which, in a nutshell, helps to make the impact of misinformation even more powerful by creating an environment or echo chamber effect. This not only reinforces individuals' existing beliefs by giving them information that they want to hear, to the exclusion of contrasting viewpoints, but also amplifies or intensifies those beliefs. Views on the actual impact of the echo chamber effect vary on its ability to shape opinion, but they do for example agree that individuals tend to have selective exposure to news sources. This can reflect their worldview and increases the possibility of 'confirmation bias', which occurs when people want a particular idea or concept to be true and, because of selective sources, end up believing it to be true (Heshmat, 2015). An immediate thought here is of the experience after the 2020 US general election when a substantial group of individuals believed and argued that the 2020 election had been lost because it had been rigged and that their party had actually won. A number of websites were reputed to have circulated misinformation, much of which amounted to little more than baseless conspiracy theories. One such website was the 4chan message board which over a decade had become notorious for 'offending, harassing or "triggering" its enemies', who were mainly but 'not exclusively liberals, minorities and establishment Republicans — for its own amusement (i.e. lulz). The Trump movement was the perfect pathway for a wider audience of targets' (Ohlheiser, 2016).

Ohlheiser observed that, although the '4chan vote was not the crucial voting block that swung the election to Trump . . . the belief that 4chan had actually contributed to or straight up caused Trump's win – was everywhere on the boards for most of the night'. A 'little fringe of Internet life made its way repeatedly into the mainstream conversation of the elections' (Ohlheiser, 2016).

It was the set of beliefs circulated by sites like 4chan that arguably contributed to the storming of the Capitol Building on 6 January 2021, despite all evidence indicating that the election result was not faked, and no substantial supporting evidence being given to argue the claim that it was. Despite the 2022/3 public inquiry, the beliefs persisted and are still strong in the lead-up to the 2024 US general election (Wendling and Sardarizadeh, 2022).

At one end of the misinformation spectrum, which shapes thoughts into action, is the spread of malicious gossip or stories which perpetuate various urban legends that intentionally or unintentionally serve to reinforce specific stereotypes. These could be humorous, ironic or made with intent to mislead. Towards the middle of the spectrum are hoax virus announcements or 'gullibility viruses' which deliberately seek to 'socially engineer' and trick individuals into opening an attachment, opening a URL or deleting part of their computer's operating system. Or they may be used as part of a fraud or romance scam (see chapter 5) to encourage an individual to part with money or perform an act. At the far end of the scale is the calculated and distributed circulation of misinformation on a grand scale to shape the broader political agenda (see the section about information warfare in chapter 4).

There are a number of means by which misleading information and misinformation can be circulated: for example, through offensive communications by email, video calls, chatrooms or discussion groups that are intended to upset, bully, stalk or groom individuals.

Offensive communications: emails, chatrooms and blogging

The growth of interactive forms of mass communication online became a vehicle for malfeasants passing off misleading information, and still is. Offensive online communications can take many forms. They can be transmitted via email communications 'spammed' to 'profiled' address lists, or they can be communicated through internet forums such as 4chan, chatrooms or blogsites.

The intensity of offensiveness varies from bullying and blackmail to threats of physical violence.[22] Some idea of the extent of the problem was exposed by a 2006 MSN/YouGov survey, which found that 10 per cent of UK teenagers were victims of online bullying (BBC, 2006b). Some fifteen years later, the UK Office of National Statistics found that one in five children (20%) in England aged 10–15 years old had experienced at least one type of online bullying (ONS, 2020). Moreover, an EU-funded survey of 8,000 young people across Europe found that one in four (25 per cent) had trolled someone online, and one in three had engaged in digital piracy (Milmo, 2022).

Serious offensive online communications are taken very seriously by the law, especially where there is a clear intent to harm or offend the recipient. The following case study of offensive communications under UK law demonstrates the breadth of legislation which covers such acts. Threats to kill tend to demonstrate clear intent and therefore fall under the Offences Against the Person Act 1861 (s. 16). However, emails that are threatening, offensive, indecent or obscene in nature, or deliberately cause annoyance or anxiety, may still constitute an offence under the Telecommunications Act 1984 (s. 43, 1a and 1b) if sufficiently serious in intent. In addition, further offences may be committed under the Malicious Communications Act 1988 (s. 1) or the Obscene Publications Act 1959 (s. 1(2)) if the emails also carry offensive and threatening attachments or embedded obscene pictures. The offending becomes even more serious if a clear intent is displayed through repeat communication by different technologies – for example, if the harassing messages are first sent by email, then followed by phone calls over a relatively short period of time. In such cases, the sender may breach the Protection from Harassment Act 1997 (ss. 1, 2 and 7).

Where the emails are sent to a publicly accessible email list and cause 'harassment, alarm or distress' to the recipients by using words or other visible representation that are threatening, abusive or insulting 'within the hearing or sight of a person', the senders could be breaching the Public Order Act 1986 under either section 4 or 5. Furthermore, if the content and manner of the communication demonstrates the sender's hostility towards the victim's membership, or presumed membership, of a racial group, then they may constitute racially aggravated offences under section 28 of the Crime and Disorder Act 1998. The final type of offensive email is the defamation arising from a libel that seeks to '"vilify a person" and bring that person into "hatred, contempt and ridicule"'.[23] Most libel cases in the UK are brought under civil proceedings; criminal prosecutions brought under the common law are rare because the harms tend to be better covered by other criminal laws.

Chatroom and discussion group communications (stalking and grooming)

Another means of circulating misleading information or misinformation is through chatroom and discussion group communications. Chatrooms are online forums which allow individuals to chat to fellow members in real time. They evolved from the usenet newsgroups (prefixed by 'alt.') into internet relay chat (IRC). The main difference between the two is that chatrooms operate in real time while newsgroups work in chosen time through the posting of messages and responses to those messages. Chatrooms provide, for all involved, a readily accessible peer group with similar interests. They are forums for living out a 'second life' away from everyday routines, giving participants an opportunity to express themselves more freely, communicate with like-minded others and indulge in their fantasies, but are often subjected to policing, or moderation, if acceptable behaviour policies are breached. For younger people, the lure of the chatroom is partly based upon the pragmatics of being able to 'play out without going out'. Chatrooms allow internet users to resolve the tensions of adolescence, namely by enabling them to conform with parental rules while communicating with and making new friends with similar interests. But chatrooms are also clearly demarcated spaces to which young people lay emotional claim through their participation with peers on their own terms and not those of their parents. This 'boundary formation' has led to public concerns about the dangers that younger people face in chatrooms, particularly because of the higher levels of trust they appear to place in their peers with whom they communicate. Not only are there societal concerns about young people's potential exposure to pornographic or other morally dangerous materials, but there are also specific parental concerns about their children being groomed online by individuals (usually adults) who wish to do them harm. Yet, Walker and Bakopoulos (2005) found in their research into patterns of internet usage that young people also expressed surprisingly similar priorities and concerns about online safety to adults: 'In the main they were concerned about security rather than pornography, which they saw as amusing rather than harmful.' This finding may allay some concerns, but it was also found that younger people tended to spend more time in chatrooms than their parents were aware of, thus increasing the potential for stalkers or groomers to establish trust relationships with them.

Chatroom and discussion list communications can be a contributory factor in 'cyber-stalking', which is where individuals become singled out as a target for subsequent harassment because of some characteristic or vulnerability that they have revealed in their online discussions. The key to dealing successfully with cyberstalking lies in being able to decide where to draw the line between the genuine threat and the nuisance. This challenge, and the need to be able to resolve it, became apparent in two early internet cases which, in retrospect, could only loosely be described as examples of stalking. In the renowned Jake Baker case (*United States* v. *Alkhabaz*, 1997) during the mid-1990s, Baker was prosecuted after publishing fantasy rape-torture and snuff stories on the 'alt.sex.stories' newsgroup. In one story called 'Doe', Baker named the victim as one of his fellow students (Wallace and Mangan, 1996: 63). Baker had not stalked the girl in the real sense of surreptitiously tracking his victim; in fact, he had not even contacted her. Moreover, it was later suggested that the girl's real name was only used because one of the syllables in it rhymed with the popular name for the male phallus. Yet, he had caused her and the others who had read the story considerable worry. In the other case, 'Mr Bungle' hijacked fellow characters in a virtual environment called LamdaMoo, 'spoofing' their words and actions and perpetrating 'acts of fictive sexual assault against the virtual reality denizens of LamdaMoo' (MacKinnon, 1997). Although none of the participants in the virtual community believed that actual bodily rape had occurred, some of the participants felt that the 'attack' was beyond fiction and they experienced a violation of their 'cyborg bodies' (see further Dibbell, 1999: 11). While 'Jake Baker' and 'Mr Bungle' brought cyber-stalking to the fore, the growing popularity of real-time internet relay chat quickly gave it a harder edge.

In a 1999 BBC interview, Parry Aftab, founder of CyberAngels (which still operate) and which are based upon the Guardian Angels model, identified three main cyber-stalking scenarios. The first was spouse abuse or revenge following the breakdown of a relationship, where offensive material is sent by email to the former partner's friends and employers. The second was the souring of internet relationships forged in a chatroom. The information shared by two people in better times was subsequently used against one of them by the other, or possibly they each used it against each other: '[p]ictures can be morphed onto pornographic pictures and emailed to employers, postings can be made which make the victim look like she is offering sexual services, giving her telephone number' (BBC, 1999a). In Aftab's third category were those who take pleasure in targeting anyone they can scare, very often children and vulnerable groups in society. At their least harmful, this third group are simply bullies; at their worst, they could be grooming for offline contacts.

Often mistakenly referred to as cyber-stalking (see Finch, 2001), internet grooming is the befriending and manipulation of children or vulnerable people online, usually in chatrooms. Groomers have the deliberate intention of gaining the confidence of their victims so that they can subsequently transfer the relationship into the offline world where the abuse can take place. Internet grooming has been of great concern for many years and with some cause. A search of the BBC news website, for example, using the key words 'internet grooming' throws up about 100 separate cases of relevant investigations or prosecutions. It was the dramatic real-time unfolding of the Studabaker case in 2003–4 which placed the issue of online grooming in the international headlines. Former US Marine Toby Studabaker had carefully groomed a 12-year-old girl in an internet chatroom, and then met up with her in Manchester before flying to Paris with her. The abduction generated considerable media attention and Studabaker was eventually tracked down and arrested in Frankfurt before being extradited to the UK for trial. He was subsequently convicted and sentenced to 4½ years in prison (BBC, 2004b). The Studabaker case not only raised public awareness of the issue of grooming, but also eased the passage of the UK Sexual Offences Act 2003, which strengthened the existing law against grooming.

Of course, the law does not always get it right and its application relies upon an appropriate level of understanding of the issues by both the general public and professionals, as the case study described in box 6.6 illustrates. The case could have been dealt with more compassionately if the parents and practitioners had more understanding of the issues and the young people involved.

Box 6.6 Facebook, flirting and threats to kill

This case study is reminiscent of the Twitter Joke Trial (*DPP* v. *Chambers*)[24] and relates to s. 127 of the Communications Act 2003 and internet threats. In the early 2010s, a teenage girl posted on Facebook a holiday picture of herself coming out of the sea wearing a bikini, with the text, 'What do you think boys?' 'Fxxxing gorgeous', came the reply from her 15-year-old boyfriend's best mate, and a flirty, but witty, banter followed. Jealous, her boyfriend told his best mate to 'back off' and a bad-tempered exchange ensued. The boyfriend angrily said (to his now former best mate) that if he said it again, he would hunt him down and kill him – actually paraphrasing Liam Neeson's speech in the 2008 Pierre Morel-directed film *Taken*. The former best mate's parents saw the exchange and, concerned for his safety, mentioned it to his teacher, who did not know what to do. She referred it to the head of year, and the situation worked its way up the school's management hierarchy to the headmaster, who also did not know what to do. He asked the local police liaison officer, who asked the Crown Prosecution Service for advice. They considered the words 'I will kill you' to be of a menacing character and a clear contravention of s. 127(1a) of the Communications Act 2003. The police arrested the boyfriend, now deemed a potential killer, with force and seized his computers. In the following investigation, the case then started to unravel and fall apart and became very public; the boyfriend was clearly not a killer and when he refused to accept a caution the case was dropped.[25]

Blogging and blogsites

'Blogs', or weblogs, are internet diaries or personal journals shared with an online audience. They emerged in the mid-1990s following advances in web publishing shareware. Diverse in format, blogs are multimedia formats with a combination of text, video and image and sometimes music. Some express the blogger's personal thoughts; others are interactions between blogging friends, or interest or occupational groups. Bloggers discuss topical or political news items or issues, or journeys through illness, religion or even sexual exploration. As with most internet activities, blogging can also be used to express grievances or to enrol public support for a cause – see, for example, 'The Queen of Sky', a former air hostess who was sacked for displaying photographs of herself taken aboard her employer's airplane (Oates, 2004b). Or it can be used as a tool of political resistance, as in the case of the 'Baghdad Blogger' (BBC, 2004c), or as a sort of hybrid newsgroup to share experience of conducting an illicit or criminal activity (hacker blogs) – see, for example, 'Belle de Jour', a self-confessed prostitute who regaled her readers with 'stories of the night' (BBC, 2004d). Before the 2010s, blogs were largely produced by single individuals, then the introduction of multi-author blogs by the news media and also social media helped make blogging a mainstream form of communication and news. Modern bloggers not only produce content, but also develop relationships with their readers, and care about their views and getting attention from them.

The important thing about blogs is that they are more than just the blogger's personal reflections on a range of issues; they bring together communities of individuals who share similar views who, in most cases, can also contribute to the blog. Gaudeul and Peroni found a positive relationship between a blogger's activities, the number of readers and the active involvement via comments (Gaudeul and Peroni, 2010), suggesting that bloggers wishing to gain an audience may be tempted to tell that audience what they want to hear.

Blogs therefore demonstrate considerable potential for transmitting good and bad information very quickly. Most contain weblinks to related information and also to other blogs. Together, this network of blogs, or 'blogroll', forms an interconnected blog environment, a 'blogosphere', in which information and debate can escalate rapidly and virally, creating a frenzy of sometimes heated discussion. According to Wikipedia and other similar sources, these 'blogstorms or swarms' occur when 'a large amount of activity, information and opinion erupts around a particular subject or controversy in the blogosphere'. Although the terminology sounds futuristic, the blogosphere constitutes a distributed network of information-sharing which can provide alternative information flows to the regular media and create a conduit for constructive and informative discussion and debate. However, in rapidly galvanizing opinion, blogging can quickly distort information, often with adverse effects, thus providing potential 'content' manipulators with access to large numbers of internet users, despite the high level of mediation and self-policing by users.

Cyber-bullying

'Cyber-bullying' is a collective term for a range of activities which include cyber-stalking, doxing and trolling (sometimes called 'flaming') using networked communications, most commonly but not exclusively social media. It is 'an aggressive, intentional act or behavior that is carried out by a group or an individual, using electronic forms of contact, repeatedly and over time against a victim who cannot easily defend him or herself' (Moreno, 2014). Importantly, the behaviour of cyber-bullies is to exert power and dominate in order to gain advantage over others for various reasons, very often for self-aggrandizement in the eyes of others, or even themselves.

Cyber-stalking is a type of bullying where offenders use the internet to stalk and harass individuals, groups or even organizations, often relentlessly, for a range of reasons. As with mainstream cyber-bullying, cyber-stalkers seek to dominate others to achieve various goals.

Doxing is the threat to publicly expose personal information of the victim and is a bullying tactic.

Trolling is the practice of intentionally provoking online users with inflammatory messages in order to elicit an emotional response that will disrupt online activities and upset those offline. Disruption rather than gain (as in extortion) seems to be the goal. 'Trolling' is identity-related because it plays upon the ambiguity of identity in a disembodied 'virtual community' and involves identity deception:

> Trolling is a game about identity deception, albeit one that is played without the consent of most of the players. The troll attempts to pass as a legitimate participant, sharing the group's common interests and concerns; the newsgroups members, if they are cognizant of trolls and other identity deceptions, attempt to both distinguish real from trolling postings, and upon judging a poster a troll, make the offending poster leave the group. (Donath, 1998: 43)

Examples of trolling have even resulted in suicide, such as the suicide of Tyler Clementi after his roommate used his webcam to video Clementi kissing another man in order to 'out' him online (Pilkington, 2010). Amanda Todd committed suicide after she was bullied online by an 'internet troll' (Wolf, 2012), and there are many more cases. The Todd case so incensed the internet vigilante group Anonymous that they subsequently revealed online the identity of her tormentor (Swash, 2012). On the subject of death, the UK Data Protection Act 1998 only applies to living people, so the memorial pages of deceased individuals are particularly prone to the posting of upsetting messages or even defacement by trolls. The callousness of such acts leaves most readers dumbfounded, though in her analysis of trolling Whitney Phillips argues that trolls are 'directly reflective of the culture out of which they emerge, immediately complicating knee-jerk condemnations of the entire behavioral category [sic]'. She argues that '[u]ntil the conversation is directed towards the institutional incubators out of which trolling emerges – as opposed to just the trolls themselves – no ground will be gained, and no solutions reached' (see discussion in Phillips, 2012).

Content that is the focus of cybercrime (stealing data, computer content and intellectual property)

The final type of content crime is where the content is the criminal's actual focus for theft or exfiltration. (Such offending includes big data theft, the denial of use of content and also the theft of digital intellectual property; each targets data stored as content on computers (including the cloud) which has value and thus attracts criminal attention, whilst also appearing as a component of other cybercrimes.)

The first type of content that is the focus of cybercrime is the big data collected about the way we use computers. As will be further explained in the next chapter, the data our computers generate about our use of different applications has commercial value to those who wish to develop data products that foretell patterns of consumer behaviour. There is a heavy demand today for big data (see chapter 7) and demand outstrips supply, increasing the value, and such data can be stolen (copied and exfiltrated) and sold on to legitimate ventures. Or it can be processed (see elsewhere in this book) and sold on the dark web through illicit online markets such as AlphaBay, Silk Road, Dream Market, Hydra Market and DarkMarket,[26] to name a few of many, for various criminal purposes, not least as credential sets for initial access to computer systems. These markets are regularly removed by law enforcement but regularly reappear in a different format.

The second type of content is data content, which we use to go about our daily personal or organizational business. This is data whose ownership we often take for granted, but it has added meaning to us when we are either deprived of its use or made aware that it could be released to others – for example, in a ransomware or data extortion attack (see elsewhere in this book). When faced with the permanent loss of data or the shame of personal data being revealed, victims are prepared to pay offenders a ransom demand. The third content-focused crime is the theft of the intellectual property of the content of computers. As mentioned in chapter 5, this content could be the victim's own creations, or copyrighted materials that victims have paid to own or stream. These three types of computer content are drivers for other types of cybercrime and are discussed more substantively in other chapters.

Can content (words and imagery) actually cause harm by turning thoughts into actions?

Of crucial importance to ascertaining the level of risk posed by offensive communications is the ability to differentiate thoughts and actions – words and conduct – in societies which value freedom of expression. It is essential, therefore, to be able to understand the ways in which the words and images that constitute content on the internet impact upon the individual. Do they simply satisfy the viewer's informational or sexual needs or curiosity? Or do they contribute to the erosion of the individual's moral bind by reaffirming and justifying deviant thoughts and then gradually exposing them to more extreme fantasies or imaginary experiences that subsequently become embedded in the individual's psyche as 'normal', thus bridging the mental divide between thoughts and actions?

Neuroscientists argue that words and actions actually shape the structure of our brains, which is one of the reasons why the human race has adapted so well over time to change. As a species, we regulate each other with words – on the one hand, they could be compliments, and on the other, constructive or destructive criticism (Barrett, 2021). From a sociological perspective, the main theoretical push towards understanding the power of words has been 'speech act theory' (Austin, 1962; Searle, 1969), though not within the context of crime. Only a few, most significantly Matsuda et al. (1993), have specifically sought to theorize and understand 'words that wound', and speech act theory has now been applied to understanding pornography (Thurley, 2005) and to the study of cybercrimes (Williams, 2001, 2006).

With some variations over time, speech act theory distinguishes between illocutionary and perlocutionary acts of speech. Illocutionary speech acts perform an act: for example, when a police officer says 'I arrest you . . .', a legal process is invoked. Perlocutionary speech acts, on the other hand, result in actions that can be very different to the words spoken, such as when a person is being persuaded to do something that subsequently leads to an action. In practice, however, the distinction is not so easy to make because speech types are not so easily disaggregated. In fact, both actions are 'performatives' which may operate simultaneously. But we can use this theory to deconstruct acts of cybercrime such as phishing. Phishers firstly perform a locutionary act by sending an email in which they present themselves to their victim as legitimate by displaying the official symbols and signs, such as a credible letter using official bank formatting and logos. Once the letter has gained the recipient's attention, then the wording – the illocutionary act – which uses the language of authority (e.g., bank speak), employs perlocutionary tactics to persuade and instruct them to comply with the request to reconfirm their personal information and financial details on the phisher's website.

Similarly, in the debate over the impact of pornography, speech act theory has usefully illuminated the discussion about the impact of pornographic text. A number of authors, including MacKinnon (1993), Langdon (1993) and Stark (1997), have argued that pornography is a performative utterance. This is because the locutionary, perlocutionary and illocutionary acts, though separate and simultaneous, are necessary for an utterance to be properly considered to be performative. 'The medium of presentation is the locutionary act, the reiteration of the subordination of women and sexual arousal is the perlocutionary act, and most importantly, assent to, legitimization of, and depiction of the subordination of women is the illocutionary act' (Thurley, 2005).

However, Thurley observes that MacKinnon and Langdon employ a very narrow definition of pornography which focuses only upon erotic material that subordinates women. Were they to broaden their definition, then the illocutionary act would disappear, refuting the argument that pornography is performative. This form of critique challenges the line of argument that led to the passing of the short-lived Communications Decency Act 1996 in the US (see Heins, 2001a, 2001b) by highlighting the broader range of expression found in pornography. Speech act theory can then provide a tool for analysing online communications in chatrooms and discussion lists, as well as blogging, to identify the words that wound.

Conclusions

This chapter has explored patterns of offending relating to the three distinct areas of content, which, respectively, is illegal, can facilitate wrongdoing and is a driver for wrongdoing.

It has demonstrated the breadth of these patterns and also the seriousness of their intent. Just because offending behaviours take place online does not mean that they are trivial or less serious. But the impacts of words and imagery are much more subtle than many of the grander theories that draw upon relationships between variables. Words and images involve a delicate interplay between thoughts and actions, and some have the capability to wound while others do not. This point was only too clear in the cases of Jake Baker and 'Mr Bungle' described earlier. Online personal contact was absent in these cases, so the words and mental images became all the more important. Applying Austin's speech act theory to the 'Mr Bungle' case, Powers (2003) argues that it 'is possible to have real moral wrongs in virtual communities . . . [and that] people can act in virtual communities in ways that both establish practices and moral expectations and warrant strong identifications between themselves and their online identities'. Williams (2001) made this point more forcefully by stating that most types of abuse online are manifested textually and the reliance by internet users on that same text to create and maintain their identities online makes them all the more psychologically vulnerable to textual attacks. 'The notion that "real" and "virtual" phenomena are inexorably connected indicates that these online abusive acts affect "actual" lives. The ability for online injurious illocutions to convey physical violence in text affords them "extraperformative muscle", where "traditional" forms of violence are re-engineered to function online' (Williams, 2001: 164).

So, not only do online words (that form content) have the capability to victimize and wound, but their effects are intensified when the online medium communicates via text and through image, thus highlighting the need to be able to assess the risk that the informational content poses to the individual (see, further, Balkin, 2004). This issue will become more relevant and pressing as new and diverse forums for communication emerge that lay participants open to new online risks.

This conveniently brings us to the next chapter, on cybercrime futures and how criminal activity online continues to adapt and change.

Some discussion questions based upon this chapter

What are the methods for identifying obscene materials online? Do you think they could be improved at all?

Where in cybercrime typology would you place interpersonal harms facilitated by cyberspace, such as image-based sexual abuse, technological domestic abuse, gendered trolling and harassment, doxing, pro-rape groups, etc. Are they cybercrime using, or in, the machine?

Why is data theft such a potentially serious crime? Explain your thinking process.

Can content actually harm individuals? Discuss with regard to obscene, violent, hateful or harmful content.

Further Reading Both the volume and depth of computer content crimes are expanding along with social media platform developments, and cybercrimes in the machine are becoming a vibrant and interesting field of study. Students and researchers who wish to further their study in this field are recommended (after first checking the titles for the suitability of their area of study) to start by exploring the following texts: Quayle and Taylor (2002); Taylor and Quayle (2003); Gillespie (2015); Williams et al. (2020).

7 The Cybercrime Ecosystem

How is the organization of criminal activity continuing to change in the information age?

Chapter contents and key points

The new technological facilitators changing cybercrime

- Cloud technologies
- The Internet of Things
- Social media networks
- Cryptocurrencies
- Datafication

The emerging cybercrime ecosystem in practice

- The various stages of a ransomware attack, showing the different functions and functionaries

The (re)organization of cybercrime and the new faces of organized crime online: the facilitators and enablers of the cybercrime ecosystem

- Phishers and infiltration brokers
- Crimeware-as-a-service brokers
- Forum brokers
- Darkmarketeers
- Databrokers
- Bulletproof hosters
- Crime IT services brokers
- Monetizers
- Cybercrime consultants

Chapter at a glance   *This chapter explores how criminal activity online is continuing to change in the information age by looking at how offenders increased scalability and sustainability in levels of cybercrime by evolving a supply chain of essential specialist skill sets that eventually became a cybercrime ecosystem.[1] By using ransomware and DDoS as examples, it becomes clear in the explorations of cybercrimes against, using and in the machine that each type of cybercrime has, in different ways, become increasingly automated by a combination of new attack vectors, technological procedures and skill sets to accompany them. The cybercrime 'issue' is no longer just a cybercrime, but also includes the processes which enable the cybercrime to take place.*

Introduction

Digital and networked technologies have both rationalized the criminal process and provided new opportunities for cybercrime. The technological advantages for crime are in terms of scale, temporality and distance. In other words, cybercrimes can, in theory, be achieved in volume, instantly and globally by one person. However, over the past two decades, offenders have realized that this possibility was hard to carry out successfully because of the increased complexity of the tasks involved, and also because of the increased risk of getting caught as cybersecurity and law enforcement techniques improved. Therefore, to achieve the scaling up of crime and increase its yield while sustaining the longevity of the criminal career or the organization, the cybercrime act had to be separated and specialized, which is what has happened. In the first edition of this book, the emergence of a new generation of cybercrime was predicted to rise as the automation of cybercrimes developed via this deskilling process (outlined earlier in chapter 2). This prediction not only came true, but in the intervening 15 years it has been superseded by a further generation of cybercrime which exists in the form of the ecosystem that exists to support offending.

The old cybercrime hacking 'technology', which combined high-level technical programming skills with expert social knowledge of communications and financial systems to enable one offender to commit the whole crime, has effectively 'disappeared'. New hacking technologies have, by comparison, replaced the old skills with purposefully designed applications which perform set functions. Their operation is now fairly intuitive and offenders no longer require the specialist programming skills they once did. Furthermore, there has also been both a drop in the cost, and an increase in the availability, of these technologies. This has dramatically reduced the start-up costs of crime, thus increasing the level of incentive, especially with the advent of cloud technologies.

The first section of this chapter briefly looks at the technological facilitators that have underpinned changes in cybercrime over the past two decades, and highlights the main changes. The second section explores the reorganization of cybercrime and identifies the new criminal actors who have entered the field to facilitate cybercrime. The third section describes the cybercrime ecosystem in practice, then follows the example of ransomware to illustrate it.

The new technological facilitators changing cybercrime

Various technological facilitators have driven changes in cybercrime over the past two decades. Cloud technologies, the Internet of Things, social media networks, cryptocurrency, and datafication (the importance of data) have facilitated important changes in both cybercrime and the ways in which it is organized. Each has created new 'affordances' and opportunities for (cyber)criminal behaviour.

Cloud technologies

Cloud technologies are a form of distributed computing which combines systems and their storage, and provides ways of accessing programmes and data across the internet. They join together a range of resources to create a 'cloud', a virtual space of almost limitless size and way beyond the capacity of a single computer drive. They have greatly increased the functionality of the internet. In addition to limitless storage capacity, cloud technologies also provide greater computing capacity, increasing the scalability of operations. This provides more capacity for collaborations between users at a lower cost. Moreover, if a system failed or data was deleted or destroyed, then the system could be recovered entirely.

The frequently used term 'cloud' is actually a distracting misnomer that obfuscates attempts to systematically understand the impact of the cloud technologies, which have driven services that provide 'on-demand' computing resources with increasing effect since the mid-2000s. Moreover, 'cloud' lacks the conceptual clarification needed to understand the implications of cloud technologies upon criminal behaviour, crime analysis and also law enforcement. Many commentators refer to 'the cloud' as a 'thing', an object, whereas others see it as simply a technological method of increasing computer storage and power. Yet others deny its very existence. 'Cloud technologies', the preferred descriptor, have impacted upon computing by *increasing power* and *storage* and delivering large-scale computing *much cheaper* and *on demand*.

All of the above are qualities that have not been lost on offenders, much to the frustration of law enforcement officers. As a consequence, cloud technologies have also impacted upon criminal behaviour online by *increasing computing power*, *increasing storage capacity* and *reducing the cost of computing power*. This means that (cyber)criminals can commit a larger volume of more complex crimes at a reduced cost per victimization. They make crime more efficient in exactly the same ways in which they make businesses and organizations more efficient. So, cloud technologies are yet another form of force multiplier that help to facilitate 'the Internet of Things', which themselves greatly increase the number of devices that can be accessed by the internet and also potentially be exploited by criminals.

As stated earlier, cloud technologies both facilitate and enable cloud cybercrimes (cloud crime). They facilitate cloud crimes via botnets, crimeware-as-a-service and also ancillary procedures such as password decryption, which requires the massive computing power that only cloud technologies can bring to the table. Cloud technologies also greatly escalate the scale of DDoS attacks, frauds and deception through spam transmission, and even the theft of complete clouds (mass data storage facilities). In a nutshell, the difference is that networked and digital technologies meant, it will be recalled from earlier, that criminals no longer needed to commit a high-risk $50 million robbery when they could commit 50 million low-risk $1 robberies using a networked computer. The changes in scalability that cloud technologies afford now enable the same criminals to commit 50 billion robberies of 0.1 cent, to achieve a greater yield and reduce the risk of prosecution even further.

The Internet of Things

The 'internet of things' (IoT) is, like 'the cloud', something of a misnomer. Rather than being a thing, it is an umbrella term that describes the proliferation of devices (or things) that now either connect directly to the internet or to an intranet or Bluetooth. These devices monitor, at an individual level, people themselves (e.g., diabetic monitors), their possessions (smartphones, household security) and the processes that control them (household energy control and the 'smart home'). At an organizational level, the devices may include the many thousands of sensors that can help a modern business or organization monitor its premises, processes and performance to operate efficiently. The list of types of devices is almost endless and is still growing. Importantly, each sensor (device) increases the potential vulnerability for the introducing of malicious software. It also increases the flow of data, much of which is sensitive to the individual or to an organization and which can be used by offenders in a criminal action.

Social media networks

Social media networks are a range of thousands of social networking services situated globally, which allow members to share information, opinion and content. Many platforms enable services which allow members to join a community; sometimes membership is open, other times it is closed and based upon some form of qualification, such as a recommendation from a trusted user or a characteristic which allows members to contribute to the community. There are billions of members of social network communities all over the world. The advantages are not lost on offenders, who can use membership to join communities to meet individuals with a view either to defrauding them or to extorting money from them, as is found with romance scams (Buchanan and Whitty, 2014). Alternatively, the aim may be to use the platforms to spread hate against an individual or a community (see Matamoros-Fernández and Farkas, 2022). As a consequence, there has been a massive rise in the number of social media network-facilitated hate crimes and frauds since their inception.

Cryptocurrencies

Cryptocurrencies are digital currencies that function as a form of decentralized exchange over computer networks. Because they use decentralized methods, usually a public ledger system, to publicly verify that the parties involved in the exchange possess the relevant funds, cryptocurrencies are not reliant upon a centralized authority such as a banking system (McDonald, 2023). They simultaneously provide convenience to users and threaten the established interests of the older institutions in the finance sector. Although cryptocurrencies have existed in one form or another for a number of decades, Bitcoin has become the most popular cryptocurrency. Founded in 2008 by the mysterious Satoshi Nakamoto (because his, her or their identity is unknown) and trading from 2009, transactions are verified through the blockchain. As with the other recent transformative technologies (the cloud, Internet of Things, social media networks), the economic advantages of cryptocurrencies are not lost on offenders. They are an 'affordance', an object or technology that creates a possibility for (rational) action – in this case, cybercrime. They provide a technological opportunity that invokes a social or emotional response which creates a 'perception' (of low risk, thrill/fun, gain) that drives offenders' rational action and transforms criminal behaviour (Goldsmith and Wall, 2022).

Cryptocurrencies facilitate criminal activity online by providing offenders with a relatively easy way of obtaining and extracting the proceeds from their cybercrimes.

They are quick to use, they are relatively anonymous, they can be easily used across physical boundaries, they are not subject to direct governance (guardianship). Furthermore, they are also risky yet fun and provide 'sneaky thrills' (Matza, 1964), plus, whilst they carry some risk, they do yield proceeds to the offender.

Although the perceived anonymity of transactions online is largely a fallacy, because those cryptocurrencies which use a blockchain, such as Bitcoin, are fairly transparent (others such as Monero are more private), offenders are advantaged by the time lag caused by the disparity between the speed at which offenders can use and remove cryptocurrency and the speed at which investigators can freeze and seize the accounts (wallets) of known offenders (see figure 7.1 for the increase in cryptocrimes).

Drawing upon the transformation thesis mentioned earlier, whereby the transforming impact of technology is understood (imagined) by what remains when it is removed, the new forms of offending facilitated by cryptocurrency can be separated into three familiar groups – cryptocurrency-assisted, cryptocurrency-enabled and cryptocurrency-dependent.

Cryptocurrency-assisted crimes are payments made in online markets, or elsewhere, for illegal goods or services, such as drugs (Hutchings and Holt, 2015). Although the payment is made online, the physical products are often posted to the client by the vendor. These payments are assisted by cryptocurrency and if the cryptocurrency was removed as the exchange medium, then the payment would still take place by other payment means. Also included in this category would be crypto-scams, such as OneCoin (see box 7.1), where the cryptocurrency is used by fraudsters to lure victims to defraud, although it could be argued that these are mainly Ponzi frauds, and if the cryptocurrency was not present, then the frauds would be organized around some other object.

Cryptocurrency-enabled crimes, in contrast to cryptocurrency-assisted crime, take advantage of the globalized qualities of cryptocurrencies. They include not only the formation of dark-web markets which host sales, but also the transactions that take place on them for illegal goods and services sold on the darkmarkets, such as ransomware and RaaS (ransomware-as-a-service), DDoS stressers and the like. Also included are the formation of grey-area cryptocurrency exchanges which manage stolen cryptocurrency.

Cryptocurrency-dependent crimes focus upon cryptocurrency as the actual object of the cybercrime, in comparison to crypto-enabled crimes. Such crimes include cryptojacking, coinmixing (bitmixers and tumblers before being turned into fiat monies) and exchange hacks. If the cryptocurrency technologies were removed, then the cryptocrimes would not be able to take place.

Box 7.1 The OneCoin scam

In 2016, OneCoin, the alleged 'Bitcoin Killer', attracted billions of dollars in investments globally. Yet the scheme was a scam as OneCoin did not exist in a viable form, it had no blockchain and was intended to steal money from investors. The scam was eventually exposed, and organizer Dr Ruja Ignatova, the self-titled 'The CryptoQueen', disappeared along with the money (BBC, 2019).

The annual rise in the number of cryptocrimes is illustrated in figure 7.1.

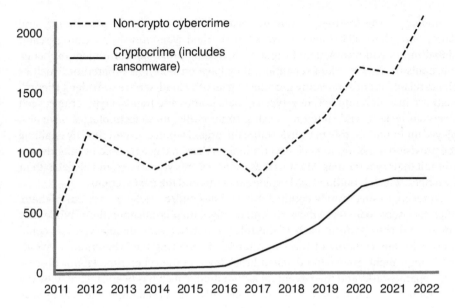

Figure 7.1 The annual rise in the number of cryptocrimes.
Source: based upon 18,000 reports of cybercrime events from author's own database.

Datafication

One of the impacts of cloud technologies and the Internet of Things has been a massive increase in the creation and flow of data, not to mention the rise in its value on the open market. At one end of the spectrum lies the 'big data' phenomenon, whereby there exists a massive (legitimate) market for big data. This data mainly comprises the usage data generated by new cloud technologies, IoTs, social network services and also the many other apps that now exist. This data can be professionally processed to increase the statistical knowledge of usage patterns, including retail and other social phenomena, and also its overall commercial value. 'Big data is the new oil' (Palmer, 2006): data, like oil, cannot be used unless it is refined into valuable products that create profit (Wall, 2018).

At the other end of the spectrum (data market), offenders can use stolen data in many ways, not least using analysed patterns of consumption to identify victim vulnerabilities. More realistically, the stolen data sets are most often sold on via the dark web (Hutchings and Holt, 2015), including users' information on healthcare, tax and insurance. These data sets can be (and are) processed for criminal purposes, such as fraud. See Porcedda and Wall (2019, 2021) for a discussion of the cascading of data from upstream data thefts to enabling further crimes downstream.

The emerging cybercrime ecosystem in practice

Three decades since the birth of the internet, the cybersecurity threat landscape has changed considerably as networked technologies have progressively transformed the way that online crime is organized. The new technologies outlined earlier (new cloud technologies, the Internet of Things, social media networks, cryptocurrency and datafication) have all in their own ways transformed cybercrime by providing greater globalization and transactional capacity, including providing convenient exchange mechanisms. At the risk of repetition, they have created new cybercrimes such as cloud-related crimes (ransomware affecting all of a cloud-service provider's clients), malware insertion into IoT, new types of hate crimes and frauds, cryptocrimes such as crypto-jacking, and stolen data sales. Importantly, these technologies have also played an important role in transforming the organization of cybercrime by enabling the provision of essential specialist criminal services that can be used by offenders to commit their cybercrimes. Many of these services are cybercrimes and illegal in their own right, which is outlined and explained in this and the next sections.

To recap, to successfully conduct cybercrimes and/or make money out of them, offenders need to increase the scale and depth of their crime operations. While they could (and can) perform each of the roles in a cybercrime themselves, few could do so with any certainty of success in terms of achieving the cybercrime or avoiding being caught. Hence the detailed breakdown of the cybercrime labour process into separate tasks and their eventual automation, which has been facilitated by the developments in technology outlined earlier. This is the deskilling and reskilling cycle previously discussed in earlier chapters. It is best explained by outlining and building upon the analysis of the various stages of a ransomware attack as referred to in chapter 4, to illustrate both the different functions and the functionaries (actors).

The various stages of a ransomware attack, showing the different functions and functionaries

Stage 1 – Reconnaissance of potential victims   The first stage of the attack is the reconnaissance of potential victims and identification of access points to networks. Knowledge is gathered about whether an organization is technologically vulnerable, socially vulnerable and also worth the effort and costs of attacking. A technological vulnerability may include an organization's network weakness, such as a zero-day exploit[2] or an unpatched operating system, which can be subsequently exploited. The attackers also look for vulnerable individuals within organizations who can be engaged with or manipulated, tricked or coerced (socially engineered) into complying. Such vulnerability may even be as simple as whether or not they reply and engage in conversation. Finally, since the costs of an attack to the attacker are very high, they identify the best victims to target by looking at weak sectors and organizations to maximize their proceeds whilst also reducing their risk. They tend to look for vulnerable companies that have a sufficiently high turnover to pay a large ransom and take out a cyber-insurance policy, but are not so large as to employ, or outsource to, a sophisticated cybersecurity department. The EMPHASIS project calculated (for this book) that almost two-thirds of the organizational victims fell into the small to medium-sized enterprise band, whereas the remainder ranged in smaller numbers from micro to massive organizations.[3] The attackers may conduct the reconnaissance work themselves or, as is increasingly the case, they may take advice from a ransomware consultant who will advise them as to which 'initial access broker' to approach via one of the forums or darkmarket sites. The 'initial access brokers' are specialists who compile access information and sell it on the various darkmarkets on the ToR (the onion router) network (a non-searchable part of the internet, see Hutchings and Holt, 2015; Cimpanu, 2020; Usman, 2020; Intel 471, 2020; FBI, 2021).

Stage 2 – Gaining initial access to the victim's network   The second stage of a ransomware attack is gaining initial access to the victim's network and infiltrating it by applying the access credentials bought or rented on advice via a forum or dark-market site. This data may typically be bought by an affiliate of a ransomware group who is trusted by the ransomware operators to use their ransomware for a fee or commission. Alternatively, they may use 'freebies', which are free access data made available (for various reasons) on the internet (ReliaQuest, 2021) – however, they are regarded as not very effective. The most important change in recent years is that it is highly unlikely today that the actual attackers will perform a phishing operation themselves as they used to do. Rather, they buy credentials from an 'initial access broker' who will have pre-assembled different types of credential data bought from 'phishers'.

Phishing for credentials involves tricking users into revealing their network access credentials or giving data that can be used to access or develop an access profile. Phishing tends to take place at lower and higher levels of data access. At the lower level, phishing starts off as a general data hunt, an indiscriminate cyber-dependent crime to get individuals to respond with some data – even a rejection shows the email is live. This data is either bought by attackers to gain low-level initial access to individuals' accounts in order to access an organization, or it may be further developed to increase its value. The information of those who respond to phishing attempts will be filtered by data specialists and classified in terms of its usability, to provide system access credentials which are then sold online as off-the-shelf live access credentials. Initial access can enable attackers to enter a system – for example, to encourage a target victim within to allow the attacker into the network via RDP methods. Or they may be used as the basis for a 'big game hunt' (or spear phishing) to target a key manager or officer within an organization in order to steal, or deceive them out of, their privileged access login credentials. Group-IB (2021) found that in 2020 phishing had been overtaken as the main means of breaking into networks by RDP credentials, followed by phishing and then exploiting public-facing applications such as Citrix, WebLogic, VPN servers or Microsoft Exchange (Group-IB, 2021).

KELA analysed 250 initial network access credential sets on sale by initial-access databrokers in Q4 2020 and found that, although the aggregate price was $1.2 million and 14 per cent of those were listed as sold, they were sold for $133,900, just over 10 per cent of the initial price (Kivilevich, 2021). Access credentials to a medium-sized company sold for as little as $1,500–$2,000, against an overall average price of $6,684 for larger companies (a 26 per cent rise from Q3). KELA argue, however, that some initial-access brokers used sales forums to showcase the types of access credentials they possessed in order to attract partners to become affiliates and work for a percentage return. So, the big money lies in the off-the-shelf access credentials, such as the RDP, VPN-based, remote code execution exploits and Citrix products offered by brokers through intermediaries (Kivilevich, 2021).

Illegal darkmarkets located on ToR operate like most online marketplaces, with a trusted payment system (in cryptocurrency, rather than via PayPal) and, importantly, a reputational management system where buyers rate the vendors to develop the

Table 7.1 The individual selling value of stolen credentials

Data type	Item being sold	Minimum price	Item being sold	Maximum Price
Credit card data	Walmart account with credit card attached	$5	Credit card details, account balance up to $5,000	$110
Payment processing services	Stolen PayPal account details, minimum $1,000 balance	$10	ING bank account logins (verified account)	$4,255
Crypto accounts	Paxful.com verified account – level 1	$20	N26 verified account (Germany)	$2,650
Social media	Spotify followers × 1,000	$1	Hacked Gmail account	$60
Hacked services	Netflix 4K 1 year	$1	Airbnb.com verified account	$300
Forged documents – scans	US business cheque templates	$8	Alberta CA driver's license (scan)	$140
Forged documents – physical	US driver's license (avg.)	$150	Maltese passport	$4,000
Email database dumps	2.4 million Canada emails	$100	10 million USA email addresses	$120
Malware	Global, low-quality, slow-speed, low success rate, per 1,000 installs	$35	Premium-quality, per 1,000	$4,500
DDoS attacks	Unprotected website, 10–50k requests per second, 1 hour	$10	Unprotected website, 10–50k requests per second, 1 month	$750

Source: adapted from the *PRIVACY Affairs* 'Dark Web Price Index 2023' (see Zoltan, 2023)

buyer's trust in the system. Table 7.1 illustrates the price range for different items of data available on the dark web. It summarizes data from the PRIVACY Affairs Dark Web Price Index (Zoltan, 2023) which publishes the contemporary prices of individual data.[4] For each category, the lowest and highest value items are contrasted. The table illustrates not only the different values of data, but, as expected, verified credentials carry more value than those that are non-verified. Also, the price varies according to what the data will do, for example, a Maltese passport at $4,000 is worth much more than a Walmart account with credit card attached at $5.

Table 7.1 also shows that, for fairly low costs, all of the basic data required to obtain initial access to a network can be acquired. This includes databases of emails, access to malware, access to hacked services, access to social media networks, even access to forged documents and financial information which can help to prove authenticity. Digital Shadows (2020) found that, in contrast to the lower access credentials, the higher-end credentials which gave access to 'organizations' key systems [were] being sold at a significant premium', with advertisements selling domain administrator access to the highest bidder for up to $140,000 (however, the average price paid was $3,139).

Stage 3 – Escalating computing access privileges in the system   The third stage is where attackers (usually the 'affiliates') get into a network and use their credentials to increase their user privileges and move laterally across it. They further infiltrate the victim's computing system to establish an independent position within it – for example, establishing a new username to hide initial access and then escalating their computing access privileges to give them control. As with information gained from earlier stages, these advanced credentials may also be sold on or developed by the attacker (the affiliate).

Once in the system, they become established and even familiar to other users – perhaps by grooming members of the IT helpdesk, giving workers genuine IT advice, helping people with their jobs. Once known in a system, they move laterally across it to further escalate their user privileges to admin status (the highest). They may even retain these credentials for future attack after this one has been completed and the victim has recovered. Various software tools exist to help hackers navigate through systems, which are usually adapted (weaponized) from proprietary brands. Cobalt Strike, for example, is a paid-for command-and-control suite which combines a collection of threat emulation tools designed to be used for cybersecurity purposes. It also has been used in a weaponized form by criminal hackers. Cisco Talos, for example, found that Cobalt Strike 'accounted for 66 per cent of all ransomware attacks [that] Cisco Talos Incident Response responded to this [Q3 2020] quarter' (Corfield, 2020). Cybersecurity researchers at SentinelOne (reported by Ilascu, 2020) explored the 'activity observed from logs on a Cobalt Strike server that TrickBot (botnet) used to profile networks and systems'. They found that, once the attackers became interested in a compromised network, they used various sophisticated (legitimate) off-the-shelf software programs to move across it. This demonstrates how adaptive attackers have become and also the range of professional routines and techniques they use to infiltrate and develop a hold over an operating system.

Stage 4 – Identifying and exfiltrating key organizational data that will cause most pain when taken   The fourth stage is the identification of the key organizational data to steal. Once inside a company's systems, attackers search through company data, emails or even cyber-insurance policies to decide upon which is the victim's most precious data, especially commercially sensitive business data in the form of personal details of employees, suppliers or clients – data that will cause the victim the most financial pain when taken. They will also use some of the financial information to ascertain the level of the ransom to be demanded: 'Sometimes they know how much that customer is losing per day by not being able to operate' (Vincent LaRocca, CEO CyberSecOp, cited by Murphy, 2021). This is a time-consuming process and attackers have been known to spend on average about two weeks inside a compromised network before encrypting the data (Ilascu, 2021), but other non-RaaS attackers can spend up to a year or more inside. Once the key organizational data and its location have been identified, it is exfiltrated.

Stage 5 –Installing ransomware and timing the encryption process to start   The fifth stage is the installation of the ransomware (malware) and timing it to begin the encryption process at a later date, often a time when the organization's security is at its weakest and the encryption can work its way through the system, such as the beginning of a long weekend or a public holiday period (Connolly and Wall, 2019).

Stage 6 – Naming and shaming victims and levying the ransom demand   Once the ransomware encryption has been activated, the attackers (affiliate) will use the ransomware brand-specific leak-site provided by the operators as part of the package to publicly name and shame the victim. In so doing, they will also levy the ransom demand, the amount of which is based upon the attackers' calculations of the organization's worth (see earlier). The attackers will usually list the victim and provide some evidence of the attack, such as a small example of data, but warn that more data will be revealed if the payment deadlines are not met. They may even threaten to begin to auction it off.

After encryption, and to encourage payment negotiations, some ransomware groups will also bombard their victims with DDoS attacks to hinder attempts to restore functionality to their systems (Abrams, 2021). Other groups also use other media, such as Facebook advertisements (e.g., RagnarLocker). To further increase the victim's pain, some attackers, such as the (now defunct) REvil ransomware group, announce that they are using VoIP to contact journalists and also their victim's business partners to inform them of their victimization.

Stage 7 – Payment of the ransom demand in cryptocurrency   Ransom payment amounts in cryptocurrency will have been set by a 'ransomware consultant' who bases the sum on an estimate of the victim's worth. This estimation is made either by subscribing to and consulting online registers of businesses which detail their worth, or from information garnered during infiltration and lateral movement across the victim's network; such information would include the existence of cyber-insurance policies. Victims are usually given precise instructions in the ransom note about their attack, how to pay the ransom and the consequences of not paying. Most ransom demands are in Bitcoin because of its ease of use and partial transnational anonymity (see earlier). In the early days of ransomware, when individuals were the prime focus of attacks, ransomware attackers would even offer a helpdesk service, very often outsourced to a legitimate call centre, where victims could ring to get advice on how to buy Bitcoin and make the payment to the attacker's Bitcoin wallet. The use of Bitcoin as the staple currency of cybercrime, and especially ransomware, has arguably driven up its market price to further advantage the attackers (Jareth, 2019).

If the victim is insured, their cyber-insurance company will often bring in a cyber-security service to help to mitigate the attack. Cyber-insurance companies, according to reports, are known to favour payment of the demands to get the organization operating again as quickly as possible. They often bring in a cyber-negotiator who will estimate what can be recovered from back-ups and then work out costs of recovery and loss, whilst also drawing upon their understanding of the previous practice of the particular ransomware gang demanding the ransom. One negotiation company, CyberSecOp, has claimed that they 'can reduce a ransom by 40–50 per cent on average' (Murphy, 2021). Interestingly, research by Chainalysis (2023) found a downturn in ransomware payments during 2022 as more victims were refusing to pay the demands, presumably mitigating the impact of the attack in other ways.

The ransomware negotiator is an entirely new role in cybercrime and involves contacting and reasoning with attackers, whilst protecting their anonymity, to get them to accept a lower payment than demanded. Tanriverdi et al. (2020) found that it is a role that demands judgement and very quick thinking in order to reduce the ransom demand. In one specific negation, they found that the negotiator tried to negotiate the ransom price down by explaining that the company only had limited resources, but the attackers were unsympathetic and immediately presented the negotiator with the company balance sheet and corporate insurance policy (which did not cover a ransom). It was only when they realized that 'real' money was on the table that they negotiated a price (Tanriverdi et al., 2020).

Although it is a lucrative occupation, the negotiators' position is also extremely vulnerable and requires due diligence to be undertaken with regard to ransomware groups before making any payments – especially to ensure they are not included on a US economic sanction which would result in severe penalties: 'One reason a lot of the boutique [Negotiation] shops shot up is that the big publicly listed companies do not want the regulatory exposure of whether they are properly conducting due diligence on the Ofac [Office of Foreign Assets Control] issues' (Murphy, 2021). The negotiation process also raises interesting questions and concerns about whether cyber-insurance is actively encouraging ransomware by effectively ensuring that payments will be made (Scroxton, 2021).

Stage 8 – Monetizing the crime   Once the ransom has been paid, offenders need to convert it from cryptocurrency into fiat (government-issued) money. The victim will have paid the ransom in cryptocurrency (usually Bitcoin) into the attackers' specified wallet. In order to extract the cryptocurrency and turn it into fiat money, the attackers will either directly use a cryptocurrency exchange, or more likely employ a professional money broker (for a fee) to launder via bitmixers and tumblers (which quickly move cryptocurrency from one type to another) and cash out the cryptocurrency via a 'tame' cryptocurrency exchange. To obtain fiat currency, the monetizers often sub-employ money mules who lend out the use of their bank accounts in exchange for a fee.

Stage 9 – Post-crime 'getting away' with it   The final part of the attack relates to the offenders actually getting away with the crime, which is a different ball game. Once the attackers have received their fiat money, they must invest it in such a way that it avoids the banks' suspicious transactions radar. Post-crime is possibly the stage which carries most risk for the offender. For this purpose, a different set of financial advice will be sought, which locates the crime gains in the legitimate economy. The monetizer who cashed out the cryptocurrency may even provide savings or investment advice to the attacker once the money has been laundered to give them a legal return on their investment. A problem for the successful attackers is that large amounts of money tend to attract attention in financial environments where there are strong money laundering rules and proceeds of crime laws, which make it harder, although not impossible, for attackers to easily spend their ill-gotten gains. So, whilst much of the cybersecurity literature discusses the offending, very little research

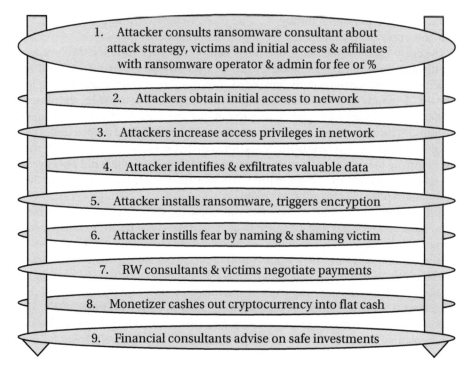

Figure 7.2 The nine different stages of a ransomware attack.
Source: Goldsmith and Wall (unpublished: 20).

discusses how offenders benefit from their crimes and this would make a useful future project.

The (re)organization of cybercrime and the new faces of organized crime online: the facilitators and enablers of the cybercrime ecosystem

The brief summary of the stages of a ransomware attack above clearly indicates that cybercrimes are organizationally complex. This breakdown gives some detail to the functions of what media reports regularly and vaguely describe as ransomware attacks being carried out by 'ransomware gangs'. Moreover, figure 7.1 and the accompanying narrative show that a detailed separation of criminal labour has occurred with regard to the organization of the ransomware operation, and that the main offenders fall into two groups: the attackers and the facilitators. Furthermore, each of these groups consists of various sub-groups. The attackers, for example, vary according to their motivation and whether they are driven by economic, political or hacktivist goals. The facilitators also separate into at least four main groups; the operators, consultants, technical facilitators and monetizers. Each of these groups of individuals has established working arrangements with the others.

Although there are some variations on the theme, the attackers (who make the actual decision to attack) are most often affiliates of the ransomware operators, who are not usually involved in any of the main stages of the attack. They facilitate the attacks by providing the ransomware as a service or set of services. To provide this service, the operators, themselves, will hire-in individuals with a range of skill sets – for example, to write code – or they will out-source services – for example, to a bulletproof web hoster to host their leak-sites (where they name and shame victims). They may also buy initial access credentials or negotiate favourable arrangements with certain trusted suppliers – for example, to monetize proceeds. Although not pursued here, it has been argued that the victims themselves constitute a fifth group, on the basis that they are indirectly complicit by either paying the ransom demands directly or through their cyber-insurance policy, but this introduces a new layer of debate about the moral politics of cybercrime and is for another forum. Here the focus is upon the transformation of criminal behaviour.

By drawing upon the above analysis of ransomware (also see Connolly and Wall, 2019; Wall, 2021) and also DDoS stressers (DDoS as a service) (see Musotto and Wall, 2022), a snapshot of the various criminal actors which make up the cybercrime ecosystem can be modelled. This is a snapshot of a picture that can quickly change as new developments in technology take place. They are listed below in rough order of their input into the ecosystem, but, in reality, they are more fluid.

Phishers and infiltration brokers

The infiltration, or 'initial access', brokers run phishing and other data collection services to obtain information that can be assembled into credentials that enable attackers to access users' personal and work accounts and also their networks. These credentials are sold on to offenders via markets or forums on the dark web to be used to perform attacks.

The process of phishing is intended to get victims to respond to the offenders' (spammers') emails, texts or voicemail – as mentioned earlier, even a 'no thanks' is crucial information that the email account is valid and being used. Phishers will use any tactic available to get recipients to respond: health cures and snake-oil remedies; income-generating offers; loans; credit options or credit rating repair; advertisements or information about products and services; offers of free or discounted products, goods and services, including free vacations, free pornography (sexualized and sexual imagery); opportunities to win something; online gambling options; surveillance software; devices and information; hoaxes; urban legends; mischief collections; jokes; and news items. Very often the phishers will have processed data to assemble lists of email addresses or phone numbers that have a common characteristic, such as a profession or a sport, etc. This way, more specific messages can be sent to victims to get them to engage and give the phisher information about themselves or their business. In so doing, the phishing attack moves from a basic 'spray and pray' phishing expedition to a more sophisticated 'prey and slay' or 'whale' phishing attack where victims are targeted in advance.

While spams may be perceived as a declining threat to those who are internet savvy, they nevertheless pose a greater danger to the more vulnerable communities in society: the poor; the newly redundant; those in remote locations; those with learning difficulties; new users who lack sufficient experience of the internet to be able to judge between the plausible and less plausible invitations; the terminally sick, ever hopeful of some relief from their pain; the poor single parent who sends off his or her last £200 for a 'work at home' scheme; youths who seek out 'cheats' for their computer games. Another particularly vulnerable group are the newly retired who have all of the internet fraudsters' most desired characteristics – impatience to invest their retirement lump sums and lack of computer knowledge and savvy. Novel forms of spamming, particularly those employing tactics based upon deception, such as phishing, pharming, 'gullibility viruses' and more recently vishing (using VoIP), frequently catch large numbers of internet users who are unaware of new risks until they are informed by word of mouth, local IT support, or web or media reporting. The offenders therefore have a particular interest in keeping one step ahead. A single spammer can repeatedly reach many millions of recipients. Wood estimated that 'more than 80 per cent of global spam originates from fewer than 200 known spammers in the USA' (2003: 4; also see Spamhaus.org).

Crimeware-as-a-service brokers

Crimeware-as-a-service brokers, as the name suggests, rent out crime services which help offenders to commit cybercrimes, such as DDoS stressers, ransomware-as-a-service, spamware-as-a-service, phishing-as-a-service, botnet services. CaaS brokers offer complete services to offenders. As indicated with the example of ransomware operators earlier, the CaaS brokers research, develop and offer their product, often buying-in services from the ecosystem in the process. They also protect the integrity of their 'brand' by setting out rules for use and often vetting potential users (affiliates) to make sure that they can trust them to pay their commission, adhere to their rules and use their service responsibly so as to reduce their (the operators') overall risk. Examples exist where affiliates overstepped boundaries – for example, attacking healthcare facilities – and the operators were sanctioned or threatened with sanctions. The high-volume CaaS can be custom-made via a dashboard, rather like buying a car, to a point of detail that fits the nature of the attack the offenders wish to make. The lesser-volume, but deeper, human-operated attacks involve more contact with the providers.

Forum brokers

Forum brokers run trusted online forums where offenders and interested parties can meet and share ideas, many of which are related to the commission of cybercrimes. Many of these forums now take the form of 'Apps'. In 2020, the 'EncroChat' chat forum was infiltrated by police forces Europe-wide and taken down. It was estimated that 60,000 people, with 10,000 in the UK, subscribed to it, and the subsequent investigations led to 746 arrests. The crimes it facilitated involved cybercrimes along with many other non-cybercrimes. The takedown disrupted 'criminal activities including violent attacks, corruption, attempted murders and large-scale drug transports' (BBC, 2020a). In his analysis of open cybercriminal marketplaces and forums using data collected over a 7-year period, Lusthaus (2019) found different layers of forums and marketplaces in which the members pursued cybercrime. At the top were open forums, the majority of which were on the dark web, although not all. A middle layer contained more closely vetted forums, whereas the bottom layer was composed of smaller and closed groupings.

Darkmarketeers

Darkmarketeers develop and run darkmarkets, which are usually located on the ToR network which provides a safe online service where offenders can buy, sell or trade a wide range of products or services using cryptocurrency as the exchange medium. Acting rather like Amazon or eBay, these underground markets offer a variety of goods and services which range from physical products to those which exist purely online. Physical products include drugs which are then posted to clients, or physical services which clients can access, and which allegedly include the services of hit men! Online goods and services, which are the topic of discussion here, include the sale of malware, crimeware-as-a-service, stolen data, money laundering services, IT services, pornographic imagery or hosting online meeting forums – in fact, everything that it takes to commit a cybercrime. In April 2023, Genesis Market, a large supplier of stolen personal data to criminals, was taken down by a 14-country multinational policing effort; 120 arrests were made. This information gives a rough idea of the transnational complexity and scale of the operation of darkmarkets. The UK NCA said it found evidence that Genesis Market had enabled ransomware attacks, because some of the corporate access credentials being sold would have offered ransomware operators initial access into the victims' computer networks (Scroxton, 2023).

Databrokers

Databrokers acquire stolen data, compile it and sell or trade the stolen data sets, mainly on darkmarket websites. This data includes processed victim profiles, but also other data, such as access to illegal data streaming.

Bulletproof hosters

Bulletproof hosters provide safe web services for offenders – see, for example, ransomware 'name and shame' leak-sites.

Crime IT services brokers

Crime IT services brokers provide offenders with access to a range of specialist IT skills ranging from writing code, to hacking for hire, to creating websites.

Monetizers

Monetizers can be hired to organize and manage the proceeds of crime: to empty cryptowallets, tumble and mix the cryptocurrencies, employ a crooked cryptoexchange to exchange cryptocurrency for fiat money, then employ money mules to extract the fiat money as cash. The monetizers may even offer financial advice on investments.

Cybercrime consultants

Cybercrime consultants (including ransom negotiators) will, for a fee, advise on different aspects of cybercrime, typically helping offenders to formulate a strategy of attack and advise on who the victims may be, and what malware or which crimeware-as-a-service to use. They can also advise on the merits and demerits of the services of those providing the different cybercrime services.

It is important to point out that these roles are in a constant state of flux as the technologies which underpin them become more sophisticated and are able to further 'automate' roles. They do, however, help to construct a hypothetical map of the ecosystem and the relationships between the various parts. Each service tends to be run by a kingpin, but the reality is that single providers tend to offer one or more service. These kingpins also tend to exert market control over the service provided, as mentioned, ensuring that they can trust the parties they work with.

As mentioned earlier, these functions can each be performed by one individual, but to reach the scalability and volume of crime needed to achieve a sizeable return, offenders outsource different crime roles for a fee. Buying-in a particular service not only saves the offender time, but also offsets risk. As stated earlier, the objective of the cybercrime ecosystem is to increase the scalability of cybercrimes whilst also reducing the risk to the purchaser. The different roles and functions are outlined in figure 7.3. Inside the circle represents the internal criminal activity, and those activities surrounded by dashed lines represent the outside-facing functions.

The relationships between the various components of the ecosystem are based upon fairly standard business models. Roberto Musotto and I analysed[5] the payment systems of a 'booter' or DDoS stresser (DDoS as a service) that had been taken down by law enforcement in 2016. We found that its operation did not fit with the prevailing organized crime (Mafia-type) narratives. It was simply constructed and employed a standard business approach. The DDoS stresser provided various levels of service, ranging from entry level through to VIP, for which customers paid accordingly. Most paid a $2 (10 min) trial in Bitcoin, a small number then bought into a higher level of service, while others bought the premium service and a few the VIP service. The analysis suggested that the 'actors' were mostly amateurs and skilled non-professionals, but a few professionals did buy the higher level of service (premium VIP), which in 2016 cost 50 bitcoins, a large sum to pay without expectation of a significant return on investment (see, further, Musotto and Wall, 2022). Similar patterns have also been found in the marketing strategies of ransomware-as-a-service.

Conclusions

As new technologies develop, the ever-changing division of criminal labour continues to transform the way cybercrimes are committed. Over the past decade, a viable ecosystem has evolved to facilitate the organization of cybercrime. As in most work patterns, technology has effectively split cybercrimes into specialist tasks which are now performed by specialists at a cost to the attacker, a cost which the attackers insert into their crime business model. What has also become clear is that the cybercrime 'attackers' are different groups of individuals from those who facilitate the crime. The facilitators not only provide specialist skills but also reduce the risk of investigation.

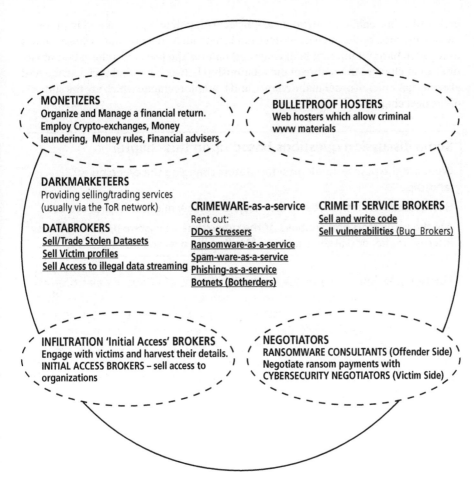

MONETIZERS
Organize and Manage a financial return.
Employ Crypto-exchanges, Money
laundering, Money rules, Financial advisers,

BULLETPROOF HOSTERS
Web hosters which allow criminal
www materials

DARKMARKETEERS
Providing selling/trading services
(usually via the ToR network)

DATABROKERS
Sell/Trade Stolen Datasets
Sell Victim profiles
Sell Access to illegal data streaming

CRIMEWARE-as-a-service
Rent out:
DDos Stressers
Ransomware-as-a-service
Spam-ware-as-a-service
Phishing-as-a-service
Botnets (Botherders)

CRIME IT SERVICE BROKERS
Sell and write code
Sell vulnerabilities (Bug Brokers)

INFILTRATION 'Initial Access' BROKERS
Engage with victims and harvest their details.
INITIAL ACCESS BROKERS – sell access to
organizations

NEGOTIATORS
RANSOMWARE CONSULTANTS (Offender Side)
Negotiate ransom payments with
CYBERSECURITY NEGOTIATORS (Victim Side)

Figure 7.3 The skills and service supply chain that forms the cybercrime ecosystem.

Their criminal businesses are based upon standard business models and reflect more a business studies manual than an organized crime playbook. The identification of the specific stages of a cybercrime and the roles of the facilitators is useful for the later discussion over policing ransomware because the findings suggest some 'pinch' points where law enforcement and cybersecurity could focus resources to disrupt the ransomware victimization cycle. Importantly, they also suggest some useful principles for understanding the structure of the way in which cybercrime is organized.

The reorganization of offending behaviour is likely to evolve as technologies continue to change. New generations of offending will continually develop and knowledge of offending patterns is a moving feast. One certainty is that while the tactics for offender–victim engagement are likely to change, many of the practices will nevertheless remain familiar. However, another certainty is that many more surprises will emerge in the future, particularly as new platforms for criminal activity emerge along with new forms of networked technologies. Offenders will find novel and innovative ways of evading technological and law enforcement attempts to stop them and will carry on exploiting new automated forms of communication to achieve their ends, thus enabling offenders to engage with potential victims and to perpetuate the infection cycle. Such news does not bring much cheer to those whose job it is to regulate harmful internet behaviour and enforce the law. The automation of victimization changes the nature of the relationship between law and social action and also the dynamics of order maintenance and law enforcement, which are the subjects of the next chapter.

Some discussion questions based upon this chapter

What are the new technological facilitators changing the cybercrime landscape?

How sustainable is the cybercrime ecosystem? How might it further evolve?

Are the facilitators and enablers of the cybercrime ecosystem becoming a new internet mafia, or will the traditional Mafia take over the internet?

Further Reading   One of the least-studied areas of cybercrime has been the changes in its organization and the emergence of a cybercrime ecosystem. As cybercrimes increasingly hit infrastructural targets, governments become more motivated to respond, hence the growing interest in this topic, but a recurrent issue has been the problems of conceptualization and also attribution of the crime. Students and researchers who wish to take this study topic further are recommended to start with the following references: Lusthaus (2018, 2019); Wall (2021); Whelan et al. (2023).

8 Policing Cybercrime: Maintaining Order and Law on the Cyberbeat

How is cyberspace regulated and policed and by whom?

Chapter contents and key points

Maintaining order in cyberspace: locating the police amongst other guardians within the networks and nodes of security within cyberspace

- Internet users and user groups
- Online virtual environment managers and security
- Network infrastructure providers / internet service providers
- Corporate organizations and corporate security
- Non-governmental, non-police organizations and agencies
- Governmental non-police organizations
- Public police organizations and agencies
- Security technologies and the internet infrastructure

Maintaining law in cyberspace: the challenges of policing cybercrime

- Cybercrimes are individually too small to deal with: 'de minimism'
- No law – no crime (*nullum crimen*) disparities
- Jurisdictional disparities
- Non-routine activity and police culture
- Under-reporting by victims
- Over-dramatization by media

The role of the public police in policing cyberspace

- The neo-Peelian agenda: renegotiating the public police role in policing cyberspace
- Multi-agency cross-sector partnerships

Conclusions: The challenge of cybercrime for the police–public mandate

---

Chapter at a glance   *This chapter explores the maintenance of order and law in cyberspace. It argues that the public police agencies are a small but important part of a broader network of security guardians who work by different means to create order on the internet. It also observes that law itself, and therefore the criminal justice system, is also challenged by cybercrime in a number of ways which have to be addressed. It concludes that the police alone cannot police cyberspace and that they have to work with other parties.*

Introduction

As the growth of criminal opportunities relating to digital and networked technologies continues, then so do the challenges for maintaining order and law for the public, the industry, the police and the courts. In fact, as explained later, the traditional dyad of law and order which dominates (mainly police-led) discussion of the regulation of the internet has been deliberately reversed here to consider the issues separately. The contents of the preceding chapters clearly constitute a thematic and descriptive justification for policing the internet to maintain order and enforce the law. Given that networked computing power has increased the offender's reach and overall capacity to exploit criminal opportunities with a high aggregate return on investment, it is hardly surprising that concerns about law and order have long dominated debates about the internet. These concerns are prolonged by the future shock (public feelings of helplessness or anxiety) generated by the poisonous combination of society's increasing reliance on networked technologies, the necessary steep learning curve demanded of users, and the popular public misperception that internet misuse cannot be controlled. Indeed, the fact that there appear to be hundreds of thousands of reported cybercrime incidents each year, compared with very few prosecutions, would seem to substantiate fears that attempts to control internet behaviour are failing. In earlier chapters we saw, for example, that during the first decade following the introduction of the Computer Misuse Act 1990 in the UK, there were only 600 or so prosecutions against hackers and even fewer convictions. This disparity is to be found not only in the UK, but elsewhere in the world too (see Smith et al., 2004). Various successful and unsuccessful attempts have been made to reform the laws in the UK and other jurisdictions. In February 2023, an open consultation to review the Act was launched to seek 'the views of stakeholders and the wider public, to identify and understand whether there is activity causing harm in the area covered by the CMA that is not adequately addressed by the current offences' (Home Office, 2023).

Does the low number of computer misuse prosecutions mean that the law has failed, or is there perhaps something about cybercrimes that makes them so different that they subvert traditional justice processes? Yet, if the internet is apparently so criminogenic, then why are more cybercrimes against individuals and organizations not reported to the police or other responding bodies? Why is there so little 'chatter' in the form of personal stories about victimization (other than fraud) across traditional pathways of communication (friendship, kinship and professional networks) verbally, by email or by letter? And if the prevalence of cybercrime is really so great, then how does life online continue to thrive? Or could it simply be the case that many of these apparent 'victimizations' are low-impact infringements that are either ignored, resolved technologically before they progressed to a victimization, or prosecuted under different laws? Remember that the more mediated by technology a criminal behaviour becomes and distanced from social interaction, the more effectively it can be governed by the same technologies and, de facto, less by law itself. This hypothesis begins to question the role of law in the information age and ask whether or not the code itself has effectively become the law, which was a theme introduced in the early writings on cyberlaw (see Lessig, 2006). Or could it be that the majority of internet harms are also being 'policed' by other means of behavioural governance?

Central to this discussion is the need to understand the role of the public police in the policing of cyberspace.

This chapter tries to address some of the questions outlined above. It focuses upon the maintenance of order and law enforcement on the internet and argues that policing online behaviour and cybercrime prevention cannot be reduced to a simple discussion about legal rules and regulations or technological solutions, because policing online crime – as in the terrestrial world – has to be understood in terms of broader frameworks of behavioural governance. The policing of cyberspace therefore is best analysed within a compliance framework composed of a multi-tiered order maintenance assemblage of networks and nodes of security that shape behaviour online.

The first section of this chapter maps out the networked and nodal architecture of internet policing in terms of networks of security that contribute to policing harmful behaviour in cyberspace before exploring how the public police are situated within them. The second section of this chapter identifies the challenges that the public police face if they are to maintain their role in policing the internet. The third section discusses the role of the public police in policing cyberspace and argues that some of the contradictions faced by 'the police' have been reconciled by the reconstitution of a neo-Peelian[1] policing agenda across a global span. While this may (re)situate the police (policing agencies) in the policing of cybercrime, it nevertheless creates a range of fresh instrumental and normative challenges.

Maintaining order in cyberspace: locating the police amongst other guardians within the networks and nodes of security within cyberspace

The public police role has to be understood within a broader and largely informal architecture of internet policing, which not only enforces norms, rules and laws, but also maintains order in very different ways. Moreover, the police are not the only 'guardians' keeping crime off the internet. Understanding this position facilitates a more realistic understanding of the police role and expectations of them. It also helps to identify the wide range of cross-jurisdictional and cross-sector networked issues that the police have to embrace in order to participate in the policing of the internet. They have to be 'networked' in their approach because new technologies have accelerated the growing tendency towards networking sources of security (Johnston and Shearing, 2003; Dupont, 2004), but also because one of the main characteristics of the internet itself is its globalizing characteristic. Table 8.1 outlines the principal interest groups that also perform a 'guardianship' role and constitute the nodes of networked internet governance. Without making any specific empirical claims, a distinction is made between the 'auspices' of governance and those who provide it. The 'auspices' are the entities that authorize governance, such as law and moral and ethical values (Shearing, 2004: 6). They shape internet behaviour (see further Wall, 2002a, 2007a) and are conceptualized here as an 'assemblage', after Deleuze and Guattari (1987), and also Haggerty and Ericson (2000: 605), because of the way that those (the providers) who constitute the nodes 'work' together as a functional entity across the network, but do not necessarily have any other unity.

Table 8.1 The internet's order-maintenance assemblage

Governance providers / guardians	Population served	Sanctions (auspices of governance)
Internet users and user groups	All internet users (inc. social media networks)	Social and moral censure, cancelling, reporting, hacktivism, digilantism
Online virtual environment managers and security	Members of online environments/ forums	The threat of, or actual, exclusion from environments
Network infrastructure providers / internet service providers	Subscribing users or clients	Contractual governance – removal of service
Corporate organizations and corporate security	Private interests of organization and organizational clientele	Contractual/corporate governance – removal of service / civil recovery / prosecution
Non-governmental, non-police organizations and agencies	All internet users	Financial sanctions / removal of service / reporting for criminal prosecution
Governmental non-police organizations and agencies	All internet users and organizations	Financial sanctions or criminal/civil prosecution
Public police organizations and agencies	All citizens	Criminal investigation and prosecution

Internet users and user groups

Internet users and user groups combine to exert a very potent influence upon online behaviour, through censure, usually after the occurrence of a 'signal' event which typically involves criminal or immoral behaviour. It will be recalled from earlier that signal events capture the media and the public's imaginations, influencing public beliefs and attitudes (Innes, 2004: 151). The more extreme behaviours may also be reported (in the UK) to relevant authorities, such as the IWF (illegal sexual materials) or Trading Standards (scams and frauds), or directly to the police, either in person or through one of the many crime-reporting websites. In addition, individual internet users may take individual action, for example for online defamation (as in *Keith-Smith* v. *Williams* (2006) – see Gibson, 2006; Sturcke, 2006), or employ a range of security software solutions to prevent themselves from becoming victims of cybercrime, solutions that range from the use of firewalls and encryption that protect personal space, through to the application of spam filters and virus checkers. Working on a self-appointed mandate, the internet users are simultaneously auspices and providers of governance. Many types of internet groupings exist, but three important issues help to coalesce them: the first is 'cancel' culture; the second, 'digilantism'; and the third, reputational management systems. At their best, they provide peer-policing and a form of governance, but at their worst they are a simultaneous threat to it.

Peer-policing 1: 'Cancel' culture   is effectively the voice of the moral majority. As various social media networks have arisen, those who express opinions or commit acts that are judged as being against the prevailing norm, who create outrage, are censured by others. Social media networks have been essential in creating such a culture because not only do they provide a platform for speech, but the same technology also gives users a voice where they can 'speak', comment or express whether they 'like' or 'dislike' someone else's posting. In extreme circumstances, the majority effectively act together to 'cancel' a disapproved user, thus removing their voice.

Peer-policing 2: 'Digilantism'   is a type of vigilantism which takes place online. Among internet users are a number of interest groups formed around specific and often controversial issues that 'police' websites and users that either threaten or offend them. These online vigilantes, or digilantes as they have become known, occupy an interesting space in the governance of the internet. On the one hand, they can help police to solve cases, providing 'eyes on the ground' with local knowledge, or simply helping to collate information. On the other hand, they can interfere with police investigations, and in some cases ruin the admissibility of evidence and any subsequent prosecution. In the Boston Bombing case, for example, internet sleuths were important in providing information, although problems arose in separating the facts from opinion when a suspected bomber was wrongly hounded, taking valuable police resources away from the hunt for the real one (see, further, Nhan et al., 2015). Largely local in operation but transnational in terms of membership and scope of function, these tend to be self-appointed and possess neither a broad public mandate nor a statutory basis. Consequently, they lack formal mechanisms of accountability for their actions, which themselves may be intrusive, illicit or even illegal. Nevertheless, they appear to be fairly potent. A number of examples of virtual community policing already exist. In addition to the various complaint 'hotlines' and the development of software to 'screen out' undesirable communications (Uhlig, 1996), some netizen groups have sought to organize internet users around particular issues. The names of the following anti-child sexual abuse/imagery sites reveal their particular mission. CyberAngels seek generally to protect children online; others are dedicated to combating child sexual exploitation: 'Ethical Hackers Against Pedophilia', 'Pedowatch', 'Se7en', 'Internet Combat Group' and 'Morkhoven' (see, further, Hughes, 1999; Gainford, 2023). The final group, The Association of Sites Advocating Child Protection (ASACP) (originally known as Adult Sites Against Child Pornography) is dedicated to the elimination of child sexual material from the internet through its reporting hotline (AIN, 2005). Other active user groups exist to combat a range of issues, such as spamming and phishing.

Peer-policing 3: reputational management systems online   The principle of peer-policing by internet users is now enshrined in e-commerce through vendor rating systems, of which the most well known is eBay's online auction trading partner profile rating system. Each eBay vendor member has his or her own profile determined by customer feedback on past sales performance. The rating system enables prospective purchasers to identify the less trustworthy sellers, thus policing undesirable behaviour within the forum: '[l]earning to trust a member of the community has a lot to do with what their past customers or sellers have to say!'[2]

Online virtual environment managers and security

As virtual environments become more popular, the need to maintain order within them becomes more pressing. To this end, most virtual environments now employ moderators or online security managers to 'police' the behaviour of their online community. The moderators ensure that community members adhere to acceptable behaviour policies and prevent discussions from becoming disruptive, libellous or being hijacked. These online security managers are collectively emerging as a new stratum of behaviour governors. A useful example of online moderation is found in the virtual world 'Habbo Hotel', which describes itself as: 'a virtual Hotel, where teenagers can hang out and chat'. It is constantly monitored by trained, police-vetted, moderators[3] and 'hotel guides' drawn from within the online community. The values and norms (auspices) that moderators maintain, as in other environments, combine the interests and norms of the particular online community with the legal and corporate responsibilities of the virtual environment 'owner'. The sanctions that moderators can invoke when community norms or rules are broken include 'timeouts' – the temporary removal of access rights if the offending is minor – or permanent exclusion from the environment if it is serious. While these 'policing' practices are generally effective in upholding community norms, they are limited in scope, especially when the offending behaviour 'crosses the line' into more serious offending. Then the concern becomes whether or not the correct action has been taken.

Network infrastructure providers / internet service providers

The network infrastructure providers, typically the internet service providers (ISPs), influence online behaviour through 'contractual governance' (Vincent-Jones, 2000; Crawford, 2003). This function is effected through the terms and conditions (auspices) of their contracts with individual clients – the internet users. The terms and conditions are largely the product of the market, the law and the ISP's commercial interests. The ISPs are also subject to contractual governance through the terms and conditions laid down in their own contracts with the telecommunications providers who host their internet services. In addition, ISPs can, because of their strategic position in the communications networks, also employ a range of software solutions to reduce offending online. Most typical of these are robust security systems accompanied by sophisticated professional spam filters.

The ISPs have a rather fluid status because, although they are physically located in a particular jurisdiction, they tend to function transnationally (Walker et al., 2000: 6). The liabilities of ISPs vary under different bodies of law and have yet to be fully established (see Rowland and Macdonald, 1997; Edwards and Wealde, 2000; Lloyd, 2000), although cases such as *Godfrey* v. *Demon Internet Ltd.* (1999) and the *League Against Racism and Anti-Semitism (LICRA) and The Union of French Jewish Students (UEJF)* v. *Yahoo Inc. and Yahoo France* (2000), *In Re: Verizon Internet Services, Inc.* (2003) (Wired, 2003) have each exerted a 'chilling' effect upon ISPs' actions and have made them very risk-averse. The fear of civil sanctions encourages ISP compliance with many of the regulatory demands made of them by the police and other state bodies. Consequently, ISPs tend to tread carefully and are fairly responsive to police requests for cooperation. In addition to being wary of their potential legal liabilities, ISPs are also fearful of any negative publicity that might arise from their failing to be seen to act responsibly. The general rule of thumb that appears to be adopted across many jurisdictions is that liability tends to arise when the ISP fails to respond to requests to remove offensive material, whether obscene or defamatory, once it has been brought to their attention following a complaint (*People* v. *Somm* (1998); *Godfrey* v. *Demon Internet Ltd.* (1999); Center for Democracy and Technology, 1998: 3; Leong, 1998: 25). ISPs tend to organize themselves both within specific jurisdictions and across them with a further level of transnational organization – for example, the Commercial Internet eXchange, the Pan-European Internet Service Providers' Association (EuroISPA) and the Internet Service Providers' Consortium (mainly US). These transnational organizations focus primarily upon technical/practical and commercial issues germane to ISPs. In addition to the ISPs are the (regional/national) domain name registries which allocate domain names under the oversight of ICANN (the Internet Corporation for Assigned Names and Numbers), an international non-profit corporation formed to assume responsibility for the IP (Internet Protocol) address space allocation, protocol parameter assignment, domain name system management, and root server system management functions. ICANN also resolves disputes over domain name registration.

Corporate organizations and corporate security

Corporate organizations protect their corporate interests by exercising contractual governance over their members (both employees and clients) and also any other outsiders. In addition, corporate security organizations may also employ a range of software solutions not just to protect themselves, but also to identify and investigate abnormal patterns of client behaviour. Contractual terms and conditions threaten the removal of privileges, or private or criminal prosecution in the case of more serious transgressions. A graphic example of the corporate exercise of contractual governance was found in the demise of JenniCAM.com, one of the original and most popular of the cam-girl sites. JenniCAM's collapse was blamed upon a change in the acceptable-use policies of the online payment service PayPal, which also affected online gambling.[4] Similarly, charities and card issuers have lobbied the UK government to change the data protection laws to allow them to cancel the credit cards of those using them to purchase child sexual materials online on the grounds that it breaches the issuers' terms and conditions of use (BBC, 2006f). Along similar lines, online stores, such as those operated by Yahoo! or Hotmail, are ceasing to enter into buyer–vendor arrangements where the seller has an easy-to-set-up webmail account (Leyden, 2006c). In March 2006, the Financial Coalition Against Child Pornography was formed to make it impossible to profit from child sexual exploitation operations on the internet. The coalition brought together a range of organizations involved in website service delivery and online payment systems to 'share information about websites that sell child porn and stop payments passing to them' (BBC, 2006a). Views vary, however, upon the effectiveness of shaping behaviour through acceptable-use strategies, and it is therefore likely that they will be more effective for some rather than others. For example, in the case of sites distributing sexual content, there is clear evidence of their immediate tactical effectiveness, as with the collapse of JenniCAM.

However, the sheer market demand for sexual materials on the internet suggests some resilience against regulation.

Following the widespread mass integration of IT within most organizational structures from the 1980s onwards, and notably since the growth of e-commerce during the late 1990s, the security departments of commercial, telecommunications and other related organizations have been strengthened to protect their interests. As e-commerce grows, it is anticipated that corporate security organizations will become major players in policing the internet. However, because their primary function is to police their own 'private' interests, it is hard to assess their overall impact on policing because of their low 'public' visibility. Importantly, they tend to pursue a 'private model' of justice because the public criminal justice system does not offer them the model of criminal justice that they want (Wall, 2001b: 174). Consequently, their relationship with the public police is often minimal. Yet the latter are organizationally ambivalent about this relationship because they resent the loss of important criminal intelligence, but simultaneously appear happy – from a managerial point of view – not to expend scarce and finite police resources on costly investigations.

Non-governmental, non-police organizations and agencies

Non-governmental, non-police organizations are a growing legion of hybrid public/private arrangements that contribute directly to the order-maintenance assemblage by acting as gatekeepers to the other levels of governance, but also by contributing towards (cyber)crime prevention. The IWF, for example, provides governance under the auspices of a mandate from the UK ISPs and UK government. One of its main functions is to bring to the attention of ISPs any illegal materials reported to its hotline, particularly child sexual materials, the eradication of which is one of the objectives of the Foundation. If deemed actionable following a judgement made against set criteria by a trained operative (see chapter 6), the IWF takes appropriate action by either informing the offender's ISP, alerting comparable hotlines in the offender's jurisdictions, or, if serious enough and within the UK, passing on details of a website directly to the police. The IWF also contributes more generally towards cybercrime prevention and public awareness. It was formed in December 1996 with the endorsement of the Metropolitan Police, the DTI, the Home Office and the associations of the ISPs, such as the Internet Service Providers Association and the London Internet Exchange (Uhlig, 1996). The standing of the IWF has increased, and it has become the quasi-public face of internet regulation in the UK, more notably since its relaunch in 2000.

Another example of a non-governmental, non-police organization are the Computer Emergency Response Teams (CERT) which have followed the model of that based at Carnegie Mellon University in Pittsburgh. It was created in 1988 in the aftermath of a devastating attack by the Morris Worm which highlighted the internet's vulnerability by bringing much of it down. Located at the Software Engineering Institute, a federally funded research and development centre of Carnegie Mellon University, the purpose of CERT was to combat unauthorized access to the internet. Its programmers would log reported hacks and carry out the initial investigations. If security breaches were found to be too complicated to deal with in-house, they were farmed out to an unofficial 'brains trust' (Adams, 1996) and to the relevant public police organizations if an offence was serious and could lead to prosecution. In 2003, CERT joined the Arlington-based US-CERT team created by the Department of Homeland Security (DHS) as part of the national infrastructure protection programme. Prior to the partnership, CERT (Carnegie Mellon) had become the model for many similar computer security organizations throughout the world. CERT was based within a non-governmental public institution but initially funded by a combination of private and governmental resources.

Although the non-governmental, non-police organizations are mainly private bodies, they often perform public functions. However, they tend to lack the formal structures of accountability normally associated with public organizations and sometimes find themselves the subject of public concern.

Governmental non-police organizations and agencies

Governmental non-police organizations provide governance under the auspices of regulations, rules and law through charges (levies), fines and the threat of prosecution. Not normally perceived as 'police', they include agencies such as customs, the postal service and trading standards organizations. In addition, these agencies may employ a range of software solutions to protect themselves and also assist in investigations. They also include a higher tier of agencies that oversee the implementation and enforcement of national internet infrastructure protection policies. Some national governments, such as those of Singapore, China, Korea and Vietnam, have at one time or another, and with varying degrees of success, actively sought to control their citizens' use of the internet. They have either required users to register with governmental monitoring organizations or sought to directly control internet traffic in their jurisdictions through government-controlled ISPs (Caden and Lucas, 1996; Center for Democracy and Technology, 1998; Standage, 1998).

At the national level, there are multi-agency cross-sector organizations, or forums, with a remit to protect the electronic infrastructure either through active interventions or through the coordination of the activities of bodies at an international level. In the UK, for example, the NISCC oversees the protection of the critical national infrastructure and covers the following sectors: telecommunications, energy, central government, financial, transport, emergency services, water and sewerage, and health services. Announced in December 1999, NISCC is an interdepartmental organization which coordinates and develops 'existing work within Government departments and agencies and organizations in the private sector to defend the Critical National Infrastructure (CNI) against electronic attack'. NISCC is also responsible for UNIRAS (the Unified Incident Reporting and Alert Scheme) – the UK CERT equivalent which gathers information about IT security incidents in government departments and agencies. Most EU members have infrastructure protection agencies with similar functions to NISCC and there are emerging a number of EU-wide agencies, such as ENISA (the European Network and Information Security Agency), whose role is to support the internal market by 'facilitating and promoting increased co-operation and information exchange on issues of network and information security'.

The US DHS was created in the aftermath of 11 September 2001. The DHS brought together twenty-two previously disparate domestic agencies into one department to protect the nation against threats to the US homeland. Among these agencies was the National Infrastructure Protection Center (NIPC) which, since 1998, had articulated the National Infrastructure Protection Plan of which the internet was part. The NIPC brought together representatives from US government agencies, state and local governments, and the private sector in a partnership to protect the nation's critical infrastructures (PDD, 1998). Within the NIPC, many state-funded non-police organizations were also involved in policing the internet to resolve specific problems. For example, the US Postal Service has a responsibility for the cross-border trading of pornography, and the US Securities and Exchange Commission is responsible for dealing with fraud.

There is a final level of very important and influential governmental non-police organizations which set regulatory policy (often secondary legislation). They are the departments of government that are responsible for trade, and therefore tend to carry the e-commerce portfolios which covered the internet: in the UK, the Department for Business and Trade (DBT) (formerly DTI); in the US, the Federal Trade Commission.

Public police organizations and agencies

Public police agencies draw upon the democratic mandate of government to impose governance by maintaining order and enforcing law. They play a comparatively small, though nevertheless significant, role in enforcing criminal sanctions upon wrongdoers online. While they are located within nation states which impose criminal definitions through the law of the jurisdiction, the public police are nevertheless networked by transnational policing organizations, such as EUROPOL and INTERPOL, whose membership requires formal status as a police force (see Sheptycki, 2002). In most Western countries, the public police are organized locally, but there also exist national police organizations that deal with the collection of intelligence and the investigation of organized crime. Within the local police services, several specialist individuals or groups of police officers are trained to respond to internet-related complaints from the public. Some police forces set up their own units, while others enter into strategic alliances with other police forces to provide such services (Wall, 2007b).

In the US, policing is delivered by about 17,000 independent local police forces (the actual number varies according to the definition of 'police' used). At a national and cross-state level, jurisdiction lies with the Federal Bureau of Investigation, although the US Secret Service – once a bureau of the Treasury, but since March 2003 part of the DHS – also carries a responsibility for investigating crimes 'involving U.S. securities, coinage, other government issues, credit and debit card fraud, and electronic funds transfer fraud' (US Secret Service, Duties and Functions). In the UK, policing is delivered by forty-three regional police forces in England and Wales, Police Scotland and the Police Service of Northern Ireland, plus a number of national police agencies such as the NCA and the British Transport Police (there are a number of smaller police agencies whose remit is to protect the armed forces, nuclear industry and the ports). Each police force now carries a capability to respond to local internet-related crimes, although the capability varies as some are more developed than others, or a strategic alliance has been forged with a neighbouring force. At a national level, the National Criminal Intelligence Service (NCIS), until 2006, was responsible for providing intelligence on serious offences, such as child sexual exploitation, which cross police force or international boundaries. From April 1998, the investigation of such offences came under the National Crime Squad (NCS), a role previously filled by the various regional crime squads. Both NCIS and the NCS were respectively defined by the Police Act 1997, parts I and II. In April 2001, the National Hi-Tech Crime Unit (NHTCU), part of the NCS, became operational to protect the UK's critical infrastructure from offences such as paedophilia, internet fraud and any other national-level offences. In April 2006, the Serious Organized Crime and Police Act 2005 brought together the NCS, NCIS, the drug trafficking investigations and intelligence branches of Customs and Excise, and the organized immigration crime component of the Immigration Service to form the Serious Organized Crime Agency (SOCA). The NHTCU became SOCA's e-Crime Unit. In 2013, SOCA was replaced by the NCA, which combined SOCA with aspects of the border force and CEOP (Child Exploitation and Online Protection) command. The NCA's cybercrime responsibility, as mentioned earlier, is headed by the National Cybercrime Unit (NCCU) which works closely with the National Cyber Security Centre (NCSC), which is part of GCHQ (Government Communications Headquarters).

The significance of presenting internet governance in terms of this order-maintenance assemblage/compliance framework is that its starting point is one of order and compliance, rather than disorder and unlawful resistance. Indeed, as stated earlier, the terms 'order' and 'law' have been deliberately reversed here to break the conceptual link that has increasingly bound the two concepts since the late 1970s (Fowles, 1983: 116; Wall, 2000). Resistance, in the form of harmful behaviours, must be understood within the compliance framework that defines it, rather than outside it (see Hermer and Hunt, 1996: 477). Furthermore, the assemblage model also has major implications for the framing of policy: the distributed nature of the internet does not allow governments the privilege of monopoly control over either the internet or user behaviour. Although the order-maintenance assemblage itself, or parts thereof, can be the subject of international policy, such as the European Commission's 1997 action plan for promoting the safe use of the internet (European Commision, 1997a), better utilization and development of the existing assemblage could lay the foundations for a more effective and more broadly democratic structure of governance. To effect this strategy, however, a plural approach is required that combines a complex web of interrelated legal, regulatory, normative and technological measures.

Security technologies and the internet infrastructure

Before progressing to the broader discussion, it is very important to mention one of the more invisible sets of guardians that exist online. These are the many layers of security technologies employed to protect citizens online by preventing cybercrimes and also protecting their data as they navigate their way around the internet to use the many services provided on it. They are rather hard to place in this schema because they are mainly conceptualized by cybersecurity professionals and produced and sold by corporate structures. They are not the focus of this book as they fall more within the remit of computer science, but their existence and function need to be recognized. Rather ironically, they mirror the cybercrime process by facilitating the work of each of the above nodes of security: the internet users (private and organizational), security managers, internet service providers, organizational security, non-government and governmental agencies and also the police. Of course, these security technologies are not free-standing, their parameters are set by different levels of laws, security policies and norms at international and national levels and also at organizational and individual levels. As Alharti (2003) has opined, they help to promote the positive governance of the internet.

Maintaining law in cyberspace: the challenges of policing cybercrime

The relationship between the public police and technology is long-standing and complex, and explains much about the positioning of the public police in late modern society. On the one hand, in Western industrial societies, the police were originally created as a response to the social disorder caused by the technologies that brought about the Industrial Revolution. On the other hand, their responsive and localized nature and response to victims always meant that the police fell behind in their access to, and use of, technology. Indeed, a long-standing complaint made by police officers, and law enforcement agencies, is that they do not have the technologies to keep up with criminals, especially with regard to offences that require what Brodeur has termed a 'high policing response' (Brodeur, 1983; Sheptycki, 2000: 11). For over a century, readers of the *Police Review* and other contemporary police journals were regularly told by their fellow police officers that they lacked the resources to obtain the latest technologies that would help them to catch offenders. In those days, the police always wanted new forms of transport (bicycles, automobiles, then helicopters) and new types of communications (telephones, radios) to keep up with offenders. More recently, complaints have focused upon obtaining modern IT skills and equipment, the latest software and high-specification broadband links, which, by and large, they have received. Of course, such complaints inevitably backfire as they make good news copy and result in – often unfounded – allegations of police ineffectiveness, which ultimately reinforce the police-originated myth that criminals are ahead of the game. But, while historical tropes can be drawn out of the woodwork, what distinguishes the modern debates from those of old is not just access to the latest technology and skill sets, but access to technology and national and international procedures that facilitate networked policing, including access to relevant networks of security. The main problem for the police is, therefore, to reconcile the dilemma that, operationally and organizationally, they are local, whereas cybercrimes are globalized.

It is one thing, however, to have all of the technological capabilities to police cybercrime, and another to be able to utilize them to great effect. There are a number of institutional obstacles to achieving this task. The public police, like the other criminal justice agencies, are reactive because they have to wait for the public (victims) to report crimes against them before they can respond. Crime prevention is both a recent and secondary goal. This reactive quality means that they have become deeply conservative institutions that have been moulded by time-honoured traditions, and therefore they do not respond readily to rapid change. Furthermore, part of this inherent conservatism stems from the police also being symbolic expressions of state sovereignty. So, contemporary debates over policing have revolved around making them more responsive to public needs, without taking away the public's liberty.

One way in which police forces generally respond to new forms of criminal behaviour, while preserving their symbolic and organizational conservatism, has been through the formation of specialist units into which officers with appropriate specialisms are placed. While this tactic constitutes an actual and visible response, it nevertheless tends to marginalize the problem it sets out to solve and runs the risk of preventing the broader accumulation of organizational and professional experience across the force in dealing with the issue at hand. Ultimately, it is the presence of a relevant body of specialist knowledge and expertise within a police force (and whether the other officers know about it) that can determine the success of the organizational and occupational response to new public concerns.

Cybercrimes introduce a new global dimension to the relationship between police, technology and the public because they clearly fall outside the traditional localized – and even national – operational purview of police. Their global and interjurisdictional reach and the new forms of technological crime organization they represent are markedly different to the daily police crime diet. As a direct consequence, cybercrimes challenge, if not contradict, the traditional Peelian policing paradigm which has long defined the local police–public mandate and shaped the organizational and professional priorities of the police, while framing their 'constitutional' position within the broader framework of policing society. This reminds us that the public police were originally introduced by Peel to 'keep the dangerous classes off the streets' by managing the present to maintain local order and investigating past events to enforce laws and ensure that the criminal justice processes were invoked where necessary. These are still their primary functions today, though performed in much more complex late modern societies (Critchley, 1978; Manning, 1978; Wall, 1998: 23; Reiner, 2000: ch 2). Modern police agencies remain largely responsive to complaints from the public; they tend to deal with routine matters and are subject to tight budgetary constraints that restrict the immediate allocation of major resources to emerging matters, and therefore their responsive capability. The problem with cybercrime is that, despite the dramatic media image, at the end of the day, like fraud, cybercrime 'does not bang, bleed or shout' (BBC, 2019) and does not grab the political agenda enough to also grab funding.

The limitations of the localized Peelian paradigm faced with transnational crime have long been understood and a number of strategies have been employed to resolve the contradictions between the two. At a procedural level, there has been the use of 'soft law' (see Trubek and Trubek, 2005) in the form of international harmonization and police coordination treaties, such as the CoE Convention on Cybercrime, which does not create law, but harmonizes the relevant criminal laws, police investigative procedures and mutual assistance arrangements of the signatory states (CoE, 2001). At an organizational level, a range of national/federal and international police organizations (e.g., EUROPOL, INTERPOL) exist to complement locally organized police forces – the hallmark of public police in most Western liberal societies. They coordinate the investigation of crimes occurring across jurisdictions and police force boundaries, collect intelligence and investigate organized crime. Despite these procedural and organizational responses, cybercrimes continue to challenge the police in a number of ways.

Cybercrimes are individually too small to deal with: 'de minimism'

The first policing challenge is to overcome the *de minimis* trap – that is, the principle whereby the 'law does not deal with trifles' (*de minimis non curat lex*). A common characteristic of many cybercrimes is that they are low-impact, bulk victimizations which are individually small but cause large losses when spread globally, potentially across all known jurisdictions. Consequently, they fall outside the traditional Peelian paradigm of policing dangerous-risk populations, which frames the police–public mandate. Since local policing strategies often depend upon decisions made at a local level about the most efficient expenditure of finite resources (Goodman, 1997: 486), it is often hard to justify the 'public interest' criteria that would release police resources for the investigation of individual cybercrime victimizations.

No law – no crime (nullum crimen) disparities

The second challenge is that legal disparities arise in some interjurisdictional cases where the laws differ. Without a law *in place*, there is no crime (*nullum crimen sine lege*). This tends to happen when new forms of cybercrime emerge, such as crypto-jacking, and legal systems take some time to adapt their laws. Protocols, including the CoE Convention on Cybercrime and the establishment of multi-agency partnerships and forums (see later), assist in facilitating interforce cooperation, but they rely upon the offence in question being given similar priority in each jurisdiction. If, for example, a case is clearly a criminal offence for which the investigation carries a strong mandate from the public, such as the investigation of online child sexual abuse, then resourcing its investigation is usually fairly unproblematic from a policing point of view. However, where there is not such an implied mandate, for example with offences other than child sexual exploitation, then resourcing becomes more problematic, especially if the deviant behaviour in question is an offence in one jurisdiction but not another. Of course, the other interjurisdictional problem is that there may be cultural differences in defining the seriousness of specific forms of offending, or some offences may fall under civil law in one jurisdiction and criminal law in another, as is the case in the theft of trade secrets, which is a criminal offence in the US but a civil offence in the UK. In the UK, only the manner by which trade-secret theft takes place falls within the criminal law (see Law Commission, 1997).

Jurisdictional disparities

A third challenge arises when a jurisdictional or evidential disparity becomes apparent. Police or prosecutors engage in a sort of policing arbitrage and use their resourcefulness to 'forum shop' (Braithwaite and Drahos, 2000) to increase the prospect of maximizing the potential for obtaining a conviction (Wall, 2002b). This process was very evident in *United States of America* v. *Robert A. Thomas and Carleen Thomas* (1996) where the prosecutors 'forum shopped' to seek a judicial site where they felt a conviction would best be secured. They chose Tennessee rather than California because of the greater likelihood of conviction. In *R.* v. *Fellows; R.* v. *Arnold* (1997), the investigation was passed from the US to the UK police because the former believed that the latter was more likely to gain a conviction because the defendants were resident in the UK. These cases illustrate some successful examples of interjuris-dictional cooperation and both cases were relatively unproblematic because they concerned extreme pornography. Where cooperation tends to fall down is with the more contentious types of non-routine offending. Either the gravity of the offence may be recognized in only one jurisdiction and not the other, or the police will simply not pass on the case because they claim ownership over it.

Non-routine activity and police culture

The fourth challenge is routinization, which affects the capacity of the police to respond to cybercrimes that are, despite the alleged volume, a 'non-routine' criminal activity. Since public policing tends to be based upon local and 'routinized' practices that define police occupational cultures, working patterns, skill sets and experiences, and ultimately the scope of professional policing, difficulties can arise when non-routine events occur (Wall, 1997: 223; Reiner, 2000). Internet-related non-routine events include cross-border investigations, or types of deviant behaviour not nor-mally regarded as criminal by police officers.

Routine events are important in the construction of a police occupational cul-ture because they generate stories that are told to others, and this 'figurative action' can eventually structure the way that police officers interpret events (Shearing and Ericson, 1991: 481). Police occupational culture is the accumulation of the collective 'routine' experience of police officers, and it is an important component of police work. With proper safeguards in place to prevent corruption and unfairness in the application of law, it enables officers to make sense of the world they have to police and enables them to apply the law appropriately (McBarnet, 1979).

Without this cultural cognitive map, police officers have little occupational under-standing of the environment they have to police. But since cybercrimes are unique events for most officers, police culture does not assist them – in fact, it can confuse rather than illuminate. Police officers tend to draw upon the 'cynical' application of conventional wisdoms (Reiner, 2000), recalling the earlier vignette about the recur-ring century-old call for more technological resources to fight crime.

It is therefore understandable that street police officers, who have close contact with the public, are unlikely to see the internet in terms of its potential for the democ-ratization of knowledge and growth in active citizenship (Walker and Akdeniz, 1998) or the levelling of ethnic, social or cultural boundaries. Rather, they are more likely to see it as an area characterized by risk (Shearing and Ericson, 1991: 500) and the crimi-nal 'other' (Garland, 2001). The internet therefore becomes understood as a place where 'criminals', notably the worst kind – paedophiles, Russian gangsters, fraud-sters and other contemporary folk-devils – ply their trade. Although police forces have made great advances in their awareness of technology during the past three decades, a cultural dissonance between traditional occupational culture and the demands created by the internet still prevails, which allows the view to persist among many officers that 'cyberspace is like a neighbourhood without a police department' (Sussman, 1995: 59).

Under-reporting by victims

A fifth, and most revealing, challenge is the under-reporting of cybercrimes to the police. Individuals and organizations are reluctant to report their victimization to the police: individuals because of embarrassment and because others, such as banks, may deal with the problem more effectively; and businesses because they are frightened of damaging their reputation and also wish to get back into business as quickly as possible. This issue was briefly discussed in chapter 2, and businesses were found to report more when the impact was greatest and as long as the victim valued cybersecurity. Also, where cybersecurity was outsourced, then reporting to public authorities was less likely, but in-house teams were more likely to report to the police (Kemp et al., 2021).

Victim reporting practices create demands upon police agencies and contribute to defining the nature of their policing services and provision. Comparisons between reporting practices, police recording procedures and prosecutions for many years revealed some startling information shortfalls (Wall, 2002b). The various cyber-crime surveys mentioned earlier (Experian, CSI/FBI, the (UK) DCMS (formerly DTI survey) and others), all of which use reputable methodologies, show a large volume of victimizations. This contrasts sharply with the findings of empirical research conducted for the UK Home Office in 2002 (Wall, 2002b), which found that relatively few internet-related offences were reported to the police (Wall, 2005), a finding echoed in the analysis of answers to the British Crime Survey's internet-related crime questions (Allen et al., 2005) and other surveys since, and still valid today. A detailed study of crime databases in one police force carried out by the author, followed up by interviews with reporting centre staff, revealed that approximately 120–150 internet-related offences per 1 million recorded crimes had been reported to the police during one year, and most of these were reasonably minor frauds, mainly credit card-related, over which no further action was taken.[5] When extrapolated to the national figures (taking into account the relative sizes of police forces), a figure was obtained of about 2,000–3,000 internet-related offences per year throughout England and Wales that were reported by the public to the police (Wall, 2003: 132). Today the reporting rate has increased many-fold, not least aided by the – often criticized – UK Action Fraud reporting system. The basic dynamics are still much the same today and, even if the figures have increased five-, ten- or even a hundred-fold or more, the reporting rate would still be relatively small by comparison to the estimated victimizations.

This apparent under-reporting could be interpreted simply as evidence of low public expectations of the ability of the police to resolve internet-related crimes. Yet, despite a gradual erosion of public confidence in the police during the past few decades, policing in the UK, US and Canada is still primarily consensual and the public still regards them as a primary emergency service. Furthermore, following the tightened security following the events of 11 September 2001 (Levi and Wall, 2004: 196), there are now in existence a range of international and national police organizations that address cybercrimes in addition to terror offences. There also exist national intelligence models – for example, in the UK, the National Intelligence Model (NIM) (NCIS, 2000: 8; Keningale, 2022), structures the collection of intelligence about all crimes, including low-level losses, to construct a national or international picture of criminal activity. Whether the NIM would pick up the very minor *de minimis* cyber-

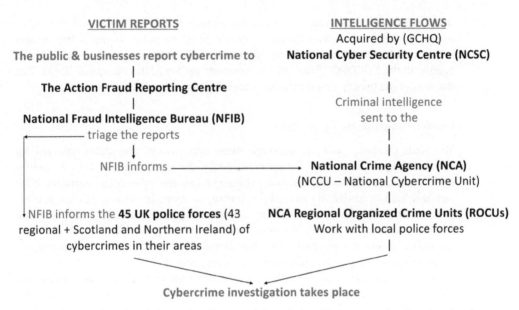

Figure 8.1 UK cybercrime information flows and the relationship between local and national authorities.

crimes is debatable, but the key issue is that a criminal intelligence model now exists in the UK to link the local with the national and international, whereas previously none existed. In addition, many of the larger local police forces/services have for some time possessed the capability to respond to internet-related complaints from the public. Some also possess local facilities to investigate computer crimes and conduct the forensic examination of computers to search for digital evidence to establish offenders' motives or whereabouts in traditional criminal code offences. Much of this evidence is located within computers, internet traffic data and mobile phone records. Finally, most major police forces around the world today now provide web portals for the public to report any cybercrime victimizations they have experienced.

The advice given to businesses and individuals in the UK is to report all cybercrime (and fraud) victimizations to Action Fraud. Action Fraud is the UK's fraud and cybercrime reporting unit and is a service run by the City of London Police, alongside the National Fraud Intelligence Bureau (NFIB) (see figure 8.1). Cybercrime reports received by Action Fraud are triaged by the NFIB Centre. Where there is sufficient evidence or intelligence to take the investigation forward, the case is passed on to the relevant local police force. The National Cyber Crime Unit (NCCU) of the NCA provides national leadership. Its nine Regional Cyber Crime Units support the local cybercrime units in each of the forty-three UK police forces and also the cybercrime units of Police Scotland and the Police Service of Northern Ireland (PSNI) (HM Government, 2022: 44).

The NCCU also responds to cross-boundary and international cybercrimes. Farther afield, the US national hub for reporting cybercrime is the IC3,[6] which is run by the FBI and provides national leadership on cybercrime. In addition, many of the larger state-located police forces also take reports from cybercrime victims in their area of jurisdiction. Similarly, in Canada, the Canadian Centre for Cyber Security[7] takes reports of cybercrime victimization from individuals, businesses and other organizations. In European countries, nearly all of the police forces of the twenty-seven member states have web portals where their citizens can report cybercrimes against them, EUROPOL,[8] the law enforcement agency of the European Union, lists the sites of the twenty-seven member states and also includes that of the UK.

Over-dramatization by media

The sixth challenge is that, although some cybercrimes are under-reported for the reasons outlined above, rather confusingly, the media tend to over-dramatize cybercrimes. It will be recalled from chapter 2 that the cybercrime narrative is far stronger than its truth and can lead to reporting bias which, in the public's eye, over-dramatizes the problem of cybercrimes, when in fact they are fairly mundane and 'boring' (Collier et al., 2021). The over-dramatization of cybercrimes tends to distort the public's view of them and increase its level of fears, which leads to demands for more police action (see later discussion of reassurance).

What we have here is a combination of different factors that can explain the simultaneous under-reporting to the police and over-dramatization of cybercrime victimization.

Box 8.1 illustrates a situation in the mid-2010s when a media frenzy following a hack and data theft caused panic and also appears to have threatened to shape the course of the investigation, whilst also creating considerable financial loss for the victim organization.

Box 8.1 The 2015 TalkTalk Hack

The hack and subsequent data theft sparked off a media frenzy, causing pundits to speculate liberally about potential terrorist involvement, vast financial losses and an impending cybercrime tsunami. This was followed by apocalyptic warnings from the business community and the announcement of government inquiries. Additionally, the media disseminated reports of customers potentially losing money, and the culture of fear around cybercrime went right through the roof (see Wall 2015b).

Placed under considerable pressure by the societal and governmental reaction to the hack, the Metropolitan Police Cybercrime Unit (FALCON) tracked the offender down and arrested him before the data could be released or sold on. FALCON also confirmed that, although some personal information could have been stolen, credit and debit card numbers had not been taken.

The initial hype of terrorist or organized crime involvement fell flat when a 15-year-old boy from Northern Ireland was arrested, followed by two 16-year-olds and a 20-year-old. The 15-year-old boy, who masterminded this heinous international crime from his bedroom, was subsequently bailed. It was alleged that he hacked into the servers of internet service provider TalkTalk by using a DDoS attack as a smokescreen, which was followed by an SQL injection to steal a data set containing personal information on 4 million TalkTalk customers.

In this case, the law was clear. Not only do DDoS attacks fall under s. 36(3) of the Police and Justice Act 2006, but the way the data was stolen also contravenes s. 1(1) and s. 1(3) of the Computer Misuse Act 1990. Furthermore, the boy was alleged to have tried to extort a ransom of about £80,000 from TalkTalk for the return of the data – otherwise, it would be released or sold.

Much of the initial media-fuelled speculation about the hack turned out to be unfounded and the whole affair began to look rather amateurish – the backlash started. More inquiries were announced and embarrassing questions asked about where TalkTalk's security personnel were at the time and exactly what was learned from the previous two attacks experienced by TalkTalk. Were they being fair to their customers? But the elephant in the room was the question of just how a 15-year-old and his associates could commit such serious crimes and create so much damage from the comfort of his bedroom? More importantly, could he get a fair trial following the wild speculation about the motives behind the attack?

The impact of media over-dramatization upon policing is contradictory. On the one hand, the public expect to be protected from harms (cyber-harms) by the police, as per the Peelian paradigm which shapes public expectations of police. On the other hand, the police are hampered by the fact that cybercrimes simply do not fit into the broader public perception of what the police actually do.

This contrast in perceptions is exacerbated by the emergence of a 'reassurance' gap between what the police and the media perceive as the problem and 'signal events' (Innes, 2004: 151). Signal events are crimes that seem to capture the media and the public's imaginations and exert 'a disproportionate impact upon public beliefs and attitudes when compared with their "objective" consequences' (Innes, 2005: 5). These 'signal events' can distort public perceptions and increase levels of fear about cybercrime. Yet they may not necessarily constitute a major infraction of criminal law, or necessarily a minor one, but 'nonetheless disrupt the sense of social order' (Innes, 2004: 151) – hence the disproportionate impact of media over-dramatization of cybercrime. The irony is that (other than online frauds), these 'events' often have little immediate impact on the public, other than temporarily tending to disrupt their internet use. And yet they may have devastating effects upon the organization involved and longer-term impacts upon the individuals involved, especially where their personal data has been stolen and can be used against them. When personal experience of these 'events' mixes with media-derived knowledge of more serious, though much less prevalent, forms of victimization, the perceived dangerousness of the internet increases.

The police gaze, therefore, tends to focus upon more serious crimes committed online, where offenders are 'dangerous', such as paedophiles and also the more notorious hackers. The dangerousness of the former is undisputed; however, it is more contestable with regard to the latter as the earlier discussion in chapter 4 illustrated. It is increasingly apparent that the under-reporting of cybercrimes to the police reflects the diverse nature of the provenance of the individual acts of cybercrime described earlier. Put simply, relatively few internet-related crimes are reported to the police because most are resolved elsewhere by the victims themselves, or by the panoply of other types of organization or groups involved in the regulation of behaviour in cyberspace. Various victim surveys show a disparity between high levels of fear of cybercrime contrasted with lower levels of actual victimization (National Statistics, 2012; Levi and Williams, 2012; Wall, 2013: 16–17).

Policing the reassurance gap in a culture of fear about cybercrime

The seventh challenge arises from the combination of over-dramatized media reportage and the under-reporting of cybercrime. This tends to confuse potential cybersecurity risks and threats with actual cybercrime harms, against a pre-existing background of dystopic conceptualizations of cybercrime, resulting in a 'culture of fear' around cybercrime (see Wall 2008). As a consequence, this 'culture of fear' has arguably led to demands for levels of security that the police agencies and government cannot realistically deliver alone (Wall 2008). The knock-on effect is that police and government have embarked upon a process of reassurance policing to bridge the gap between the demands for security and safety and its actual supply. But the results have been mixed, because some of the tactics employed amount to important and novel developments in policing (e.g., disruptive policing models), whereas others seem to be little more than PR exercises to appease the public. What seems to be happening is that in the current politicization of cybercrime, police agencies often tend to respond to the micro-politics of the situation, especially to the 'voices of concern', rather than to the justice needs of individual victims. The upshot here, it is argued, is that the loudest voices tend to prevail, and policing agencies feel pressure to police the reassurance gap, rather than police cybercrimes in order to achieve justice. This phenomenon is supported by an analysis of local police data which shows emphasis towards policing internet bad behaviour (under s. 127 of the Communications Act 2003) rather than Computer Misuse, but can be seen more broadly – for example, locally and nationally – in the various responses to three case studies outlined earlier in box 6.4 ('Snapchat and "sexting"'), box 6.6 ('Facebook, flirting and threats to kill') and box 8.1 ('The TalkTalk hack').

The culture of fear about cybercrime and the reassurance gap arising from the mismatch between expectations of security and its delivery mean that police and related agencies will have to work towards managing public and business expectations of the levels and types of security that police and government can deliver. The public's first point of contact, the police call centre, for example, is the most logical starting point for this. Current practice in many police force call-centres with regard to reports of frauds and cybercrime seems to be to redirect callers to report them to Action Fraud (the UK national economic and cybercrime reporting centre). It has been argued elsewhere that if call-centre staff across the UK spent two or three minutes or more with each caller to give advice and reassurance and explain to victims that their information is very important even though less serious cases may not result in a police investigation, then the public might be more inclined to report a cybercrime (Wall, 2017). If they did, important strategic intelligence may also be collected, including vital information about the many attempted frauds and related inchoate offences, which can be used by the National Fraud Intelligence Bureau to develop the UK Fraud Strategy and also to identify the tactical information that is needed to investigate online crimes (see Wall, 2013: 18, and references at the rear).[9]

The role of the public police in policing cyberspace

The answer to the earlier questions about the effectiveness of the role of the public police in cyberspace is quite simple: they only play a very small part in overall policing of the internet. This is not, however, to say that cyberspace goes unpoliced. As Robert Reiner has observed more generally: 'not all policing lies in the police' (Reiner, 2000). Similarly, Stenning and Shearing have argued that the public police are neither in control of, nor necessarily at the centre of, the governance of crime because there are so many other actors involved (Stenning and Shearing, 2005: 167). It is also important to bear in mind that the poor visibility of traditional police performance indicators that measure online order, for example, contrasts sharply against high levels of police science which can catch infringers by using surveillant technology. This debate is taken forward in the next chapter.

The governance of online behaviour is characterized by a sense of order that results from the complex order-maintenance 'assemblage' of networked nodes of security described earlier. These networks not only effect compliance, but also continually shape virtual behaviour (Wall, 1997, 2001b: 171, 2002a: 192; Walker and Akdeniz, 1998: 8; Newman and Clarke, 2003: 160). In so doing, they transcend the 'state/non-state binary' (Dupont, 2004: 76) and also state sovereignty (Shearing, 2004: 6). The term 'assemblage' is particularly useful in this context to explore the relationships between nodes, and also within them. In some of these networked relationships, there may be consensus about the policing process, while in others the consensus may be in the outcomes or goals achieved. Consequently, there is a replication of the bifurcation found in terrestrial policing between the maintenance of order and the enforcement of law. By separating the two, some sense can be made of the rather conflicting messages emerging in debates over policing the internet. Networked security, for example, exploits the 'natural surveillance' implicit in networked technologies to enable both primary and secondary social control functions to operate. It also tends to mediate, to some extent, global disparities arising from national or jurisdictional legal differences in definition.

Furthermore, looking at the policing of the internet in this way exposes countervailing tensions and helps to unravel the apparently rather tangled role of the public police. On the one hand, the overall public police role is comparatively small, with the other networks playing the larger role in policing and regulating online behaviour. As indicated above, since many cybercrimes fall outside traditional police crime diets, they become unproblematic from a police resourcing point of view – they simply do not get resourced. On the other hand, the public police not only tend to lay claim culturally (in an organizational and occupational sense) to a greater ownership of policing the internet than 'they actually own', but, more importantly, they are also expected to do so by the public because of their traditional consensual relationship with the state and the citizen. In most common-law countries, the public still regard the public police as an emergency service. So, even though the public police do not actually police some parts of cyberspace, an echo of their Peelian heritage reminds them of their symbolic duty to protect the public from danger.

We see in the debates over the policing of the internet a replication of the terrestrial reassurance policing debate (Crawford and Lister, 2004), though with a slight twist.

Whereas the reassurance policing debate is born out of the 'increasing recognition that the police alone cannot win the fight against crime and disorder nor meet the public's seemingly insatiable demand for a visible policing presence' (Crawford and Lister, 2004: 413), when shifted into cyberspace, the debate takes for granted that the police alone cannot win the fight against crime, but nevertheless demands a more visible policing presence. This raises important questions as to how they deal with those challenges.

The neo-Peelian agenda: renegotiating the public police role in policing cyberspace

The earlier discussion situated the police as a relatively minor, but important, player in the broader network of security that constitutes the policing of cyberspace. By outlining the various challenges faced by local police with regard to globalized offending online, the preceding analysis suggests that the police are in fact fairly ill equipped organizationally, occupationally and culturally to deal with it. However, that is only part of the story. As Crawford and Lister (2004: 414) have observed, during the past decade or so we have witnessed the increasing pluralization of terrestrial policing. The 'public police are becoming part of a more varied and complex assortment of organizations and agencies with different policing functions together with a more diffuse array of processes of control and regulation' (Crawford and Lister, 2004: 414). They show that while 'much policing is now taking place beyond the auspices' of the public police (p. 426), it would be premature to view the partnerships that form plural policing as facilitating a form of 'networked governance'. In the British terrestrial policing context, '[t]he reality, at the moment at least, is that crime and disorder partnerships remain state-dominated institutions' (p. 426). But these observations can still inform our understanding of the police role in cyberspace because of its networked and nodal architecture. The earlier discussion about situating the police demonstrated considerable pluralism in the policing of cyberspace beyond the auspices of the public police. However, the emerging role of the police as (digital) information brokers (Ericson and Haggerty, 1997) has led, during the past decade, to a new neo-Peelian role for the public police in which the original Peelian principles and values are promoted, but within the networks and nodes of multi-agency cross-sector partnerships, forums and coalitions. Just as ideas about crime have become globalized, then so have ideas about policing.

Multi-agency cross-sector partnerships

Three main tensions arise in the order-maintenance 'assemblage' outlined above, which public police forces have to reconcile in their working relationships or partnerships with others. These are the public-to-public police tensions, which have to be resolved in order to facilitate working relationships between public police forces and agencies, both formal and informal, at local, national and international levels. More problematic are the public-to-private tensions in relationships between public police and private organizations, and, thirdly, the tensions arising from private-to-private relations between private organizations which effectively exclude the public police (see McKenzie, 2006).

To varying degrees, multi-agency cross-sector partnerships and forums help to resolve some of the potentially destructive conflicts between private/commercial and public policing interests. They also mediate potential 'turf wars' between different police agencies that can impede cooperative efforts between organizations and levels of cooperation between individuals. Traditionally, the tensions between the commercial and public sectors arise because the primary function of the former is to police their own 'private' interests. In so doing, they pursue a 'private model' of justice that does not expose publicly their organization's weaknesses, and thereby maintains the confidence of the market. The public criminal justice model, on the other hand, is public, and the prosecution of offenders is carried out in the public interest and in the public gaze – not a model of criminal justice that many corporate entities want (Wall, 2001b: 174). Within the public sector are found equally destructive tensions between different policing agencies. Not only do 'turf wars' take place between national and local police forces for ownership of cases, but there are also distinct contrasts between the organizational and occupational ethos of law enforcement and police agencies that can damage the collective effort. Such contrasts are highlighted in Gorman's (2003) analysis of governmental responses to the 11 September terrorist attacks. Gorman argues that the 'FBI [are] from Mars, and the CIA from Venus . . . it's not that [FBI agents and CIA officers] don't like each other . . . they're really different people . . . they have a hard time communicating' (2003: paras. 1, 4).

Through what is effectively a form of 'peacebuilding' (J. Wood, 2004: 41), the purpose of multi-agency cross-sector partnerships is to build up networked trust relationships that engender a willingness to share information. Although these partnerships tend to be driven by internet security and law enforcement initiatives, it would be wrong simply to assume they are the product of formal policy, and also that they are necessarily dominated by state law-enforcement imperatives. The following three examples from North America, involving many similar enterprises, illustrate how the partnerships, forums and coalitions of interest can vary in terms of their being multi-agency or cross-sector, or both, and also how the boundaries between them can overlap. POLCYB (the Society for the Policing of Cyberspace), for example, is both multi-agency and cross-sectoral, existing to share information across micro-networks of trusted individuals and agencies to promote cooperation between sectors while actively inviting international involvement from law enforcement, corporate entities and interest groups. The High-Tech Crime Consortium (HTCC), on the other hand, is more multi-agency than cross-sectoral. Largely internet based, it provides a closed forum for law-enforcement and security officers – mostly, but not exclusively, from North America – to discuss matters within a secure environment. Whereas POLCYB tends to discuss policy-end issues face to face, HTCC is more about sharing information, day-to-day problem solving, providing solutions and identifying emerging problems. Other forums are much looser coalitions or friendship associations of law-enforcement and security experts. The AGORA security group, for example, encourages informal cross-sector relationships and provides a face-to-face environment for information exchange between members/associates about internet-related security matters. In a similar manner to POLCYB, the discussion about information sharing in AGORA tends to take place at a policy or procedural level, rather than specifically sharing substantive intelligence data – for example, developing ideas about security issues and good practice, but also identifying, even agreeing (pre-policy), possible acceptable limits for data storage about economic transactions and internet traffic flows and also the standards to be employed in responding to requests to store and/or provide data. However, the networked trust relationships established within the forums also facilitate the subsequent sharing of intelligence, including information about commercial victimizations and related criminal intelligence. Importantly, the personal and occupational interests of the members indicate a substantial cross-over of membership between the three partnerships.

The tightening of security after 11 September brought together multi-agency partnerships driven by specific national policies or legislation, and drew together relevant aspects of (governmental and non-governmental) agencies under the auspices of a coordinating body. Appel (2003) provides a very detailed and useful list of the many private–public cybercrime-related multi-sector partnerships operating in the USA which are associated with the Department of Justice and the DHS. The nearest EU-wide equivalent is the European Network and Information Security Agency (ENISA). In the UK, the key co-ordinating organization is the NISCC, which coordinates the principal agencies. In the US context, Appel argues that public–private collaborations are currently working in states, counties, regions and cities, and cites many examples of effective solutions with different approaches that involve law enforcement, business, private security, government and academia (Appel, 2003).

Specific emerging concerns have also stimulated demand for specialist coalitions to be set up by a broad range of interested organizations, often with some governmental input. One such example is the CNSA (the Contact Network of Spam Authorities) which coordinates efforts under the EU anti-spam directive. Existing on the margins of policing – though within the broader context of EU-wide responses to spamming, which includes spam generation as well as spam content – the anti-spam enforcement authorities of thirteen European countries (Austria, Belgium, Cyprus, the Czech Republic, Denmark, France, Greece, Ireland, Italy, Lithuania, Malta, the Netherlands and Spain, with others invited to join) have agreed to work together to investigate complaints about cross-border spams from within the EU. However, since the majority of spam originates outside the EU, it is planned that the CNSA will work in cooperation with other countries, 'both bilaterally and in international forums like the OECD and the International Telecommunication Union' (European Commission, 2005). In 2004, a similar agreement was reached between the US, UK and Australia to coordinate anti-spam efforts (electricnews, 2005). Another example of such a coalition is the APWG, mentioned in chapter 5, which now has about 2,000 members.

It is very difficult to assess the effectiveness of these partnerships and forums in achieving their respective tasks because there are few visible performance indicators, and the multiple flows of information generated between the many nodes in security networks can paint different pictures at different points. However, by creating environments of openness through the establishment of trust, then the networks created by the partnerships, forums and coalitions facilitate the flow of essential information to the nodes. At the centre of the establishment of trust appears the 'police' link.[10] A brief examination of the composition of the many partnership management boards indicates a mix of law-enforcement and other organizations. Their activities, mainly conferences, workshops and meetings, also display a similar balance. What comes across very strongly, from a cursory examination of their activities, is that former and current police officers clearly play an important, though not always leading, role in these multi-agency and cross-sector partnership forums. But there remain, as yet, a number of unanswered questions about the nature of their role, because the actual working of the partnership operation often lacks oversight and transparency – although discretion, of course, is one of the main reasons why the partnerships work. Also relatively unknown is the extent to which the non-police contacts in these networks of trust are themselves former police officers. Again, a brief look at the composition of the boards of these agencies and their working parties suggests that the number is fairly high. At the heart of the trust-building dynamics appears to be a meeting of minds that possess a similar *Weltanschauung*, which is probably the main reason why the networks actually work (this would be another research project in itself). The shared occupational values appear to sustain and culturally reproduce the Peelian policing paradigm, so that, while the milieu of policing cybercrimes may be different, the public policing mandate remains much the same.

Conclusions: the challenge of cybercrime for the police–public mandate

This chapter has explored the challenges that cybercrimes pose for the police and their mandate from the public. It has examined the role played by the public police in policing the internet within the broader architecture of internet governance and its order-maintenance assemblage/compliance framework. It has illustrated how the internet, and the criminal behaviour it transforms, challenge the processes of order maintenance and law enforcement. Not only does internet-related offending take place within a global context while crime tends to be nationally defined, but the public police mandate prioritizes some offending over others, particularly where there is a dangerous 'other', as in the production of child sexual images. Furthermore, policing the internet is a very complex affair by the very nature of policing and security being networked and nodal. It is also complex because within this framework the public police play only a small part in the overall policing process, yet the Peelian heritage of the police that has long defined their relationship with the state and the public has caused the police instinctively to assert ownership over the policing function.

Cyberspace thus places the public police in a rather contradictory position – on the one hand, the characteristics of cybercrimes contradict the basic Peelian principles of policing, yet those very same principles lead the public to rely upon the police for protection. This contradiction can be observed in most jurisdictions where policing takes place by consent, and even in some where the consent is less apparent. Cybercrimes generate many questions about whether the public police's cultural heritage and traditional constitutional position actually fit them organizationally for a role in policing cyberspace. However, the contradictions faced by 'the police', particularly the 'reassurance gap' between crimes experienced and those felt (Innes, 2004: 151), have led to public concern about 'cybercrime'. This has subsequently shaped the demands made of the police for reassurance, which have been reconciled by the reconstitution of the Peelian principles of policing and the emergence of a neo-Peelian agenda across a global span. While this resituates the police as an authority within the networks of security, it nevertheless creates a range of instrumental and normative challenges for them. One of those challenges is to temper the potentially dangerous drift towards the very edge of 'ubiquitous law enforcement' (Vinge, 2000) and to excite a range of opposing debates. But there is also optimism in the potential for those same technologies to provide important opportunities for police reform (Chan et al., 2001). The surveillant characteristics that make technology a powerful policing tool also make it a natural tool for overseeing police practice and for increasing broader organizational and public accountability (see debate in Newburn and Hayman, 2001).

The future of the public police role in policing the internet is about more than simply acquiring new expert knowledge and capacity. It is about forging new types of working relationships with the other nodes within the networks of internet security. Such relationships require a range of new transformations to take place in order to enhance the effectiveness and legitimacy of the nodal architecture – for example, a further flattening of policing structures, parity of legal definitions across boundaries, broadly accepted frameworks of accountability to the public, shared values, multi-agency and cross-sectoral dialogues. There is also the need for steering the mindset of police officers away from a 'warrior' mentality (good guy / bad guy binary) and developing more of a mindset of a guardianship role.[11] Without these new relationships, there will be one less check on the danger of a drift towards 'ubiquitous law enforcement' and 'ubiquitous crime prevention'.

The long-standing myth that the internet is a lawless and disordered environment – a place where people go for a moral holiday (see Baron and Straus, 1989: 132) – continues to endure, but it is wholly mistaken. Rather, the evidence points to the contrary. In this chapter, it was demonstrated that there exists an order-maintenance assemblage – almost a compliance framework – that intervenes in many different ways and for many different reasons to police behaviour on the internet. In this, law remains an important reference point, but it is not the sole driver of behaviour, and in itself it is certainly not a sound basis for cybercrime-prevention policy. Any policy needs to recognize not just law, but also social values, market forces and especially the extent to which the behaviour to be prevented has been mediated by technology. This latter point is important because many offences currently called 'cybercrimes' are actually traditional (or unmediated) crime. The true cybercrimes are only just beginning to emerge. Whereas this chapter has focused upon the present and the past, the next chapter looks to the future and focuses on the architecture of regulating and preventing cybercrimes.

Some discussion questions based upon this chapter

Who polices cybercrime and how?

What are the main challenges that cybercrime poses for police and criminal justice systems?

Are the police the best agency for responding to victims of cybercrime. If not, then what approach would you suggest?

Further Reading   Formulating appropriate policing responses to cybercrimes by responsible agencies has been a recurring problem for many years. As various preventative, mitigative and investigatory responses improve, policing becomes quickly left behind by more adaptive offenders who employ more ruthless techniques. Important questions arise as to whether or not conventional policing agencies are best equipped to police this area solely – or should they be assisted by other agencies, or even replaced in this role? Students and researchers who wish to take this field of study further are recommended to start with the following sources: Wall and Williams (2014); Holt et al. (2015); PNLD and Staniforth (2017); Saunders (2017).

9 Controlling, Preventing and Regulating Cybercrime

How are cybercrimes to be controlled, regulated and prevented?

Chapter contents and key points

Law and legal action
- A case study in making law: regulating spamming as a cybercrime

Technological controls: cybercrime control and prevention using technology

Social controls: social values

Economic controls: market forces

Code and the public v. private interest

Technologies of control or the control of technology

Chapter at a glance *This chapter looks at the issues relating to controlling, reducing and generally regulating cybercrime. It explores the formal role of law and legal action, but also the various technical, social and economic (market) controls which combine to reduce the different ways in which cybercrime is prevented, mitigated, investigated and prosecuted.*

Introduction

The previous chapter discussed how cybercrimes are policed and showed that state-appointed police play a relatively small (although important) role in the larger picture of policing the internet. This chapter broadens the governance perspective even further to include the wider regulation of cyberspace (the internet) as the environment in which cybercrimes take place. It explores the roles played by law, technological architecture, social values and the market in maintaining order and law on the internet. After all, ideally, a good system of regulation should enable good behaviours as well as disabling bad behaviours, to promote positive as well as negative governance (Alharthi, 2023).

It was established earlier in this book that the 'digital' realism of cybercrime is that, although laws define the boundaries between acceptable and unacceptable behaviours in society, including virtual society, cybercrimes are the product of a range of legal, technical, social and economic 'affordances'[1] or opportunities. As a reminder, the legal affordances arise from offenders feeling comfortable to commit cybercrimes because of a relatively low risk of detection, either because of inadequate or ill-fitting law, or because cybercrime is low on the criminal justice system's list of priorities. They are technical because the technology provides an 'affordance' (Gibson, 1979) or enabler for cybercrime. They are social in that the act of cybercrime is socially rewarding for offenders, by providing satisfaction and 'sneaky thrills' (Katz, 1988) for their efforts, and a degree of social status within their communities. Finally, the opportunities are economic as they reward offenders with money for their efforts.

It therefore follows that these 'affordances', which enable offending, can be turned on their head and used as points from which to regulate, police and prevent cybercrime. In an ideal world, the solution is to strengthen law and its enforcement, make the technology more secure and reduce the social and economic rewards. The real world, however, is more complex, but there are a number of aspects of these opportunities which can be exploited, especially the technology. More specifically, the surveillant and 'dataveillant' (Clarke, 1994), panoptic and synoptic (Mathieson, 1997: 215) qualities of networked technologies that enable cybercrime also provide potentially powerful new tools for policing the internet and collecting new sources of evidence with which to secure prosecutions and convictions. They also provide 'disciplinary' tools that can facilitate cybercrime control and prevention. But it does not stretch the libertarian imagination too much to see where this is going, because these technical 'tools' also take us to the very edge of 'ubiquitous law enforcement', to 'ubiquitous crime prevention' and even to the policing of pre-crime[2] by anticipating intent. Not surprisingly, they excite a range of opposing debates about the nature of privacy and freedom in the information age. Are current expectations of privacy and freedom now dead in an information age where it is almost impossible to evade the surveillant gaze? Do we therefore need to revise current ideas about privacy to fit today (Sprenger, 1999), or do we protect the old values or completely rethink them? These questions are for another book as this chapter is about how we regulate and prevent cybercrimes at the cyber-assisted, cyber-enabled and cyber-dependent levels. Should the balance of the four affordances be applied equally, or proportional to the type of offence? Should, for example, cyber-assisted crime be treated mainly as a communications issue? Should cyber-enabled crimes be treated as they are offline? Should cyber-dependent crimes, which are wholly mediated by technology, be regarded mainly as a scientific technical problem to which a technical solution (sanctioned by law) should be applied, or are they an aggravation that should be considered by existing laws? Will, for example, the exercise of 'perfect control' (Post, 2000: 1450) be based upon scientific or commercial considerations that will override the influence of law, social values and market forces which normally combine with technology to form the architecture of environments that shape the behaviour that takes place within them? Is perfect control ever possible? The answers to these questions will become progressively significant as the scale of cybercrimes continues to become larger and the cybercrimes become more and more automated.

The first part of this chapter looks briefly at the role of law and legal action in regulating the internet. The second part explores technological controls and the existing use of technology in cybercrime control and prevention. The third part looks at societal (social) controls, and the fourth part at market or economic controls that can be brought to bear to regulate internet activity. The final part of this chapter explores the issue of embedding law and policy into computer code.

Law and legal action

Hard law outlines the boundaries between acceptable and unacceptable behaviours, often in great detail. There are a number of laws that respond to each of the different types or levels of cybercrime (mainly using the UK law as an example). The Computer Misuse Act 1990 (ss. 1–3) and its various amendments, for example, respond to cyber-dependent crimes, the cybercrimes that take place against the machine, as described in chapter 4. These include hacking systems, denial of service attacks, malware. Cyber-enabled crimes (crimes which use the machine, described in chapter 5) include fraud, covered by the Fraud Act 2006; theft, by the Theft Act 1998; and/or extortion or blackmail, by the Theft Act 1968 and s. 29 and s. 30 of the Larceny Act 1916. Finally, cybercrimes in the machine (chapter 6), depending on which type, are covered by the Obscene Publications Act 1959 and Criminal Justice and Immigration Act 2008, Pt 5, for extreme pornography; the Regulation of Investigatory Powers Act 2000 for terror materials; the Fraud Act 2006 for content that deceives; and the Copyright Designs and Patents Act 1988 for intellectual property.[3] Similar bodies or types of law exist in other jurisdictions.

In addition to hard law, which remains a crucial source of authority, is soft law, which is formed of agreed rules, recommendations or guidelines. It emerged in international law (Boyle, 1999; Trubek and Trubek, 2005) and is perhaps best expressed in the various UN treaties. *The UN norms of responsible state behaviour in cyberspace* is one soft law which provides guidance for countries to introduce measures that increase stability and security in the use of information and communications technologies (ICTs) and prevent practices that are acknowledged to be harmful or pose threats to international peace and security (ASPI, 2022: 13). Reproduced in Box 9.1, the norms, in a nutshell, recommend that states approach ICT incidents responsibly, work cooperatively, protect human rights, protect their infrastructures, ensure the integrity of their supply chains and share information and good practice. Finally, they should not allow their territories to be used for wrongful ICT acts or support the harming of the ICT systems of another state.

Box 9.1 Full text of the UN cyber norms

a. Consistent with the purposes of the United Nations, including to maintain international peace and security, States should cooperate in developing and applying measures to increase stability and security in the use of ICTs and to prevent ICT practices that are acknowledged to be harmful or that may pose threats to international peace and security;
b. In case of ICT incidents, States should consider all relevant information, including the larger context of the event, the challenges of attribution in the ICT environment and the nature and extent of the consequences;
c. States should not knowingly allow their territory to be used for internationally wrongful acts using ICTs;
d. States should consider how best to cooperate to exchange information, assist each other, prosecute terrorist and criminal use of ICTs and implement other cooperative measures to address such threats. States may need to consider whether new measures need to be developed in this respect;

e. States, in ensuring the secure use of ICTs, should respect Human Rights Council resolutions 20/8 and 26/13 on the promotion, protection and enjoyment of human rights on the Internet, as well as General Assembly resolutions 68/167 and 69/166 on the right to privacy in the digital age, to guarantee full respect for human rights, including the right to freedom of expression;

f. A State should not conduct or knowingly support ICT activity contrary to its obligations under international law that intentionally damages critical infrastructure or otherwise impairs the use and operation of critical infrastructure to provide services to the public;

g. States should take appropriate measures to protect their critical infrastructure from ICT threats, taking into account General Assembly resolution 58/199 on the creation of a global culture of cybersecurity and the protection of critical information infrastructures, and other relevant resolutions;

h. States should respond to appropriate requests for assistance by another State whose critical infrastructure is subject to malicious ICT acts. States should also respond to appropriate requests to mitigate malicious ICT activity aimed at the critical infrastructure of another State emanating from their territory, taking into account due regard for sovereignty;

i. States should take reasonable steps to ensure the integrity of the supply chain so that end users can have confidence in the security of ICT products. States should seek to prevent the proliferation of malicious ICT tools and techniques and the use of harmful hidden functions;

j. States should encourage responsible reporting of ICT vulnerabilities and share associated information on available remedies to such vulnerabilities to limit and possibly eliminate potential threats to ICTs and ICT-dependent infrastructure;

k. States should not conduct or knowingly support activity to harm the information systems of the authorized emergency response teams (sometimes known as computer emergency response teams or cybersecurity incident response teams) of another State. A State should not use authorized emergency response teams to engage in malicious international activity.

The EU (European Parliament) harmonizing directive provides soft law guidance on how to implement laws locally. In 2022, the EU's Network and Information Security directive (NIS2) introduced new rules designed to increase the level of cybersecurity across EU member states. The rules also strengthen the cybersecurity requirements for medium-sized and large organizations that operate and provide infrastructural services in the key sectors (EU, 2023). This legislation is in addition to the CoE Cybercrime (Budapest) Convention (ETS No. 185) and additional protocols which create a framework for permitting practitioners from across the CoE's member states and additional signatories to facilitate cooperation and share experiences of policing cybercrime. It supports, for example, a 24/7 network for law enforcement agencies which helps to expedite international cooperation on matters relating to cybercrime and securing electronic evidence. These international laws, treaties and conventions exist on top of the laws of individual nation states.

But law also provides an authority for legal tactics which may be intended to fall short of formal prosecution, but which have a 'chilling effect' on behaviour, particularly relating to warnings about the consequences of wrongdoing at one end of the spectrum, and formal 'sanctions' at the other end. See, for example, US sanctions[4] imposed against cybercriminals. Executive Order 13694 (2015) imposes sanctions on individuals and groups who are responsible for or complicit in malicious cybercrime activities that materially threaten or harm 'national security, foreign policy, or economic health or financial stability of the United States', including election processes (USDOS, 2023). Executive Order 13757 (2016) was amended (EO13694) to include the harms caused by malicious cyber-enabled activities and directs the Secretary of State of the Treasury (after consulting with the Attorney General and Secretary of State) to impose sanctions on individuals determined to be responsible for or complicit in harmful cyber-activities. These individuals (and groups) are included on the Treasury's Office of Foreign Assets list of Specially Designated Nationals and Blocked Persons and can be subject to extradition proceedings. See, for example, the May 2023 indictment charging a Russian national with conducting ransomware attacks against US critical infrastructure: 'From his home base in Russia, Matveev allegedly used multiple ransomware variants to attack critical infrastructure around the world, including hospitals, government agencies, and victims in other sectors' (USDOJ, 2023a).

Matveev is alleged to have worked as an affiliate of the Lockbit, Hive and Babuk ransomware groups and is believed to have attacked law enforcement and other government agencies, hospitals, and schools in three global ransomware campaigns. The ransom demands totalled $400 million, and the total payments were as much as $200 million (USDOJ, 2023a). Because Matveev is based in Russia, to whom he has pledged support, and there is not an extradition order in place, it is unlikely that Russian police will cooperate with the FBI. However, prosecutors were clear that the indictment was intended to send a strong message to wrongdoers that they were on the US radar and their safe harbour would not last for ever.

> We want the indictment, sanctions and reward for Mikhail Matveev to sound an alarm in the ranks of cyber criminals all over the world . . . The FBI and our law enforcement partners, as well as our international partners, are coming after you. These malicious actors believe they can operate with impunity – and don't fear getting caught because they sit in a country where they feel safe and protected. That may be the case now, but the safe harbor may not exist forever. When we have an opportunity, we will do everything in our power to bring Matveev and his ilk to justice. (USDOJ, 2023b)

Evidence of the impact of sanctions is found in the case of the ransomware attack on Colonial Pipeline by the Darkside Ransomware group. The attack resulted in the shutdown of the fuel supply to the US Eastern Seaboard. The US Department of State offered a $10 million reward for information leading to the identification of the leaders of Darkside, and a further $5 million for information leading to their arrest and conviction (USDOS, 2021). In response to the reward bounty, the Darkside operators[5] closed down their website and withdrew their ransomware service, stating on its website that 'Our goal is to make money and not creating problems for society' (Russon, 2021).

But law is more than the black letters on the pages of a law book, and it works in different ways. Not only are there national and international hard and soft laws and rules, but the laws and rules also have to be implemented and enforced by various 'guardians' each of which exercises discretion in their application of law. As we saw in chapter 8, although police agencies are primarily responsible for investigating and prosecuting criminal offenders, they are only one of a number of groups which enforce laws. In fact, the police are neither best placed to do the whole job of polic-ing, nor able to work in isolation, so various other 'guardians' in society contribute to the overall policing function. As will be recalled, internet users and user groups, online virtual environment managers and security, network infrastructure provid-ers, corporate organizations and corporate security, non-governmental non-police organizations, governmental non-police organizations also play different roles in policing online behaviours and enforcing laws and rules, in addition to the public police organizations. Each of these brings to bear a range of different forms of govern-ance, often relating to the contract between user and service provider. And the list of guardians is growing, along with an expanding debate about encouraging more active public participation in policing, and there are various cross-sector partner-ships which bring together police, industry and other organizations.

Below the exercise of hard law lie other forms of legal action which range from 'cease and desist' tactics (letters before action in the UK) to private criminal court actions. Cease and desist is effectively a warning to an offender to stop a behaviour before formal action (usually civil) is brought. It also has a chilling effect and has been used with mixed effects by the music and film industry (see, further, Wall, 2015a), but also the police. The UK NCA's Cyber Choices programme, for example, works with individuals whose behaviour indicates that they may be possible cyber-offenders.[6] The programme explains them the difference between legal and illegal cyberactivity, and also the range of choices that they have for using their skills, such as the advan-tages of working in the legitimate cybersecurity industry.

Chilling effects can also be created by mobilizing an outraged public. In the early 2000s, the Institute for Spam and Internet Public Policy (ISIPP) proposed mass pri-vate legal action to 'chill' spamming behaviour through its 'death by 1000 paper cuts' strategy. ISIPP encourages victims of spam, mainly domain name owners, to 'sue a spoofer'. ISIPP wants domain owners to stand up for themselves, by shouting '"We're not going to take it", and fighting back, spammers will have to stop spoofing, if not stop spamming altogether' (ISIPP website). Taking forward the idea of consumer action against spam, Nigel Roberts was successful in suing an email marketing com-pany for £300 for sending him unsolicited emails about contract car hire and their fax broadcasting service (*Roberts* v. *Media Logistics (UK) Ltd*, 2006). Fortified by his suc-cess, Roberts formed 'spam legal action' as a rallying call to victims of spam to bring their own actions against spammers. To assist them, he provides a do-it-yourself spam suing kit containing sample documents through his Spam Legal Action web-site. So, in this sense, law is the authority, and legal action can shape market demand by moulding social values about new types of activities.

Actions such as Roberts's were an early form of digilantism (internet vigilantism), which has evolved in the 2000s with the advent of social media into a rather large movement where internet users who are disappointed at what they see as a lack of police action take justice into their own hands. They hack or bait and publicly shame or denounce individuals who they feel are a danger to society. On the one hand, when conducted correctly, digilantism can act democratically and help authorities to act by providing them with essential community-based information. On the other hand, it can go wrong as the digilantes are usually self-appointed and their zeal often blurs boundaries between right and wrong, frequently hiding their own bullying behaviours (Trottier et al., 2020; Gainford, 2023).

A case study in making law: regulating spamming as a cybercrime

Although spamming is often regarded as trivial, its use is significant for cybercriminals because it delivers phishing messages to 'phish' personal information, causes BEC crimes and furthers cybercrimes (see chapter 5). The regulation of spamming is therefore a useful case study here to illustrate not only the impact of introducing law when there was previously none, but also the potential for introducing law into 'code'.

As outlined in earlier chapters, spamming is currently an automated tactic to enable online offenders to engage with their victims. With spamming emails and text messages, the spammer's clients elicit a direct response by getting victims either to give personal information, to open an infected attachment or to click onto an infected web link. The act of spamming itself has been a criminal act in many jurisdictions since the early 2000s, and spams rain upon users daily in their billions. Figure 9.1 shows the top ten countries by number of daily spam emails (in billions) as of January 2023. The US and India were the main senders, by a small margin, and also significant recipients. It is important to note that these statistics are only an indicator of volumes of spam because they can differ daily as rogue servers are legally removed by authorities and new servers are illegally set up by offenders.

Two major schools of thought currently dominate the debates over spamming: the legal determinists and the technological determinists (crime science, if you like).

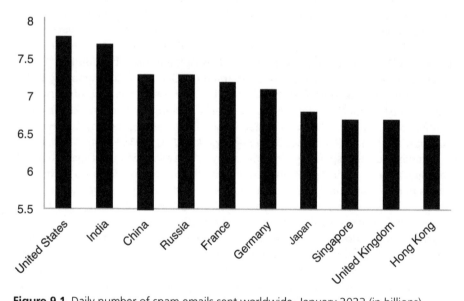

Figure 9.1 Daily number of spam emails sent worldwide, January 2023 (in billions).
Source: adapted from data published by Statista[7] from Cisco Talos Intelligence Group; 16 January 2023.

The legal determinists believe that norms embodied in legislation condition social change, whereas the technologists believe that technology can perform this role. The legal determinist solution to an undesirable behavioural problem is to introduce new laws to curtail it, and there has been no shortage of laws to deal with spamming. On 11 December 2003, the UK introduced compulsory opt-in legislation in the form of the Privacy and Electronic Communications (EC Directive) Regulations 2003 (SI/2003/2426). These regulations brought into effect Article 13 of EU Directive 2002/58/EC[8] on privacy and electronic communications, which had been passed in July of the previous year. Prior to December 2003, the UK had adopted a self-regulatory model in which spammers were supposed to provide those on their mail lists the facility to opt out. The 2003 EU Directive outlawed spamming unless consent had previously been obtained from the recipient. The main problem for the UK, for example, is that the majority of spam received originates outside the UK, with the bulk originating in the US and the Far East.

In the US, federal legislation entitled 'Controlling the Assault of Non-Solicited Pornography and Marketing Act of 2003', or the 'CAN-SPAM Act of 2003' (s. 877), was passed by Congress in early December 2003 and came into effect on 1 January 2004. It imposed 'limitations and penalties on the transmission of unsolicited commercial electronic mail via the Internet'. The US legislation sits on top of a patchwork of state legislation, some of which is strong, as in California, and other parts either weak or non-existent. Unlike the EU legislation which requires recipients to have previously opted-in to spam lists, the CAN-SPAM Act made it a compulsory requirement that spammers provide an opt-out facility (the UK/EU's previous position). However, despite the discordance between the EU/UK and US approaches to spamming and criticisms of their respective legal shortcomings, the bodies of legislation were brought into effect from early 2004 where neither previously existed.

The legislation was timely because it coincided with a rise in the number of 'botnets' (Race, 2005) which acted as a force multiplier for spammers. In their Global Internet Security Threat Report 2004, Symantec found a huge increase in zombie PCs between January and June 2004, from under 2,000 to more than 30,000 per day – peaking at 75,000 on one day (Leyden, 2004e). Since the early 2000s, the number of botnet command and control servers has grown a hundredfold. The main botnets in 2021 worldwide were, in order of percentage of traffic, Trickbot (29%), Qbot (14%), Emotet (13%), Dridex (12%), Clupteba (10%), Phorpiex (10%), other bots (12%).[9] These are the malware that draw together the botnet; they do, however, often serve more than one function – for example, also stealing personal information (information guzzlers). Sending out spam is therefore only one of their functions. In their 2020 Botnet Report, ENISA, the European Union Agency for Cybersecurity, estimated that Emotet, a botnet source comprising 10% of traffic, sent out 11 million emails (ENISA, 2020). Spamhaus found that, although botnet command and control servers were found in 193 countries, the top 3 ranked by volume were Russia (4,712), the USA (4,007) and the Netherlands (1,441) (Spamhaus, 2020).

As figure 9.1 suggests, the overall number of spams being circulated daily falls in the billions. What is reassuring is that most spams do not reach their destinations because of filtering systems that are ultimately empowered by law. In the early 2000s, I collected spam emails received on a research email account. The monthly spam totals received by this email account from January 2000 until July 2004 are

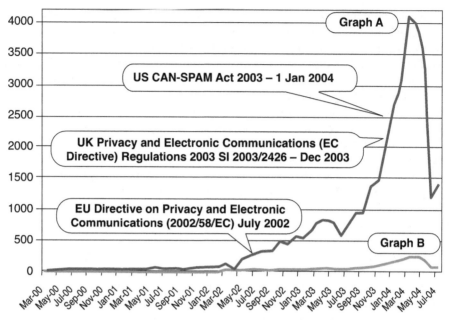

Figure 9.2 The monthly receipt of emails into a research email account from 2000 to 2004 and the impact of regulation (Graph line A represents spam emails and Graph B the 'legitimate' emails).

represented in figure 9.2. It would be easy to construct a case which shows the (delayed) positive impact of law in reducing spamming (or increasing it, if one were to be cynical!). However, the facts of the story are a little different.

The number of spam emails received increased exponentially around 2002, when botnets became more established. Also note the timeline of anti-spam legislation. After April/May 2004, Graph A departs from other contemporary sources of data on spams being sent (not shown here) and shows that the number of spams received by the account reduced considerably compared to those being sent. Race (2005), for example, in contrast to figure 9.2, illustrated that the number of spams in circulation remained more or less constant after April/May 2004. The explanation for the drop in spams received after April/May 2004 shown by Graph line A (and also Graph line B) was that, following the spam legislation, the ISP holding the research email account restructured its service provision and moved the account to another server which automatically ran anti-spam software on all incoming emails. Many confirmed spams were then intercepted in transit before they reached the recipient's mailbox. Previously, the software had only flagged potential spams before placing them into the mailbox, thus giving the account owner the choice over what to do with them.

So, this 'technological' event, and not the emergence of new law, explains a dramatic fall in spams received by the test account after April 2004 and gives weight to the technological determinist argument that technology can be used to reduce opportunities for crime by suppressing, or 'designing out', the opportunities that encourage the offending behaviour. Without the intervention of anti-spam technology in April 2004, the number of spams received would have continued at roughly the same level as the peak in April. But, to reiterate the earlier point, the law empowered the introduction of the technology; otherwise, the ISP would have been vulnerable to charges of restricting email traffic and possibly freedom of expression.

These observations demonstrate that code can trump the law (Edwards, 2004). They show the power of code to interrupt information flows and therefore how technology can have a greater impact upon online behaviour than law in this context. They also appear to lend some support to Room's argument that the real weapons against spam may not actually be found in the law contained in Directive 2002/58 or SI 2003/2426 or in the CAN-SPAM Act (Room, 2003: 1780), but in using 'code' in the form of anti-spam technology (also see Race, 2005). Similarly, Starr questions the use of law as a solution to spam: 'Trying to clamp down upon spammers with ever-more pedantic legislation could penalize email users while having a negligible effect on spam. If legislation consistently fails to meet the expectations of those seeking to suppress spam, then perhaps those expectations are being invested in the wrong thing' (Starr, 2004a: para. 25). Starr argued that expectations should be invested in technology instead of in law, because the sooner we recognize that 'spam is nothing more than a thorny practical problem, the sooner we will develop technology that can solve that problem' (Starr, 2004b: para. 22). This is the direction that has been taken ever since, with the application of artificial intelligence (AI) into modern sophisticated spam detection systems.

Spam has been made into a moral and even a comical issue, where those accused of sending it or apologising for it are automatically vilified, and those who oppose it are thought to occupy the moral high ground. This has left us without the perspective necessary to deal with spam effectively. The sooner we recognize that spam is nothing more than a thorny practical problem, the sooner we will develop technology that can solve that problem (Starr, 2004b: para. 22).

The problem with the crime science / technological determinist position is, however, that, while technology in the form of 'code' clearly disrupts the flow of spam, spams are not simply technological occurrences but the combined effect of a number of different variables. Simply to apply technological remedies does not solve the initial problem, but addresses the effect rather than the cause. What is actually happening is not that spamming behaviour and its attendant dangers are necessarily being deterred, but that the spams are now being identified and deleted en route to the recipient. Although this interception brings internet users some respite from the seemingly never-ending spam tsunami, there is no reason to believe that purely 'technological' solutions can stem spamming behaviour – they have merely reduced the number of spams received. The solution to spamming is therefore much more complex than a technological fix. More worrying is that the decisions to impose policies to intercept spams appear to be based upon scientific considerations, often in the private interest, and made in the absence of any critical debate. Using technology to change the architecture in which the behaviour takes place wrongly assumes that spammers are heterogeneous, and act rationally and intentionally; it also contravenes the internet's established principle of openness and network neutrality.

Additionally, for many of the reasons outlined earlier, law is an imperfect tool, and so is law enforcement, enabling entrepreneurial individuals to seize opportunities to make money / commit crimes, in much the same way as occurred in the West five or more years ago. Much less easy to explain, however, was the greater than 10 per cent increase in spamming from Europe, where the opt-in law, as opposed to the US opt-out, is stronger and arguably more enforceable. It is probable that this rise is mainly due to the presence of more insecure computers, especially in the new EU countries, which means a greater possibility of their being used as zombies. In addition, it is likely (though the evidence is not conclusive) that there may have been some displacement from the US, because the number of spammers has not noticeably increased according to the Spamhaus ROKSO database (Register of Known Spam Operations). It shows that '80% of spam received by Internet users in North America and Europe can be traced via aliases, addresses, redirects, locations of servers, domains and DNS setups, to around 100 known spam operations listed in the ROKSO database' (Spamhaus, 2020). In fact, the daily number of active spam operations (which use the botnets) is much less. On 18 May 2023, for example, 21 active spammers were listed in ROKSO.[10]

The decrease in spams received appears to be related to an increase in security empowered by law and also to users becoming more security conscious (and new computers coming with stronger security), combined with the impact of US-based sanctions against known spammers which has put some key spammers out of business and may have deterred others. We see, then, the influence of law in conjunction with other variables, or 'modalities of constraint': technological controls, social values and the market. Here they are explored in more detail.

Technological controls: cybercrime control and prevention using technology

The use of technology to effect crime control and prevention is long-standing, as illustrated earlier by the example of protecting the pyramids from grave robbers (chapter 1) or, at an everyday level, the invention of the lock and key to provide only the key holder with access. But the difference today is that those wanting to gain access do not have to be physically present and they can also remove entire contents without physical constraints.

Crime control and prevention initiatives have tended to fall into one of two distinct strategies: designing crime out of systems, or designing crime control into them. Each strategy finds a resonance in the broader literature on crime prevention (Clarke and Mayhew, 1980; Newman and Clarke, 2003; Clarke, 2004; and others). Situational crime prevention, as it is often known, draws upon the criminologies of everyday life (Garland, 2001: 127) to focus upon the reduction of opportunity by increasing the effort needed to commit a crime, increasing the risks to the offender, or reducing the reward of crime, but regardless of intent. At its heart is what Lessig has termed the 'old Chicago School' argument that if 'forces outside law regulate, and regulate better than law, the old school concludes that law should step aside' (Mitchell, 1995; Lessig, 1998b: 661).

Crucial to the success of crime control policies is the ability of the implementer not only to control the design process of the technology and its support systems, but also to identify any vulnerabilities and then to modify designs accordingly, prior to production. This is arguably more feasible with networked technologies (the internet) since the codes that make them work can easily be manipulated, which is a very appealing quality for crime scientists whose focus is on crimes rather than criminals, and who take a multidisciplinary approach to understanding, preventing and detecting them (see Pease, 2001: 18). It is also attractive to governments who have made it part of their broader agenda for protecting trade development. In the UK, for example – although similar examples exist in other jurisdictions – the DTI's 'Foresight' and 'Cyber-Trust' initiatives actively sought to identify the vulnerabilities in new technologies to encourage industry to modify designs and reduce the opportunities for crime without compromising usability (DTI, 2000; OST, 2004; Pease, 2001).

A useful example of designing crime out of an online payments system is the (policy) decision made by some online retailers to generally not accept direct credit card payments and only allow escrowed payment services (such as PayPal). This decision effectively reduced some types of card-not-present frauds. Such decisions can be implemented by changing the software codes which operate the financial transactions aspect of the website. A particularly relevant example of designing out crime was the inclusion of security facilities into computer operating systems that keep the system automatically updated by the manufacturer. Another was the implementation of a further policy which changed the security default position in operating systems from 'off' to 'on'. But designing crime out of technologies or systems is not without its problems, because it is very hard to ascertain how effective an intervention has been at the design stage, particularly when any means of measuring its success has also been designed out – measurement which budget managers like to see. This is especially the case in a networked virtual environment where functionality is primarily determined by software and its accompanying procedures, rather than by the hardware itself. The strategy can also have undesirable knock-on effects which have to be taken into consideration. There is, for example, the ever present conflict between the level of security provided and functionality of the product, because security measures will always compete with the user's instinctive preference for ease of use. If security measures are too complicated, users will tend to switch them off. Similarly, if a system is too secure, displacement may take place to one that is less secure, or even different part of the system, inadvertently creating new crime incentives. We saw in chapter 5, for example, how criminal attention focused upon the input or output stages of the transaction process as payment systems became more secure.

A more visible strategy is to design crime control into a system. Perhaps the most common, if not universal, experience of crime control is the use of usernames/ID and passwords to gain access to secure networks. Without these symbols of trust, the system will not allow access to individuals. Further crime control is also exercised through the retrieval and analysis of records of internet transactions. Although largely an afterthought in the original network design, the surveillant qualities of networked technologies can be utilized to effect crime control over individuals in a number of ways. Data mining is the analysis of collected and retained internet traffic data which records every internet transaction. The internet's 'fine-grained distributed systems' are linked to 'every part of social life' (Lessig, 2006: 1) and establish the potential for online monitoring and also the mining of the various databases of network traffic. Potentially analysed at speeds akin to real time to identify specific deviant activities or patterns of behaviour (Gandy, 2003: 26), data mining is the key to unlocking the 'disciplinary' potential of networked technology. One of the great public misperceptions about the internet is the myth of anonymity. In fact, networked technology leans in the opposite direction, to the point that we are now in danger of experiencing what was described earlier as the 'disappearance of disappearance' (Haggerty and Ericson, 2000: 619). This adds further weight to Ericson and Haggerty's (1997) arguments that policing 'the risk society' is increasingly about information brokering, and that relations between policing bodies are becoming largely concerned with negotiating the exchange of information. In this case, the information in question is internet traffic data, which can be used more broadly to gather intelligence about deviant – including terrorist – networks, or to establish conclusive evidence of wrongdoing (Walker and Akdeniz, 2003). These negotiations lead to the emergence of formal and informal relationships that underpin the networks of security mentioned in the previous chapter. Nowhere is this information brokering more apparent than with the proposed Dragnet intelligence systems, which rely upon the data-mining principle to combine and analyse various databases created by converged digital technologies to identify a range of harmful and criminal intentions. The Terrorism (previously 'Total') Information Awareness (TIA), for example, was proposed in the US after 11 September specifically to join all key national databases together to 'drain the swamp to catch the snake' (Evans-Pritchard, 2001; Levi and Wall, 2004: 207). Another, the 'Nice'[11] system, advertised in the 2000s to provide 'policing with a more human face', claimed to use AI to analyse different multimedia intelligence sources to detect abnormal behavioural patterns that it identifies as a possible sign of illegal activity. In public spaces, the manufacturers of Nice claimed that it 'can alert police when it detects loitering, crowd gathering, people running when they should be walking, tailgating, parking in the wrong place, unauthorized entry, or any sort of behaviour the police want to track' (Ballard, 2006). There were at the time some concerns as to whether or not the claims could be met. Nearly two decades later, the debate has developed into the merits and demerits of using AI and advanced surveillance technology to create predictive policing which anticipates crime hot spots in advance, so that the police can manage their resources more effectively. On this, there have been some claims of success using AI-analysed 'big data' in the US to reduce gun incidents, and in the UK (Manchester) to reduce robberies, burglaries and thefts from motor vehicles (Isafiade, 2022). Whilst these systems can replace laborious manual procedures and place police officers in the right position on the ground, they cannot, with any great degree of success that complies with contemporary privacy laws, predict an individual's criminal intentions (Kaufmann et al., 2018; Moses and Chan, 2018). Moreover, research by the Royal United Services Institute (RUSI) found that machine-learning algorithms can replicate and amplify bias on race, sexuality and age (Grierson, 2019).

A second way of introducing crime control is to utilize the 'code' that controls networked technologies by actively designing in security / crime prevention without changing the hardware. Katyal argues that solutions to cybercrime must try to exploit the internet's potential for natural surveillance, territoriality (stewardship of a virtual area) and its capacity for building online communities without damaging its principal design innovation – its openness (Katyal, 2003: 2268). These characteristics can also be used to generate a range of automated active 'policing' tools that seek to identify wrongdoing, of which 'honeypots' are an example. Honeypots are a computer program, usually a website (the Honeynet), which seeks to attract offenders and counter their intentions. Although fake, the 'honeynet' has the outward appearance of the 'real thing' but constructed to display the 'key words' that offenders search for when trawling, say, for illegal images (Honeynet Project, 2002). Various honeypot operations have been used by police forces all over the world with some success, to deter people developing an interest in viewing extreme pornographic imagery (see chapter 6).

When seeking to view or search for illegal content, the viewer will be directed to the 'honeynet' site and, after trying to refine the search, will be redirected to another police-owned site which will warn them that their actions are illegal and that to seek the illegal content again will constitute an offence for which they will be prosecuted. Honeynets have been used by law enforcement to identify offenders wishing to access illegal imagery and pass wilfully through various levels of security, agreeing at each stage that they are aware of the content and indicating their intent. They eventually find themselves facing a law enforcement message – a 'gotcha' – and a notice that their details will be recorded or, in cases where intent is clear, subsequently become the subject of investigation. Traditionally used against hackers, Scanlan et al. used a honeynet organized via social networks to educate users against developing an interest in the child exploitation material. They recruited and observed 947 participants during an eleven-month period to 'demonstrate the ability to capture, observe, and educate a cohort that would otherwise have been difficult to isolate in a meaningful way' (Scanlan et al., 2022).

Honeynets exploit the discipline of the panopticon (Foucault, 1983: 206) to become the 'electronic' (Gordon, 1986: 483; Lyon, 1994: 69), 'virtual' (Engberg, 1996) or 'super panopticon' (Poster, 1995). Their purpose is to acquire intelligence about criminality, but also simultaneously to create a preventative 'chilling effect', which, through the awareness of being surveilled, tempers the actions of consumers of child sexual materials, fraudsters, spammers and hackers.

Designing in crime control, like designing out crime, is not without its problems and critics. The downside of using technological solutions to achieve crime prevention goals is that an acceptable balance has to be found between providing security and also maintaining fundamental rights such as privacy. While there often appears to be a 'common-sense' security logic to crime control policies, they are not always desirable and may even conflict with the public interest, especially when they interfere with the free flow of information or invade individual privacy. It was precisely such concerns that undermined US government attempts in the mid-1990s to introduce devices into computer design to 'protect the interests of US industry' (Reno, 1996). The V-chip technology was designed to filter out violence and pornography, and the 'clipper chip' was an 'escrowed encryption system' that would have provided government with codes to unscramble encrypted files (Post, 1995; Akdeniz, 1996: 235). A not dissimilar fate was experienced by the previously mentioned intrusive Dragnet intelligence-gathering proposals for automated mass surveillance systems introduced in the US after the events of 11 September. The TIA (terrorism information awareness) system failed largely because of the political and commercial backlash from challenges to the legality and efficacy of its objectives – as well as a funding shortfall because such systems are very expensive. Whether the likes of the 'clipper chip', V-chip and TIA programs would have delivered fully as intended is another matter; the crucial factor here is that the legal and political process intervened to protect the broader public interest.

The more vociferous critics of situational crime prevention and crime science argue that its major flaw is that, while offending behaviour is the province of comparatively few individuals, all users are unfairly affected by what has been called an 'anti-social criminology of everyday life' (Hughes et al., 2001). Whereas the utilitarian argument may find some justification in the physical world, it begins to fall down in the online world. This is because the manipulation of software codes can have such an absolute impact on users' ability to exercise their rational choice, thus undermining the logic of the internet, which is to facilitate free communications between users. No longer is cyberspace the environment 'where everyone has the same level of access to the web and . . . all data moving around the web is treated equally' (Berners-Lee, cited by Fildes, 2006). The hope that 'end-to-end' architecture will value free communication, while leaving the choice over what to receive and what not to receive to the user, is rapidly being undermined (Saltzer et al., 1984). Lessig (1998b) has argued in his 'new Chicago School' argument that the special characteristics of the internet are such that it is not possible or feasible to reject law even where alternative forms of regulation such as technology are found to be stronger; he also argues that state involvement cannot be avoided – indeed it can do more (1998b: 661). The big question is 'how', with regard to alternative forms of regulation, and 'how', with regard to the role of the state.

Social controls: social values

The social values held by the individual constitute their *Weltanschauung*, their worldview, and are crucial in turning individual thoughts into social action and influencing the decision to act, not to act, or how to act. Two quite different tactics have been employed to reduce spamming by shaping values. In both examples, law provides both a reference point and the means of empowerment. The first is by actively encouraging the building, or galvanizing, of online communities of users against the behaviour. A number of counter-spam communities already exist, which individuals can consult to find out how they can remove their own addresses from existing spam lists. See, for example, Spamhaus.org, Junkbusters.com and Spambusters.com. Of course, these active groups also provide passive information which is educational. Alternatively, spam groups may go further and actively push the political process for change, for example by lobbying politicians to bring about a more coordinated international response. The parliamentary APIG (apig.org.uk) has been very active in this endeavour, as has CAUCE (Coalition Against Unsolicited Commercial Email), resulting in legislative responses by the EU Parliament and US Congress.

The second way in which social values are shaped is by providing information sources to educate spammers and users more generally as to what is, or is not, acceptable behaviour (i.e., what is and what is not spam) and also what the risks are. Education also equips users to make up their own minds and express their own choices by linking their own experiences with information made available to them by coalitions of interested parties, NGOs and government organizations. Especially informative are Spamhaus.org, CAUCE (cauce.org) and also David Sorkin's spam laws.com site. Increased user awareness makes users begin to deal with their own spams, though with a sense of realism: '[d]on't think technology is ever going to be able to completely solve these problems because there is a human aspect . . . you need a lot of education to change behavior' (Timo Skytta, cited by Clarke, 2005). Increased user awareness, resulting from various educational sources, is a contributing factor to the overall drop in complaints to ISPs about unsolicited bulk emails (Wall, 2002b, 2003).

Economic controls: market forces

In addition to the technological protection and the market disincentives created by legal action and the social values that law shapes, but which also shape law, the market can also determine the desirability of behaviour. Clearly, the high return on investment demonstrated in chapter 7 is the principal driver of spamming. Conversely, the negative impacts of spam on commerce have put pressure on ISPs and other organizations providing networked services to introduce increasingly robust policies against spamming. Aside from technological and legal actions, examples of such policies include giving recipients the choice over whether or not to accept attachments with their emails, thus reducing the risk of infection. Alternatively, it has been proposed to introduce a very small charge for each email transaction to make the cumulative cost of distribution expensive and reduce the return on investment, thereby reducing spamming by reducing incentives (BBC, 2006d, 2006e).

What the above analysis illustrates is that, while technology can effect almost 'perfect control', law and legal action, social values and market demands also shape behaviour. It shows that the law plays a particularly important role in the governance of spamming (and cybercrime) by also indirectly moulding its physical and mental architecture. Under the 'shadow of law', technology is effective in shaping the architecture of spamming to prevent it from reaching its destination. But the shadow of law also strengthens social values against spammers by stating that spamming is wrong. It also mobilizes the market against spammers by reducing the return on investment and pressurizing ISPs to protect their customers. However, faced with the choice, most would go for the technological fix. The fact that the receipt of spam in mailboxes can decline considerably, possibly by as much as 95 per cent, is certainly good news (Leyden, 2004a), but the problem is that the technological interventions have not been the product of a coherent policy formation process that has taken all implications into consideration. Technological interventions represent a marked shift away from the principle of network neutrality ('end-to-end') outlined earlier, towards the embedding of filtering and access policy into the very codes that facilitate communications. We therefore need to explore the governance of online behaviour as a multidisciplinary activity, but also to respect the digital realism of cybercrime.

Code and the public v. private interest

Invoking the earlier discussion about regulating spams, while it is highly unlikely that any internet users would actually wish to receive more spams (other than perhaps spammers!), the uncritical adoption of technological interventions has much broader implications for the general flow of information across the internet. The fact that such interventions appear to be intuitive and logical belies the fact that they are policy decisions embedded in 'code'. Because of this, users can no longer exercise a free choice to mediate their own communications, and the big question is: where does the restriction of free choice end? Which brings us back to Lessig, and his ideas on the role of government and law within the context of the origination and application of cybercrime prevention policy. Lessig shows us that the confluence of codes as regulators and codes as definers of architecture leaves the internet vulnerable because of a lack of acceptable mechanisms for providing oversight. Remember that Lessig's primary concern has been to 'build a world of liberty' into an internet whose future looks increasingly to be controlled by technologies of commerce and backed by the rule of law (Lessig, 2006: x), but also unnervingly controlled by distributed, rather than centralized, sources of authority:

> The challenge of our generation is to reconcile these two forces. How do we protect liberty when the architectures of control are managed as much by government as by the private sector? How do we assure privacy when the ether perpetually spies? How do we guarantee free thought when the push is to propertize every idea? How do we guarantee self-determination when the architectures of control are perpetually determined elsewhere? (Lessig, 2006: x–xi)

In much the same way as Lessig, Sir Tim Berners-Lee, the originator of the World Wide Web, has warned of the dangers of a two-tier internet, in which broadband providers will become gatekeepers to the web's content and companies or institutions that can pay will have priority over those that cannot. However, whereas Berners-Lee and the net-libertarians are optimistic that the internet will resist attempts to fragment it (Fildes, 2006), others (including Lessig) make convincing arguments in support of third-party intervention to maintain the public interest over the private – which begs the question: who should intervene?

Katyal (2003) seeks pragmatically to reconcile Lessig's concept of digital architecture with ideas of crime prevention that employ the manipulation of real-space architecture to show that the four digital design principles of natural surveillance, territoriality, community building and protecting targets can be employed to prevent cybercrime. As noted earlier, Katyal has argued that solutions to cybercrime must utilize the internet's distinctive qualities for control without damaging its openness (2003: 2268). Yet he notes the merits of balancing the advantages with the disadvantages, because this 'openness' can be 'both a blessing and a curse'. On the one hand, it helps software, particularly open-source code, to adapt when vulnerabilities are found, but, on the other hand, 'the ease with which architecture is changed can also facilitate exit and network fragmentation' (Katyal, 2003: 2267). Also, closed or hidden code in the hands of the private sector can lead to similar fragmentations, especially that which creates the higher-end, structural, internet architecture. Lessig himself has long argued that private ordering can 'pose dangers as severe as those levied by the state' (Katyal, 2003: 2283; Lessig, 2006: 208), which he similarly fears because of its lack of transparency. But Katyal claims that, since architecture is such an important tool of control, then this lack of transparency is precisely the reason why the government 'should regulate architecture, and why such regulation is not as dire a solution as Lessig portrays' (Katyal, 2003: 2283). Government regulation, for Katyal, is the lesser of the two evils because it works within more transparent frameworks of accountability. This view is also shared by Zittrain, who argues that government-mandated destination-based intervention 'stands the greatest chance of approximating the legal and practical frameworks by which sovereigns currently sanction illegal content apart from the Internet' (Zittrain, 2003: 688). Indeed, this interventionist position is really not so far removed from Lessig's, who subsequently recognizes, like Katyal, that 'the invisible hand of cyberspace is building an architecture for cyberspace that is quite the opposite of what it was at cyberspace's birth' (Lessig, 2006: 5). He has therefore expressed concern that if governments cannot regulate conduct directly, then they will 'regulate the regulatability of cyberspace' (Post, 2000: 1450; Lessig, 2006: 198). Even worse is the inevitability that the forces of commerce will do it for them by constructing architectures of identity to effect 'perfect control' (Lessig, 2006: 30).

The above arguments bring us back to the issue of the uncritical application of anti-spam technology. In discussing 'Realtime Blackhole Listing' spam filtering, a process at the heart of many spam-filtering systems which identifies emails that might be spams, Lessig argues that the decision to introduce it (prior to the Spam laws) was not reasoned, deliberative or political. It was not a policy 'made by a collective process capable of expressing collective values' (Post, 2000: 1456). The argument here is that the 'invisible hand' of market forces is guided by the private rather than the public interest. Any dispute between Katyal and Lessig is over whether or not the public interest should be represented, respectively, by government or by a more broadly constituted democratic body. Although it is the case that government has since intervened in the case of spam since Lessig wrote in the late 1990s, the intervention did not include full consideration of the application of technological solutions. If anything, the position with regard to technological intervention is less clear now, because public law is, in effect, being used de facto to justify the inclusion of anti-spam filters to serve private interests.

Conclusions: technologies of control or the control of technology

In the shadow of technology, law has only a limited direct impact upon online behaviour because software codes ultimately determine what can and cannot be done. Lessig, and others such as Greenleaf (1998), have stated, using a digital realist argument, that law does have the capacity to shape not only the environment that influences the formation of the code which forms the architecture of cyberspace, but also the social norms which internet users take with them online and the incentives and disincentives created by the market which shape the behaviour within. Of particular interest is the capacity of these four distinct, but interdependent, modalities of constraint, as Lessig calls them (1998a, 2006) to shape criminal or deviant behaviour positively or negatively – depending upon where one stands. At first glance, the broader themes are not so far removed from situational crime prevention theories that advocate the use of technological means to change the physical environment of criminal opportunity so as to reduce it. Indeed, there is also a resonance here with Foucault's analysis of Bentham's Panopticon prison design which shapes the physical and mental architecture of the prison and therefore the relationships within it, especially the power relationship between the observer (guard) and the observed (prisoner) (Foucault, 1983: 223). Where the digital realist argument departs from the more conventional crime prevention theories is in its consideration of the architecture of the internet as 'codes' which reactively create the online environment – and also the moral and economic framework within which it operates. In the following paragraphs, the roles of, and indeed interplay between, law, architecture, social structure and economy are explored with regard to the regulation of spamming as a new form of automated offender–victim engagement.

The literature from Karl Marx through to Gary Marx (2015), via many others, illustrates quite conclusively that the application of technologies of control alone tends to inscribe distrust into the process. In so doing, it leads to the breakdown of trust relationships because they fail to reassure, creates fresh demands for novel forms of trust, and then institutionalizes them (paraphrasing Crawford, 2000). In fact, history shows generally that technologies of control can often make much worse the very problems they were designed to solve, especially if, in the case of spam, they end up hardening the spammer's resolve, which is a possibility. Already there is evidence to show that the means of circumventing anti-spam measures is becoming more sophisticated (BBC, 2003a; McCusker, 2005: 3) and that there have been marked signs of resistance in the form of hacktivism, denial of service attacks and various forms of ethical and non-ethical hacking. This is in addition to the increasing convergence of the (cyber) criminal skill sets belonging to fraudsters, hackers, virus writers and spammers that led to the rise of the botnets.

This does not mean, however, that law has failed; rather, the preceding analysis reveals that the law works in a number of different ways and at a number of different levels to achieve its desired end. Basically, if law cannot shape behaviour directly, then it can regulate the factors that shape behaviour. In many ways, the discussion over spamming is fairly unproblematic because of the overwhelming support for anti-spam measures, so it is therefore harder to make stick some of the arguments posed earlier. But what the discussion has exposed is the necessity to ensure that there is in place legal authority which justifies and legitimizes action, provides some transparency and allows recourse in cases where injustice occurs. This is because there is no agreed meaning as to what constitutes 'online order' which is common enough to render it simply and uncritically reducible to a set of formulae and algorithms that can be subsequently imposed (surreptitiously) by technological imperatives. The imposition of order online, as it is offline, needs to be subject to critical discussion and also checks and balances that have their origins in the authority of law, rather than technological capabilities.

When the discussion shifts to the contravention of the 'end-to-end' principle, using wholesale technological interventions, the importance of law becomes visible. Some measure of legal support for this principle might, interestingly, be found in the US case of *Metro-Goldwyn-Mayer Studios, Inc.* v. *Grokster, Ltd.* (2004), in which various facets of the music industry attempted to curtail use of peer-to-peer technology (in the distribution of MP3s). The 9th Circuit decided (and upheld on first appeal) against the plaintiffs on the basis that 'significant non-infringing uses' would be inconvenienced were the decision to be made in favour of MGM et al. That decision effectively begins to support generally the principle of 'end-to-end' because technological interventions also ensnare legitimate users of the technology. It will be interesting to see whether a similar argument will be launched against the design of anti-spam filters, or any other form of intervention, at some point in the future.

All the indications suggest that spamming and new methods of offender–victim engagement are here to stay in one form or another. Not only do they continue to increase in volume, but spammers and their successors will become even more inventive and reflexive in overcoming security measures (P. Wood, 2004: 31–2). Unfortunately, this enduring reflexivity means that we have some hard decisions to make if we are to maintain current internet freedoms and openness and not become strangled by security. Either we continue to allow decisions to be made on scientific grounds and allow the mission or 'control creep' (Innes, 2001) that is endemic to the present climate of post-11-September security consciousness to continue (Levi and Wall, 2004), or we work towards developing workable, law-driven frameworks in which a range of considerations – including technology, but also social and market values – are employed to reduce harmful online behaviour. There is a hard message here: we need to take a much more holistic approach. Governments alone cannot tackle cybercrime, and nor should they; a multifaceted approach needs to be taken (McCusker, 2005). But it is an approach in which government can take a lead in establishing a framework for the different interventions.

Having argued for a governmental or democratic steer, we certainly need to counter the prevailing tendency towards over-regulation, and also consider alternatives. To what extent, for example, can we learn from laissez-faire or deregulation approaches to the governance of behaviour? Could we, perhaps, draw some lessons from the concept of 'safety through danger', which is a road safety policy currently being evaluated. Introduced to improve road safety (Hamilton-Baillie, 2004), the concept of 'safety through danger' removes all of the rules and their visible expression from an environment to make the space in which social activity takes place less predictable. The actors can no longer make any assumptions about each other because the absence of apparent rules removes any indications of the likely actions of others – or their relationship with their immediate physical environment. As a consequence, the actors have to interact with each other continually to negotiate a safe way through an environment and to ensure their own safety. They have to make hard decisions about their actions and, in so doing, take more responsibility for those same actions. After all, rules make the environment more predictable and the rights they create actually reduce the need for interaction between participants in transactions. In so doing, they also reduce individuals' decision-making abilities. But is this laissez-faire approach what was actually being originally proposed in the end-to-end principle, and is it a position that cannot be sustained in the light of more powerful interests? What is certain is that retaining personal responsibility and online control is very important because of the constant threat of censorship and the need to retain the ability to determine truth.

> Citizens must do their best to guard against government censorship for political purposes. At the same time, they are responsible for trying to distinguish useful and truthful information from bad quality information and must therefore exercise critical thinking about what they see and hear. And that responsibility extends to all media, not only the internet. Moreover, where disinformation or misinformation exists, thoughtful citizens have a responsibility to draw attention to the problem, possibly even to provide information to counteract the bad data. (Cerf, 2003: 9)

This begs the ever-important question, raised at the beginning of this chapter, as to whether or not we should simply regard true cybercrimes as a scientific problem to which a technical solution should be applied. The answer is that if we regard it as a technical problem, we lose too much information in the process. There is too strong a case against leaving decisions about whether or how to intervene to science or to the market. Rather, they should be made in the public, rather than private, interest, and should therefore rest with government (Katyal) or a responsible, democratically elected body (Lessig). These are important considerations; however, it is inevitable that in practice ideals will become moulded by the politics of compromise. If this means that we may have to tolerate spam and other incivilities to a small degree in order to preserve what is good about the internet, then it will arguably be a small price to pay.[12] Given that purely technological solutions are problematic for the reasons outlined earlier, a digital realist approach can inform (social) policy formation to constitute the most viable and effective attack upon what has quickly become 'the white noise' of the internet. To paraphrase Nate Silver (2012),[13] we have to separate the signal from the noise and focus upon the real message from multiple sources, rather than seeking answers by reducing complex questions to simple and decontextualized statistical tests.

Some discussion questions based upon this chapter

Why is it so important to regulate spamming?

Is law generally an effective way of controlling cybercrime? Say why it is or why it is not.

How do you measure how effective law is in regulating cybercrime?

What other methods of control can be utilized to regulate cybercrime?

Further Reading   As with the policing of cybercrime, the measures introduced to control, prevent and regulate cybercrime require regular update, if not a complete rethink. Clearly, the law alone is not strong enough and needs to be supplemented by other methods of control, which takes the study beyond the legal into the socio-legal. Students and researchers wishing to follow this area of study further are recommended to begin with the following sources: Lessig (2006); Clough (2015); Walden (2016); Gillespie (2019).

10 Conclusions: The Transformation of Crime in the Information Age

Chapter contents and key points

Differentiating between the ways in which cybercrimes use digital and networked technologies

Differentiating between the varying modi operandi of cybercrimes

Differentiating between the different victim groups

Differentiating between law, law enforcement and public security when developing responses to cybercrime. The police cannot work alone on cybercrime!

Conclusions: living with and responding to constantly transforming criminal behaviour in the information age

Chapter at a glance   *This chapter concludes the book by bringing together the themes of each chapter, explaining why the answers to the questions outlined in each chapter are so important in understanding the transformation of crime in the information age.*

Introduction

Along the pathway followed by this book, it has become clear that cybercrime means different things to different people and the meaning keeps changing, not least since cybercrimes such as DDoS, hacks, ransomware and data theft, etc., have recently become an established part of warfare to support kinetic warfare tactics. Importantly, contemporary debates encompass a range of legal, administrative, political, technological, cybersecurity expert, academic, social and economic discourses that have led to some very different epistemological constructions of cybercrime. The legal and administrative (rule-creation) discourse defines what *should* happen by establishing and clarifying the laws and rules that identify boundaries of acceptable and unacceptable behaviour; the political (and international relations) discourse hypothesizes about what outcomes parties *would like to happen* on a broader political stage; the technological (including computer science) discourse shows what *could happen* by demonstrating technological proof of concept; the cybersecurity expert community suggests what *the tactical solutions might be*; the academic discourse (including criminological) provides an informed analysis about *what has happened and why*; the social or lay discourse reflects what the person on the street *thinks is happening*. Moreover, the demands for cybersecurity are often mingled, or even confused, with the demands to respond to cybercrime. So, while concerns about cybercrime are expressed by a range of voices, they are often looking at the same thing from different perspectives, but do not always articulate a common understanding. At a more constructive level, these observations suggest that a more rounded approach needs to be taken, which respects each of the above perspectives. But until this is achieved, the everyday experience is that the different experiences result in a rather confused media point of view that just about any offence involving a computer nowadays becomes regarded as a 'cybercrime'. This itself results in a broad tendency to confuse crimes that use the internet with those created by the internet. It is the differences between the former and the latter which this book has sought to address – the ways in which crime has become, and is being, transformed by networked technologies. The first part of this short concluding chapter briefly retraces the steps of the book's journey, and gives some important messages to those responsible for developing policy and practice responses to cybercrime. The second part draws some broader conclusions and messages from the main themes and observations.

Differentiating between the ways in which cybercrimes use digital and networked technologies

Whatever its merits and demerits, the term 'cybercrime' has now entered the public parlance and we are stuck with it. The term has a greater meaning if it is understood in terms of the level of dependency on digital and networked technologies which cause the transformation of criminal or harmful behaviour, rather than an exhaustive listing of the acts themselves. If the hallmark of the internet and cyberspace is its informational, networked and global qualities, then they should also be characteristic of cybercrimes. So, a simple 'transformation test', whereby we think about what happens if the internet is removed from the activity, enables us to identify the different levels of transformation by technology which the informational, networked and global characteristics of the internet bring about in substantive cyber-criminal behaviours.

Cyber-assisted crimes are traditional or ordinary crimes using computers, usually as a method of communication or to gather precursor information to assist in the organization of a crime. Remove the internet and the behaviour persists because offenders will revert to other forms of available communication. The second level of cybercrimes are *cyber-enabled (hybrid) cybercrimes*, which are 'traditional' crimes in law, for which network technology has created entirely new global opportunities. Take away the internet and the behaviours continue by other means, but not upon such a global scale or across such a wide span of jurisdictions and cultures. The third generation of cybercrimes are *cyber-dependent (true) cybercrimes* that are solely the product of the internet. Take away the internet and they vanish – the problem goes away. This last generation includes spamming, 'phishing' and 'pharming', cryptojacking, variations of online intellectual property piracy and many other emerging cybercrimes.

The practical reality of cybercrimes is that the commission of a cybercrime often involves more than one level, especially when the cybercrime ecosystem facilitates the criminal's ambitions. The offenders communicate using the internet, usually through a crime forum (cyber-assisted). They may transact to buy or sell skill sets or code (cyber-enabled) which they may use themselves to commit a crime (cyber-dependent). These different levels and types of distinctions are important to identify for analytical and also policy reasons, because they can inform the application of law and resources to responses to cybercrime and also law-enforcement practice. Any legal problems arising therefore relate more to legal procedures than to substantive law. The greater challenge lies with cyber-dependent crimes, which emerge quickly and mercilessly with great impact upon society. But these different levels of transformation say little about how the offenders set about cybercrime (*modus operandi*).

Differentiating between the varying modi operandi of cybercrimes

Chapters 4, 5 and 6 successively explored the different *modi operandi* of cybercrime: *cybercrimes against the machine, cybercrimes using the machine* and *cybercrimes in the machine.*[1] Cybercrimes against the machine assault the integrity of network access mechanisms (and include hacking and cracking, cyber-vandalism, spying, DDoS and viruses). They often pave the way for other forms of more serious offending; identity theft from computers only becomes serious when the information is used against the owner. Similarly, zombie computers (infected by remote administration trojans malware: RATware) may be later used by 'bot herders' to run phishing expeditions or even infect computers. Cybercrimes using the machine use networked computers to engage with victims with the intention of dishonestly acquiring cash, goods or services ('phishing', advance-fee frauds, etc.). They also involve internet scams perpetrated by fraudsters in collusion with spammers, which tend to be relatively minor in individual outcome, but serious by nature of their aggregate volume. Cybercrimes in the machine relate to the illegal content on networked computer systems, and include the trade and distribution of pornographic materials as well as the dissemination of hate-crime materials. They are informational, and those that are not directly illegal may be extremely personal and/or politically offensive and may contribute to the incitement of violence or prejudicial actions against others.

Despite the existence of applicable bodies of national and international law, cybercrimes and offenders often conspire to impede the traditional investigative process. Particularly significant is the observation that the actual, rather than perceived, dangers posed by them are not always immediately evident to potential or actual victims. Either they are not individually regarded as serious, or they are genuinely not serious, but possess a latent danger in their aggregation or in being precursors to more serious crimes. Each of the substantive criminal behaviours (in addition to the main offence) illustrates this latency.

So, an evolving picture of cybercrimes emerges which contrasts their informational, networked and globalized characteristics with the physical and local qualities of the more traditional and routine patterns of offending – offending that is still defined by law, the criminal justice processes and crime debates which underpin the criminal justice paradigm and therefore continue to shape expectations of it. Within the literature, cybercrimes may find some resonance with the study of white-collar crimes because they are both commonly regarded as soft or hidden crimes. However, they differ from what are regarded as white-collar crimes because they are not necessarily crimes of the powerful, but of the new 'knowledged' classes.

Differentiating between the different victim groups

Although the above differentiations between cybercrimes separated out levels of technology and *modi operandi*, they say little about the intended victims. This is why it is important to also separate out the victim groups into individuals, organizations and nation states, because of their different wealth, power and position, each being factors that can motivate offenders. Victim groups therefore differ in terms of whether offenders are targeting individual citizens, organizations and businesses, or whether they have a bigger political picture in mind and seek to victimize nation states via their economies or infrastructures. *Individual citizens* are typically affected by frauds, scams, extortion, but also political, sexual and religious hate speech. *Organizations and businesses* tend to fall victim to larger-scale frauds, extortion or data theft, which are often highly publicized fraud in order to increase the possibility not only of direct economic gain, but also of an indirect gain – for example, to enable a competitor to gain an advantage because of the reputational damage caused. *Nation states* fall victim to attacks that are tactically designed to alter the political status quo. These can either be direct attacks on infrastructure which can cause inconvenience to citizens and embarrass governments who may be prevented from delivering key services, or can be indirect, but orchestrated, misinformation (fake news) campaigns, designed to shape and change citizens' views in a particular direction.

Together, these three dimensions of cybercrime (technology dependency, modi operandi, intended victims) provide a conceptual language frame that helps to explain cybercrime and its variations more accurately – not least, the ways in which internet technologies affect cybercrime in terms of being cyber-assisted, cyber-enabled or cyber-dependent, but also what the offender's intentions are, such as 'against the machine', 'using it' or 'in it', and who they are levelled against, whether it be individuals, organizations or nation states. Of course, reality challenges theory because, as identified in earlier chapters, serious offenders can target individuals to access organizations that they are linked to which may serve the infrastructure of nation states. But the dimensions remain important beginnings for analysis and assessment of risk.

Differentiating between law, law enforcement and public security when developing responses to cybercrime. The police cannot work alone on cybercrime!

The general public can be forgiven for their inability to square the apparent 'cybercrime' wave portrayed by the news media and cybersecurity sector with the relatively few arrests and prosecutions of so-called cybercriminals. This shortfall can be explained partly through local police forces working within tightly prescribed budgetary parameters and being simply unable to cope with demands to investigate crimes arising from globalized electronic networks. But the shortfall mainly arises because of the contrast between expectations and actuality, as the public police only play a very small part in the overall policing and nodal network of the governance of cyberspace. For various reasons outlined earlier, the demand for cybersecurity is greater than that which government can provide.

In the twenty-first century, the police still continue to work much along the lines of their 170-year-old Peelian public mandate to regulate the 'dangerous classes' – hence the understandable focus upon policing paedophiles, child sexual exploitation, fraudsters and those who threaten the infrastructure, such as, but not solely, terrorists. This is not to say, however, that cyberspace goes unpoliced, nor is it the case that police activity is either inefficient or ineffective. Rather, the police role has to be understood within its mandate and within a framework of the broader and largely informal networked and nodal architecture of internet policing, composed of internet users and user groups; network infrastructure providers; corporate security organizations; non-governmental, non-police organizations; governmental non-police organizations; and public police organizations. These not only enforce laws but also maintain order in very different ways (see, further, Wall, 2007a).

Joining these networks together is a range of initiatives that are designed to make their governance function more effective: international coalitions of organizations; multi-agency, cross-sectoral partnerships and coalitions; and also international coordination policies. Active public police participation in these partnerships and coalitions performs a number of functions. It enables 'the police' to extend their own reach at a symbolic and normative level by reconstituting the fundamental Peelian principles of policing across a global span, and thereby resolving some of the contradictions they face. At a more practical level, it enables them to perform their emerging function as information brokers. The information in this sense relates to internet traffic data and its intelligence and evidential value.

While this neo-Peelian agenda enables police to resituate themselves as a lawful and legitimate authority within the broader networks of security, it nevertheless institutes a range of instrumental and normative challenges. A major challenge is to work effectively in partnership with the private sector to temper the latter's unreflective drift towards the routine use of the surveillant technologies to strengthen security by catching offenders and preventing crime by exclusion. The 'digital' realism of cyberspace is that the very technology which causes cybercrimes also has the potential to become part of the solution, but only partly, because the solutions also have to be set in accepted legal, social, economic and technological frameworks, which frame the digital realist position. Unless checked, the 'ubiquitous policing' that follows this 'hard-wiring of society' (Haggerty and Gazso, 2005)[2] could contribute to the destruction of the democratic liberal values which currently bind most societies. For the time being, this adverse potential is tempered by the intervention of constitutional law, the imperfect human condition that results in inaccurate data entry and resistance against intrusion, and some theory failure in crime prevention caused by an inadequate conceptualization and understanding of cybercrime and its associated risks. However, if this tendency is contained within a supportive socio-legal context, for there is still time to achieve this, those same technologies could – optimistically – assist the process of police reform. This is because the same surveillant characteristics that make network technology a powerful policing tool also make it a natural tool for overseeing police and regulatory practice, and also for creating broader organizational and public accountability.

Conclusions: living with and responding to constantly transforming criminal behaviour in the information age

The transformation of crime in the information age is characterized by the fact that society's response to cybercrime is greatly improving, but cybercriminals are being more adaptive to stay ahead of their pursuers. The good news is that we are progressively learning more and more about the impact of networked technologies upon criminal behaviour and therefore learning more effective and acceptable ways of dealing with it. Increasingly rigorous empirical research is now being conducted on different aspects of internet victimization by a wide range of organizations, particularly the academic funding councils. The findings of this research are challenging narratives promoted by organizations that have a stake in the high prevalence of cybercrimes. Furthermore, the inclusion of relevant questions in the US National Crime Victimization Survey (NCVS), and the British Crime Survey (as a test in 2003–5) and its successor the Crime Survey of England and Wales (from 2017), yields useful empirical data about victimization that counter some of the cybersecurity narratives that have accrued during the past few decades. Within UK police organizations, hi-tech crime-policing capabilities have matured through the NCA Cyber Crime Unit (NCCU)[3] working with local police forces through its regional offices (ROCUs). Importantly, this also works closely with the National Cybersecurity Centre (part of GCHQ) along with Get Safe Online and Cyber Aware[4] in the UK, and with international law enforcement partners such as EUROPOL, the FBI and the US Secret Service to share intelligence and coordinate action.[5] This expansion of policing beyond the basic responsive policing role has allowed the amassing of a wide corpus of knowledge and policing experience in the field. This is also the case in the US and other jurisdictions. Laws are being revised and harmonized in many different ways, because of variations in public and political concerns expressed in national debates. In the UK, for example, the Computer Misuse Act 1990 has been reviewed by the APIG (2004) and its scope expanded by sections 35–38 of the Police and Justice Act 2006 to make DDoS attacks and the distribution of hacking tools illegal. Then it was reviewed again in 2023, pending report. These new powers are in addition to the host of new state powers created in the UK, and also the US and beyond, by the anti-terrorism and domestic security legislation following the events of 11 September 2001. Of course, in the common-law jurisdictions, the laws are also constantly being clarified by case law precedent.

Rather worryingly, however, it is apparent that, while the actions of public police officers are framed by legislation and codes of practice, many of the other partners in policing the internet are not, other than by the narrower confines of their responsibilities in law. Not all sharing partnerships are truly sharing, and protocols on sharing data, or even what data to share, are still to be agreed upon. Also worrying is the lack of checks and balances on the noticeable shift towards the technological determinism of automated policing initiatives, influenced largely by the cybersecurity industry. There are, for example, a broad range of moral, ethical and legal concerns about the implications of the high degree of entrapment when employing 'honeypots' and 'honeynets', not least in the validity and strength of evidence presented to the court, assuming that this form of policing is in fact designed to capture offenders rather than simply to deter offending through the technological imposition of panoptic 'discipline' and its 'chilling effect'. Then there are the ethical concerns about the application of predictive policing technologies and some of the pre-crime claims made of them.

Beyond policing, there have been technological interventions into something as seemingly innocuous as spamming, a cyber-dependent cybercrime in more ways than one, and one of a new legion of networked crimes that generates further cybercrime. Many ISPs have introduced anti-spam software into the delivery process, which contravenes the long-standing end-to-end principle of the internet, which is freedom of movement across the network to its nodes, while leaving choice and mode of receipt to the end users. Yet, the hundredfold increase in spams over the last few decades has necessitated this action. No one wants spam and few would be unhappy to see it disappear, yet there has as yet been little critical discussion about the insertion of spam filters into the delivery mechanisms. The spam filters are one of many such technological solutions. Also currently emerging, to deal with other true cybercrimes, are software devices that identify and track the appropriation of various types of electronically conveyed intellectual property with increasing levels of efficiency. There is a danger that true cybercrime will generally come to be regarded as a 'technical problem' and that, as a consequence, important decisions are being made largely on scientific grounds – mainly because a filter can be made. In the case of spam, there is understandably little objection, but since the technological solutions clearly work, what is to stop the application of filtering software to images or to certain words or combinations of words and thereby filtering out everything that is deemed undesirable and against private interests? Are we witnessing the gradual embedding of private interpretations of law into code, into the technological fix?

What we do not want is for all users to be affected by the sins of the few, and freedom of expression, privacy of use and freedom from interference have to be important values to maintain. So, applying 'policing software' to exclude everything undesirable is extremely problematic, because, as Cerf has observed, '[t]here are no electronic filters that separate truth from fiction' (Cerf, 2003: 10). But the technological fix is becoming easier and less contestable, especially when it is being carried out automatically on our behalf by technology. Although our concerns may not warrant the dystopic hysteria invoked by George Orwell's *1984*, we may do well to heed Horkheimer and Adorno's warning in their *Dialectic of Enlightenment* about solving problems using technology: 'Once we assume that scientific methodology can solve all intellectual problems, science becomes mythology, aware of everything but itself and its own blind spots and biases. This results in authoritarianism, especially where science is harnessed to industrial-age technology and nature is conceptualised as a sheer utility for the human species' (Agger, 2004: 147).

A delicate balance has therefore to be drawn between the need to maintain order and the enforcement of laws, in order to provide a balance between the desires of law and the procedural protections it affords and the desires of law enforcement to catch offenders. The danger, in the words of Adams (1998: 194), is that 'new technology will allow the police to solve 100 percent of all crimes. The bad news is that we'll realize 100 percent of the population are criminals, including the police.' Without such a balance, we will descend into a world of de facto strict liability and reverse burden of proof. Worse still, the practical realities of the transparent society may produce exactly the opposite effect (Brin, 1998) and '[a]s the Internet continues to become more transparent, the risk is that the stage may be set for a twenty-first century witch-hunt' (Campbell, 2005b). Let us hope that a balance can be achieved and that these dark predictions are unfounded and simply part of a societal reaction to the future shock of technology.

Finally, since the internet became part of our lives over three decades ago, it has transformed not only our lives but also crime into cybercrime. During the first decade and a half of its public existence, the internet was still establishing itself and offenders were also doing the same. Most significantly during this early period, digital technologies enabled the technological deskilling and reskilling of crime. They effectively democratized crime by enabling anybody (with computer knowledge) to carry out crimes that were previously the preserve either of organized crime groups or of a privileged group of powerful people. After the internet (at the risk of repeating myself), a person could conduct the whole crime process: why commit a risky $50 million robbery when you can conduct 50 million $1 dollar robberies from the comfort of your own home? The problem was that, whilst this was true in theory, the practice became very different. Until the late 2000s, committing small to large-scale thefts in bulk from a distance was impractical because offenders had to use fiat money as there was no alternative exchange mechanism. The next 15–20 years, however, look to be as eventful as the last 15–20. Not only has the introduction of cryptocurrencies, botnets, cloud computing and social media begun to make criminal ambitions more possible, but the emergence of an ecosystem to facilitate cybercrime has enabled those ambitions much more than anticipated. Cybercrime has become industrialized on a scale not previously anticipated, and will continue to do so – what is next?

Some final discussion questions based upon this concluding chapter (at the risk of repetition from earlier)

Why is it important to differentiate between the ways in which cybercrimes use digital and networked technologies?

Why is it important to differentiate between the varying modi operandi of cybercrimes?

Why is it important to differentiate between the different victim groups?

Why is it important to differentiate between law, law enforcement and public security when developing responses to cybercrime. The police cannot work alone on cybercrime!

How can we live with and respond to constantly transforming criminal behaviour in the Information Age?

Appendix: The Cybercrime Curriculum

Below is a detailed breakdown of a Cybercrime Module comprised of sessions that are based upon the book, its chapter structure and also chapter-at-a-glance summaries that were outlined earlier. Some discussion questions are listed at the end of each chapter which could provide ideas for assignment questions or themes to organize seminars. NB: as many of the examples of law and procedure refer to the UK legal system, teachers outside the UK should adapt these materials and references to their own jurisdictions.

1 **Introduction to the Cybercrime Module**
    Session one describes the aim of this module, for whom it is intended and the key questions that will be answered throughout it. The session then outlines the questions to briefly introduce the students to, and get them to develop a critical appreciation for: (a) what cybercrimes are; (b) what we know about them and how; (c) how networked technologies have changed opportunities for criminal activity; (d) what those criminal opportunities are; (e) how criminal activity is continuing to change in the information age; (f) how cyberspace is policed and by whom; (g) how cybercrimes are to be regulated and prevented; and (h) finally, why the answers to these questions are so important.

2 **How is Knowledge about Cybercrime Produced?** Reflecting upon how we know how criminal behaviour has changed online
    Session two seeks to critically explore how we know what cybercrimes are and, importantly, the nature of problems and tensions that arise from the competing (inter-disciplinary) viewpoints that constitute the production of knowledge about them. The session also reconciles different versions of events with the narratives that frame the cybercrime narrative. The first part, therefore, looks at the cultural origins of the term 'cybercrime' and outlines the various sources of knowledge that inform our understanding of crime in the information age, in particular identifying various 'voices' that are present within the literature. The second part identifies the various tensions and competing views in the production of knowledge about cybercrimes, and the culture of fear around cybercrime which can shape understandings of it.
    More specifically:

   a) *Producing knowledge about cybercrimes?*
      - *Cyberpunk and the conceptual origins of cyberspace*
      - *What, then, are cybercrimes?*
      - *The origins of the terms 'cyberspace' and 'cybercrime' in social science fiction*

- *Hacker and haxploitation movies*
- *Academic literature*
- *Statistical sources: state and the cybersecurity industry*

b) **Tensions in the production of knowledge about cybercrimes?**
- *Over-problematizing cybercrime: reporting bias and media construction – Changes in the news process: churnalism – The lack of reliable statistics*
- *Under-reporting of cybercrimes*
- *The power struggle for control over cyberspace as a contested space*
- *Competing expert claims*
- *Conflicts and confusions between public and private-sector interests*
- *The danger of confusing the rhetoric with reality*
- *Criminological theory and cybercrime*

c) **So, what are cybercrimes and what do we know about them?**

3 **How Has Criminal Activity Been Transformed in Cyberspace?** How have networked technologies changed opportunities for criminal activity?

This session explains how the technologies of cyberspace have transformed criminal activity, and then looks at the changes in the organization of criminal behaviour online. It then describes changes in the modus operandi of criminal behaviour online and changes in the organization, scope, types and focus of criminal activity online.

More specifically, it covers:

a) **The internet and the information society**
b) **The transformative impacts of cyberspace upon criminal activity**
- *Networking and the convergence of digital and networked technologies*
- *Informational transfer and value*
- *Globalization*
c) **Changes in the organization of crime and the division of criminal labour**
- *Greater control over the criminal process by the individual*
- *New forms of criminal organization through collaborations between different skill sets*
- *Deskilling criminal labour online*
- *Reskilling criminal labour online: automation and facilitation – towards the ecosystem*
d) **Changes in the scope of criminal opportunity online**
- *Cyber-assisted – crimes using computers to assist traditional offending*
- *Cyber-enabled – opportunities for crimes across a global span of networks*
- *Cyber-dependent – cybercrimes mediated by technologies*
e) **Changes in the type of criminal opportunity online**
- *Cybercrimes against the machine (computer integrity crimes)*
- *Cybercrimes using the machine (computer-enabled (or computer-related) crimes)*
- *Cybercrimes in the machine (computer content crimes)*
f) **Changes in the victim focus of criminal opportunity online**
- *Individual, organizational and nation-state victims*

4   **Cybercrimes against the Machine: Hacking, Cracking and Denial of Service** –
    How have crimes against the machine changed in the information age?
    This session explores cybercrimes taking place *against the* machine, such as
    hacking, cracking and denial of service attacks. These are specifically the cyber-
    crimes intended to attack computer systems and networks. These are sometimes
    as crimes in their own right – for example, to prevent users from gaining access;
    at other times to gain entry to a system with a view to stealing content or holding
    the content to ransom. The first part looks at the different types and variation of
    hackers. The second part discusses the tactics used by hackers to attack machines.
    The third part explores the different motivations and attractions for this type of
    cybercrime offending.
    More specifically, the session explores:

    a) The different types of hacking and hackers
        – *The ethical hackers*
        – *The unethical hackers*
        – *Cyber-conflict and espionage actors*
        – *Cyber-terrorists and information warfare*
    b) Hacker tactics to compromise the integrity of networked computers
        – *Social engineering*
        – *Inserting malicious software and code*
        – *Using spyware and surveillance software*
        – *Attacking services used by victims*
    c) Motivations for offending and reproducing criminal knowledge online
        – *Criminal gain or commercial advantage*
        – *Revenge*
        – *Self-satisfaction*
        – *The need for peer respect*
        – *To get 'sneaky thrills'*
        – *To impress potential employers*
        – *Distance from victim*
        – *Politically motivated protest, conflict*

5   **Cybercrimes Using the Machine: Virtual Robberies, Scams and Thefts, Social
    Media Network Crime, Violent, Offensive Communications, Largescale
    Privacy Violations** – How have crimes using the machine changed in the infor-
    mation age?
    This session explores cybercrimes in which offenders *use 'the machine'*
    (computer devices) to commit virtual robbery, fraud and theft by exploiting the
    internet's scalable and globalizing qualities. These cybercrimes differ from crimes
    against the machine, such as hacking (see session four) and those where the
    cybercrime is in the machine, such as content crimes (see session six). To illus-
    trate the point, this session will look at virtual bank robbery (cybercrimes against
    financial and billing systems online); virtual stings (deceptions, frauds and extor-
    tion); virtual scams (which are mainly deceptions); and virtual theft and digital
    burglary (cyber-piracy and 'stealing' informational intangibles).

More specifically:

a) Virtual bank robbery: *identity theft and exploiting online financial and billing systems*
- *Electronic input frauds*
- *Input fraud (identity theft)*
  - *Identity theft through phishing.*
  - *Identity theft through DNS cache poisoning (pharming).*
  - *Identity theft using surveillance software (spyware).*
- *Output frauds*
- *Card-not-present and other payment frauds (output frauds)*

b) Virtual stings, *online deceptions, frauds and extortion*
- *Business email compromise (BEC)*
- *Authorized push payment (APP) scams*
- *Online gambling scams*
- *Internet advertising frauds*
- *Premium line switching frauds*
- *'Short-firm' frauds*
- *Ransomware and data extortion*

c) Virtual scams, *using e-commerce as a means to deceive individuals*
- *Scareware scams*
- *Arbitrage / grey market exploitation*
- *Pyramid selling scams online*
- *Direct investment scams*
- *Loans, credit options or the repair of credit ratings*
- *Website domain name scams*
- *Deceptive advertisements for products and services*
- *Entrapment marketing scams*
- *Internet auction frauds*
- *Advance-fee frauds (419 scams and romance fraud)*
- *Online ticket scams*
- *Drug sales / health cures / snake-oil remedies*
- *Cryptocurrency scams*

d) Virtual theft and digital burglary: *'stealing' informational intangibles and cyber-piracy*
- *Informational services*
- *Streaming*
- *Intellectual property piracy and the internet*
- *Intellectual property piracy: music*
- *Intellectual property piracy: video (film and television)*
- *Intellectual property piracy: software*
- *The theft of virtual artefacts*

6 **Cybercrimes in the Machine: Extreme Sexual Abuse Materials, Hate and Violent Speech** – How have crimes in the machine changed in the information age?

This session explores cybercrimes *within the machine,* or content crime. These crimes typically involve some form of informational materials or data held on a computer or device which either are illegal to possess, constitute evidence of wrongdoing or have contents that are the focus of cybercrime. The structure of this session represents these aspects of cybercrimes in the machine.

More specifically:

a) **Computer content that is illegal**
   - Obscene materials online
     - Sexually explicit materials
     - Extreme sexual abuse materials (extreme pornography)
     - Child sexual abuse materials and the internet
   - Violent or harmful content
     - Terror materials
     - Violent imagery / murder video nasties
     - Hate speech, including racism and radical politics
     - Using websites to circulate information used in the organization of harmful activities
     - Circulating information about making drugs and weapons

b) **Content contributing to wrongdoing** – Offensive or harmful-content emails, chatrooms and blogging
   - Circulating misinformation online
   - Chatroom and discussion group communications (stalking and grooming)
   - Blogging and blogsites
   - Cyber-bullying

c) **Content that is the focus of cybercrime**
   - Data theft
   - Computer content
   - Intellectual property

d) **Can content (words and imagery) actually cause harm by turning thoughts into actions?**
   - Impact of harmful content upon conduct (social action)
   - The boundary between harmful thoughts and harmful actions
   - The boundary between words and conduct
   - The tension between offensive content and freedom of expression.

7 **How Criminal Activity Is Continuing to Change in the Information Age** – Cybercrime futures – the (re)organization of the cybercrime supply chain as an ecosystem

This session explores how criminal activity online is continuing to change in the information age by looking at how offenders increased scalability and sustainability in levels of cybercrime by evolving a supply chain of essential specialist skill sets that eventually became a cybercrime ecosystem. By using ransomware and DDoS (distributed denial of service) as examples, it becomes clear in the explorations of cybercrimes against, using and in the machine that each type of cybercrime has, in different ways, become increasingly automated by a combination of new attack vectors, technological procedures and skill sets to accompany them. The cybercrime 'issue' is no longer just a cybercrime, but also includes the processes which enable the cybercrime to take place.

More specifically:

a) ***The new technological facilitators changing cybercrime***
  - *Cloud technologies; The Internet of Things; social media networks; – Cryptocurrencies: datafication*

b) ***The cybercrime ecosystem in practice, using the example of ransomware***

c) ***The various stages of a ransomware attack, showing the different functions and functionaries***

d) ***The (re)organization of cybercrime and the new face of organized crime online*** – *the facilitators and enablers of the cybercrime ecosystem*
  Infiltration brokers (initial access and phishers); Darkmarketeers; Forum brokers; Databrokers; Crimeware as a service; Bulletproof hosters; Crime IT services brokers; Monetizers; Cybercrime consultants (inc. ransom negotiators)

8 **Policing Cybercrime: Maintaining Order and Law on the Cyberbeat** – How is cyberspace regulated and policed, and by whom?
    This session explores the maintenance of order and law in cyberspace. It argues that the public police agencies are a small but important part of a broader network of security guardians who work by different means to create order on the internet. It also observes that law itself, and therefore the characteristics of cybercrime, challenge the criminal justice system in various ways which require further explanation. It concludes that the police alone cannot police cyberspace and that they have to collaborate with other parties.
    More specifically:

  a) **Maintaining order in cyberspace** – Locating the police amongst other guardians within the networks and nodes of security within cyberspace
    - *Internet users and user groups*
    - *Online virtual environment managers and security*
    - *Network infrastructure providers*
    - *Corporate organizations and corporate security*
    - *Non-governmental, non-police organizations*
    - *Governmental non-police organizations*
    - *Public police organizations*

  b) **Maintaining law in cyberspace** – The challenge of cybercrime for the public police
    - *Crimes too small to deal with* – *'De minimis' crimes*
    - *No law no crime* (nullum crimen*) disparities*
    - *Jurisdictional disparities*
    - *Non-routine activity and police culture*
    - *Under-reporting by victims*
    - *Over-dramatization by media*

  c) **The role of the public police in policing cyberspace**
    - The neo-Peelian agenda: renegotiating the public police
    - Police role in policing cyberspace
    - Multi-agency cross-sector partnerships

  d) **The challenge of cybercrime for the police–public mandate**

9   **Controlling and Preventing Cybercrime** – How are cybercrimes to be regulated and prevented?

This penultimate session looks at the issues relating to controlling, reducing and generally regulating cybercrime. It explores the formal role of law and legal action, but also the various technical, social and economic (market) controls which combine to reduce the different ways in which cybercrime is prevented, mitigated, investigated and prosecuted.

More specifically:

a)   **Law and legal action**
b)   **Technological controls – cybercrime control and prevention using technology**
c)   **Social controls – social values**
d)   **Market forces – economic controls**
e)   **Code and the public v. private interest**
f)   **Technologies of control or the control of technology**

10 **Conclusions: The Transformation of Crime in the Information Age** – It is important to differentiate between the ways in which cybercrimes use digital and networked technologies.

This final session concludes the module by bringing together the themes of each session, explaining why the answers to the questions outlined in each are so important in understanding the transformation of crime in the information age.

More specifically:

a)   **It is important to understand the ways in which technology has impacted upon crimes**
b)   **It is important to differentiate between the modi operandi of cybercrimes**
c)   **It is important to differentiate between the different victim groups**
d)   **We have to learn to live with a constantly transforming online crime landscape in the information age and keep adapting to the new challenges it presents to us**

A further note on broadening the curriculum

Where teachers are interested in fleshing out some of the issues further, as might be the case in some different disciplines, I would also recommend that they explore the Cybercrime module of the United Nations Office on Drugs and Crime (UNODC), Education for Justice (E4J) University Module Series, which is part of the Global Programme for the Implementation of the Doha Declaration. The UNODC Cybercrime module contains additional cybercrime-related topics and also further references. The UNODC E4J University Module teaching guide can be found at www .unodc.org/documents/e4j/Cybercrime/Cybercrime_Teaching_Guide_final.pdf; and the cybercrime module at www.unodc.org/e4j/en/tertiary/cybercrime.html.

Notes

Preface and Acknowledgements to the Second Edition

1 See later discussion about 'affordances' – in this case, technologies which 'afford' opportunities (here, cybercrime).

1 Introduction

1 These include the UK Home Office, Department of Trade and Industry (Foresight Initiative), European Commission, AHRC (Arts and Humanities Research Council), ESRC (Economic and Social Research Council) and EPSRC (Engineering and Physical Sciences Research Council), and also agencies such as CEPOL and thinktanks such as GI-TOC.

2 Producing Knowledge about Crime in Cyberspace

1 Not to be confused with Gibson's 1986 book of short stories called *Burning Chrome*, though the short story is reproduced in this collection at p. 176.
2 There are a few exceptions, such as in Australia, where a Cybercrime Act was introduced in 2001, and in Nigeria, where a Draft Cybercrime Act has been proposed.
3 Writer Bruce Bethke is credited with coining the word 'Cyberpunk' in his 1980 story 'Cyberpunk'. See Jamneck (2005).
4 A very popular make of Russian automobile.
5 Earlier versions of this section appeared in the first edition, and Wall, 2008 and 2012.
6 As Bruce Sterling once accused me of arguing in his *Wired* magazine blog (Sterling, 2008).
7 I use the word 'factional' because there is some science behind the ideas used. The early social science fiction authors – for example, William Gibson, Bruce Sterling and others – often consulted scientists and built their ideas on contemporary scientific ideas and theories.
8 H. G. Wells's better-known science fiction novels are *The Time Machine* (1895), *The Island of Dr Moreau* (1896), *The Invisible Man* (1897), *The War of the Worlds* (1898) and *The First Men in the Moon* (1901).
9 Hackmageddon (aka Paolo Passeri – www.hackmageddon.com).
10 www.cambridgecybercrime.uk/process.html.
11 Mainly the EPSRC (Engineering, Physics and Science Research Council) CRITiCAL/EMPHASIS projects Cybercrime Db and Ransomware Db.
12 Original statistics at CERT/CC Statistics 1988–2005 (www.cert.org/stats/cert_stats.html) are no longer available, but information can be found at www.sei.cmu.edu/about/divisions/cert.
13 A separate debate exists about the methodological rigour of automated data collection systems, which I am not addressing here.
14 See, for example, the Software Engineering Institute Cybercrime Survey Collection 2006ß2015: https://resources.sei.cmu.edu/library/asset-view.cfm?assetid=484019.
15 NB: please note that this is not conducted annually.
16 NB: there have been a number of studies of specific types of cybercrime, such as sexual offending online, not included here.

3 Cyberspace and the Transformation of Criminal Activity

1 Please note that I am using the phrases 'information society' and 'information age', also 'internet' and 'digital and networked technologies' rather interchangeably and loosely here. They are meant to be indicative rather than prescriptive.
2 I am extending Braverman's (1976) deskilling hypothesis to social skills and the construction of virtual social life.
3 In previous literature, I have referred to this as the 'elimination test'. Upon reflection, 'transformation' is a more useful concept.
4 The terms peer-to-peer and grid technologies are often used interchangeably.
5 See later comment upon crackers.
6 NISCC was an inter-departmental centre of UK government, formed to minimize risk to national infrastructure. In 2007 it was merged with NSAC, the National Security Advice Centre, to form CPNI, the Centre for the Protection of National Infrastructure.
7 NB: please do not confuse the generations of cybercrime with generations of hackers mentioned in the previous chapter.
8 To paraphrase one of the anonymous reviewers of an early draft of this book to whom I am very grateful for pointing this issue out.
9 'Deepweb' and 'dark web' tend to refer to activities on the ToR, or onion, router. 'Deepweb' identifies the more legal uses of ToR, and 'dark web' the illegal spaces used to trade.
10 For a very useful overview of the UK law in these three areas of behaviour, see Walden (2003: 295; 2016).

4 Cybercrimes against the Machine (Computer Integrity Crime)

1 Please note that in the previous edition 'cybercrimes against the machine' were referred to as 'computer integrity crimes'. The term 'machine' is a euphemism for hardware and also computer systems and networks.
2 The Department of Culture, Media & Sport now conducts the Cyber Security Breaches Survey.
3 NB: the data for prosecutions in more recent years was not available at the time of writing.
4 Two cases involved malware and 12 unauthorized access to personal information.
5 These issues were (are being) discussed by the UK government's Review of the Computer Misuse Act 1990: www.gov.uk/government/consultations/review-of-the-computer-misuse-act-1990.
6 An example of computer spying was illustrated by the case of the Hanover Group (Hafner and Markoff, 1995; Young, 1995: 11).
7 'Guest' being a default username as well as the password.
8 A brute-force attack is usually carried out by using a 'bot' which runs a massive range of number and letter combinations against a username. Credential stuffing uses bots to bombard login portals with usernames and previously used passwords.
9 A 'bot' is an automated software program that follows a set of instructions to achieve a pre-determined goal. Some bots may incorporate applications of artificial intelligence.
10 'All about PC, W97m/Michael-B' (www.all-about-pc.de/english/Virus%20Corner/Michael-B.asp) [no longer available].

5 Cybercrimes Using the Machine (Computer-Enabled Crime)

1 In the previous edition, the title of this chapter was 'Computer-Assisted Crime'. This earlier title conflicted with the descriptor of the basic level of technology employed in cybercrime and was changed.
2 Sutton's law is used in medical schools and teaches doctors to look for the most obvious cause when making a diagnosis.

3 Micro-robberies or micro-frauds are individually too small to investigate by law enforcement, but become significant when the proceeds from all are aggregated (Wall, 2010a).

4 For further information about identity theft, see Finch (2002); also see UK Finance (2022a).

5 See, further, Action Fraud: www.actionfraud.police.uk/a-z-of-fraud/identity-fraud-and-identity -theft.

6 The statistics for input frauds are sent by the banks to CIFAS, the UK's Fraud Prevention Community (www.cifas.org.uk).

7 These marketplaces are mentioned by name only because they are the most popular retail outlets; there are many others. They also provide levels of protection and information for clients - see, for example, eBay's Rules & Safety Overview (SafeHarbor) for concerned clients at https://pages .ebay.com/services/tsindex.html?mkevt=1&mkcid=1&mkrid=711-53200-19255-0&campid=5337 590774&customid=&toolid=10001.

8 From (one of many) phishing emails received by the author.

9 'RWdb' stands for 'Ransomware Database', which contains open-source data on ransomware attacks collated for the EPSRC Critical Project.

10 These are the five most popular platforms, but many others exist. For more useful details on social media phishing, see, further, TrendMicro, 'What is social media phishing?', www.trendmicro .com/en_us/what-is/phishing/social-media-phishing.html.

11 Ofcom, '45 million people targeted by scam calls and texts this summer', Ofcom News, 20 October 2021, www.ofcom.org.uk/news-centre/2021/45-million-people-targeted-by-scams.

12 Zeus malware is a Windows-based trojan horse package that can be used to carry out a number of criminal and otherwise malicious tasks. Zeus can be used to steal personal banking information as well install malicious software such as ransomware.

13 Please note that the man-in-the-middle attack is a different technical process to pharming, but the similarity is that both alter the communications process to deceive victims into thinking they are in a familiar and safe place, where they will reveal and give personal information freely.

14 Interview conducted with convicted offender for this book. Note that credit card issuers now require more information about the billing address and that CVC2 information and additional-factor authorization are now often required for card payments.

15 See, further, 'business email compromise (BEC)' defined: www.microsoft.com/en-us/security /business/security-101/what-is-business-email-compromise-bec.

16 See further PayPal's acceptable use policy with regard to gambling at www.paypal.com.

17 eBay, Security Center, https://pages.ebay.com/securitycenter/?mkevt=1&mkcid=1&mkrid=711 -53200-19255-0&campid=5337590774&customid=&toolid=10001.

18 The drop in percentage was due to an overall increase in other forms of internet-related frauds.

19 In Q4 2022, the average advance fee fraud loss was £2,813, and was converted to dollars for the comparison.

20 See Action Fraud, Ticket scams, www.actionfraud.police.uk/a-z-of-fraud/ticket-scams.

21 For a philosophical discussion about virtual theft, see Wildman and McDonnell (2020).

22 Section 1, Theft Act 1968.

23 'Dilution' is a term frequently used in intellectual property law to describe the reduction in value through unrestricted use, but also to justify sustaining intellectual property rights.

24 Akdeniz (1997) describes the case of the Jet Report (on satanic abuse and witchcraft) which was released into the public domain on ethical grounds.

25 Although this is not to understate the resources required for research and development.

26 See 'Quick Reference Sheet of Felony Charges to Consider and Relevant Issues to Consider in Typical Intellectual Property Cases' at www.usdoj.gov/criminal/cybercrime/ipmanual/chart .htm.

27 It must be pointed out that various organizations now exist to police such marketplaces, alongside the markets' own quality control. Most Trading Standards Authorities have an internet unit, and a number of police forces also have intellectual property units, for example PIPCU (Police Intellectual Property Crime Unit), which is a department of the City of London Police.

6 Cybercrimes in the Machine (Computer Content Crime)

1 JenniCAM was formed in 1996 and was the first 'cam-girl' site. The original Jennicam pages at JenniCAM.com have now been removed, along with a history of the site and archives. But a brief history can be found in Reynolds (2015) and a more detailed analysis of the cam-girl phenomenon at Jimroglou (1999).

2 The word 'porn' is used colloquially here to mean sexually explicit materials performed by consenting adults. The term 'pornography' is contentious because it is sometimes used too broadly by regulators to include morally rather than legally outlawed imagery. There is also an argument that the subjects are unwillingly trafficked into taking part even though they appear to have given their consent.

3 Pornhub, according to Wikipedia, 'is a pornographic video sharing website and the largest pornography site on the Internet': https://simple.wikipedia.org/wiki/Pornhub.

4 Criminal Justice and Immigration Act 2008, Part 5, www.legislation.gov.uk/ukpga/2008/4/part/5.

5 The Audiovisual Media Services Regulations 2014 (UK SI 2014 No. 2916): www.legislation.gov.uk /uksi/2014/2916/contents/made.

6 See the IWF's 'Our vision & mission', www.iwf.org.uk/about-us/why-we-exist/our-vision-and -mission.

7 See the Chart of Signatures and Ratifications of Treaty 201: www.coe.int/en/web/conventions /full-list?module=signatures-by-treaty&treatynum=201.

8 See the Status of Ratification, Optional Protocol to the Convention on the Rights of the Child on the sale of children, child prostitution and child pornography, OHCHR (Office of the High Commissioner for Human Rights): www.ohchr.org/en/instruments-mechanisms/instruments /convention-rights-child.

9 The legal arrangements are slightly different in Scotland and are covered by section 51 (Obscene Material), section 52 (Indecent Photographs of Children) and section 52a (Possession of Indecent Photographs of Children) of the Civic Government (Scotland) Act 1982.

10 Statistics from the 'Operation Ore' pages of Survivors Swindon, at www.survivorsswindon.com /ore.htm.

11 Comprises sexual exploitation of children through photographs (making, distributing, showing, advertising) (75%), Possession of an indecent photograph (22%) or prohibited image of a child (3%).

12 Statistics obtained through Freedom of Information requests.

13 For example, the Commission's recommendation on measures to effectively tackle illegal content online of March 2018.

14 It must be noted here that there is some contention about Harding's claims. He states that 'snuff movies' are hard to find on the internet but a 'user comment' from 2006 states that he/she had no problem in finding such sites.

15 http://protest.net/activists_handbook/economist_article.html.

16 DrinkOrDie was a renowned underground software piracy and trading group in the 1990s. It was forced to close following a major law enforcement raid called Operation Buccaneer. See Jamez (1997).

17 Also see the 'Gangs or Us' pages on gangs and the internet at www.gang-sorus.com/Internet .html.

18 See Mann and Sutton (1998) for a very useful description of the use of news groups for the distribution of information about the technologies used for committing offences.

19 See Schneier on 'Security', a weblog covering security and security technology at www.schneier .com/blog/archives/2005/08/london_bombing_1. html.

20 In the USA by the First Amendment to the US Constitution, and in Canada by the Canadian Charter of Rights, section 2.

21 Doxing is a practice of publishing personally identifiable information about an individual or organization, usually on the internet, to expose irregularities, extract revenge, create fear to extort money or otherwise intimidate them.

22 For a useful overview of the legislation applying to offensive emails, see Angus Hamilton's 'Awkward Customers' at www.hamiltons-solicitors.co.uk/archive-docs/awkward-customers1 .htm; also Neil Addison's web pages at www.harassment-law.co.uk.

23 See www.hamiltons-solicitors.co.uk/archive-docs/awkward-customers1.htm.

24 In the Twitter Joke Trial, Chambers sent a tweet saying that he would destroy Doncaster Airport, while in a fit of pique, and was subsequently prosecuted under s. 127 of the Communications Act 2003. The conviction was quashed after a third appeal, as it was deemed that 'a message which does not create fear or apprehension in those to whom it is communicated, or who may reason-ably be expected to see it, falls outside this provision' (of the Communications Act 2003). See *DPP v. Paul Chambers* [2012] EWHC 2157: www.judiciary.gov.uk/wp-content/uploads/JCO/Docu ments/Judgments/chambers-v-dpp.pdf.

25 This is based upon a real case told to the author; see Wall (2017).

26 All now defunct for various reasons.

7 The Cybercrime Ecosystem

1 'Ecosystem' is used here to describe a socio-technological environment in which the various components continually organize themselves by interacting and adapting to each other in order to manage scalability and sustainability (see, further, Briscoe and De Wilde, 2009).

2 A zero-day exploit is a software vulnerability that has previously been undetected by those writing, selling or operating it. Until the vulnerability is resolved, then hackers can exploit it, and regularly do. Many software providers seek to reduce the number of zero-day exploits by offering rewards known as 'bug bounties' to hackers who identify them and bring them to their attention.

3 The sizes of the organizations are as follows: Micro (rev<$2m-staff>1<10); Small (rev>$2m<$10m-staff>10<50); Medium (rev>$10m<$50m-staff>50<250; Large a (rev>$50m<$250m-staff>250<1.5k); Large b (rev>$250m<$1b-staff>1.5k<5k); V. large a (rev>$1b<$10b-staff>5k<20k); V. Large b (rev>$10b<$50b-staff>20k<150k); Massive (rev>$50b+-staff>150k).

4 Included are prices for credit card data, payment processing services (e.g. Paypal, etc.), crypto-currency accounts, social media, hacked services, forged documents – scans, forged documents – physical, email database dumps, DDoS attacks.

5 For the EU Horizon 2020 project 'TAKEDOWN 700688'.

8 Policing Cybercrime

1 Sir Robert Peel, the founder of the Metropolitan Police, is alleged to have set out nine fundamental principles of democratic policing which outline the ethics of policing. There exists some contro-versy over whether or not he actually wrote these principles down (see Lentz and Chaires, 2007) – rather, they are thought to be a romantic aggregation of his and other luminaries' thoughts on policing by police historians, not least Charles Reith in his 1948 *Short History of the British Police*. Regardless of authorship, they have come to encapsulate the principle of democratic policing in Western common-law countries and also farther afield.

2 See, further, the 'Resolving Feedback Disputes' pages at http://pages. ebay.com/help/feedback /feedback-disputes.html. Note that the eBay system operates very differently to Amazon's book rating system.

3 I must thank Sophie Wall for enlightening me on the intricacies of the Habbo world.

4 See PayPal acceptable-use policy with regard to gambling (18 May 2006) at www.paypal.com.

5 Conducted in 2005.

6 Internet Crime Complaint Center (IC3): www.ic3.gov.

7 Canadian Centre for Cyber Security (the Cyber Centre): www.cyber.gc.ca/en.

8 EUROPOL: www.europol.europa.eu/report-a-crime/report-cybercrime-online.

9 At the time of writing, many UK police forces have reviewed their call-centre advice to the public with regard to cybercrimes. There has also been a review of the Action Fraud system.

10 This is a hypothesis based upon observations and requires further research.

11 Although related more to positioning the police approach, see the debates in McLean et al. (2020).

9 Controlling, Preventing and Regulating Cybercrime

1 Affordance theory originated in psychology to explain how animals adapt to their environment. It is used here in a context that helps to explain how offenders adapt to their environments, especially cyberspace and cybercrime (see, further, Goldsmith and Wall, 2022).

2 This is a deliberate reference to the Stephen Spielberg film *Minority Report* in which a special police unit working with psychics sought to arrest murderers before they killed their victims. This pre-crime meme is often misquoted in relation to artificial intelligence when in fact the murder visions were from psychic humans and the examples of applied artificial intelligence failed, yet the term is frequently used as an AI meme.

3 Please note that this spread of law is intended to be illustrative and there are many other applicable laws.

4 Note that the US both imposes the most sanctions and has the strongest set available.

5 Note from chapters 4 and 7 that the ransomware operators make the malware available to affiliates for a fee.

6 Individuals who are offered a place on the programme are identified by police through information from concerned parents, carers or guardians, or teachers or safeguarding staff. This is my interpretation because the entry criteria do not seem to be published. See Cyber Choices: www.nationalcrimeagency.gov.uk/cyber-choices.

7 Data published by Statista: www.statista.com/statistics/1270488/spam-emails-sent-daily-by-country.

8 See paragraphs 40, 41, 42, 43, 44, 45. The full text of the EU Directive on Privacy and Electronic Communications (concerning the processing of personal data and the protection of privacy in the electronic communications sector) is available at europa.eu.int/eur-lex/pri/en/oj/dat/2002/l_201/l_20120020731en00370047.pdf.

9 Data published by Statista, see www.statista.com/statistics/1270488/top-botnets-worldwide (drawn from Checkpoint's ThreatMap).

10 See, further, the Register of Known Spam Operations database at www.spamhaus.org/rokso.

11 Originally known as Neptune Intelligence Computer Engineering: www.nice.com.

12 I am referring here only to nuisance and minor infringements.

13 My interpretation of Silver.

10 Conclusions

1 In the first edition, I referred to these as computer integrity crimes, computer-assisted crimes and computer content crimes (Wall, 2007a).

2 Hard-wiring is a metaphor that signifies the construction of permanent structures of surveillance. Of course, the future structures will in fact be soft-wired through ambient technologies.

3 Its predecessors were the NHTCU, formed as part of the NCS, which was then absorbed into SOCA, which then became part of the NCA, which succeeded SOCA and parts of other agencies.

4 Get Safe Online provides general information and advice on how to keep safe online; Cyber Aware provides alerts about threats and provides advice.

5 NCA, 'Cyber crime': https://nationalcrimeagency.gov.uk/what-we-do/crime-threats/cyber-crime%20.

Glossary

advance-fee frauds are fraudulent tactics that deceive victims into paying fees in advance to facilitate a transaction which purportedly benefits them. Nigerian, or 419, frauds (after the Nigerian penal code which criminalizes them) deceive recipients into allowing the use of their bank account to help fraudsters to supposedly remove money out of their country. Once involved in the scam, the victim is required to pay a series of advance fees to facilitate the transaction, which never takes place. Variations use internet auctions or online dating forums to obtain advance fees.

arbitrage is the exploitation of pricing differentials between different markets.

article spinning is an unethical practice of hashing and rehashing published articles and blog entries to appear as new and discrete writing for dissemination to various online media sources. By using careful editing techniques, article spinners avoid infringing copyright laws. Some automated applications are now available for use by article spinners that exchange parts of sentences and change words for alternatives. 'Spun' articles are usually for sale, but the practice can also assist *search engine optimization* because interesting articles can also be laced with keywords.

assemblage is a concept derived from Deleuze and Guattari (1987) which explains that phenomena may have an association with each other and even work together as a functional entity, but do not necessarily have any other unity.

asymmetry literally means the absence of symmetry. It is used in this book to describe the way that one individual can interact with many others simultaneously. Asymmetric relationships lead to *viral information flows*.

asynchronicity describes communications that take place outside conventional time-frames, for example in 'chosen-time': chosen by the end users in an email communication stream.

attack vectors describes the ways in which (usually unauthorized) access to a system can be obtained to exploit vulnerabilities within it.

auction frauds are the use of internet auction sites to commit fraudulent acts, usually luring bidders into a transaction outside the auction site, or by selling fake or poor-quality goods. Alternatively, the bank cheque clearance processes may be exploited.

avatars are graphical depictions of a computer user that express their alter ego through the depiction of real or imaginary characteristics or qualities. They can vary in type and form depending upon the context in which they are being used. They can be graphical (animated) depictions of the self in virtual worlds, or they can be (typically) a 100 × 100 pixel (postage stamp size) graphical representation on posts to internet forums.

big data is the transactional and content-viewing data generated by our interactions with the internet; to be used further it must be analysed, or refined by using data analytics to make it into informational products.

big game hunting is the practice of aiming cybercrime attacks specifically at wealthy individuals and organizations (usually businesses). See *whale* and *spear phishing*.

Bitcoin is a *cryptocurrency* begun in 2009 following a paper by a person using the name Satoshi Nakamoto, and the releasing of open-source software supporting the cryptocurrency. Bitcoin differs from fiat currency (government-supported) because there is no central authority and transactions are validated by a decentralized blockchain which records them in a public ledger.

black hat – see *hacker*.

Black hat SEO – see *search engine optimization*.

black swan events (after Taleb, 2007) are rarely occurring situations which, like *signal events*, have a disproportionately high impact on society, are 'beyond the realm of normal expectations in history, science, finance and technology' and are hard, if not impossible, to predict.

blended threats are a type of malicious software that employs simultaneously, through multiple infection, a combination of attack techniques that make the viruses and worms even more potent and also much harder to detect.

blogs or **blogsites** are internet diaries or personal online journals shared with an online audience. They tend to be interlinked and the network of blogs forms an interconnected blog environment, a 'blogosphere', in which information and debate can escalate rapidly and virally, creating a frenzy of, sometimes heated, discussion known as a blogstorm.

bot herders – see *botnets*.

botnets comprise lists of the *internet protocol (IP) addresses* of 'zombie' computers that have been infected by *RATware / remote administration tools* and which can subsequently be controlled remotely. Botnets are valuable commodities because of the power they can place in the hands of the remote administrators (bot herders) to deliver a range of harmful malicious software (*malware or malcode*). For this purpose, they can be hired out, sold or traded.

browser-in-the-middle attack (sometimes called a 'man in the middle' or 'man in the browser' attack) is an information-gathering scam technique. Usually, some malicious software (*malware or malcode*) impersonates a browser that the user wishes to log on to, in order to steal their login credentials and other personal information. The browser looks the same as the intended log-on frontpage, but it may seek additional personal information 'for verification'. Once the user has logged on, then they are redirected seamlessly to the intended site to do their business.

bulletproof hosting services are provided by some web or domain hosters which: (a) host services or materials often prohibited by jurisdictions by exploiting differences in national laws; or (b) have loose terms and conditions that allow clients to bypass regulations. They are popular with those providing illegal content services, but also spammers and online gambling hosts.

cam-girls – see *webcams*.

chat rooms are online forums that allow individuals to chat to fellow members in real time. They evolved from the usenet *newsgroups* (prefixed by 'alt.') into *internet relay chat (IRC)*. The main difference between the two is that chat rooms operate in real time, whereas newsgroups work in chosen time through the posting of messages and responses to those messages.

child sexual imagery or child sexual exploitation is the use of 'obscene' images of children by viewers to elicit sexual arousal.

chilling effect describes the way that a fear of legal or economic action encourages self-censorship.

churnalism is a term coined by BBC journalist Waseem Zakir. It is a form of instant journalism that has emerged as the impact of the twin pressures of time and money, and which does not follow the traditional journalistic practice of confirming the integrity of a news story by seeking two or more independent sources of information. Instead, churnalists utilize 'information subsidies' in the form of press releases, wire stories and other forms of pre-packaged material to create articles in newspapers and other news media without undertaking further research or checking. Churnalists combine with bloggers to become an important component of *viral information flows*. Also see *article spinning* and *clickbait*.

click fraud / bogus click syndrome defrauds the internet advertising billing systems by bulk clicking advertisements, by using either low-wage labour or automated scripts.

cloud computing is a metaphor that refers to a form of on-demand computing that provides intuitive information technology capabilities without the need for the user to gain prior knowledge and skills in order to control the technological infrastructure that supports the services. In recent years, the term has been used to refer to data centres which control the storage data 'in the cloud'. Cloud technologies enable those facilities.

code can have two meanings. The first is with regard to codes that grant owners access to a secure environment. The second is a more colloquial term for software programming language.

computer is an electronic device that executes pre-determined instructions in the form of a program to manipulate data and, when networked, it becomes the platform from which networked activity takes place.

cookies trade data that authenticate visitors' access to www sites and can be used to track their sessions. Whilst these functions can assist the user, tracking cookies also help to maintain specific information about users' choices of www sites and their purchasing preferences (from their shopping carts). Tracking cookies are not *spyware* as such because they merely trade data; however, the fact that they allow users to be tracked from site to site does raise concerns and lead to them being regarded as intrusive and therefore treated by some anti-virus packages in the same manner as they treat spyware.

copyright trolling or speculative Invoicing is the practice of obtaining information about downloaded copyright materials from an ISP (usually by a court order) and sending invoices for the materials to alleged downloaders, with warnings that legal action will be taken if they do not pay the invoice. The practice brought bad press to the music industry and it shifted to pornographic materials.

counterfeits are imitations of an object or virtual artefact constructed intentionally to deceive users into thinking that they possess the qualities and characteristics of the original.

cracker – see *hacker.*

credential stuffing is an automated method of attack on businesses to achieve a type of account takeover. It uses email addresses and passwords purchased as credential databases on the *dark web* to target many user accounts via *botnets*. Financial services and retailers are the main targets. It relies upon users employing the same email and password address across multiple accounts and sites. Not to be confused with *credential cracking.*

crimeware differs from malicious software (viruses, worms, trojans) in that it is not normally self-reproducing. It results from the injection of malicious code via a flaw in existing software. It can exploit vulnerabilities in web browsers, reach its target via emails or be disseminated via peer-to-peer networks. Once installed, the malicious code steals information which it returns to its sender.

crimeware-as-a-service (CaaS) is, as the name suggests, a criminal variant of 'software as a service' (SAAS) which, upon payment of a fee, provides users with access to a suite of software which can then be downloaded without further payment. In the CaaS variant, offenders pay a fee to gain access to a range of *crimeware* (malicious software) and other custom exploits. Also see *crimeware, wizards.*

cryptocrime refers to criminal behaviours that involve the use of encryption in the modus operandi for the crime. Encryption can be used in different ways, for example in a *ransomware* crime to make a computer system unusable and leverage a ransom, or more simply in the use of value exchange (using cryptocurrency).

cryptocurrencies secure virtual monetary schemes that are based upon encryption to allow exchange; their anonymity, ease of use and novelty enable offenders to use them in criminal activities.

crypto-wallets (cryptocurrency wallets) are a safe space where *cryptocurrencies* can be kept; they can be provided either as a service or as a program.

culture of fear describes the exaggeration of fear, whether through an intentional policy or as a knock-on effect of media sensationalized reporting, and its normalization to the point that the fear of *cybercrimes* is not only accepted as a normal part of everyday life, but also anticipated. This 'culture of fear' is, according to many commentators, used by modern governments as a tool of governance – a political tool that justifies increased governmental power and control over society.

cybercrimes are criminal or harmful activities that are informational, global and networked, and are to be distinguished from crimes that simply use computers. They are the product of digital and networked technologies that have transformed the division of criminal labour to provide entirely new opportunities for, and new forms of, crime, which typically involve the acquisition or manipulation of information and its value across global networks for gain. They can be broken down into crimes which are related to the integrity of the system, crimes in which networked computers are used to assist the perpetration of crime, and crimes which relate to the content of computers. They tend to be individually small in impact, though their harms are caused by their sheer volume.

cybercrime wave describes the very quick and almost 'viral' proliferation of *cybercrimes* across globalized networks. They have sometimes been referred to as cyber-tsunamis, although the term has been used less following the 2004 and 2011 tsunamis.

cyberpunk authors joined the concept of cybernetics with the sensibilities of the late 1970s punk movement to form a genre of science fiction that thematically combined ideas about dystopic advances in science and information technology with their potential capability to break down the social order.

cyberspace is the mentally constructed *virtual environment* within which networked computer social activity takes place. The term was first used by novelist William Gibson in the early 1980s, then developed conceptually by John Perry Barlow. It is a place that is not inside the *computer* or inside the technology of communication, but in the imaginations of those individuals who are being connected. Although imaginary, it is nevertheless real in the sense that the things that happen in that space have real consequences for those who are participating.

cyber-terrorism uses computers to attack the physical infrastructure, to generate mass fear and anxiety and, in theory, manipulate the political agenda.

cyberworlds – see *virtual environment*.

dark web is a hidden part of the deep web where criminal activity takes place. The deep web exists below the surface web and enables many different legitimate surface web functions to take place, such as social media. The deep web and the dark web are accessible via the anonymous ToR router and are not indexed, so not searchable by a normal search engine.

data doubling refers to the comparing of an individual's access codes (personal information) with data already held by the computer system to verify his or her access rights and identity.

data mining – see *dataveillance*.

data theft (hack) is the theft of bulk data by *hackers* who have, to date, tended to perform a DDoS attack as a decoy to confuse the computer security before breaching the system (via an SQL injection) to steal the data.

data trails are left by the informational transactions required to secure access to, and navigation around, the *internet*. They are also sometimes known as 'mouse droppings'.

dataveillance is the use of *data trails*, usually by mining databases, to provide evidence of transactions or to identify abnormal patterns of behaviour.

de minimism is from *de minimis non curat lex*, which means 'the law does not deal with trifles'. It is used in this book to describe the attitude of the law to low-impact, bulk victimizations that are individually too small to investigate because it would not be in the public interest. Yet these bulk offences which are unique to the internet cause great losses when globally aggregated across the network.

deskilling describes the process of rationalizing and 'degrading' labour by breaking it down into essential tasks which are then automated to increase the efficiency and economy of the operation. The deskilling process is accompanied by a reskilling process, whereby fewer people gain control over the whole automated process.

digital natives is a term that describes those individuals who grew up with the *internet*. The implication is that digital natives find the technologies intuitive and are predisposed towards it.

digital realism is a term used in this book to emphasize that the more a behaviour is mediated (shaped) by the architecture of networked technology, the more it can be governed by that same technology. The potential concerns arising from this *ubiquitous law enforcement* invoke debates about the role of technology and other forms of control (law, social values, market control) in tempering or legitimizing the use of technology as a means of governing online behaviour.

distributed denial of service (DDoS) attacks prevent legitimate users from gaining access to their web space (networks and computer systems) by bombarding access gateways with a barrage of data.

DMS (domain name systems) servers translate domain names into *internet protocol (IP) addresses* that facilitate access to, and navigation around, the World Wide Web.

drive-by downloads are a method of infection by malicious software disguised as images or software that are downloaded during the course of browsing the web.

end-to-end describes the internet's original principle of free communications online while leaving the end users the choice over what to, and what not to, receive.

entrapment marketing is a form of extreme 'lock-in' marketing that is designed to trap victims into buying products or services that they do not want. Internet variations of entrapment marketing typically entice (some would say mislead) the victim into buying software (see *scareware*) and/or entrap them into making (usually) small repeat payments for services that they either: (a) originally understood were free; or (b) signed up to on trial but (i) forgot to terminate, or (ii) subsequently found too complicated to terminate (e.g. written notice required), or (iii) are embarrassed to terminate or complain about.

escrow is an arrangement whereby two sides involved in a transaction supply a trusted third party with finance, objects or access codes that are released once the conditions of the transaction have been fulfilled.

fraud is a deception perpetrated by one individual in order to obtain an advantage over another. The object of the fraud may be purely financial or informational. See *advance-fee frauds, click fraud, input fraud, output fraud, payment fraud, salami fraud, scams, short-firm fraud.*

gambling scams – see *scams.*

Gemeinschaft/Gesellschaft are sociological terms used by Ferdinand Tönnies in 1887 to describe the transition from (*Gemeinschaft*) organic communities based upon neighbourhood and familial bonds to (*Gesellschaft*) communities of association defined by a common instrumental goal.

globalization is a social process that configures and reconfigures the relationships that exist between multiple entities, from individuals to international agencies, which are widely distributed in space.

glocalization describes the impact of globalized ideas upon a locality.

google bombing is a form of *search engine optimization* which uses various techniques to deliberately influence the ranking of web pages in the Google search engine (the most popular search engine) in order to increase the traffic onto those pages. See *search engine optimization.*

graphics user interface (GUI) uses graphical images in the form of pictures and words to represent information. GUI is associated with the advent of Windows and replaced the older text-based displays.

grey hat hackers – see *hacker.*

grid computing/technology – see *peer-to-peer networks.*

gullibility viruses use *social engineering* to trick individuals into deleting part of their computer's operating system.

gurus are expert 'white hat' *hackers.*

hacker is a term that has a history in the experimentation of often illicit access to communications systems. Computer hackers evolved to explore the boundaries of informational access and also the integrity of secure systems. Hacker actions basically fall into ethical and unethical activities. They meet online in chat forums to discuss their actions. See *darkside hackers, gurus, samurai, script kiddies* and *wizards.*

hacktivism is a fusion of ethical hacking and the use of computer technique to effect political protest.

hate speech seeks intentionally to degrade, exclude, intimidate, or incite violence or prejudicial action against someone based on their race, ethnicity, national origin, religion, sexual orientation or disability.

haxploitation is the deliberate exploitation of the public fear of *hackers* for entertainment purposes. The imagery that haxploitation generates becomes more powerful when the boundaries between the individual hacker and the state – as hacker – merge (as in, for example, movies like *Die Hard 4.0*) to redress the imaginary power imbalance (state impotence in the face of the hacker) created by the earlier hacker movies.

honeynets are fake websites constructed to socially engineer offenders into accessing them and showing intent by wilfully passing through various levels of security, agreeing at each stage that they are aware of the content and indicating their intent. Offenders eventually find themselves facing a law enforcement message (a 'gotcha') and a notice that their details will be recorded or that they will become subject to investigation in cases where intent is clear.

hotspot paranoia is the fear that free public *wi-fi* hotspots will create new opportunities for *cybercrime*.

identity theft / ID theft is the fraudulent acquisition of personal information that can be used to obtain credit facilities or take control of existing accounts online. It is often mistakenly used to describe credit card theft.

informational property is a term that refers to the rights of ownership over information. Although narrower in scope than *intellectual property*, the two are, however, often used interchangeably.

information society is a society in which the relationships of production/consumption, power and experience have been transformed by information technology. It is a product of the *network society*.

information warfare is a term commonly used today in a non-militaristic context to describe the use of information, misinformation or disinformation to shape public confidence with regard to patterns of consumption or participation in the democratic process. It is often confused with *cyberterrorism*. Also see *SCADA* and *Stuxnet*.

input fraud refers to the illegal acquisition of credit facilities, typically credit cards.

intellectual property covers a range of claims and entitlements to the ways that ideas are expressed. The laws that establish and define intellectual property include copyright, trademarks, patents and designs.

internet is a global network of interconnected government, military, corporate, business and domestic computer networks. It is not a network but a network of networks. It is the platform upon which the *World Wide Web* operates.

Internet of Things arises from the convergence of multiple technologies that connect and transfer information to and from everyday devices such as the smart home or medical monitors. The purpose of the data collection is to improve the functionality of devices and also the quality of the lives of the users who own them.

internet protocol (IP) addresses are unique numerical identifiers that networked devices use to identify each other and then communicate once a route has been opened.

internet relay chat (IRC) – see *chat rooms*.

internet service providers (ISPs) are businesses that provide internet users access to internet and related services through a range of media that include dial-up, digital subscriber line (DSL) through telephone wires, Integrated Services Digital Network (ISDN) switched through telephone wires, broadband *wireless*, broadband through cable TV.

internet year: Moore's Law states that hardware evolution is increasing desktop computing power by 2 to the power *n*. Calculations based upon this 1965 formula estimate that the rate of change is such that one internet year equals approximately three months or less in real time.

jailbreaking is a type of hacking that seeks to remove restrictions that manufacturers place upon the use of their devices, in order to modify their purpose.

Java applets are small programs written in the Java programming language that can be included in an HTML web page. They are used to provide interactive features to web applications that cannot be provided by the HTML (HyperText Markup Language), which is the main language used for creating web pages.

key-stroke loggers are diagnostic tools that record a user's keystrokes. Originally designed to identify errors in systems, they were subsequently put to use measuring employees' work output. More recently, they have been incorporated in *spyware* to keep a log of the victim's keystrokes (including passwords, etc.) and return the information to a web address. They have also been used to spy upon offenders.

keyword stuffing (or Randomly Repeated Keywords) is the loading of keywords into the HTML or XHTML metatags that provide hidden information about the Web page that is used by a search engine. Used properly it can be ethical and useful to users as it guides them to relevant web pages. It can also be used unethically to artificially increase internet traffic to web pages. See *search engine optimization*.

link farming is a form of *spamdexing* that uses hyperlinks to cause a group of websites to link to all sites in its particular group. Initially created manually, link farming has become automated via specific software designed to create links.

Local Area Networks (LAN) are local computer networks that serve small defined areas, such as an office, and usually link to WANs (wide area networks). Their advantage is to increase the speed of access in sharing files – plus, they can be configured to suit particular office work practices.

logic bomb is a type of malicious software that activates once predetermined criteria are met, such as a specific date or after a system has been accessed a specified number of times. The best known of these is 'Michelangelo' which only activates on 6 March, Michelangelo's birthday.

lottery scams – see *scams*.

malware or malcode (from 'malicious software') comprises software scripts that seek to disrupt, damage or steal information from computer systems. 'Worms' self-propagate themselves across networks by exploiting security flaws and are distinguished from 'viruses' which tend to infect static files and therefore require the actions of users to assist with their propagation. *Blended threats* are meta-trojans which can embody a combination of worms and viruses depending upon their intended purpose.

man-in-the-middle attack – see *browser-in-the-middle*

micro-frauds are mass frauds that are individually small in impact, but significant in their aggregate. They are mainly online frauds that are deemed to be too small to be acted upon by law enforcement. As a consequence, they tend to be written off by victims, both individuals and corporate, or are deemed not to be sufficiently significant to devote policing resources towards in the public interest. See *de minimism*.

money mule is a third party who is involved in a fraud. In *cybercrimes*, the money mule is typically the person who uses stolen identity information to extract money from a bank. A proportion of the gains will be forwarded to the phishers. The money mules tend to be the ones that get caught in successful policing operations, but are the 'low-hanging fruit' in the fraud operation as they only play a small part (see *phishing*).

MP3 (full name MPEG-1 Audio Layer 3) is an audio compression format, which exploits the fallibility of the human ear by removing inaudible analogue sounds. By saving space, it enables sound files to be efficiently transmitted across the *internet*.

MP4 (MPEG-4) is a computer file compression format like *MP3* which allows video, audio and other information to be stored efficiently on one file and transmitted across the *internet*.

networked technology consists of the various hardware and software technologies plus protocols that enable computing devices to communicate with each other.

network society was coined in 1991 by Van Dijk (see Van Dijk, 1999) and later argued by Manuel Castells (2000a) to be one of the hallmarks of the *information society*/age. It emerged from the historical convergence of three independent processes during the late twentieth century: the information technology revolution in the 1970s; the restructuring of capitalism and of statism in the 1980s; the cultural social movements of the 1960s and their 1970s aftermath. Often attributed to the *internet*, the network society actually predated it by a number of decades; however, while the information technology revolution did not create the network society, the network society as we know it today would arguably not exist without it.

newsgroups – see *chat rooms*.

non-fungible tokens are individual digital assets that carry rights of ownership. They are unique digital identifiers which can be neither copied, substituted nor divided. The asset is recorded on a blockchain which certifies its authenticity and ownership.

obscene materials are ideas and thoughts expressed in words, images and actions which offend the prevailing social morality. Most jurisdictions have laws which define where the boundaries of obscenity lie, but definitions are not always the same. Although the term 'obscene' can be applied broadly, legal and moral debates over 'obscene' materials tend to focus upon the depiction of sexual activities (extreme *pornography*).

output fraud refers to the use of credit facilities to obtain goods, services or money fraudulently.

Panopticon is a term used by Jeremy Bentham to describe a design of prison which allowed prison officers to see their prisoners without being seen. It became an important concept in the formation of Foucault's disciplinary theory (1983: 223). In the panopticon, prisoners never knew when they were being watched and therefore obeyed prison rules of conduct because they feared punishment. After a period of time under the panoptic gaze, prisoners eventually adhered to the regime and modified their behaviour to comply with the rules. The panopticon illustrates how prison architecture shapes the physical and mental architecture of the prison and therefore the relationships within it, especially the power relationship between the observer (guard) and the observed (prisoner). This theory lends itself to internet surveillance and to theorizing about the governance of online behaviour.

payment fraud is fraud that takes place in the payment phase of a transaction.

peer-to-peer networks (P2P) rely upon user participation to create networks to generate new forms of decentralized commercial and informational relationships between individuals. Variations of P2P are business to business (B2B) and business to consumer (B2C) and vice versa. The term is often confused with *grid computing* which connects distributed computers to create a virtual computer architecture that has a computing power that is greater than the sum of its parts.

people hacking – see *social engineering*.

personal digital assistants (PDAs) are small, but powerful, handheld computers that can be connected to the *internet* by *wireless technologies*.

pharming is an automated version of *phishing* that does not rely upon *social engineering* to trick the recipient, because it automatically redirects the recipient to the offending site.

phishing is the use of internet communications, e.g. emails, to *socially engineer* (trick) people out of personal financial information. Variations include *spear phishing*, where specific, rather than blanket, targets are chosen. Also *pharming, smishing, vishing*. Also *whale phishing* and *big game hunting*. Phishing tends to exploit human emotions such as greed, guilt, pride, compassion, curiosity.

phlooding is a multiple *distributed denial of service (DDoS)* attack caused by a group of simultaneous, though geographically distributed, attacks which target the network login structure of a particular business to overload its central authentication server.

piracy is a term frequently used to describe the unauthorized reproduction and distribution of electronic and audio-visual media that are protected by *intellectual property* copyright laws. It is most commonly used with regard to the unauthorized distribution of *MP3* and *MP4* files.

policing is a term used broadly within this book to describe the act of regulating the behaviour of a population, usually to maintain order and enforce law. Although this function is commonly performed by the police (public police organizations), they are not the sole actors performing this function – indeed, they arguably perform only a small part of 'policing'.

pornography describes the visual, textual or oral depiction of the human body with the intention of sexually arousing those who experience it. It is often linked to, but is distinguishable from, erotica, which also has artistic merit. While pornography may be morally illicit, pornography is not necessarily illegal unless it is deemed to be *obscene*.

premium line service scams – see *rogue dialler*.

pseudo-photographs use new graphics technologies to 'morph' or graphically blend two photographic images together to make a new image with new meaning. The various laws relating to *pornographic* 'pseudo photographs' were amended in the early to mid-1990s to make possession of them illegal because they weakened the case for the prosecution, which had long relied upon the fact that an individual (usually a child) had been abused in the construction of the picture.

'pump and dump' scams deceive stock market investors through the circulation of information on the *internet* that misrepresents the value and potential of real stock. This misinformation artificially drives up the price of the stock (the pump), which is then sold off at inflated prices (the dump).

pyramid selling scams (Ponzi frauds) have migrated online and are elaborate confidence tricks that promise a good return on investment. The return on investment is, however, paid from money derived from new investors, rather than profits, and the schemes mathematically eventually run out of investors. The schemes are fuelled by the fact that the very early investors often do get a good return on their money, and their enthusiasm advertises their apparent authenticity.

ransomware (or ransom virus) is malicious software that hijacks a computer system until it is neutralized by a code provided by a blackmailer once a ransom has been paid. The original practice of locking access to *computers* was replaced in the 2010s by crypto-ransomware which encrypts complete data systems. This practice was followed in late 2019 by an aggressive ransomware tactic that targets and enters organizations' systems and moves laterally to identify and exfiltrate key data before encrypting the data on the system. Victims are named on a 'wall of shame' WWW site and the data is published in segments if the ransom is not paid by the deadline (also known as 'reverse double jeopardy ransomware').

RATware / remote administration trojans (RATs) are a form of malicious software that makes an infected 'zombie' computer become susceptible to remote administration and inclusion in a *botnet*.

reputation management systems: vendors build up profiles based upon customer feedback on their past sales performance, which enables potential purchasers to vet them before making bids. Good reputations are highly valued and maintaining them discourages dishonest behaviour by vendors and bidders. See '*short-firm' frauds*.

reskilling – see *deskilling*.

reverse social engineering – see *social engineering*.

rogue dialler is a type of malicious software that automatically and discreetly transfers users' existing telephone services from the normal domestic rate to a premium line service in order to defraud them.

rogueware is software that has a dark motive. Mostly, but not exclusively criminal, it includes malicious software generally, but also *scareware* and *spyware*.

salami fraud describes the perpetration of many small frauds from different sources, or over a long time span, which are individually minor but large in aggregate.

samurai are *ethical hackers* who hire themselves out to undertake legal 'cracking' tasks and assist those who have legitimate reasons to use an electronic locksmith.

SCADA (Supervisory Control And Data Acquisition) systems are computing systems that are used to monitor and also to control major industrial processes ranging from some manufacturing processes to the utilities (electricity, water, etc.) that comprise the infrastructure. There has been much concern that SCADA systems will become the focus for *cyber-terrorists* or become the target in cyber-warfare and, after many years of prophesizing, proof of concept arrived with the discovery of the Stuxnet. See *Stuxnet* and *information warfare*.

scams are confidence tricks, typically undertaken to engage and defraud a victim. Internet scams commonly originate in *spam* communications and include: (a) healthcare scams which seek to deceive victims by offering the promise of improvements to health – say, through performance-enhancing drugs or surgery, or they may claim to cure ill health through various snake-oil remedies; (b) finance scams, which seek to deceive victims by offering the promise of improvements to their finances, and include *phishing, pyramid selling, pump and dump*; (c) advertising scams, which lure victims by offering free or discounted products, goods and services; (d) *pornography* scams which lure victims with offers of free access to sexual imagery; (e) others, which include 'lottery scams', in which victims are lured by telling them that they have won a prize which they can claim once advance fees are paid or personal information is provided, and 'gambling scams', which entrap victims with a free line of gambling credit.

scareware (sometimes known as *rogueware or shockware*) is an aggressive sales technique through which 'scare-mongers' inundate computer users with misleading messages that emulate Windows security messages. They are sometimes delivered by Windows messenger, or via Twitter, Facebook and other social networking sites, or else by a spam email message. These messages are often referred to as malverts – a combination of '*malware*' and 'adverts' – that are intended to socially engineer recipients into believing that their computer has been infected or, as in the case of messages alleged to contain important breaking news, into clicking onto a URL in order to gain further information, which then tells them via a pop-up message that their computer is infected. These scare or shock tactics convince recipients that their personal *computer* has been infected by malicious software and therefore requires fixing. Of course, the solution recommended is usually the scare-mongers' own brand of software (see *entrapment marketing*) which downloaders have to pay for and which is usually ineffective, or may give an impression that it is having some impact, or else it may contain malicious software.

script kiddies are inexperienced and unskilled *hackers* who seek peer respect for their audacity by infiltrating or disrupting computer systems by using cracking scripts that they have designed.

search engine optimization (SEO) is a legitimate marketing strategy that increases the relevance and ranking of a www site according to specific keywords. The higher a www site ranks with a search engine, then the more traffic will go its way. The SEO process can take place by editing the content of a www site either to make it relevant to keywords or to remove barriers that exist to the indexing functions of search engines. Search engine optimization can have positive impact by creating incentives to enable more accessible web pages in order to increase web traffic naturally. It can also have its downside because it creates an unethical practice and associated dark economy, or 'Black hat SEO' as it is often referred to, which encourages the use of devious methods to increase rankings – for example, see *spamdexing, link farming, keyword stuffing, article spinning, google bombing.*

the semantic web refers to a future vision of the evolution of the World Wide Web so that it will become the universal medium for the exchange of data, information and knowledge. Prospective in design, the semantic web envisages the development of the www along the lines of its original open flow principles, but incorporating aspects of AI so that users' needs and demands are understood. Some aspects of the semantic web have been developed; others exist as specification only. The success of the semantic web requires, amongst other technological developments, the construction of new formats for data interchange, such as the Ontological Web Language (OWL), Resource Description Frameworks (RDF) and Scheme (RDFS), which describe the operating concepts, relationships and terminology within knowledge domains.

sexting is the sending of sexually explicit materials via SMS messaging. The materials are usually in image and text format and are produced by the sender usually for consumption by the recipient or recipients who are part of the sender's social network.

shockware – see *scareware.*

short-firm fraud is a term used in this book to describe the fraudulent exploitation of online auction reputation management systems. Typically, once a good vendor 'trust' rating has been acquired, then items are sold, usually offline, to runners-up in the bidding war, and the vendor disappears without supplying the goods once the money has been received.

signal events are events – such as, but not exclusively, crime – that capture the media's attention and heighten existing public anxieties. Although not necessarily major, they nevertheless have a significant impact upon public beliefs compared with their actual consequences and they can artificially increase levels of fear about *cybercrime.* See *black swan events.*

simulacra (simulacrum in singular) is a term used by Jean Baudrillard (1994) to describe a situation where one can have copies without originals. It introduces a useful language to describe the construction and dissemination of multi-media materials in computer file format.

simulation captures the essence of a real object in such a way that it can be used to observe and predict how that object may behave when subject to changing inputs.

situational crime prevention focuses upon the reduction of criminal opportunity by increasing the effort needed to commit a crime, increasing the risks to the offender, or reducing the reward of crime. It tends to ignore consideration of intent.

smishing is a form of *phishing* which uses bulk text messaging facilities to target mobile devices such as phones or *personal digital assistants (PDAs)* with urgent text requests for the recipient to call an alleged bank phone number or log onto a website and change their security information, thereby revealing it.

snake-oil scams – see *scams.*

social engineering or 'people hacking' is the use of interpersonal deceptions to trick staff within organizations into giving out personal information such as passwords to secure systems, by building up trust relationships with them and exploiting their personal weaknesses. 'Reverse social engineering' is where a *hacker* causes a technical problem within a system and then positions himself or herself to be commissioned to fix it, thereby gaining access.

social networking websites offer interactive, user-submitted networks of friends, personal profiles, *blogs*, groups, photos, music and videos. They connect people who possess different types of interests. Examples include MySpace, LiveJournal.com.

Software Defined Radio – see *wireless technology*.

spam/spamming is the distribution of unsolicited bulk emails that deliver invitations to participate in schemes to earn money; to obtain free products and services; to win prizes; to spy upon others; to obtain improvements to health or well-being; to replace lost hair; to increase one's sexual prowess; or to cure cancer. They choke up bandwidth and present risks to the recipient should they respond.

spamdexing is a technique that specifically uses *spams* containing a range of keywords to increase the ranking of web pages in a search engine's index. The keywords can be hidden in the content of the spammed email in the form of text or a URL link to a www site (see *keyword stuffing*). It is an illicit, or unethical, form of *search engine optimization*.

spear phishing is the deliberate targeting of emails to specific groups in society in order to socially engineer them into giving their personal information, opening attachments, downloading malicious websites or engaging directly in a fraud. The 'spear' phish hooks the target group by using specific information which they can resonate with. See *whale phishing* and *big game hunting*.

spoofing is a term that describes an act where people, through software, falsify information in order to pretend to be someone or something else so as to deceive another to gain an illicit advantage over them.

spyware is software that covertly surveils the user's computer files to obtain and return personal information about the user.

stressers (booter services) are quasi-legal online services that enable *hackers* to launch DDoS attacks. Usage is legitimate if the www site being attacked gives its consent – for example, by penetration testers. Most stresser usage by hackers is, however, illegal.

Stuxnet is a form of *malware* that can be used to sabotage industrial control systems (*SCADA*). It represents a 'paradigm shift' in malware threats and is distinct from other malicious worms because: (a) its primary method of entry into operating systems is (amongst other potential entry means) through USB sticks; (b) like other worms, it establishes a rootkit, as well as a backdoor connection which allows external control; (c) unlike other worms, it aggressively attacks specific types of SCADA systems produced by particular manufacturers; (d) the July 2010 Stuxnet worm had a kill date and limited scope and sought particular system configurations – indicating that it was intended to hit specific targets, but did not find its target this time. In the absence of further information, conspiracy theories quickly evolved which mapped the Stuxnet threat onto contemporary political divisions. A particular concern was that the 2010 attack was specifically targeted at Iranian (nuclear) processes. See *information warfare*.

surveillance is the act of monitoring the behaviour of another, either in real time using cameras, audio devices or key-stroke monitoring, or in chosen time by *data mining* records of internet transactions. Surveillance can be overt or covert. User awareness of being surveilled in real or chosen time can shape their online behaviour. See *panopticon*.

tabnapping is a form of *phishing* that overlays browser pages that have been open and unused for some time with a logon panel which informs users that they have to log into their page again in order to gain access to it once more. Once users have logged on, the panel disappears and they can access the page once again. In so doing, users innocently give their valuable login information to identity thieves who can subsequently use the information against them.

TCP/IP (transmission control protocol / internet protocol) are layered protocols that enable internet communications to take place, and form the technical core of the *internet*. They were adopted in 1982 by the US Department of Defense and ratified in 1985 by the Internet Architecture Board.

technology is a term which describes the expression of ideas about methods that rationalize human activity. Usually such expression involves the use of tools – in this book, hardware and software – but it is the ideas and rationale behind the tools that are of primary interest.

tracking (HTTP) cookies trade data that authenticate visitors to www sites and can track their sessions. Whilst these functions can assist the user, tracking cookies also help to maintain specific information about users' choices of www sites and also their purchasing preferences (from their shopping carts). Tracking cookies are not *spyware* as such because they merely trade data; however, the fact that they allow users to be tracked from site to site does raise concerns and lead to them being regarded as intrusive and therefore treated by some anti-virus packages in the same manner as they treat spyware.

trojans – see *malware or malcode.*

ubiquitous law enforcement arises from the *digital realism* that the same technologies which provide opportunities for *cybercrime* also provide opportunities for law enforcement and crime prevention. It creates a new agenda with regard to debate over the appropriate use of technologies in the policing function.

unethical hackers evolved from *script kiddies* and are driven by financial or other types of gain. They used to be called 'crackers' by the cybersecurity media to distance them from ethical hackers, but the term caused offence because it was historically used as a racial slur and so is rarely used today.

URL (uniform resource locator) is simply another name for a web address (begins http://).

viral information flow is a term that describes how information proliferates across distributed networks by word of 'mouse' (rather than mouth). The information flows can be almost viral in the way that they are distributed exponentially from node to node across networks. The term 'viral' is now used colloquially to describe the internet video phenomenon; indeed, they are actually called 'virals'. See *churnalism* and *asymmetry.*

virtual environment is a term often used synonymously with *cyberspace*, but virtual environments, such as Habbo Hotel or Second Life, to name but two, are actually the localities of cyberspace.

virus – see *malware or malcode.*

vishing is another form of *phishing* that uses *VoIP (voice over internet protocol)* to *spam* recorded messages to telephone numbers. The VoIP messages purport to be from banks, other financial institutions, online merchants such as Amazon or internet auction houses such as eBay, and warn that their credit card has been used for fraudulent transactions. As with *phishing* and its variations, recipients are asked to contact a phone number or log on to a website to verify and change their security information. Also referred to as 'robocalling'.

VoIP (voice over internet protocol) is a method of enabling telephone conversations to take place over the *internet* or through any other internet protocol-(IP-)based network.

webcams are cameras linked to networked *computers* via a website whose real-time images can be watched from afar by all who access the particular site. Their use ranges from closed circuit *surveillance* to video-conferencing. They were made popular in the mid-1990s by cam-girls, such as JenniCAM, who broadcast voyeuristic images of themselves for a fee.

webmail is email that can be sent through a web browser, e.g. hotmail or Yahoo, rather than a dedicated email program such as Microsoft Outlook.

whale phishing is the practice of specifically targeting phishing emails at wealthy individuals and business organizations to socially engineer the infection of their *computers* or to directly defraud them. See *big game hunting* and *spear phishing.*

white-collar crime is a term that describes crimes of the powerful and crimes that are normally hidden from 'blue collar' criminologies of street crime. *Cybercrime* shares many of the characteristics of hidden crimes and can be informed by those debates; however, the fit with white-collar crime is not so easy since informational knowledge is power within *cyberspace.*

white hat – see *hacker.*

wi-fi is the form of *wireless technology* that enables wireless internet connections, but it is increasingly becoming the basis for connecting many other domestic electronic appliances.

wizards are 'white hat' *hackers* who are renowned for their hacking knowledge.

World Wide Web (www) runs on the *internet* and is a network of interlinked and hypertext multimedia documents known as web pages.

worms – see *malware or malcode.*

Zeus is a trojan, a form of malware that is distributed by spammed email. It looks benign, but infects the insecure *computers* of small businesses and individuals in order to steal bank login information and has a built-in capacity to evade detection. It has evolved through a number of iterations.

Earlier versions sought user names and passwords for *social networking websites* and online services as well as online banking credentials. More sophisticated later versions focus solely on collecting banking information, which is subsequently sent to a collecting database via encrypted communications (see *malware or malcode* and *phishing*).

zombies – see *botnets* and *RATware*.

Cases and References

Cases

ACLU et al. *v.* Reno (1997), 117 S Ct 2329.

Ashcroft *v.* Free Speech Coalition (2002) 535 US 234 (2002) 198 F 3d 1083.

DPP *v.* Paul Chambers (2012) EWHC 2157.

Godfrey *v.* Demon Internet Ltd. (1999) 4 All ER 342.

In re Doubleclick Inc. (2001) 154 F Supp 2d 497 – SDNY, 28 March.

In re Verizon Internet Services, Inc. (2003); at http://news.findlaw.com/hdocs/docs/verizon/inreveri zon12103opn.pdf.

Keith-Smith *v.* Williams (2006) EWHC 860.

Lauri Love *v.* The Government of the USA [2018] EWHC 172 (Admin.).

League Against Racism and Anti-Semitism (LICRA) and The Union of French Jewish Students (UEJF) *v.* Yahoo Inc. and Yahoo France (2000), Interim Court Order, 20 November, The County Court of Paris, No. RG: 00/05308.

Metro-Goldwyn-Mayer Studios, Inc. *v.* Grokster, Ltd. (2004) 9th Circuit Court of Appeals, 19 August; at www.eff.org/IP/P2P/MGM_v_Grokster/20040819_mgm_v_grokster_decision.pdf.

Paris Adult Theater I *v.* Slaton (1973) 413 US 49.

People *v.* Somm (1998), Amtsgericht Munich [Local Court], File No. 8340.

Planned Parenthood *v.* ACLA (2001) (Planned Parenthood of the Columbia/Willamette, Inc. *v.* American Coalition of Life Activists), No. 99–35320, 2001, US App. LEXIS 4974 (9th Cir. 28 Mar. 2001).

R. *v.* Jonathan Bowden (2000) 1 Cr App Rep 438.

R. *v.* Brown (1993) 97 Cr App Rep 44, (1994) 1 AC 212.

R. *v.* Fellows; R. *v.* Arnold (1997) 2 All ER 548.

R. *v.* Handyside *v.* United Kingdom (1976) 1 EHRR 737.

R. *v.* Wilson (1996) 2 Cr App Rep 241.

R. *v.* Zundel (1992) 95 DLR (4th) 202 (1992) and (Can Sup Ct 27 Aug. 1992, unreported).

Roberts *v.* Media Logistics (UK) Ltd (2006); http://spamlegalaction.pbwiki. com.

United States *v.* Alkhabaz (1997); US App LEXIS 9060; (1996) 104 F 3d 1492; (1995) 48 F 3d 1220 and US App LEXIS 11244.

United States *v.* Dost (1986) 636 F Supp 828.

United States of America *v.* Robert A. Thomas and Carleen Thomas (1996) 74 F 3d 701; 1996 US App LEXIS 1069; 1996 Fed App 0032P (6th Cir).

References

Abou-Assaleh, T. and Das, T. (2008) 'Combating spamdexing: incorporating heuristics in link-based ranking'. In W. Aiello, A. Broder, J. Janssen and E., Milios (eds.), *Algorithms and Models for the Web-Graph. WAW 2006.* Lecture Notes in Computer Science, 4936, Berlin: Springer.

Abrams, L. (2021) 'Another ransomware now uses DDoS attacks to force victims to pay', *BleepingComputer*, 24 January, www.bleepingcomputer.com/news/security/another-ransom ware-now-uses-ddos-attacks-to-force-victims-to-pay.

Action Fraud (2023) 'Ticket to nowhere: don't get ticked off with ticket fraud this summer', Action Fraud Press Release, 10 April, www.actionfraud.police.uk/ticketfraud.

Adams, J. A. (1996) 'Controlling cyberspace: applying the computer fraud and abuse act to the internet', *Santa Clara Computer and High Technology Law Journal*, 12: 403–34.

Adams, S. (1998) *The Dilbert Future: Thriving on Business Stupidity in the 21st Century*, London: Harper Business.

Adler, A. (2001) 'The perverse law of child pornography', *Columbia Law Review*, 101: 209–73.

Afifi-Sabet, K. (2020) '36 billion personal records exposed by hacks in 2020 so far', *ITPro*, 29 October, www.itpro.com/security/357578/exposed-records-top-36-billion-in-2020-so-far.

Agger, B. (2004) *The Virtual Self: A Contemporary Sociology*, Oxford: Blackwell.

AIN (2005) 'ASACP changes name: Association of Sites Advocating Child Protection', *Adult Industry News*, 2 March, www.ainews.com/story/8557.

Akdeniz, Y. (1996) 'Computer pornography: a comparative study of US and UK obscenity laws and child pornography laws in relation to the internet', *International Review of Law, Computers and Technology*, 10 (2): 235–61.

Akdeniz, Y. (1997) 'The regulation of pornography and child pornography on the internet', *Journal of Information Law and Technology*, (1), www2.warwick.ac.uk/fac/soc/law/elj/jilt/1997_1/akdeniz1.

Akdeniz, Y., Walker, C. P. and Wall, D. S. (eds.) (2000) *The Internet, Law and Society*, London: Longman.

Alharthi, M. (2023) *The Positive Governance of the Internet in the Kingdom of Saudi Arabia*, PhD thesis, University of Leeds.

Allen, J., Forrest, S., Levi, M., Roy, H. and Sutton, M. (2005) 'Fraud and technology crimes: findings from the 2002/03 British Crime Survey and 2003 Offending, Crime and Justice Survey', *Home Office Online Report 34/05*, www.homeoffice.gov.uk/rds/pdfs05/rdsolr3405.pdf.

Anderson, A. (2000) *Snake Oil, Hustlers and Hambones: The American Medicine Show*, Jefferson, NC: McFarland.

Anderson R., Barton, C., Böhme, R., et al. (2013) 'Measuring the cost of cybercrime', *The Economics of Information Security and Privacy*, 265: 300.

Andrews, J. (2023) 'Fraud and cyber crime report 2022', *Money*, 12 January, www.money.co.uk/credit-cards/fraud-report.

APIG (2004) *Revision of the Computer Misuse Act: Report of an Inquiry by the All Party Internet Group*, June, www.apig.org.uk/CMAReportFinal Version1.pdf.

Appel, E. (2003) 'US cybercrime: model solutions', paper presented to 'Technologies for Public Safety in Critical Incident Response', National Institute of Justice, Office of Science and Technology, 23 September, www.nlectc. org/training/nij2003/Appel.pdf.

APWG (2022) 'APWG phishing activity trends report, 3rd Quarter, 2022', 22 September, https://docs.apwg.org/reports/apwg_trends_report_q3_2022.pdf.

Arthur, C. (2005) 'Interview with a link spammer', *The Register*, 31 January, www.theregister.co.uk/2005/01/31/link_spamer_interview.

Artosi, A. (2002) 'On the notion of an empowered agent', paper presented to the 2002 Workshop on the Law of Electronic Agents, Bologna, www.cirfid.unibo. it/~lea-02/pp/Artosi.pdf.

ASPI (2022) *The UN Norms of Responsible State Behaviour in Cyberspace*, International Cyber Policy Centre, Canberra: Australian Strategic Policy Institute, March.

Austin, J. (1962) *How to Do Things with Words*, Oxford: Clarendon Press.

Balkin, J. (2004) 'Virtual liberty: freedom to design and freedom to play in virtual worlds', *Virginia Law Review*, 90 (8): 2044–98, www.yale.edu/lawweb/jbalkin/articles/virtual_liberty1.pdf.

Ballard, M. (2006) 'Police offered robot eye: intelligence gets "intelligent"', *The Register*, 1 June, www.theregister.co.uk/2006/06/01/ police_eye.

Barlow, J. P. (1994) 'The economy of ideas: a framework for rethinking patents and copyrights in the digital age (everything you know about intellectual property is wrong)', *WIRED*, 2 (3): 84.

Barlow, J. P. (1996) 'A declaration of the independence of cyberspace', *John Perry Barlow Library*, www.eff.org/Misc/Publications/John_Perry_ Barlow/barlow_0296.declaration.txt.

Baron, L. and Straus, M. (1989) *Four Theories of Rape in American Society: A State-Level Analysis*, New Haven and London: Yale University Press.

Barone, M. (2004) 'The national interest: absence of evidence is not evidence of absence', *US News & World Report*, 24 March, www.usnews.com/usnews/opinion/baroneweb/mb_040324.htm.

Barrett, L. (2021) *Seven and a Half Lessons about the Brain*, London: Picador.

Barrett, N. (2004) *Traces of Guilt*, London: Bantam Press.

Baudrillard, J. (1988) 'Consumer society'. In M. Poster (ed.), *Jean Baudrillard: Selected Writings*, Oxford: Blackwell, 32–59.

Baudrillard, J. (1994) *Simulacra and Simulation*, Ann Arbor: University of Michigan Press.

Baudrillard, J. (1998) *The Consumer Society: Myths and Structures*, London: Sage.

Baudrillard J. (2009) 'The precession of simulacra'. In J. Storey (ed.), *Cultural Theory and Popular Culture: A Reader*, 4th edn, Harlow: Pearson, 409–15.

Bauman, Z. (1998) *Globalization: The Human Consequences*, Cambridge: Polity.

BBC (1999a) 'Cyberstalking: pursued in cyber space', *BBC News Online*, 26 June, http://news.bbc.co .uk/1/hi/uk/378373.stm.

BBC (1999b) 'Internet football hooligan probe', *BBC News Online*, 8 August, http://news.bbc.co.uk /1/hi/uk/414634.stm.

BBC (2001) 'Briton kidnapped in money scam', *BBC News Online*, 13 July, http://news.bbc.co.uk/2/ hi/uk_news/1438082.stm.

BBC (2002) 'Shoe bomb suspect "did not act alone"', *BBC News Online*, 25 January, http://news.bbc .co.uk/1/hi/world/americas/1783237.stm.

BBC (2003a) 'Spammers and virus writers unite', *BBC News Online*, 30 April, http://news.bbc.co.uk /1/hi/technology/2988209.stm.

BBC (2003b) 'Extortionists target technology', *BBC News Online*, 12 November, http://news.bbc.co .uk/1/hi/business/3265423.stm.

BBC (2003c) 'E-commerce targeted by blackmailers', *BBC News Online*, 26 November, http://news .bbc.co.uk/1/hi/technology/3238230.stm.

BBC (2004a) 'Hacker threats to bookies probed', *BBC News Online*, 23 February, http://news.bbc.co .uk/1/hi/technology/3513849.stm.

BBC (2004b) 'Ex-marine jailed for abduction', *BBC News Online*, 2 April, http://news.bbc.co.uk/1/hi /england/manchester/3594235.stm.

BBC (2004c) 'Iraqis seek a voice via blogs', *BBC News Online*, 8 September, http://news.bbc.co.uk /1/hi/technology/3632614.stm.

BBC (2004d) 'London "call girl" gives up blog', *BBC News Online*, 17 September, http://news.bbc.co .uk/1/hi/technology/3665440.stm.

BBC (2005a) 'Rich pickings for hi-tech thieves', *BBC News Online*, 25 January, http://news.bbc.co.uk /1/hi/technology/4203601.stm.

BBC (2005b) 'Net regulation "still possible"', *BBC News Online*, 27 January, http://news.bbc.co.uk /1/hi/technology/4211415.stm.

BBC (2005c) 'How eBay fraudsters stole £300k', *BBC News Online*, 28 October, http://news.bbc.co.uk /1/hi/uk/4386952.stm.

BBC (2005d) 'Internet piracy pair facing jail', *BBC News Online*, 6 May, http://news.bbc.co.uk/1/hi/te chnology/4518771.stm.

BBC (2005e) 'Tools drive point-and-click crime', *BBC News Online*, 15 August, http://news.bbc.co.uk /1/hi/technology/4152626.stm.

BBC (2006a) 'Sites selling child porn targeted', *BBC News Online*, 16 March, http://news.bbc.co.uk /1/hi/technology/4812962.stm.

BBC (2006b) 'Cyber bullies haunt young online', *BBC News Online*, 14 March, http://news.bbc.co.uk /1/hi/technology/4805760.stm.

BBC (2006c) 'Extortion virus code gets cracked', *BBC News Online*, 1 June, http://news.bbc.co.uk /1/hi/technology/5038330.stm.

BBC (2006d) 'E-mail charging plan to beat spam', *BBC News Online*, 6 February, http://news.bbc.co .uk/1/hi/technology/4684942.stm.

BBC (2006e) 'E-mail delivery "tax" criticised: protests about the plan have come from many non-profit groups', *BBC News Online*, 6 March, http://news.bbc.co.uk/1/hi/technology/4778136.stm.

BBC (2006f) 'Paedophiles face cancelled cards', *BBC News Online*, 19 July, http://news.bbc.co.uk/1/hi/business/5194150.stm.

BBC (2006g) 'UK hackers condemn McKinnon trial', *BBC News Online*, 8 May, http://news.bbc.co.uk/1/hi/technology/4984132.stm.

BBC (2006h) 'McKinnon's extradition condemned', *BBC News Online*, 7 July, http://news.bbc.co.uk/1/hi/technology/5157674.stm.

BBC (2006i) 'Spammers manipulate money markets', *BBC News Online*, 25 August, http://news.bbc.co.uk/1/hi/technology/5284618.stm.

BBC (2006j) '"Tower of Babel" technology nears', *BBC News Online*, 27 September, http://news.bbc.co.uk/1/hi/technology/5382086.stm.

BBC (2009) '"Scareware" scams trick searchers', *BBC News Online*, 23 March, http://news.bbc.co.uk/1/hi/technology/7955358.stm.

BBC (2015) '"Sexting" boy's naked selfie recorded as crime by police', *BBC News Online*, 3 September, www.bbc.com/news/uk-34136388.

BBC (2019) 'Fraud victims let down by "inconsistent policing"', *BBC News Online*, 2 April, www.bbc.com/news/uk-47781981.

BBC (2020a) 'Hundreds arrested as crime chat network cracked', *BBC News Online*, 2 July, www.bbc.co.uk/news/uk-53263310.

BBC (2020b) 'Woman loses £320,000 in "romance fraud" scam', *BBC News Online*, 20 October, www.bbc.co.uk/news/uk-england-somerset-54613937.

Beck, U. (1992) *Risk Society*, London: Sage.

Beck, U. (1999) *World Risk Society*, Cambridge: Polity.

Becker, H. (1963) *Outsiders: Studies in the Sociology of Deviance*, London: Press of Glencoe.

Bell, D. (2001) *An Introduction to Cybercultures*, London: Routledge.

Berger, A. (1996) 'The low-tech side of information warfare', *Air & Space Power Chronicles – Chronicles Online Journal*, www.airpower.maxwell.af.mil/airchronicles/cc/berger.html.

Berinato, S. (2006) 'Attack of the bots', *WIRED*, 14 (1), www.wired.com/wired/archive/14.11/botnet_pr.html.

Berkowitz, B. and Hahn, R. W. (2003) 'Cybersecurity: who's watching the store?', *Issues in Science & Technology*, 19 (3): 55–63, www.issues.org/issues/19.3/berkowitz.htm.

Bevan, M. (2001) 'Confessions of a hacker', *Sunday Business Post Online*, 1 April, www.kujimedia.com/modules.php?op modload&nameNews&file article&sid 60.

Biever. C. (2004) 'How zombie networks fuel cybercrime', *New Scientist.Com*, 3 November, www.newscientist.com/news/news.jsp?id ns99996616.

Bischoff, P. (2021) 'How to Recognize and Avoid eBay Scams', *comparitech*, 6 September, www.comparitech.com/identity-theft-protection/ebay-scams.

Bossler, A. and Berenblum, T. (2019) 'Introduction: new directions in cybercrime research', *Journal of Crime and Justice*, 42 (5): 495–9 (special issue: 'New Directions in Cybercrime Research', www.tandfonline.com/toc/rjcj20/42/5).

Bottoms, A. and Wiles, P. (1996) 'Understanding crime prevention in late modern societies'. In T. Bennett (ed.), *Preventing Crime and Disorder: Targeting Strategies and Responsibilities*, Cambridge: University of Cambridge, Institute of Criminology.

Boyle, A. (1999) 'Some reflections on the relationship of treaties and soft law', *International and Comparative Law Quarterly*, 48 (4): 901–13.

Boyle, J. (1996) *Shamans, Software and Spleens: Law and the Construction of the Information Society*, Cambridge, MA: Harvard University Press.

Braithwaite, J. (1992) *Crime, Shame and Reintegration*, Cambridge: Cambridge University Press.

Braithwaite, J. and Drahos, P. (2000) *Global Business Regulation*, Cambridge: Cambridge University Press.

Braverman, H. (1976) *Labour and Monopoly Capital*, New York: Monthly Review Press.

Brenner, S. (2001) 'Is there such a thing as "virtual crime"?', *California Criminal Law Review*, 4 (1): 11.

Brenner, S. (2002) 'Organized cybercrime? How cyberspace may affect the structure of criminal relationships', *North Carolina Journal of Law & Technology*, 4 (1): 1–41.

Brewer R., Fox, S. and Miller, C. (2019) 'Applying the techniques of neutralization to the study of cybercrime'. pp. 547–565 In T. Holt and A. Bossler (eds.), *The Palgrave Handbook of International Cybercrime and Cyberdeviance*, London: Palgrave Macmillan, 547–65.

Brin, D. (1998) *The Transparent Society: Will Technology Force Us to Choose between Privacy and Freedom?*, London: Addison-Wesley.

Briscoe, G. and De Wilde, P. (2009) 'Digital ecosystems: evolving service-oriented architectures', *IEEE First International Conference on BIO Inspired models of NETwork, Information and Computing Systems* (BIONETICS) (2006), *arXiv*, https://doi.org/10.48550/arXiv.0712.4102.

Britz, M. T. (2003) *Computer Forensics and Computer Crime*, New Jersey: Upper Saddle River, NJ: Pearson Prentice Hall.

Broadhurst, R. and Grabosky, P. (eds.) (2005) *Cyber-Crime: The Challenge in Asia*, Hong Kong: Hong Kong University Press.

Brodeur, J.-P. (1983) 'High policing and low policing: remarks about the policing of political activities', *Social Problems*, 30 (5): 507–20.

Broersma, M. (2004) 'Boost UK govt cybercrime resources', *ComputerWeekly*, 17 May.

Buchanan, T. and Whitty, M. (2014) 'The online dating romance scam: causes and consequences of victimhood', *Psychology, Crime & Law*, 20 (3): 261–83.

Burrows, R. (1997) 'Cyberpunk as social theory'. In S. Westwood and J. Williams (eds.), *Imagining Cities: Scripts, Signs and Memories*, London: Routledge, 235–48.

Button, M. and Cross, C. (2017) *Cyber Frauds, Scams and Their Victims*, London: Routledge.

Button, M., Hock, B. and Shepherd, D. (2022) *Economic Crime: From Conception to Response*, London: Routledge.

C'T (2004) 'Uncovered: trojans as spam robots', *C'T Magazine*, 23 February, www.heise.de/english/newsticker/news/44879.

Caden, M. L. and Lucas, S. E. (1996) 'Accidents on the information superhighway: on-line liability and regulation', *Richmond Journal of Law & Technology*, 2: 1.

Cain, M. (2002) 'International crime and globalisation', *Criminal Justice Matters*, 46: 34–5.

Campbell, D. (1997) 'More Naked Gun than Top Gun', *The Guardian*, 27 November, 2.

Campbell, D. (2005a) 'A flaw in the child porn witch-hunt', *Sunday Times*, 26 June, www.timesonline.co.uk/article/0,,2092-1669131,00.html.

Campbell, D. (2005b) 'Operation Ore exposed', *PC Pro*, 1 July, www.pcpro.co.uk/features/74690/operation-ore-exposed.html.

Cards International (2003) 'Europe "needs mag-stripe until US adopts chip"', *epaynews.com*, 28 July, www.epaynews.com/index.cgi? survey &ref browse&f view&id 1059392963622215212&block.

Carey, M. and Wall, D. S. (2001) 'MP3: more beats to the byte', *International Review of Law, Computers and Technology*, 15 (1): 35–58.

Carr, J. H. (2004) *Child Abuse, Child Pornography and the Internet*, London: NCH (National Children's Home).

Cashell, B., Jackson, W. D., Jickling, M. and Webel, B. (2004) *The Economic Impact of Cyber-Attacks*, Order Code RL32331, Government and Finance Division, Congressional Research Service, Library of Congress.

Castells, M. (1997a) 'An introduction to the Information Age', *City*, 7: 6–16.

Castells, M. (1997b) *The Information Age: Economy, Society, and Culture*, Volume II: *The Power of Identity*, Oxford: Blackwell.

Castells, M. (2000a) 'Materials for an explanatory theory of the network society', *British Journal of Sociology*, 51 (1): 5–24.

Castells, M. (2000b) *The Information Age: Economy, Society, and Culture*, Volume I: *The Rise of the Network Society*, 2nd edn, Oxford: Blackwell.

Castells, M. (2000c) *The Information Age: Economy, Society, and Culture*, Volume III: *End of Millennium*, 2nd edn, Oxford: Blackwell.

Castells, M. (2013) 'The impact of the internet on society: a global perspective', in *Ch@nge: 19 Key Essays on How the Internet Is Changing Our Lives*. Madrid: BBVA, 127–41.

Center for Democracy and Technology (1998) *Regardless of Frontiers: Protecting the Human Right to Freedom of Expression on the Global Internet*, Washington: Global Internet Liberty Campaign.

Cerf, V. (2003) 'The internet under surveillance: obstacles to the free flow of information online', *Reporters Without Borders*, www.rsf.org/IMG/ pdf/doc-2236.pdf.

Chainalysis (2023) 'Ransomware revenue down as more victims refuse to pay', *Chainalysis Blog*, 19 January, https://blog.chainalysis.com/reports/crypto-ransomware-revenue-down-as-victims-refuse-to-pay.

Chan, J., Brereton, D., Legosz, M. and Doran, S. (2001) *E-Policing: The Impact of Information Technology on Police Practices*, Brisbane: Queensland Criminal Justice Commission.

Chandler, A. (1996) 'The changing definition and image of hackers in popular discourse', *International Journal of the Sociology of Law*, 24: 229–51.

Chatterjee, B. (2001) 'Last of the rainmacs? Thinking about pornography in cyberspace'. In D. S. Wall (ed.), *Crime and the Internet*, London: Routledge, 74–99.

Chicago Crime Commission (2000) 'Internet gang sites', Chicago Crime Commission Press Release, 28 November, http://ccc.dr-technology.com/ gangsites.html.

CIFAS (2021) 'Surge of identity fraud hits the UK as criminals capitalise on recovering economy', CIFAS Press Release, 12 July, www.cifas.org.uk/newsroom/identity-fraud-surge-2021.

CIFAS (2023) 'This is fraudscape 2023', *Cifas*, https://www.fraudscape.co.uk/old-home-2#welcome.

Cimpanu, C. (2020) 'A hacker group is selling more than 73 million user records on the dark web', *ZDNET*, 9 May, www.zdnet.com/article/a-hacker-group-is-selling-more-than-73-million-user-records-on-the-dark-web.

Cimpanu, C. (2021) 'Scam-as-a-service operation made more than $6.5 million in 2020', *ZDNet*, 14 January, www.zdnet.com/article/scam-as-a-service-operation-made-more-than-6-5-million-in-2020.

Claburn, T. (2010) 'Tabnapping attack makes phishing easy', *Information Week*, 25 May, www.informationweek.com/news/storage/security/showArticle.jhtml?articleID=225200157&subSection=News.

Claburn, T. (2022) 'Scanning phones to detect child abuse evidence is harmful, "magical" thinking', *The Register*, 13 October, www.theregister.com/2022/10/13/clientside_scanning_csam_anderson.

Clarke, G. (2005) 'Liberty goes after phishers', *The Register*, 15 June, www.theregister.co.uk/2005/06/15/_liberty_phishing.

Clarke, R. (1994) 'Dataveillance: delivering 1984'. In L. Green and R. Guinery (eds.), *Framing Technology: Society, Choice and Change*, Sydney: Allen & Unwin, 117–30.

Clarke, R. (2004) 'Technology, criminology and crime science', *European Journal on Criminal Policy and Research*, 10 (1): 55–63.

Clarke, R. and Felson, M. (eds.) (1993) *Routine Activity and Rational Choice*, London: Transaction Press.

Clarke, R. and Mayhew, P. (eds.) (1980) *Designing Out Crime*, London: HMSO.

Clough, J. (2015) *Principles of Cybercrime*, 2nd edn, Cambridge: Cambridge University Press.

CNN (2005) 'Video shows executions, life inside North Korea', *CNN.Com*, 14 November, www.cnn.com/2005/WORLD/asiapcf/11/13/nkorea.hiddenvideo/index.html.

CoE (2001) *Convention on Cybercrime*, Council of Europe, Budapest, 23 November (ETS No. 185), http://conventions.coe.int/Treaty/EN/Treaties/Html/185.htm.

CoE (2003) *Additional Protocol to the Convention on Cybercrime, Concerning the Criminalisation of Acts of a Racist and Xenophobic Nature Committed through Computer Systems*, Council of Europe, Strasbourg, 28 January (ETS No. 189), http://conventions.coe.int/Treaty/en/Treaties/Html/189.htm.

CoE (2006) *Council of Europe Convention on the Protection of Children against Sexual Exploitation and Sexual Abuse* (CETS No. 201), Council of Europe, www.coe.int/en/web/conventions/full-list?module=signatures-by-treaty&treatynum=201.

Cohen, L.. and Felson, M. (1979) 'Social change and crime rate trends: a routine activity approach', *American Sociological Review*, 44: 588–608.

Collier, B., Clayton, R., Hutchings, A. and Thomas, D. (2021) 'Cybercrime is (often) boring: infrastructure and alienation in a deviant subculture', *The British Journal of Criminology*, 61 (5): 1407–23.

Computing (2005) 'Sentences should deter virus writers', *Computing*, 13 July, www.computing.co.uk/computing/comment/2139739/sentences-should-deter-virus.

Connolly, A. and Wall, D. S. (2019) 'The rise of crypto-ransomware in a changing cybercrime landscape: taxonomising countermeasures', *Computers and Security*, 87 (Nov), available online 10 July, https://doi.org/10.1016/j.cose.2019.101568.

Corera, G. (2021) 'Fraud epidemic "is now national security threat"', *BBC News Online*, 25 January, www.bbc.co.uk/news/business-55769991.

Corfield, G. (2019) 'If there were almost a million computer misuse crimes last year, Action Fraud is only passing 2% of cases to cops', *The Register*, 21 October, www.theregister.com/2019/10/21/action_fraud_computer_misuse_crimes_decrease.

Corfield, G. (2020) 'We need to talk about criminal hackers using Cobalt Strike, says Cisco Talos', *The Register*, 24 September, www.theregister.com/2020/09/24/cobalt_strike_cisco_talos.

Cowan, R. (2005) 'Arrests of internet paedophiles quadruple over two years', *The Guardian*, 5 March, http://society.guardian.co.uk/children/story/0,1074,1430881,00.html.

Cowie, H. (2013) 'Cyberbullying and its impact on young people's emotional health and well-being', *The Psychiatrist*, 37 (5): 167–70.

CPS (2016) *Pornography – Child Abuse Images Offences 2009–2016*, Crown Prosecution Service, www.cps.gov.uk/underlying-data/pornography-child-abuse-images-offences-2009-2016.

CPS (2019) 'Extreme pornography', *The Code for Crown Prosecutors*, 10 September (updated 15 Nov. 2021), www.cps.gov.uk/legal-guidance/extreme-pornography.

Crawford, A. (2000) 'Situational crime prevention, urban governance and trust relations'. In A. von Hirsch, D. Garland and A. Wakefield (eds.), *Ethical and Social Perspectives on Situational Crime Prevention*, Oxford: Hart, 193–213.

Crawford, A. (2003) 'Contractual governance of deviant behaviour', *Journal of Law and Society*, 30 (4): 479–505.

Crawford, A. and Lister, S. (2004) 'The patchwork future of reassurance policing in England & Wales: integrated local security quilts or frayed, fragmented and fragile tangled webs?', *Policing: An International Journal of Police Strategies & Management*, 27 (3): 413–30.

Creighton, S. (2003) 'Child pornography: images of the abuse of children', *NSPCC Information Briefings*, NSPCC Research Department, November, www.nspcc.org.uk/inform/Info_Briefing/ChildPornography.pdf.

Critchley, T. A. (1978) *A History of the Police in England and Wales*, London: Constable.

Croall, H. (2001) *Understanding White Collar Crime*, 2nd edn, Buckingham, Open University Press.

David, M. (2010) *Peer to Peer and the Music Industry: The Criminalization of Sharing*, London: Sage.

Davies, M., Croall, H. and Tyrer, J. (2015) *Criminal Justice*, Harlow: Pearson.

Davies, N. (2008) 'Our media have become mass producers of distortion', *The Guardian*, 4 February, www.theguardian.com/commentisfree/2008/feb/04/comment.pressandpublishing.

Davies, N. (2010) *Flat Earth News*, London: Chatto.

Davies, P., Francis, P. and Jupp, V. (eds.) (1999) *Invisible Crimes: Their Victims and Their Regulation*, London: Macmillan.

DCMS (2021) *Cyber Security Breaches Survey 2021*, Department for Digital, Culture, Media & Sport, www.gov.uk/government/statistics/cyber-security-breaches-survey-2021/cyber-security-breaches-survey-2021.

DCMS (2022) *Cyber Security Breaches Survey 2022*, 11 July, Department for Digital, Culture, Media & Sport, www.gov.uk/government/statistics/cyber-security-breaches-survey-2022/cyber-security-breaches-survey-2022.

Deflem, M. (1997) 'The globalization of heartland terror: reflections on the Oklahoma City bombing', *The Critical Criminologist, Newsletter of the ASC Critical Criminology Division*, Fall: 5.

Deleuze, G. and Guattari, F. (1987) *A Thousand Plateaus: Capitalism and Schizophrenia*, Minneapolis: University of Minnesota Press.

Denning, D. (2000) 'Cyberterrorism', *Testimony before the Special Oversight Panel of Terrorism*

Committee on Armed Services, US House of Representatives, 23 May, www.cs.georgetown.edu/~denning/infosec/ cyberterror.html.

Diamond, M. and Uchiyama, A. (1999) 'Pornography, rape and sex crimes in Japan', *International Journal of Law and Psychiatry*, 22 (1): 1–22, ww.hawaii.edu/PCSS/online_artcls/pornography/prngrphy_rape_jp.html.

Dibbell, J. (1999) *My Tiny Life: Crime and Passion in a Virtual World*, New York: Henry Holt.

Digital Shadows (2020) *From Exposure to Takeover: The 15 Billion Stolen Credentials Allowing Takeovers*, Digital Shadows Photon Research Team, www.hackread.com/wp-content/uploads/2020/07/from-exposure-to-takeover-the-15-billion-stolen-credentials-allowing-account-takeover.pdf.

Dodt, C. (2020) 'Top 8 world crises exploited by cybercriminals and lessons learned', *Infosec*, 10 August, https://resources.infosecinstitute.com/topic/top-8-world-crises-exploited-by-cyber criminals-lessons-learned.

Dolinar, L. (1998) 'Hackers hit Pentagon system: organised attack highlights flaws', *Newsday*, 26 February, A03.

Donalds, C. and Osei-Bryson, K. M. (2019) 'Toward a cybercrime classification ontology: a knowledge-based approach', *Computers in Human Behavior*, 92 (3): 403–18.

Donath, J. (1998) 'Identity and deception in the virtual community'. In P. Kollock and M. Smith (eds.), *Communities in Cyberspace*, London: Routledge.

Downey R. (2002) 'Victims of wonderland', *Community Care*, 1412: 30–1.

DTI (2000) *Turning the Corner*, London: Department of Trade and Industry.

DTI (2002) *Information Security Breaches Survey 2002*, London: Department of Trade and Industry.

DTI (2004) *Information Security Breaches Survey 2004*, London: Department of Trade and Industry.

Duff, L. and Gardiner, S. (1996) 'Computer crime in the global village: strategies for control and regulation – in defence of the hacker', *International Journal of the Sociology of Law*, 24: 211–28.

Dumais, E. (2022) 'Counterfeit medications are taking over the internet: here's how to spot them', *Vice*, 12 September, www.vice.com/en/article/xgyy9k/fake-medications-sold-online.

Dupont, B. (2004) 'Security in the age of networks', *Policing and Society*, 14 (1): 76–91.

Dupont, B. and Holt, T. (2023) 'Advancing research on the human factor in cybercrime', *Computers in Human Behavior*, 138.

Edwards, L. (2000) 'Canning the spam: is there a case for the legal control of junk electronic mail?'. In L. Edwards and C. Wealde (eds.), *Law and the Internet: A Framework for Electronic Commerce*, 2nd edn, Oxford: Hart.

Edwards, L. (2004) 'Code and the law: the next generation', paper presented at the LEFIS workshop 'Lessig's Code: Lessons for Legal Education from the Frontiers of IT law', Queen's University, Belfast.

Edwards, L. and Wealde, C. (eds.) (2000) *Law and the Internet: A Framework for Electronic Commerce*, 2nd edn, Oxford: Hart.

Edwards, S. (2000) 'Prosecuting "child pornography": possession and taking of indecent photographs of children', *The Journal of Social Welfare & Family Law*, 22 (1): 1–21.

electricnews (2005) '13 EU countries link up to fight spam', *The Register*, 7 February, www.theregister.co.uk/2005/02/07/ec_antispam_campaign.

Engberg, D. (1996) 'The virtual panopticon', *Impact of New Media Technologies*, Fall, http://is.gseis.ucla.edu/impact/f96/Projects/dengberg.

ENISA (2020) *Botnet from January 2019 to April 2020*, ENISA Threat Landscape, European Union Agency for Cybersecurity, www.enisa.europa.eu/topics/cyber-threats/threats-and-trends/etl-review-folder/etl-2020-botnet.

Ericson, R. and Haggerty, K. (1997) *Policing the Risk Society*, Oxford: Oxford University Press.

EU (2023) 'Fighting cybercrime: new EU cybersecurity laws explained', *European Parliament News*, 16 February, www.europarl.europa.eu/news/en/headlines/security/20221103STO48002/fighting-cybercrime-new-eu-cybersecurity-laws-explained.

European Commission (1996) *Green Paper on the Protection of Minors and Human Dignity in*

Audio-visual and Information Services, European Commission Select Committee, Brussels: European Commission, COM (96) 483.

European Commission (1997a) *Action Plan on Promoting Safe Use of the Internet*, COM (97) 582 final, 26 November, http://aei.pitt.edu/5894/01/001336_1.pdf.

European Commission (1997b) *Green Paper on the Convergence of the Telecommunications, Media and Information Technology Sectors, and the Implications for Regulation: Towards an Information Society Approach*, Brussels: European Commission, COM (97) 623, 3 December, http://aei.pitt.edu/archive/00001160/01/telecom_convergence_gp_COM_97_623.pdf.

European Commission (2005) 'European countries launch joint drive to combat "spam"', Press Release, IP/05/146, Brussels, 7 February.

European Commission (2021) *Regulation to Address the Dissemination of Terrorist Content Online*, EU Commission, https://home-affairs.ec.europa.eu/policies/internal-security/counter-terrorism-and-radicalisation/prevention-radicalisation/terrorist-content-online_en.

Evans-Pritchard, A. (2001) 'US asks Nato for help in "draining the swamp" of global terrorism', *The Daily Telegraph*, 27 September, www. telegraph.co.uk/news/main.jhtml?xml /news/2001/09/27/wusa27.xml.

Fafinski, S. (2009) *Computer Misuse: Response, Regulation and the Law*, London: Willan.

Fay, J. (2005) 'WTO rules in online gambling dispute', *The Register*, 8 April, www.theregister.co.uk/2005/04/08/wto_online_gambling.

FBI (2019) 'Worldwide sweep targets business email compromise', *FBI News*, 10 September, www.fbi.gov/news/stories/operation-rewired-bec-takedown-091019.

FBI (2021) *Internet Crime Report 2020*, FBI / Internet Crime Complaint Center (IC3), March, www.ic3.gov/Media/PDF/AnnualReport/2020_IC3Report.pdf.

Felson, M. (2000) 'The routine activity approach as a general social theory'. In S. Simpson (ed.), *Of Crime and Criminality: The Use of Theory in Everyday Life*, Thousand Oaks, CA: Sage.

Fildes, J. (2006) 'Web inventor warns of "dark" net', *BBC News Online*, 23 May, http://news.bbc.co.uk/1/hi/technology/5009250.stm.

Finch, E. (2001) *The Criminalisation of Stalking: Constructing the Problem and Evaluating the Solution*. London: Cavendish.

Finch, E. (2002) 'What a tangled web we weave: identify theft and the internet'. In Y. Jewkes (ed.), *dot. cons: Crime, Deviance and Identity on the Internet*, Cullompton: Willan, 86–104.

Finch, E. and Fafinski, S. (2010) *Legal Skills*, Oxford: Oxford University Press.

Findlay, M. (1999) *The Globalisation of Crime: Understanding Transitional Relationships in Context*, Cambridge: Cambridge University Press.

Finnemann, N. (2002) 'Perspectives on the internet and modernity: late modernity, postmodernity or modernity modernized?'. In N. Brügger and H. Bødker (eds.), *The Internet and Society?*, Centre for Internet Research, University of Aarhus, Denmark, 29–39.

FireEye (2012) *FireEye Advanced Threat Report – 2H 2012*, FireEye, https://icscsi.org/library/Documents/Threat_Intelligence/FireEye%20-%20Advanced%20Threat%20Report%20-%202H-2012.pdf.

Foreman, T. (2013) '"Cracker" conveys history of bigotry that still resonates', *CNN*, 2 July, https://edition.cnn.com/2013/07/01/us/zimmerman-trial-cracker/index.html.

Foucault, M. (1983) 'Afterword: the subject and power'. In H. Dreyfus and P. Rainbow (eds.), *Michel Foucault: Beyond Structuralism and Hermeneutics*, 2nd edn, Chicago: University of Chicago Press, 208–26.

Fowles, A. J. (1983) 'Order and the law'. In K. Jones, J. Brown and J. Bradshaw (eds.), *Issues in Social Policy*, London: Routledge & Keegan Paul.

Francisco, J. (2003) 'Defensive information warfare: a review of selected literature', *Eller College Working Paper No. 1004-04*, December, http://ssrn.com/abstract 607443.

Frieder, L. and Zittrain, J. (2006) 'Spam works: evidence from stock touts and corresponding market activity', *Working Paper, Krannert School of Management and Oxford Internet Institute*, 25 July, http://ssrn. com/abstract 920553.

Friedewald, M., Vildjiounaite, E. and Wright, D. (eds.) (2006) *The Brave New World of Ambient Intelligence: A State-Of-The-Art Review*, Safeguards in a World of Ambient Intelligence (SWAMI),

European Commission, January, http://swami.jrc.es/pages/documents/SWAMI_D1_Final_000. pdf.

Furedi, F. (2002) *Culture of Fear*, London: Continuum.

Furedi, F. (2006) 'What is distinct about our rules of fear?', Leeds Social Sciences Institute Public Guest Lecture, Leeds, 23 October.

Furnell, S. (2005) *Computer Insecurity – Risking the System*, London: Springer.

Gainford, A. (2023) *The Challenges of Digilantism for Law Enforcement and Public Order*, PhD thesis, University of Leeds.

Gambling Commission (2021) *Gambling Behaviour in 2020: Findings from the Quarterly Telephone Survey: Statistics on Participation and Problem Gambling, Year to December 2020*, Gambling Commission, 23 February, www.gamblingcommission.gov.uk/statistics-and-research/publi cation/year-to-december-2020.

Gandy, O. (1982) *Beyond Agenda Setting: Information Subsidies and Public Policy*, New York: Ablex Publishers.

Gandy, O. (2003) 'Data mining and surveillance in the post-9.11 environment'. In F. Webster and K. Ball (eds.), *The Intensification of Surveillance: Crime Terrorism and Warfare in the Information Age*, London: Pluto Press, 26–41.

Garland, D. (2000) 'The culture of high crime societies: some preconditions of recent "law and order" policies', *British Journal of Criminology*, 40 (3): 347–75.

Garland, D. (2001) *The Culture of Control*, Oxford: Oxford University Press.

Garland, D. and Sparks, R. (2000) 'Criminology, social theory and the challenge of our times', *British Journal of Criminology*, 40 (2): 189–204.

Gaudeul, A. and Peroni, C. (2010) 'Reciprocal attention and norm of reciprocity in blogging networks', *Economics Bulletin*, 30 (3): 2230–48.

Geer, D. (2004) 'The physics of digital law', Plenary Speech at the 'Digital Cops in a Virtual Environment' Conference, Information Society Project, Yale Law School, 26–28 March 2004.

Geist, M. (2006) 'Video and the net: an explosive mix', *BBC News Online*, 17 July, http://news.bbc.co .uk/1/hi/technology/5188482.stm.

Gey, S. G. (2000) 'The Nuremberg files and the First Amendment value of threats', *Texas Law Review*, 78: 541.

Gibson, J. (1966) *The Senses Considered as Perceptual Systems*, London: Allen and Unwin.

Gibson, J. (1979) *The Ecological Approach to Visual Perception*, Boulder, CO: Taylor & Francis.

Gibson, O. (2006) 'Warning to chatroom users after libel award for man labelled a Nazi', *Guardian Online*, 23 March, www.guardian.co.uk/law/ story/0,,1737445,00.html.

Gibson, W. (1982) 'Burning chrome', *Omni Magazine*, July.

Gibson, W. (1984) *Neuromancer*, London: HarperCollins.

Gibson, W. (1986) *Count Zero*, London: Grafton.

Gibson, W. (1988) *Mona Lisa Overdrive*, London: Grafton.

Giddens, A. (1990) *The Consequences of Modernity*, Cambridge: Polity.

Gillespie, A. (2015) 'Hate and harm: the law on hate speech'. In A. Savin and J. Trzaskowski (eds.), *Research Handbook on EU Internet Law*, Cheltenham: Edward Elgar, 488–507.

Gillespie, A. (2019) *Cybercrime: Key Issues and Debates*, 2nd edn., London: Routledge.

Glaser, B. and Strauss, A. (1967) *The Discovery of Grounded Theory: Strategies for Qualitative Research*. Chicago: Aldine.

Glenny, M. (2012) *DarkMarket*, New York: Vintage Books.

Goldsmith, A. and Brewer, R (2015) 'Digital drift and the criminal interaction order', *Theoretical Criminology*, 19 (1): 112–30.

Goldsmith, A. and Wall, D. S. (2022) 'The seductions of cybercrime: adolescence and the thrills of digital transgression', *European Journal of Criminology*, 19 (1): 98–117, https://journals.sagepub .com/doi/full/10.1177/1477370819887305.

Goldsmith, A. and Wall, D. S. (unpublished) 'Weaponising ransomware: cybercrime and geopolitical strategy', Vienna: GI-TOC, 2023.

Goodin, D. (2017) 'NSA-leaking Shadow Brokers just dumped its most damaging release yet', *Ars*

Technica, 14 April, https://arstechnica.com/information-technology/2017/04/nsa-leaking-sha
dow-brokers-just-dumped-its-most-damaging-release-yet.

Goodman, M. (1997) 'Why the police don't care about computer crime', *Harvard Journal of Law and Technology*, 10: 645–94.

Goodman, M. (2016) *Future Crimes: Everything Is Connected, Everyone Is Vulnerable and What We Can Do About It*, London: Corgi.

Goodman, M. and Brenner, S. (2002) 'The emerging consensus on criminal conduct in cyberspace', *UCLA Journal of Law and Technology*, 3, www.lawtechjournal.com/articles/2002/03_020625_good manbrenner.pdf.

Goodman, R. (2023) 'Romance fraud losses up 95% in three years', *YourMoney.Com*, 2 February, www.yourmoney.com/saving-banking/romance-fraud-losses-up-95-in-three-years.

Gordon, D. (1986) 'The electronic panopticon: a case study of the development of the National Criminal Records System', *Politics and Society*, 15: 483–51.

Gordon, D. (2010) 'Forty years of movie hacking: considering the potential implications of the popular media representation of computer hackers from 1968 to 2008', *International Journal of Internet Technology and Secured Transactions*, 2 (1/2): 59–87.

Gordon, S. and Chess, D. (1999) 'Attitude adjustment: trojans and malware on the internet – an update', Proceedings of the 22nd National Information Systems Security Conference, 18–21 October, Crystal City, Virginia, http://csrc.nist.gov/nissc/1999/proceeding/papers/p6.pdf.

Gorman, S. (2003) 'FBI, CIA remain worlds apart', *The National Journal*, 1 August, reproduced at http://198.65.138.161/org/news/2003/030801-fbi-cia01.htm.

Goss, A. (2001) 'Jay Cohen's brave new world: the liability of offshore operators of licensed internet casinos for breach of United States' anti-gambling laws', *Richmond Journal of Law & Technology*, 7 (4): 32, www.richmond.edu/jolt/v7i4/article2.html.

Gostev, A., Shevchenko, A. and Nazarov, D. (2006) *Malware Evolution: January–March 2006*, Kaspersky Labs, https://securelist.com/malware-evolution-january-march-2006/36080.

Grabosky, P. N. (2016) *Cybercrime*, Oxford: Oxford University Press.

Grabosky, P. N. and Smith, R. G. (1998) *Crime in the Digital Age: Controlling Communications and Cyberspace Illegalities*. Piscataway, NJ: Transaction.

Grabosky, P. N., Smith, R. G. and Dempsey, G. (2001) *Electronic Theft: Unlawful Acquisition in Cyberspace*, Cambridge: Cambridge University Press.

Granovsky, Y. (2002) 'Yevroset tainted by gray imports', *The Moscow Times*, 9 July: 8, www.themosco wtimes.com/stories/2002/07/09/045.html.

Green, E. (1999) FUD 101 v1.0, November 15, http://badtux.org/home/eric/editorial/fud101-1.0 .0.html.

Greenberg, A. (2012) '3D-printable gun project hits its fundraising goal despite being booted off Indiegogo', *Forbes Magazine*, 20 September, www.forbes.com/sites/andygreenberg/2012/09/20 /3d-printed-gun-project-hits-its-fundraising-goal-despite-being-booted-off-indiegogo.

Greenberg, A. (2017) 'The WannaCry ransomware has a link to suspected North Korean hackers', *WIRED*, 15 May, www.wired.com/2017/05/wannacry-ransomware-link-suspected-north-korean -hackers.

Greenberg, A. (2019) 'Hackers are passing around a megaleak of 2.2 billion records', *WIRED*, 30 January, www.wired.com/story/collection-leak-usernames-passwords-billions.

Greenberg, S. (1997) 'Threats, harassment and hate on-line: recent developments', *The Boston Public Interest Law Journal*, 6: 673.

Greenleaf, G. (1998) 'An endnote on regulating cyberspace: architecture vs. law?', *University of New South Wales Law Journal*, 21 (2). Reproduced in D. S. Wall (ed.), *Cyberspace Crime*, Aldershot: Dartmouth, 2003, 89–120.

Grierson, J. (2019) 'Predictive policing poses discrimination risk, thinktank warns', *The Guardian*, 16 September, www.theguardian.com/uk-news/2019/sep/16/predictive-policing-poses-discrimi nation-risk-thinktank-warns.

Grimes, R. (ed.) (2017) *Hacking the Hacker: Learn from the Experts Who Take Down Hackers*, New York: John Wiley & Sons, Inc.

Group-IB (2021) 'Under the hood. Group-IB threat intelligence. Part 1: Dive into breached DB section, *Group-IB Blog*, 29 July, www.group-ib.com/blog/gib-tia-db.

Hafner, K. and Markoff, J. (1995) *Cyberpunk: Outlaws and Hackers on the Computer Frontier*, London: Simon & Schuster.

Haggerty, K. and Ericson, R. (2000) 'The surveillant assemblage', *British Journal of Sociology*, 51 (4): 605–22.

Haggerty, K. and Gazso, A. (2005) 'Seeing beyond the ruins: surveillance as a response to terrorist threats', *The Canadian Journal of Sociology*, 30 (2): 169–87.

Hall, C. (2005) 'Internet fuels boom in counterfeit drugs', *Sunday Telegraph*, 16 August, www.telegra ph.co.uk/news/main.jhtml?xml /news/2005/08/16/ndrugs 16.xml.

Hamilton-Baillie, B. (2004) 'Urban design: why don't we do it in the road? Modifying traffic behaviour through legible urban design', *Journal of Urban Technology*, 11 (1): 43–62, www.hamilton-baillie .co.uk/papers/urban_ design.pdf.

Hanoch, Y. and Wood, S. (2021) 'The scams among us: who falls prey and why', *Current Directions in Psychological Science*, 30 (3): 260–6.

Hansard (2002) 'Answer to the Earl of Northesk's question HL3294 about the number of prosecutions under the provisions of the Computer Misuse Act 1990 in each year since its implementation', *Hansard*, HL, 26 Mar. 2002, col. WA36, https://publications.parliament.uk/pa/ld200102/ldhansrd /vo020326/text/20326w02.htm.

Harcup, T. (2008) 'Reporters need to ask what they're not being told', *Press Gazette*, 18 February, www .pressgazette.co.uk/story.asp?storycode=40268.

Harding, K. (2001) 'Snuff films', *Planet Papers*, www.planetpapers.com/ Assets/2136.php.

Harvey, B. (1985) 'Computer hacking and ethics', *ACM Select Panel on Hacking*, www.cs.berkeley .edu/~bh/hacker.html.

Hayes, P. (2005) 'No "sorry" from Love Bug author', *The Register*, 11 May, www.theregister.co.uk/20 05/05/11/love_bug_author.

Hayward, D. (1997) 'Censorship coming to the Continent', *TechWeb*, 13 March, www.techweb.com /wire/news/mar/0314porn1.html.

Heins, M. (2001a) *Not in Front of the Children: Indecency, Censorship and the Innocence of Youth*, New York: Hill and Wang.

Heins, M. (2001b) 'Criminalising online speech to "protect" the young: what are the benefits and costs?'. In D. S. Wall (ed.) *Crime and the Internet*, London: Routledge, 100–12.

Hermer, J. and Hunt, A. (1996) 'Official graffiti of the everyday', *Law and Society Review*, 30 (3): 455–80.

Hern, A. (2021) 'Streaming was supposed to stop piracy: now it is easier than ever', *The Guardian*, 2 October, www.theguardian.com/film/2021/oct/02/streaming-was-supposed-to-stop-piracy -now-it-is-easier-than-ever.

Heshmat, S. (2015) 'What is confirmation bias?', *Psychology Today*, 23 April, www.psychologytoday .com/intl/blog/science-choice/201504/what-is-confirmation-bias.

Hetler, A. (2022) '9 common cryptocurrency scams in 2023', *WhatIs.com*, 2 November, www.techtar get.com/whatis/feature/Common-cryptocurrency-scams.

Hewson, B. (2003) 'Fetishising images', *Spiked Online*, 23 January, www.spiked-online.com/Prin table/00000006DC06.htm.

HM Government (2022) *National Cyber Strategy 2022*, Cabinet Office, https://assets.publishing.ser vice.gov.uk/government/uploads/system/uploads/attachment_data/file/1053023/national-cyber -strategy-amend.pdf.

HOC (2009) *Press Standards, Privacy and Libel, Second Report of Session 2009–10*, Volume II: *Unprinted Evidence*, House of Commons: Culture, Media and Sport Committee, HC 362-II, April [Nick Davies's evidence on Tuesday 21 April 2009, Q402–Q495, 125–49], www.publications.parlia ment.uk/pa/cm200910/cmselect/cmcumeds/362/362ii.pdf.

Holt, T. and Bossler, A. (2015) *Cybercrime in Progress: Theory and Prevention of Technology-Enabled Offenses*, London: Routledge.

Holt, T., Bossler, A. and Seidfried Spellar, K. (2022) *Cybercrime and Digital Forensics: An Introduction*, 2nd edn, London: Routledge.

Holt, T., Burruss, G. and Bossler, A. (2015) *Policing Cybercrime and Cyberterror*, Durham, NC: Carolina Academic Press.

Home Office (2005) 'Crackdown on violent pornography', Home Office Press Release, Ref: 125/2005, 31 August, http://press. homeoffice.gov.uk/press-releases/Crackdown_On_Violent_Por nography? version 1.

Home Office (2006) *Consultation on the Possession of Extreme Pornographic Material: Summary of Responses and Next Steps*, Home Office, August, www.homeoffice.gov.uk/documents/cons-ext remeporn-3008051/Gvt-response-extreme-porn2.pdf?view Binary.

Home Office (2015) *Indecent and Obscene Materials, Guidance*, 14 October, https://assets.publish ing.service.gov.uk/government/uploads/system/uploads/attachment_data/file/468768/Indecent _and_obscene_materials_v_1_0.pdf.

Home Office (2023) *Review of the Computer Misuse Act 1990*, Open Consultation, 7 February, www .gov.uk/government/consultations/review-of-the-computer-misuse-act-1990.

Honeynet Project (2002) *Know Your Enemy: Revealing the Security Tools, Tactics, and Motives of the Blackhat Community*, Essex: Addison Wesley.

Howie, M. (2006) 'Accused in child porn inquiry to sue police', *The Scotsman*, 15 September, http:// news.scotsman.com/uk.cfm?id1362272006.

Hughes, D. (1999) *Pimps and Predators on the Internet Globalizing the Sexual Exploitation of Women and Children*, University of Rhode Island, January, www.researchgate.net/profile/Donna-Hughes -2/publication/237531290_Pimps_and_Predators_on_the_Internet_Globalizing_the_Sexual_Exp loitation_of_Women_and_Children/links/00b4952c713e600830000000/Pimps-and-Predators-on -the-Internet-Globalizing-the-Sexual-Exploitation-of-Women-and-Children.pdf.

Hughes, G., McLaughlin, E. and Muncie, J. (2001) 'Teetering on the edge: the futures of crime control and community safety'. In G. Hughes, E. McLaughlin and J. Muncie (eds.), *Crime Prevention and Community Safety: Future Directions*, London: Sage, 318–34.

Humble, C. (2005) 'Inside the fake Viagra factory', *Sunday Telegraph*, 21 August, www.telegraph.co .uk/news/main.jhtml?xml /news/2005/08/21/nviag21.xml.

Hutchings, A. and Holt, T. J. (2015) 'A crime script analysis of the online stolen data market', *British Journal of Criminology*, 55: 596–614.

Hutchings, A. and Holt, T. J. (2018) 'Interviewing cybercrime offenders', *Journal of Qualitative Criminal Justice & Criminology*, 7 (1): 75–94.

IC3 (2022) *Federal Bureau of Investigation, Internet Crime Report 2022*, Internet Crime Complaint Center, www.ic3.gov/Media/PDF/AnnualReport/2022_IC3Report.pdf.

ICMEC (2019) 'Child sexual abuse material: model legislation & global review (9th Review)', *International Centre for Missing and Exploited Children*, February, www.icmec.org/wp-content/up loads/2019/02/One-Pager-9th-Edition.pdf.

IFAW (2005) *Born to Be Wild: Primates Are Not Pets*, London: International Fund for Animal Welfare, www.ifaw.org/ifaw/dfiles/file_553.pdf.

Ilascu, I. (2020) 'Ryuk ransomware deployed two weeks after Trickbot infection', *BleepingComputer*, 23 June, www.bleepingcomputer.com/news/security/ryuk-ransomware-deployed-two-weeks-af ter-trickbot-infection.

Ilascu, I. (2021) 'Ransomware is a multi-billion industry and it keeps growing', *Bleeping Computer*, 4 March, www.bleeping.computer.com/news/security/ransomware-is-a-multi-billion-industry -and-it-keeps-growing.

Illuminati News (2004) 'What's wrong with the "execution videos"?', *Illuminati News*, 10 October, www.illuminati-news.com/executionvideos.htm.

Innes, M. (2001) 'Control creep', *Sociological Research Online*, 6 (3), www.socresonline.org.uk/6/3/in nes.html.

Innes, M. (2004) 'Reinventing tradition? Reassurance, neighbourhood security and policing', *Criminal Justice*, 4 (2): 151–71.

Innes, M. (2005) 'Why disorder matters? Antisocial behaviour and incivility as signals of risk', paper presented to the Social Contexts and Responses to Risk (SCARR) Conference, Kent, UK, 28–29 January, www.kent.ac.uk/ scarr/papers/papers.htm.

Intel 471 (2020) 'Steal, then strike: access merchants are first clues to future ransomware attacks',

Intel 471 Blog, 1 December, https://intel471.com/blog/ransomware-attack-access-merchants-in fostealer-escrow-service.

IPTS (2003) *Security and Privacy for the Citizen in the Post-September 11 Digital Age: A Prospective Overview. Report by the Institute for Prospective Technological Studies, Joint Research Committee, Seville, to the European Parliament Committee on Citizens' Freedoms and Rights, Justice and Home Affairs*, European Commission, July (EUR 20823 EN-ISBN: 92-894-6133-0).

Isafiade, O. (2022) 'Artificial intelligence is used for predictive policing in the US and UK – South Africa should embrace it, too', *The Conversation*, 24 October, https://theconversation.com/artificial-intelligence-is-used-for-predictive-policing-in-the-us-and-uk-south-africa-should-embrace-it-too-191266.

ITRC (2023) *2022 Annual Data Breach Report*, Identity Theft Resource Center, 25 January, www.idtheftcenter.org/post/2022-annual-data-breach-report-reveals-near-record-number-compromises.

ITV (2023) 'Police target 1,000 homes for illegally watching sport streams without a subscription', *ITV.Com*, 11 January, www.itv.com/news/2023-01-11/police-to-visit-1000-homes-for-illegally-watching-sport-streams.

IWF (2023) *The Annual Report 2022*, Internet Watch Foundation, April, https://annualreport2022.iwf.org.uk/wp-content/uploads/2023/04/IWF-Annual-Report-2022_FINAL.pdf.

Jackson, W. (2005) 'Is a new ID theft scam in the wings?', *Government Computer News*, 14 January, www.gcn.com/vol1_no1/security/34815-1.html.

Jamez, J. (1997) 'DRINK OR DIE HISTORY: Warez bears from Russia & beyond 1993–1997', *The Evil Advisor*, 1 April, https://web.archive.org/web/19970611213535/http://www.drinkordie.com:80/history.html.

Jamneck, L. (2005) 'Interview: Bruce Bethke', *Strange Horizons*, 11 July, www.strangehorizons.com/2005/20050711/bethke-int-a.shtml.

Jareth (2019) 'Is ransomware driving up the price of Bitcoin?', *EMISOFT Blog*, 3 September, https://blog.emsisoft.com/en/33977/is-ransomware-driving-up-the-price-of-bitcoin.

Javelin (2009) 2009 *Identity Fraud Survey Report: Consumer Version*. Pleasanton, CA: Javelin Strategy and Research.

Jewkes, Y. (ed.) (2003) *Dot.Cons: Crime, Deviance and Identity on the Internet*, Cullompton: Willan.

Jewkes, Y. (ed.) (2006) *Crime Online*, Cullompton: Willan.

Jewkes, Y. and Andrews, C. (2005) 'Policing the filth: the problems of investigating online child pornography in England and Wales', *Policing & Society*, 15 (1): 42–62.

Jewkes, Y. and Yar, M. (eds.) (2009) *Handbook of Internet Crime*, Cullompton: Willan.

Jimroglou, K. (1999) 'A camera with a view: JenniCAM, visual representation, and cyborg subjectivity', *Information, Communication & Society*, 2 (4): 439–53.

Johnson, P. (1996) 'Pornography drives technology: why not to censor the internet', *Federal Communications Law Journal*, 49 (1): 217–26.

Johnston, L. and Shearing, C. (2003) *Governing Security: Explorations in Policing and Justice*, London: Routledge.

Jones, R. (2003) 'Review of "Crime in The Digital Age" by P. Grabosky and R. Smith', *International Journal of Law and Information Technology*, 11: 98.

Jones, T. and Newburn, T. (2002) 'The transformation of policing? Understanding current trends in policing systems', *British Journal of Criminology*, 42: 129–46.

Jordan, T. (1999) *Cyberpower: The Culture and Politics of Cyberspace and the Internet*, London: Routledge.

Jurgenson, N. (2011) 'Digital dualism versus augmented reality', *The Society Pages*, 24 February, https://thesocietypages.org/cyborgology/2011/02/24/digital-dualism-versus-augmented-reality.

Kabay, M. E. (2002) 'Salami fraud', *Network World Security Newsletter*, 24 July, www.networkworld.com/newsletters/sec/2002/01467137.html.

Kaonga, G. (2023) 'Donald Trump's trading cards collapse in value', *Newsweek*, 19 April, www.newsweek.com/donald-trump-trading-cards-value-collapse-cryptocurrency-nft-1795229.

Katyal, N. K. (2001) 'Criminal law in cyberspace', *University of Pennsylvania Law Review*, 149: 1003.

Katyal, N. K. (2003) 'Digital architecture as crime control', *Yale Law Journal*, 112: 2261–89.

Katz, J. (1988) *The Seductions of Crime*, New York: Basic Books.

Kaufmann, M., Egbert, S. and Leese, M. (2018) 'Predictive policing and the politics of patterns', *The British Journal of Criminology*, 59 (3): 674–92, https://doi.org/10.1093/bjc/azy060.

Kemp, S., Buil-Gil, D., Miró-Llinares, F. and Lord, N. (2021) 'When do businesses report cybercrime? Findings from a UK study', *Criminology & Criminal Justice*, online first, https://doi.org/10.1177/17488958211062359.

Keningale, P. (2022) 'The National Intelligence model: the barriers to its success', *BSC Policing Network*, 31 May, https://bscpolicingnetwork.wordpress.com/2022/05/31/the-national-intelligence-model-the-barriers-to-its-success.

Kerr, Orin S. (2003) 'Cybercrime's scope: interpreting "access" and "authorization" in computer misuse statutes', *New York University Law Review*, 78 (5): 1596–668.

Kewney, G, (2005) 'Hotspot paranoia: try to stay calm', *The Register*, 24 January, www.theregister.co.uk/2005/01/24/wi_fi_hotspot_security.

Kitsuse, J. (1962) 'Societal reaction to deviant behavior: problems of theory and method', *Social Problems*, 9: 247–56.

Kivilevich, V. (2021) 'The secret life of an initial access broker', *KELA*, 6 August, https://ke-la.com/the-secret-life-of-an-initial-access-broker.

Knight, P. (2000) *Conspiracy Culture: From Kennedy to the X-Files*, London: Routledge.

Koops, B. J., Lüthy, C., Nelis, A., Sieburgh, C., Jansen, J. and Schmid, M. (2013) *Engineering the Human: Human Enhancement between Fiction and Fascination*, New York: Springer.

Kozlovski, N. (2004) 'Designing accountable online policing', paper presented to the 'Digital Cops in a Virtual Environment' Conference, Information Society Project, Yale Law School, 26–28 March.

Kravetz, A. (2002) 'Qatari national taken into federal custody in wake of terrorist attacks allegedly committed credit card fraud', *Peoria Journal Star*, 29 January, www.collegefreedom.org/AMpsj02.htm.

Krone, T. (2004) 'A typology of online child pornography offending', *Trends and Issues in Crime and Criminal Justice*, 279, Canberra: Australian Institute of Criminology, www.aic.gov.au/publications/tandi2/ tandi279.pdf.

Krupp, J., Backes, M. and Rossow, C. (2016) 'Identifying the scan and attack infrastructures behind amplification DDoS attacks', Proceedings of the 2016 ACM SIGSAC Conference on Computer and Communications Security, ACM: 1426–37.

Kshetri, N. (2019) 'How cryptocurrency scams work', *The Conversation*, 13 May, https://theconversation.com/how-cryptocurrency-scams-work-114706.

Landau, M. (2002) 'The First Amendment and "virtual" child pornography', *Gigalaw*, www.gigalaw.com/articles/2002-all/landau-2002-07-all.html.

Lane, A. (2022) 'Crypto theft is on the rise. Here's how the crimes are committed, and how you can protect yourself', *The Conversation*, 3 February, https://theconversation.com/crypto-theft-is-on-the-rise-heres-how-the-crimes-are-committed-and-how-you-can-protect-yourself-176027.

Langdon, R. (1993) 'Speech acts and unspeakable acts', *Philosophy and Public Affairs*, 22 (4): 293–330.

Lastowka, G. and Hunter, D. (2005) 'Virtual crime', *New York Law School Law Review*, 49 (1), 293–316.

Lavorgna, A. (2020) *Cybercrimes: Critical Issues in a Global Context*, London: Bloomsbury Academic.

Lavorgna, A. and Holt, T. (eds.) (2021) *Researching Cybercrimes: Methodologies, Ethics, and Critical Approaches*, London: Palgrave Macmillan.

Law Commission (1997) *Legislating the Criminal Code: Misuse of Trade Secrets*, Consultation Paper 150, www.lawcom.gov.uk/library/lccp 150/summary.htm.

Legal Betting Online (2023) 'State-by-state legal US gambling guide for 2022', *Legal Betting Online*, www.legalbettingonline.com/states.

Lemert, E. (1951) *Social Pathology*, New York: McGraw-Hill.

Lemos, R. (2000) 'Script kiddies: the Net's cybergangs', *ZDNet*, 13 July, www.zdnet.com/article/script-kiddies-the-nets-cybergangs.

Lemos, R. (2005) 'Phishers look to net small fry', *The Register*, 20 June, www.theregister.co.uk/2005/06/20/phishers_target_us_credit_unions/.

Lentz, S. and Chaires, R. (2007) 'The invention of Peel's principles: a study of policing "textbook" history', *Journal of Criminal Justice*, 35 (1): 69–79, https://doi.org/10.1016/j.jcrimjus.2006.11.016.

Leong, G. (1998) 'Computer child pornography – the liability of distributors?', *Criminal Law Review* (December), special edition: 'Crime, Criminal Justice, and the Internet', 19–28.

Leppard, D. (2005) 'Child porn suspects set to be cleared in evidence "shambles"', *Sunday Times*, 3 July, www.timesonline.co.uk/printFriendly/0,,1-523-1678810-523,00.html.

Lessig, L. (1998a) 'The laws of cyberspace', paper presented at the Taiwan Net '98 Conference, Taipei, March.

Lessig, L. (1998b) 'The New Chicago School', *Journal of Legal Studies*, 27 (2): 661–91.

Lessig, L. (2006) *Code and Other Laws of Cyberspace, Version 2.0*, New York: Basic Books.

Leukfeldt, R. (2016) *Cybercriminal Networks: Origin, Growth and Criminal Capabilities*, The Hague: Eleven International Publishing.

Leukfeldt, R. and Holt, T. (eds.) (2021) *Human Factor of Cybercrime, 2nd Edition*, London: Taylor & Francis.

Levi, M. (2001) '"Between the risk and the reality falls the shadow": evidence and urban legends in computer fraud'. In D. S. Wall (ed.), *Crime and the Internet*, London: Routledge, 44–58.

Levi, M. and Maguire, M. (2004) 'Reducing and preventing organised crime: an evidence-based critique', *Crime, Law and Social Change*, 41: 397–469.

Levi, M. and Wall, D. S. (2004) 'Technologies, security and privacy in the post-9/11 European information society', *Journal of Law and Society*, 31 (2): 194–220.

Levi, M. and Williams, M. (2012) *eCrime Reduction Partnership Mapping Study*, Cardiff: NOMINET/Cardiff University.

Levi, M., Doig, A., Gundur, R., Wall, D. and Williams, M. (2017) 'Cyberfraud and the implications for effective risk-based responses: themes from UK research', *Crime, Law and Social Change*, 67 (1): 77–96.

Lewis, J., Williams, A. and Franklin, R. (2008) 'Four rumours and an explanation: a political economic account of journalists' changing newsgathering and reporting practices', *Journalism Practice*, 2 (1): 27–45.

Leyden, J. (2002) 'Online gambling tops internet card fraud league', *The Register*, 28 March, www.theregister.co.uk/content/23/24633.html.

Leyden, J. (2004a) 'IBM dissects the DNA of spam', *The Register*, 23 August, www.theregister.co.uk/2004/08/23/spam_or_ham.

Leyden, J. (2004b) 'The rise of the white collar hacker', *The Register*, 30 March, www.theregister.co.uk/content/55/36663.html.

Leyden, J. (2004c) 'WTO rules against US gambling laws', *The Register*, 11 November, www.theregister.co.uk/2004/11/11/us_gambling_wto_rumble.

Leyden, J. (2004d) 'Gizza job, virus writers ask AV industry', *The Register*, 10 September, www.theregister.co.uk/2004/09/10/mydoom_job_plea.

Leyden, J. (2004e) 'Rise of the botnets', *The Register*, 20 September, www.theregister.co.uk/2004/09/20/rise_of_the_botnets.

Leyden, J. (2005a) 'Phishing morphs into pharming', *The Register*, 31 January, www.theregister.co.uk/2005/01/31/pharming.

Leyden, J. (2005b) 'Fight fraud not ID theft', *The Register*, 28 April, www.theregister.co.uk/2005/04/28/id_fraud.

Leyden, J. (2005c) 'UK under cyber blitz', *The Register*, 16 June, www.theregister.co.uk/2005/06/16/uk_cyber-blitz.

Leyden, J. (2005d) 'Hacker magazine shuts up shop', *The Register*, 11 July, www.theregister.co.uk/2005/07/11/phrack_shuts.

Leyden, J. (2005e) 'Webroot guesstimates inflate UK spyware problem', *The Register*, 20 October, www.theregister.co.uk/2005/10/20/webroot_uk_ spyware_guesstimates.

Leyden, J. (2005f) 'Victims coughing up to online extortionists', *The Register*, 6 October, www.theregister.co.uk/2005/10/06/ibm_botnet_vb.

Leyden, J. (2006a) 'Spear phishers target eBay', *The Register*, 5 January, www.theregister.co.uk/2006/01/05/ebay_spear_phishing.

Leyden, J. (2006b) 'Phishing fraudsters offer cash reward', *The Register*, 14 March, www.theregister.co .uk/2006/03/14/chase_phishing_scam.

Leyden, J. (2006c) 'Online fraudsters love webmail – true: easier to block accounts linked to spamming than fraud', *The Register*, 19 July, www.theregister.co.uk/2006/07/19/online_fraud_survey.

Leyden, J. (2006d) 'MySpace adware attack hits hard', *The Register*, 21 July, www.theregister.co.uk/20 06/07/21/myspace_adware_attack.

Leyden, J. (2012) 'If you see "URGENT tax rebate download" in an inbox, kill it with fire', *The Register*, 26 September, www.theregister.co.uk/2012/09/26/spear_phishing_hooks.

Leyden, J. (2013) 'Trying to kill undead Pushdo zombies? Hard luck, Trojan is EVOLVING', 17 May, www.theregister.com/2013/05/17/pushdo_extra_stealth.

Libbenga, J. (2004) 'Trojans as spam robots: the evidence', *The Register*, 22 February, www.theregister .co.uk/2004/02/22/trojans_as_spam_robots.

Licklider, J. and Taylor, R. (1990[1968]) 'The computer as a communication device'. In R. Taylor (ed.), *In Memoriam: J. C. R. Licklider 1915–1990*, Palo Alto, CA: Digital Research Center, 21–41 (reprinted from *Science and Technology*, April 1968).

Liedtke, M. (2005) '"Click fraud" threatens online advertising boom', *Legal Technology*, 14 February, www.law.com/jsp/ltn/pubArticleLTN.jsp? id 1107783347883.

Lindsay, J. (2017) 'Restrained by design: the political economy of cybersecurity', *Digital Policy, Regulation and Governance*, 19 (6): 493–514.

Lindsey, N. (2019) 'Cyber insurance payouts are only encouraging more ransomware attacks', *CPO Magazine*, 1 October, www.cpomagazine.com/cyber-security/cyber-insurance-payouts-are-only -encouraging-more-ransomware-attacks.

Littman, J. (1997) *The Watchman: The Twisted Life and Crimes of Serial Hacker Kevin Poulsen*, Boston, MA: Little, Brown and Company.

Lloyd, I. J. (2000) *Information Technology Law*, London: Butterworths.

Loader, B. and Thomas, D. (eds.) (2000) *Cybercrime: Security and Surveillance in the Information Age*, London: Routledge.

Loader, I. and Walker, N. (2001) 'Policing as a public good: reconstituting the connections between policing and the state', *Theoretical Criminology*, 5 (1): 9–35.

Longworth, K. (2007) 'Jean Baudrillard and American popular culture', *International Journal of Baudrillard Studies*, 4 (3), www.ubishops.ca/baudrillardstudies/vol4_3/v4-3-article58-longworth .html.

Lueck, M. (2005) 'UK in grip of hi-tech crime wave', *BBC News Online*, 17 June.

Lusthaus, J. (2018) *Industry of Anonymity: Inside the Business of Cybercrime*, Cambridge, MA: Harvard University Press

Lusthaus, J. (2019) 'Beneath the dark web: excavating the layers of cybercrime's underground economy', Proceedings of the 2019 IEEE European Symposium on Security and Privacy Workshops, DOI 10.1109/EuroSPW.2019.00059.

Lyon, D. (1994) *The Electronic Eye: The Rise of Surveillance Society*, Minneapolis: University of Minnesota Press.

Mac, R. (2018) 'Bitcoin Scammers Are Using This App to Fleece People', *BuzzFeed.News*, 25 January, www.buzzfeednews.com/article/ryanmac/cryptocurrency-scammers-are-running-wild-on-tele gram.

MacColl, J., Nurse, J. and Sullivan, J. (2021) *Cyber Insurance and the Cyber Security Challenge*, Royal United Services Institute (RUSI Occasional Paper), June, https://kar.kent.ac.uk/89041/1/RUSI-Ke nt-OP-Cyber-insurance.pdf.

MacKinnon, C. (1993) *Only Words*, Cambridge, MA: Harvard University Press.

MacKinnon, R. (1997) 'Virtual rape', *Journal of Computer Mediated Communication*, 2 (4), www.ascu sc.org/jcmc/vol2/issue4/mackinnon. html.

Madow, M. (1993) 'Private ownership of public image: popular culture and publicity rights', *California Law Review*, 81: 125–240.

Mann, D. and Sutton, M. (1998) 'Netcrime: more change in the organisation of thieving', *British Journal of Criminology*, 38 (2): 210–29.

Manning, P. (1978) 'The police: mandate, strategies, and appearances'. In P. Manning and J. Van Maanen (eds.), *Policing: A View from the Street*, New York: Random House, 7–32.

Maras, M.-H. (2016) *Cybercriminology*, Oxford: Oxford University Press.

Marshall, L. (2002) 'Metallica and morality: the rhetorical battleground of the Napster Wars', *Entertainment Law*, 1 (1): 1.

Martin, J. and Barratt, M. (2020) 'Dark web, not dark alley: why drug sellers see the internet as a lucrative safe haven', *The Conversation*, 4 March, https://theconversation.com/dark-web-not-dark-alley-why-drug-sellers-see-the-internet-as-a-lucrative-safe-haven-132579.

Marx, G. (2001) 'Technology and social control: the search for the illusive silver bullet', *International Encyclopaedia of the Social and Behavioral Sciences*, Amsterdam: Elsevier, 15506–12.

Marx, G. (2015) 'Technology and social control'. In *International Encyclopedia of the Social & Behavioral Sciences*, 2nd edn, New York: Elsevier, 117–24.

Masnick, M. (2010a) 'Extortion-like mass automated copyright lawsuits come to the US: 20,000 filed, 30,000 more on the way', *techdirt*, 30 March, www. techdirt.com/articles/20100330/1132478790 .shtml.

Masnick, M. (2010b) 'ACS: law now using dubious legal theories to threaten Slyck.com', *techdirt*, 22 May, www.techdirt.com/articles/20100321/ 2136068650.shtml.

Matamoros-Fernández, A. and Farkas, J. (2022) 'Racism, hate speech, and social media: a systematic review and critique', *Television & New Media*, 22 (2), online first.

Mathieson, T. (1997) 'The viewer society: Foucault's Panopticon revisited', *Theoretical Criminology*, 1: 215–34.

Matsuda, M. J., Lawrence, C. R., Delgado, R. and Crenshaw, K. W. (1993) *Words that Wound: Critical Race Theory, Assaultive Speech, and the First Amendment*, Boulder, CO: Westview Press.

Matza, D. (1964) *Delinquency and Drift*, New York: John Wiley & Sons.

Maynard, D. (2001) 'Circuit Court case notes: violence in the media', *Communications Lawyer*, Spring: 41–2.

McBarnet, D. (1979) 'Arrest: the legal context of policing'. In S. Holdaway (ed.), *The British Police*, London: Arnold.

McConnell International (2000) *Cyber Crime . . . and Punishment? Archaic Laws Threaten Global Information*, Washington, DC: McConnell International, www.witsa.org/papers/McConnell-cybercrime.pdf.

McCusker, R. (2005) 'Spam: nuisance or menace, prevention or cure?', *Trends and Issues in Criminal Justice*, 294 (Canberra: Australian Institute of Criminology), March, www.aic.gov.au/publications /tandi2/tandi294.pdf.

McDonald, O. (2023) *Cryptocurrencies: Money, Trust and Regulation*, 2nd edn, Northwood: Agenda Publishing.

McDowell, R. (1994) 'Do snuff films really exist, or are they merely popular myth?', *San Francisco Chronicle*, 7 August.

McGoogan, C. (2016) 'British hacker Lauri Love to be extradited to the US for "accessing government computers"', *The Daily Telegraph*, 16 September, www.telegraph.co.uk/technology/2016/09/16 /british-hacker-lauri-love-to-be-extradited-to-the-us-for-access.

McGuire, M. (2007) *Hypercrime: The New Geometry of Harm*, London: Routledge-Cavendish.

McKenzie, S. (2006) *Partnership Policing of Electronic Crime: an Evaluation of Public and Private Police Investigative Relationships*, PhD thesis, University of Melbourne.

McLean, K., Wolfe, S., Rojek, J., Alpert, G. and Smith, M. (2020) 'Police officers as warriors or guardians: empirical reality or intriguing rhetoric?', *Justice Quarterly*, 37: 1096–1118.

McLemee, S. (2007) 'Remember Baudrillard', *Inside Higher Ed*, 14 March, www.insidehighered.com /views/mclemee/mclemee135.

McQuade, S. (2006a) 'Technology-enabled crime, policing and security', *Journal of Technology Studies*, 32 (1): 32–42.

McQuade, S. (2006b) *Understanding and Managing Cybercrime*, Boston, MA: Allyn & Bacon.

Mead, N., Hough, E. and Stehney, T. (2005) *Security Quality Requirements Engineering (SQUARE) Methodology Report*, 31 October, Carnegie Mellon University.

Melossi, D. (1994) 'Normal crimes, élites and social control'. In D. Nelken (ed.), *The Futures of Criminology*, London: Sage, 202–19.

Mendelson, H. and Pillai, R. (1999) 'Information Age organisation, dynamics and performance', *Journal of Economic Behaviour and Organization*, 38 (3): 253–81.

Menn, J. (2010) *Fatal System Error: The Hunt for the New Crime Lords Who Are Bringing Down the Internet*, New York: PublicAffairs.

Miller, P. and Rose, N. (1990) 'Governing economic life', *Economy and Society*, 1 (1): 1.

Milmo, D. (2022) 'Risky online behaviour "almost normalised" among young people, says study', *The Guardian*, www.theguardian.com/technology/2022/dec/05/risky-online-behaviour-almost-nor malised-among-young-people-says-study.

Mitchell, W. (1995) *City of Bits: Space, Place, and the Infobahn*, Cambridge, MA: MIT Press.

Mitnick, K. and Simon, W. L. (2002) *The Art of Deception: Controlling the Human Element of Security*, New York: John Wiley and Sons.

Mitnick, K. and Simon, W. L. (2012) *Ghost in the Wires: My Adventures as the World's Most Wanted Hacker*, Boston, MA: Back Bay.

Modine, A. (2009) 'Sports site sues Facebook for click fraud', *The Register*, 14 July, www.theregister .com/2009/07/14/rootzoo_sues_facebook_for_click_fraud.

Moitra, S. (2003) *Analysis and Modelling of Cybercrime: Prospects and Potential*, Freiburg: Max-Planck Institute for Foreign and International Criminal Law.

Moore, G. E. (1965) 'Cramming more components onto integrated circuits', *Electronics*, 38 (8): 114–17.

Morales, C. (2018) 'NETSCOUT Arbor confirms 1.7 Tbps DDoS attack; the terabit attack era is upon us', *Arbor Networks*, 5 March, www.arbornetworks.com/blog/asert/netscout-arbor-confirms-1-7 -tbps-ddos-attack-terabit-attack-era-upon-us.

Moreno, M. (2014) 'Cyberbullying', *JAMA Pediatrics*, 168 (5): 500, doi:10.1001/jamapediatrics.2013 .3343. PMID 24791741.

Morris, M. and Ogan, C. (1996) 'The Internet as mass medium', *Journal of Communication*, 46 (1): 39–49.

Morris, S. (2004) 'The future of netcrime now: part 1 – threats and challenges', *Home Office Online Report 62/04*, www.homeoffice.gov. uk/rds/pdfs04/rdsolr 6204.pdf.

Moses, L. and Chan, J. (2018) 'Algorithmic prediction in policing: assumptions, evaluation, and accountability', *Policing and Society*, 28 (7): 806–22.

Muncaster, P. (2021) 'BEC costs UK firms £140M over past year', *InfoSecurity Magazine*, 26 October, www.infosecurity-magazine.com/news/bec-costs-uk-firms-140m-past-year.

Murphy, H. (2021) 'The negotiators taking on the ransomware hackers', *Financial Times*, 17 February, www.ft.com/content/c0def43a-6949-44ca-86ff-f28daa3818be.

Musotto, R. and Wall, D. S. (2022) 'More Amazon than Mafia: analysing a DDoS stresser service as organised cybercrime', *Trends in Organized Crime*, 25: 173–91.

Naraine, R. (2005) 'Triple-barrelled trojan attack builds botnets', *eweek.com*, 4 June, www.eweek.com /article2/0,1759,1823690,00.asp.

National Statistics (2012) '2010/11 Scottish Crime and Justice Survey: Main Findings', *National Statistics/Scottish Government*, https://lx.iriss.org.uk/sites/default/files/resources/0122316.pdf.

NCA (2017) *Pathways into Cyber Crime, Intelligence Assessment*, January, www.nationalcrimeagency .gov.uk/who-we-are/publications/6-pathways-into-cyber-crime-1/file.

NCIS (2000) *The National Intelligence Model*, London: National Criminal Intelligence Service.

NCIS (2003) *United Kingdom Threat Assessment of Serious and Organised Crime 2003*, London: National Criminal Intelligence Service.

Newburn, T. and Hayman, S. (2001) *Policing, CCTV and Social Control: Police Surveillance of Suspects in Custody*, Cullompton: Willan.

Newcomb, A. (2016) 'Study reveals the age, nationality, and motivation of hackers', *NBCNews.com*, 13 September, www.nbcnews.com/tech/security/study-reveals-age-nationality-motivation-hac kers-n647171.

Newman, G. R. and Clarke, R. V. (2003) *Superhighway Robbery: Preventing e-Commerce Crime*, Cullompton: Willan.

Newman, L. (2017a) 'The ransomware meltdown experts warned about is here', *WIRED*, 12 May, www.wired.com/2017/05/ransomware-meltdown-experts-warned.

Newman, L. (2017b) 'How an accidental "kill switch" slowed Friday's massive ransomware attack', *WIRED*, 13 May, www.wired.com/2017/05/accidental-kill-switch-slowed-fridays-massive-ransomware-attack.

Newman, L. (2021) 'Colonial Pipeline paid a $5m ransom – and kept a vicious cycle turning', *WIRED*, 14 May, www.wired.com/story/colonial-pipeline-ransomware-payment.

Nhan, J., Huey, L. and Broll, R. (2015) 'Digilantism: an analysis of crowdsourcing and the Boston Marathon bombings', *The British Journal of Criminology*, 57 (2): 341–61, https://doi.org/10.1093/bjc/azv118.

NHTCU (2002) *Hi-Tech Crime: The Impact on UK Business*, London: National Hi-Tech Crime Unit.

NISCC (2005) 'Targeted trojan email attacks', *NISCC Briefing 08/2005*, 16 June, www.niscc.gov.uk/niscc/docs/ttea.pdf.

Nissenbaum, H. (2004) 'Hackers and the contested ontology of cyberspace', *New Media & Society*, 6 (2): 195–217.

NSPCC (2021) 'Child abuse image crimes in the UK have risen – we urgently need a stronger Online Safety Bill', *NSPCC News*, 12 March, www.nspcc.org.uk/about-us/news-opinion/2021/indecent-image-offences-online-safety-bill.

NSPCC (2022) 'Child sexual abuse prosecutions and convictions roughly halve in 4 years', *NSPCC News*, 19 January, www.nspcc.org.uk/about-us/news-opinion/2022/child-sexual-abuse-prosecutions-convictions-halve.

O'Connor, P. (2003) *Oppression and Responsibility: A Wittgensteinian Approach to Social Practices and Moral Theory*, University Park: Penn State Press.

O'Malley, P. (1999) 'Governmentality and the risk society', *Economy and Society*, 28: 138–48.

Oates, J. (2004a) 'Email fraud soars', *The Register*, 18 February, www.theregister.co.uk/content/55/35635.html.

Oates, J. (2004b) 'Queen of the Sky gets marching orders', *The Register*, 3 November, www.theregister.co.uk/2004/11/03/airline_blogger_sacked.

Oates, J. (2006) 'Online attack holds files to ransom: Rochdale nurse hit by ransomware', *The Register*, 31 May, www.theregister.co.uk/2006/05/31/virus_ransoms_files.

Ohlheiser, A. (2016) '"We actually elected a meme as president": how 4chan celebrated Trump's victory', *The Washington Post*, 9 November, www.washingtonpost.com/news/the-intersect/wp/2016/11/09/we-actually-elected-a-meme-as-president-how-4chan-celebrated-trumps-victory.

Ohm, P. (2007) 'The myth of the superuser: fear, risk, and harm online', University of Colorado Law Legal Studies Research Paper No. 07-14, May 22 [online], http://papers.ssrn.com/sol3/papers.cfm?abstract_id=967372.

Oliver, C. (2006) 'All sides of the story?', BBC Editor's Blog, 31 August, www.bbc.co.uk/blogs/theeditors/index.html#a003979.

ONS (2020) 'Online bullying in England and Wales: year ending March 2020', Office of National Statistics, 16 November, www.ons.gov.uk/peoplepopulationandcommunity/crimeandjustice/bulletins/onlinebullyinginenglandandwales/yearendingmarch2020.

ONS (2022) 'Nature of fraud and computer misuse in England and Wales: year ending March 2022', Office for National Statistics, 26 September, www.ons.gov.uk/peoplepopulationandcommunity/crimeandjustice/articles/natureoffraudandcomputermisuseinenglandandwales/yearendingmarch2022#trends-in-fraud.

ONS (2023) 'Crime in England and Wales: other related tables', 26 January, www.ons.gov.uk/file?uri=/peoplepopulationandcommunity/crimeandjustice/datasets/crimeinenglandandwalesotherrelatedtables/yearendingseptember2022/otherrelatedtablesyesept22.xlsx.

Osborne, H. (2020) 'Revealed: fake "traders" allegedly prey on victims in global investment scam', *The Guardian*, 1 March, www.theguardian.com/world/2020/mar/01/revealed-fake-traders-allegedly-prey-on-victims-in-global-investment-scam.

OST (2004) 'Cybertrust and Crime Prevention Project: executive summary', Office of Science and Technology, www.foresight.gov.uk/Previous_Projects/Cyber_Trust_and_Crime_Prevention/Reports_and_Publication/Executive%20Summary.pdf.

Palmer, D. (2021) '"Like playing whack-a-mole": do cyber-crime crackdowns have any real impact?', *ZDNet*, 25 March, www.zdnet.com/article/like-playing-whack-a-mole-do-cyber-crime-crackdowns-have-any-real-impact.

Palmer, M. (2006) 'Data is the new oil', *ANA Marketing Maestros*, 3 November, http://ana.blogs.com/maestros/2006/11/data_is_the_new.html.

Pattavina, A. (ed.) (2005) *Information Technology and the Criminal Justice System*, Thousand Oaks, CA: Sage.

PDD (1998) 'The Clinton Administration's policy on critical infrastructure protection', *Presidential Decision Directive (PDD) no. 63*, 22 May, www.cybercrime.gov/white_pr.htm.

Pearce, F. (1976) *Crimes of the Powerful: Marxism, Crime, and Deviance*, London: Pluto Press.

Pease, K. (2001) 'Crime futures and foresight: challenging criminal behaviour in the information age'. In D. S. Wall (ed.), *Crime and the Internet*, London: Routledge, 18–28.

Person, L. (1998) 'Notes toward a postcyberpunk manifesto', *Nova Express 1998* (archived in SCRIBD, www.scribd.com/document/463211695/Notes-Toward-a-Postcyberpunk-Manifesto).

Phillips, W. (2012) 'What an academic who wrote her dissertation on trolls thinks of Violentacrez', *The Atlantic*, 15 October, www.theatlantic.com/technology/archive/2012/10/what-an-academic-who-wrote-her-dissertation-on-trolls-thinks-of-violentacrez/263631.

Pilkington, E. (2010) 'Tyler Clementi, student outed as gay on internet, jumps to his death', *The Guardian*, 30 September, www.theguardian.com/world/2010/sep/30/tyler-clementi-gay-student-suicide.

PNLD and Staniforth, A. (eds.) (2017) *Blackstone's Handbook of Cyber Crime Investigation*, Oxford: Oxford University Press.

Porcedda, M. G. and Wall, D. S. (2019) 'Cascade and chain effects in big data cybercrime: lessons from the TalkTalk hack', Proceedings of WACCO 2019: 1st Workshop on Attackers and Cyber-Crime Operations, IEEE EuroS&P 2019, Stockholm, Sweden, 20 June 2019, https://papers.ssrn.com/sol3/papers.cfm?abstract_id=3429958.

Porcedda, M. G. and Wall, D. S. (2021) 'Modelling the cybercrime cascade effect of data theft', Proceedings of the IEEE Workshop on Attackers and Cyber-Crime Operations (WACCO 2021), Montreal, 29 October, DOI:10.1109/EuroSPW54576.2021.00025.

Post, D. (1995) 'Encryption vs. the alligator clip: the Feds worry that encoded messages are immune to wiretaps', *American Lawyer*, January/ February: 111.

Post, D. (2000) 'What Larry doesn't get: code, law, and liberty in cyberspace', *Stanford Law Review*, 52: 1439–59.

Poster, M. (1995) *Second Media Age*, Cambridge: Polity.

Powell, O. (2022) 'The most dangerous cyber security threats of 2023', *Cyber Security Hub*, 27 December, www.cshub.com/attacks/articles/the-most-dangerous-cyber-security-threats-of-2023.

Power, R. (2000) *Tangled Web: Tales of Digital Crime from the Shadows of Cyberspace*, Indianapolis: Que.

Powers, T. (2003) 'Real wrongs in virtual communities', *Ethics and Information Technology*, 5 (4): 191–8.

Presdee, M. (2000) *Cultural Criminology and the Carnival of Crime*, London: Routledge.

Quayle, E. and Taylor, M. (2002) 'Child pornography and the internet: perpetuating a cycle of abuse', *Deviant Behavior*, 23 (4): 331–61.

Race, J. (2005) 'You needn't eat spam (or worms): the real reasons why spam still exists today – and what to do about it', *Free Software Magazine*, 6 (July), www.ftc.gov/os/comments/canspam3/516736-00048.pdf.

Rainie, L. and Wellman, B. (2012) *Networked: The New Social Operating System*, Boston, MA: MIT Press.

Rathmell, A. (1998) 'The world of open sources (2): information warfare and hacking', paper presented to 1998 International Conference for Criminal Intelligence Analysts: 'Meeting the Challenge from Serious Criminality', Manchester, UK.

Rathmell, A. (2001) 'Controlling computer network operations', *Information & Security*, 7: 121–44.

Rauterberg, M. (2004) 'Positive effects of entertainment technology on human behaviour'. In R. Jacquart (ed.), *Building the Information Society*, London: Kluwer, 51–8.

Reed, C. and Angel, J. (eds.) (2003) *Computer Law*, Oxford: Oxford University Press.

Reiner, R. (2000) *The Politics of the Police*, 3rd edn, Oxford: Oxford University Press.

ReliaQuest (2021) 'The rise of initial access brokers', *ReliaQuest Blog*, 22 February, www.reliaquest .com/blog/rise-of-initial-access-brokers.

Reno, J. (1996) 'Law enforcement in cyberspace', address to the Commonwealth Club of California, San Francisco Hilton Hotel, 14 June.

Reuters (2005) 'Microsoft, Nigeria fight e-mail scammers', *e-week.com*, 14 October, www.eweek.com /article2/0,1895,1871565,00.asp.

Reynolds, E. (2015) 'Patient Zero of the selfie age: why JenniCam abandoned her digital life', *News .com.au*, 16 April, www.news.com.au/technology/online/social/patient-zero-of-the-selfie-age -why-jennicam-abandoned-her-digital-life/news-story/539cd1b26016fcee1a51cfca3895a7b5.

Rheingold, H. (1994) *The Virtual Community: Homesteading the Electronic Frontier*, New York: Harper Perennial.

Rhodes, R. (1996) 'The new governance: governing without government', *Political Studies*, 44: 652–67.

Richardson, T. (2005) 'BT cracks down on rogue diallers', *The Register*, 27 May, www.theregister.co.uk /2005/05/27/rogue_bt_diallers.

Rimm, M. (1995) 'Marketing pornography on the information superhighway: a survey of 917,410 images, descriptions, short stories, and animations downloaded 8.5 million times by consumers in over 2000 cities in forty countries, provinces, and territories', *Georgetown Law Review*, 83: 1849–934.

Ritzer, G. and Jurgenson, N. (2010) 'Production, consumption, prosumption: the nature of capitalism in the age of the digital "prosumer"', *Journal of Consumer Culture*, 10: 13–36.

Robertson, R. (1995) 'Globalisation'. In M. Featherstone, S. Lash and R. Robertson (eds.), *Global Modernities*, London: Sage, 40–65.

Ronson, J. (2005) 'Game over: interview with Gary McKinnon', *The Guardian*, 9 July, www.theguardi an.com/theguardian/2005/jul/09/weekend7.weekend2.

Room, S. (2003) 'Hard-core spammers beware?', *New Law Journal*, 28 November: 1780.

Rosenberger, R. (2003) 'Computer viruses and "false authority syndrome"', *Vmyths.com*, https:// www.philo5.com/Textes-references/RosenbergerRob_ComputerViruses_1997.pdf.

Ross, A. (1990) 'Hacking away at the counterculture', *Postmodern Culture*, 1/1, http://jefferson.villa ge.virginia.edu/pmc/issue.990/contents.990.html.

Rotenberg, R. (2001) 'What Larry doesn't get: fair information practices and the architecture of privacy', *Stanford Technology Law Review*, February, http://stlr.stanford.edu/STLR/Symposia/ Cyberspace/00_rotenberg_1/ article.htm.

Rothman, J. E. (2001) 'Freedom of speech and true threats', *Harvard Journal of Law & Public Policy*, 25 (1): 1.

Rowland, D. and Macdonald, E. (1997) *Information Technology Law*, London: Cavendish.

RSA (2011) 'The psychology of social engineering', RSA, July, www.rsa.com/solutions/consumer_aut hentication/intelreport/11477_Online_Fraud_report_0711.pdf.

Rupnow, C. (2003) 'Not "made of money"', *Wisconsin Leader-Telegram*, 23 April, www.xpressmart .com/thebikernetwork/scam.html.

Russon, M. (2021) 'US fuel pipeline hackers "didn't mean to create problems"', *BBC News Online*, 10 May, www.bbc.com/news/business-57050690.

Ryan, J. and Jefferson, T. (2003) 'The use, misuse and abuse of statistics in information security research', Proceedings of the 2003 ASEM National Conference, St Louis, MO, www.attrition.org/ archive/misc/use_misuse_ abuse_stats_infosec_research.pdf.

Saltzer, J., Reed, D. and Clark, D. (1984) 'End-to-end arguments in system design', *ACM Transactions in Computer Systems*, 2 (4): 277–88.

Sambrook, R. (2006) 'How the net is transforming news', *BBC News Online*, 20 January, http://news .bbc.co.uk/1/hi/technology/4630890.stm.

Sandars, N. K. (1972) *The Epic of Gilgamesh: An English Version with an Introduction*, Harmondsworth: Penguin Classics.

Saunders, J. (2017) 'Tackling cybercrime – the UK response', *Journal of Cyber Policy*, 2 (1): 4–15.

Satchwell, G. (2004) *A Sick Business: Counterfeit Medicines and Organised Crime*, Lyon: INTERPOL, www.interpol.int/Public/FinancialCrime/IntellectualProperty/Publications/SickBusiness.pdf.

Savvy Security (2021) '8 Types of man in the middle attacks you need to know about', *Savvy Security Blog*, 10 November, https://cheapsslsecurity.com/blog/types-of-man-in-the-middle-attacks.

Scanlan, J., Watters, P., Prichard, J., Hunn, C., Spiranovic, C. and Wortley, R. (2022) 'Creating honeypots to prevent online child exploitation', *Future Internet*, 14 (2): 121–35.

Schneider, J. L. (2003) 'Hiding in plain sight: an exploration of the illegal(?) activities of a drugs newsgroup', *The Howard Journal of Criminal Justice*, 42 (4): 374–89.

Schneier, B. (2003) *Beyond Fear: Thinking Sensibly about Security in an Uncertain World*, New York: Springer-Verlag.

Scroxton, A. (2021) 'Is it time to ban ransomware insurance payments?', *ComputerWeekly.com*, 11 Feb., www.computerweekly.com/feature/Is-it-time-to-ban-ransomware-insurance-payments.

Scroxton, A. (2023) 'Cops bust Genesis cyber crime marketplace', *ComputerWeekly.com*, 5 April, www.computerweekly.com/news/365534857/Cops-bust-Genesis-cyber-crime-marketplace.

Searle, J. (1969) *Speech Acts: An Essay in the Philosophy of Language*, Cambridge: Cambridge University Press.

Sennett, R. (1992) *The Fall of Public Man*, New York: W. W. Norton.

Sentencing Advisory Panel (2002) *The Panel's Advice to the Court of Appeal on Offences Involving Child Pornography*, London: Sentencing Guidelines Council, 15 August, www.sentencing-guidelines.gov.uk/docs/advice_child_porn.pdf.

Sentencing Council (2013) *Sexual Offences: Response to Consultation*, December, www.sentencingcouncil.org.uk/wp-content/uploads/Final_Sexual_Offences_Response_to_Consultation_web1.pdf.

Shantz, J. and Tomblin, J. (2014) *Cyber Disobedience: Re://Presenting Online Anarchy*, Alresford: John Hunt Publishing.

Shea, S. (2019) '6 different types of hackers, from black hat to red hat', *TechTarget*, October, www.techtarget.com/searchsecurity/answer/What-is-red-and-white-hat-hacking.

Shearing, C. (2004) 'Thoughts on sovereignty', *Policing and Society*, 14 (1): 5–12.

Shearing, C. and Ericson, R. (1991) 'Culture as figurative action', *British Journal of Sociology*, 42 (4): 481–506.

Shenon, P. (2001) 'Internet piracy is suspected as U.S. agents raid campuses', *New York Times*, 12 December, www.criminology.fsu.edu/ transcrime/articles/Internet%20Piracy%20Is%20Suspected%20as%20_S_%20Agents%20Raid%20Campuses.htm.

Sheptycki, J. (2000) 'Introduction'. In J. E. Sheptycki (ed.), *Issues in Transnational Policing*, London: Routledge, 1–20.

Sheptycki, J. (2002) *In Search of Transnational Policing: Towards a Sociology of Global Policing*, Aldershot: Ashgate.

Sherman, B. and Bently, L. (1999) *The Making of Modern Intellectual Property Law*, Cambridge: Cambridge University Press.

Sherriff, L. (2004) 'Child porn suspect suicide tally hits 32', *The Register*, 21 December, www.theregister.co.uk/2004/12/21/child_porn_suicide_shame.

Shinder, D. and Tittel, E. (2002) *Scene of the Cybercrime*, Rockland, MA: Syngress Media.

Siegelman, W. (2021) 'Did Cambridge Analytica collude with Russia's intelligence services to interfere in US elections?', *Byline Times*, 20 April, https://bylinetimes.com/2021/04/20/did-cambridge-analytica-collude-with-russias-intelligence-services-to-interfere-in-us-elections.

Silver, N. (2012) *The Signal and the Noise: Why Most Predictions Fail – but Some Don't*, New York: Penguin.

Simon, J. (2007) *Governing through Crime: How the War on Crime Transformed American Democracy and Created a Culture of Fear*, New York and Oxford: Oxford University Press.

Singleton, T. (2002) 'Stop fraud cold with powerful internal controls', *Journal of Corporate Accounting & Finance*, 13 (4): 29–39.

Smith, G. (1998) 'Electronic Pearl Harbor? Not likely', *Issues in Science and Technology*, 15 (3): 68–73, www.nap.edu/issues/15.1/smith.htm.

Smith, R. G., Grabosky, P. N. and Urbas, G. (2004) *Cyber Criminals on Trial*, Cambridge: Cambridge University Press.

Solove, D. (2008) *Understanding Privacy*, Cambridge, MA: Harvard University Press.

Sommer, P. (2004) 'The future for the policing of cybercrime', *Computer Fraud & Security*, 1: 8–12.

Spadafora, A. (2021) 'Hackers are using DDoS attacks to squeeze victims for ransom', *techradar.pro*, January, www.techradar.com/news/hackers-are-using-ddos-attacks-to-squeeze-victims-for-ran som.

Spamhaus (2020) 'Botnet threat report 2019', Spamhaus Malware Labs, 28 January, www.spamhaus .org/news/images/full-2019/spamhaus-botnet-threat-report-2019.pdf.

Sprenger, P. (1999) 'Sun on privacy: "Get Over It"', *WIRED*, 26 January, www.wired.com/news/polit ics/0,1283,17538,00.html.

Stajano, F. and Wilson, P. (2011) 'Understanding scam victims: seven principles for systems security', *Communications of the ACM*, 543: 70–5 (early version available at www.cl.cam.ac.uk/techreports /UCAM-CL-TR-754.pdf).

Standage, T. (1998) *The Victorian Internet: The Remarkable Story of the Telegraph and the Nineteenth Century's Online Pioneers*, London: Phoenix.

Stanley, R. (2013) 'Album sales are declining, but it's part of the battle between art and commerce', *The Guardian*, 24 November, www.theguardian.com/commentisfree/2013/nov/24/album-sales -declining-battle-art-commerce.

Stark, C. (1997) 'Is pornography an action? The causal vs. the conceptual view of pornography's harm', *Social Theory and Practice*, 10 (2): 277–305.

Starr, S. (2004a) 'Can the law can spam? Legislation is a blunt instrument with which to beat junk email', *Spiked*, 7 April, www.spikedonline.com/articles/0000000CA4BF.htm.

Starr, S. (2004b) 'Can technology can spam? IT companies do battle with bulk email', *Spiked*, 5 May, www.spiked-online.com/Articles/0000000CA50F.htm.

Statista (2023) 'Number of active online banking users worldwide in 2020 with forecasts from 2021 to 2024, by region', *Statista Financial Information*, www.statista.com/forecasts/1169529/online-ban king-penetration-by-country.

Steinmetz, K. (2016) *Hacked: A Radical Approach to Hacker Culture and Crime*, New York: New York University Press.

Stenning, P. (2000) 'Powers and accountability of private police', *European Journal on Criminal Policy and Research*, 8 (3): 325–52.

Stenning, P. and Shearing, C. (2005) 'Reforming police: opportunities, drivers and challenges', *Australian and New Zealand Journal of Criminology*, 38 (2): 167–80.

Stenson, K. and Edwards, A. (2003) 'Crime control and local governance: the struggle for sovereignty in advanced liberal polities', *Contemporary Politics*, 9 (2): 203–17.

Stephenson, N. (1992) *Snowcrash*, London: ROC/Penguin.

Sterling, B. (1994) *The Hacker Crackdown: Law and Disorder on the Electronic Frontier*, London: Penguin.

Sterling, B. (2008) 'Cybercrime: cyberpunk writers made it all up', 'Bruce Sterling Blog', WIRED, 30 August, www.wired.com/2008/08/cybercrime-cybe.

Strozewski, Z. (2022) 'US airport hit with cyber-attack: "No one is afraid of you"', *Newsweek*, 29 March, www.newsweek.com/us-airport-hit-cyberattack-over-ukraine-no-one-afraid-you-1692903.

Sturcke, J. (2006) 'Expert warns of more chatroom libel awards', *Guardian Online*, 22 March, www.gu ardian.co.uk/uk_news/story/0,,1737000,00.html.

Surman, D. (2003) *CGI animation: Pseudorealism, Perception and Possible Worlds*, MA thesis, Warwick University, UK, www.academia.edu/168038/CGI_Animation_Pseudorealism_Perception _and_Possible_Worlds.

Sussman, V. (1995) 'Policing cyberspace', U.S. News & World Reporting, 23 January: 54–61.

Sutherland, E. (1949) *White Collar Crime*, New York: Dryden.

Sutton, W. and Linn, E. (1976) *Where the Money Was: The Memoirs of a Bank Robber*, New York: Viking Press.

Swash, R. (2012) 'A new internet age? Web users turn on "trolls"', *BBC News Online*, 19 October, www .theguardian.com/technology/2012/oct/19/new-internet-age-trolls.

Swift, R. (2002) 'Rush to nowhere', *New Internationalist*, 343, March, www.newint.org/issue343/key note.htm.

Swinhoe, D. (2022) 'Man-in-the-middle (MitM) attack definition and examples', *CSO online*, 25 March, www.csoonline.com/article/3340117/man-in-the-middle-attack-definition-and-exam ples.html.

Szafranski, R. (1995) 'A theory of information warfare: preparing for 2020', *Airpower Journal*, Spring, www.airpower.maxwell.af.mil/airchronicles/apj/szfran.html.

Taleb, N. (2007) *The Black Swan: The Impact of the Highly Improbable*, New York: Random House.

Tannenbaum, F. (1951[1938]) *Crime and the Community*, New York: McGraw-Hill.

Tanriverdi, H., Weber, R. and Sachsinger, C. (2020) 'How cyber criminals blackmail corporations', *ta gess-chau.de*, 11 November, www.tagesschau.de/wirtschaft/ransomware-101.html.

Taylor, M. (1999) 'The nature and dimensions of child pornography on the Internet', paper presented to the 'Combating Child Pornography on the Internet' conference, Vienna, September.

Taylor, M. and Quayle, E. (2003) *Child Pornography: An Internet Crime*, London: Brunner-Routledge.

Taylor, P. (1999) *Hackers: Crime in the Digital Sublime*, London: Routledge.

Taylor, P. (2001) 'Hacktivism: in search of lost ethics?'. In D. S. Wall (ed.), *Crime and the Internet*, London: Routledge, 59–73.

The Mentor (1986) 'The conscience of a hacker (Hacker's Manifesto)', *Phrack*, 1 (7): phile 3, www. phrack.org/show.php?p 07.

Thurley, P. (2005) 'Pornography as performative utterance', paper presented to the Northwest Student Philosophy Conference, Washington State, 29 May, http://artsweb.uwaterloo.ca/~pthur ley/index/Pornography.htm.

Toffler, A. (1970) *Future Shock*, New York: Bantam Books.

Tombs, S. and Whyte, D. (2003) 'Unmasking the crimes of the powerful', *Critical Criminology*, 11 (3): 217–36.

Toyne, S. (2003) 'Scam targets NatWest customers', *BBC News Online*, 24 October, http://news.bbc .co.uk/1/hi/business/3211635.stm.

Trottier, D., Gabdulhakov, R. and Huang, Q. (2020) *Introducing Vigilant Audiences*, Cambridge: Open Book Publishers.

Trubek, D. and Trubek, L. (2005) 'Hard and soft law in the construction of social Europe: the role of the open method of co-ordination', *European Law Journal*, 11 (3): 343–64.

Turner, G. (2004) *Celebrity*, London: Sage.

Uhlig, R. (1996) 'Hunt is on for internet dealer in child porn', *Electronic Telegraph*, 518, 23 October, www.telegraph.co.uk/htmlContent. jhtml?html /archive/1996/10/23/nporn23.html.

UK Finance (2022a) *Annual Fraud Report 2022*, UK Finance, 28 June, www.ukfinance.org.uk/policy -and-guidance/reports-and-publications/annual-fraud-report-2022.

UK Finance (2022b) 'Nearly 40 per cent of people looking for love online were asked for money', UK Finance, www.ukfinance.org.uk/press/press-releases/nearly-40-cent-people-looking-love-online -were-asked-money.

UN (1989) *Convention on the Rights of the Child*, United Nations, General Assembly resolution 44/25, 20 November, www.ohchr.org/en/instruments-mechanisms/instruments/convention-rig hts-child

Ungoed-Thomas, J. (1998) 'The schoolboy spy', *Sunday Times*, 29 March, 1–2.

USDOJ (2002) 'Warez leader sentenced to 46 months', US Department of Justice Press Release, 17 May, www.cybercrime.gov/sankusSent.htm.

USDOJ (2004) 'Computer programmer arrested for extortion and mail fraud scheme targeting Google, Inc.', US Department of Justice Press Release, 18 March, www.usdoj.gov/usao/can/press /html/ 2004_03_ 19_ bradley.html.

USDOJ (2018) 'Latvian national pleads guilty to "scareware" hacking scheme that targeted Minneapolis Star Tribune website', *U.S. Department of Justice News*, 6 February, www.justice.gov /opa/pr/latvian-national-pleads-guilty-scareware-hacking-scheme-targeted-minneapolis-star- tribune.

USDOJ (2019) '281 arrested worldwide in coordinated international enforcement operation targeting hundreds of individuals in business email compromise schemes', *US Department of Justice News*, 10 September, www.justice.gov/opa/pr/281-arrested-worldwide-coordinated-international-enforcement-operation-targeting-hundreds.

USDOJ (2023a) 'Russian national charged with ransomware attacks against critical infrastructure', *US Department of Justice News*, 16 May, www.justice.gov/opa/pr/russian-national-charged-ransomware-attacks-against-critical-infrastructure.

USDOJ (2023b) 'Ransomware charges unsealed against Russian national', *US Department of Justice News*, 16 May, www.justice.gov/usao-dc/pr/ransomware-charges-unsealed-against-russian-national.

USDOS (2021) 'Reward offers for information to bring DarkSide ransomware variant co-conspirators to justice', US Department of State Press Statement, 4 November, www.state.gov/reward-offers-for-information-to-bring-darkside-ransomware-variant-co-conspirators-to-justice.

USDOS (2023) *Cyber Sanctions*, US Department of State, www.state.gov/cyber-sanctions.

Usman, M. (2020) 'PIA data hacked: Threat Actor put databases up for sale at dark web', *Bol News*, 24 November, www.bolnews.com/latest/2020/11/pia-data-hacked-threat-actor-put-databases-up-for-sale-at-dark-web.

Vallance, C. (2022) '3D printed guns: warnings over growing threat of 3D firearms', *BBC News Online*, 9 November, www.bbc.com/news/technology-63495123.

Van Dijk, J. (1999) 'The one-dimensional network society of Manuel Castells: a review essay', *New Media & Society*, 1 (1): 127–38, www.thechronicle.demon.co.uk/archive/castells.htm.

Vincent-Jones, P. (2000) 'Contractual governance: institutional and organisational analysis', *Oxford Journal of Legal Studies*, 20: 317–51.

Vinge, V. (2000) 'The digital Gaia: as computing power accelerates, the network knows all – and it's everywhere', *WIRED*, 8 (1), www.wired.com/ wired/archive/8.01/forward.html.

Wadhwani, S. (2022) 'Medibank confirms data leak following refusal to pay ransom', *spiceworks*, 10 November, www.spiceworks.com/it-security/data-security/news/medibank-data-leak.

Wakefield, J. (2005) 'Online service foils ransom plot', *BBC News Online*, 31 May, http://news.bbc.co.uk/1/hi/technology/4579623.stm.

Walden, I. (2003) 'Computer crime'. In C. Reed and J. Angel (eds.), *Computer Law*, Oxford: Oxford University Press, 295–329.

Walden, I. (2016) *Computer Crimes and Digital Investigations*, Oxford: Oxford University Press.

Walker, C. and Akdeniz, Y. (1998) 'The governance of the internet in Europe with special reference to illegal and harmful content', *Criminal Law Review*, special issue on 'Crime, Criminal Justice and the Internet', 5–18.

Walker, C. P. and Akdeniz, Y. (2003) 'Anti-terrorism laws and data retention: war is over?', *Northern Ireland Legal Quarterly*, 50 (2): 159–82.

Walker, C. and Conway, M. (2015) 'Online terrorism and online laws', *Dynamics of Asymmetric Conflict*, 8: 156–75.

Walker, C. P., Wall, D. S. and Akdeniz, Y. (2000) 'The internet, law and society'. In Y. Akdeniz, C. P. Walker and D. S. Wall (eds.), *The Internet, Law and Society*, London: Longman, 3–24.

Walker, D. (2004) 'Who watches murder videos?', *BBC News Online*, 12 October, http://news.bbc.co.uk/1/hi/magazine/3733996.stm.

Walker, R. and Bakopoulos, B. (2005) 'Conversations in the dark: how young people manage chatroom relationships', *First Monday*, 10 (4), http:// firstmonday.org/issues/issue10_4/walker/index.html.

Wall, D. S. (1997) 'Policing the virtual community: the internet, cybercrimes and the policing of cyberspace'. In P. Francis, P. Davies and V. Jupp (eds.), *Policing Futures*, London: Macmillan, 208–36.

Wall, D. S. (1998) *The Chief Constables of England and Wales: The Socio-Legal History of a Criminal Justice Elite*, Aldershot: Dartmouth. Republished 2019 by Routledge.

Wall, D. S. (2000) 'The theft of electronic services: telecommunications and teleservices', Essay 1 on the CD-ROM annex to DTI, *Turning the Corner*, London: Department of Trade and Industry.

Wall, D. S. (ed.) (2001a) *Crime and the Internet*, London: Routledge.

Wall, D. S. (2001b) 'Maintaining order and law on the internet'. In D. S. Wall (ed.) *Crime and the Internet*, London: Routledge, 167–83.

Wall, D. S. (2002a) 'Insecurity and the policing of cyberspace'. In A. Crawford (ed.), *Crime and Insecurity*, Cullompton: Willan, 186–210.

Wall, D. S. (2002b) 'DOT.CONS: internet related frauds and deceptions upon individuals within the UK', Final Report to the Home Office, March (unpublished).

Wall, D. S. (2003) 'Mapping out cybercrimes in a cyberspatial surveillant assemblage'. In F. Webster and K. Ball (eds.), *The Intensification of Surveillance: Crime Terrorism and Warfare in the Information Age*, London: Pluto Press, 112–36.

Wall, D. S. (2004) 'Policing Elvis: legal action and the shaping of postmortem celebrity culture as contested space', *Entertainment Law*, 2 (3): 35–69 (published in 2004, journal dated 2003).

Wall, D. S. (2005) 'The internet as a conduit for criminals'. In A. Pattavina (ed.), *Information Technology and the Criminal Justice System*, Thousand Oaks, CA: Sage, 77–98. Updated in 2015, https://papers.ssrn.com/sol3/papers.cfm?abstract_id=740626.

Wall, D. S. (2007a) 'Policing cybercrime: situating the public police in networks of security in cyberspace', *Police Practice and Research: An International Journal*, 8 (1); updated in 2011: https://papers.ssrn.com/sol3/papers.cfm?abstract_id=853225.

Wall, D. S. (2007b) *Cybercrime: The Transformation of Crime in the Information Age, 1st Edition*, Cambridge: Polity.

Wall, D. S. (2008) 'Cybercrime and the culture of fear: social science fiction and the production of knowledge about cybercrime', *Information Communications and Society*, 11 (6): 861–84.

Wall, D. S. (2010a) 'Micro-frauds: virtual robberies, stings and scams in the information age'. In T. Holt and B. Schell (eds.), *Corporate Hacking and Technology-Driven Crime: Social Dynamics and Implications*, Hershey, PA: IGI Global, 68–85.

Wall, D. S. (2010b) 'The organization of cybercrime and organized cybercrime'. In M. Bellini, P. Brunst and J. Jaenke (eds.), *Current Issues in IT security*. Freiburg: Max-Planck-Instituts für ausländisches und internationales Strafrecht, 53–68.

Wall, D. S. (2012) 'The devil drives a Lada: the social construction of hackers as cybercriminals'. In C. Gregoriou (ed.), *Constructing Crime: Discourse and Cultural Representations of Crime and 'Deviance'*, London: Palgrave Macmillan, 4–18.

Wall, D. S. (2013) 'Enemies within: redefining the insider threat in organizational security policy', *Security Journal*, 26 (2): 107–24.

Wall, D. S. (2015a) 'Copyright trolling and the policing of intellectual property in the shadow of law'. In M. David and D. Halbert (eds.), *The SAGE Handbook of Intellectual Property*, London: Sage, 607–26.

Wall, D. S. (2015b) 'The TalkTalk hack story shows UK cybersecurity in disarray', *The Conversation*, 28 October, https://theconversation.com/the-talktalk-hack-story-shows-uk-cybersecurity-in-disarray-49909.

Wall, D. S. (2017) 'Crime, security and information communication technologies: the changing cybersecurity threat landscape and implications for regulation and policing'. In R. Brownsword, E. Scotford and K. Yeung (eds.), *The Oxford Handbook of the Law and Regulation of Technology*, Oxford: Oxford University Press, 1075–96.

Wall, D. S. (2018) 'How big data feeds big crime', *Current History: A Journal of Contemporary World Affairs* (University of California Press), January, 117 (795): 29–34.

Wall, D. S. (2019) 'Cybersecurity'. In J. Muncie and E. McLoughlan (eds.), *The SAGE Dictionary of Criminology (4th Edition)*, London: Sage, 140.

Wall, D. S. (2021) 'The transnational cybercrime extortion landscape and the pandemic: ransomware and changes in offender tactics, attack scalability and the organisation of offending', *European Law Enforcement Research Bulletin* (SCE 5), 5 Oct., 45–60.

Wall, D. and Williams, M. (eds.) (2014) *Policing Cybercrime: Networked and Social Media Technologies and the Challenge for Policing*, London: Routledge.

Wallace, J. and Mangan, M. (1996) *Sex, Laws and Cyberspace*, New York: Henry Holt.

Ward, M. (2005) 'Key hacker magazine faces closure', *BBC News Online*, 9 July, http://news.bbc.co.uk/1/hi/technology/4657265.stm.

Warren, P. (2005) 'UK trojan siege has been running over a year', *The Register*, 17 June, www.theregis ter.co.uk/2005/06/17/niscc_warning.

Wasik, M. (2000) 'Hacking, viruses and fraud'. In Y. Akdeniz, C. P. Walker and D. S. Wall (eds.), *The Internet, Law and Society*, London: Longman, 272–93.

Weale, S. (2023) '"We see misogyny every day": how Andrew Tate's twisted ideology infiltrated British schools', *The Guardian*, 2 Feb., www.theguardian.com/society/2023/feb/02/andrew-tate-twisted -ideology-infiltrated-british-schools.

Weaver, N., Paxson, V., Staniford, S. and Cunningham, R. (2003) 'A taxonomy of computer worms', paper presented at the workshop on Rapid Malcode (WORM), at the Tenth ACM Conference on Computer and Communications Security, Washington, DC, 27 October, www.cs. berkeley.edu/ ~nweaver/papers/taxonomy.pdf.

Webroot (2005) *The State of Spyware, Q2*, Webroot Software Inc., October, www.webroot.com/pdf/20 05-q2-sos.pdf.

Webster, F. (2002) *Theories of the Information Society*, 2nd edn, London: Routledge.

Weimann, G. (2006) *Terror on the Internet: The New Arena, the New Challenges*, Washington, DC: United States Institute of Peace Press.

Weisburd, D., Wheeler, S., Waring, E. and Bode, N. (1991) *Crimes of the Middle Classes: White-Collar Offenders in the Federal Courts*, New Haven, CT: Yale University Press.

Welsh, I. (2002) *Porno*, London: Vintage.

Wendling, M. and Sardarizadeh, S. (2022) 'US midterms: the election deniers running to control 2024 vote', *BBC News Online*, 3 November, www.bbc.co.uk/news/world-us-canada-63490938.

Whelan, C., Bright, D. and Martin, J. (2023) 'Reconceptualising organised (cyber)crime: The case of ransomware', *Journal of Criminology*, online first, https://journals.sagepub.com/doi/epub/10.11 77/26338076231199793.

White, M. (2019) 'Drug dealers "moving from street corners to social media"', *Sky News*, 8 September, https://news.sky.com/story/one-in-four-youngsters-exposed-to-illegal-drug-ads-on-social-media -11804202.

WHO (2004) *Report of Pre-eleventh ICDRA Satellite Workshop on Counterfeit Drugs*, Madrid, Spain, 13–14 February, www.who.int/medicines/organization/qsm/activities/qualityassurance/cft/Pre -ICDRA_Counterfeit_report.pdf.

Wildman, N. and McDonnell, N. (2020) 'The puzzle of virtual theft', *Analysis*, 80 (3): 493–9, https://doi .org/10.1093/analys/anaa005.

Williams, M. (2001) 'The language of cybercrime'. In D. S. Wall (ed.), *Crime and the Internet*, London: Routledge, 152–66.

Williams, M. (2006) *Virtually Criminal: Crime, Deviance and Regulation Online*, London: Routledge.

Williams, M., Burnap, P., Javed, A., Liu, H. and Ozalp, S. (2020) 'Hate in the machine: anti-black and anti-Muslim social media posts as predictors of offline racially and religiously aggravated crime', *The British Journal of Criminology*, 60 (1): 93–117.

Wilson, D., Patterson, A., Powell, G. and Hembury, R. (2006) 'Fraud and technology crimes: findings from the 2003/04 British Crime Survey, the 2004 Offending, Crime and Justice Survey and admin- istrative sources', *Home Office Online Report 09/06*, www.homeoffice.gov.uk/rds/pdfs06/rdsolr09 06.pdf.

Wired (2003) 'Verizon must reveal song swappers', *WIRED*, 24 April, www.wired.com/news/digiwo od/0,1412,58620,00.html.

Wolf, N. (2012) 'Amanda Todd's suicide and social media's sexualisation of youth culture', *The Guardian*, 26 October, www.theguardian.com/commentisfree/2012/oct/26/amanda-todd-suici de-social-media-sexualisation?view=mobile.

Wood, J. (2004) 'Cultural change in the governance of security', *Policing and Society*, 14 (1): 31–48.

Wood, P. (2003) 'The convergence of viruses and spam: lessons learned from the SoBig.F experience', *MessageLabs White Paper*, www.nframe.com/PDF/VirusSpam.pdf.

Wood, P. (2004) 'Spammer in the works: everything you need to know about protecting yourself and your business from the rising tide of unsolicited "spam" email', *MessageLabs White Paper*, April 2004, www.security. iia.net.au/downloads/spammer%20in%20works%20-%20an%20update%20 14.5.pdf.

Wordtracker (2005) 'Top 500 search engine keywords of the week', *Wordtracker*, 3 May, www.search
engineguide.com/wt/2005/0503_wt1.html.

Yar, M. (2005a) 'Computer hacking: just another case of juvenile delinquency?', *Howard Journal of Criminal Justice*, 44 (4): 387–99.

Yar, M. (2005b) 'The novelty of "cybercrime": an assessment in light of routine activity theory', *European Journal of Criminology*, 2: 407–27.

Yar, M. (2006) *Cybercrime and Society*, London: Sage.

Yar, M. (2018) 'Doing criminological research online – Majid Yar'. In P. Davies and P. Francis (eds.), *Doing Criminological Research, 3rd Edition*, London: Sage.

Yar, M. and Steinmetz, K. (2023) *Cybercrime and Society*, 4th edn, London: Sage.

Young, J. (1997), 'Left realism: the basics'. In B. MacLean and D. Milovanovic (eds.), *Thinking Critically about Crime*, Vancouver: Collective Press.

Young, L. F. (1995) 'United States computer crime laws, criminals and deterrence', *International Yearbook of Law, Computers and Technology*, 9: 1–16.

Zetter, K. (2011) 'How digital detectives deciphered Stuxnet, the Most menacing malware in history', *WIRED*, 11 July, www.wired.com/2011/07/how-digital-detectives-deciphered-stuxnet.

Zittrain, J. (2003) 'Internet points of control', *Boston College Law Review*, 44 (2): 653–88.

Zoltan, M. (2023) 'Dark Web Price Index 2023', *PRIVACY Affairs*, 23 April, www.privacyaffairs.com/dark-web-price-index-2023.

Index